A Short History of Writing Instruction

D0933050

Short enough to be synoptic, yet long enough to be usefully detailed, *A Short History of Writing Instruction* is the ideal text for undergraduate courses and graduate seminars in rhetoric and composition. It preserves the legacy of writing instruction from antiquity to contemporary times with a unique focus on the material, educational, and institutional context of the Western rhetorical tradition. Its longitudinal approach enables students to track the recurrence over time of not only specific teaching methods, but also major issues such as social purpose, writing as power, the effect of technologies, the rise of vernaculars, and writing as a force for democratization.

The collection is rich in scholarship and critical perspectives, which is made accessible through the robust list of pedagogical tools included, such as the Key Concepts listed at the beginning of each chapter, and the Glossary of Key Terms and Bibliography for Further Study provided at the end of the text. Further additions include increased attention to orthography, or the physical aspects of the writing process, new material on high school instruction, sections on writing in the electronic age, and increased coverage of women rhetoricians and writing instruction of women. A new chapter on writing instruction in late medieval Europe has also been added to augment coverage of the Middle Ages, fill the gap in students' knowledge of the period, and present instructional methods that can be easily reproduced in the modern classroom.

James J. Murphy is Professor Emeritus in the Department of English and the Department of Communication at the University of California, Davis.

A Short History of Writing Instruction

From Ancient Greece to Contemporary America

Third Edition

Edited by
James J. Murphy

Routledge
Taylor & Francis Group

NEW YORK AND LONDON

Third Edition published 2012
by Routledge
711 Third Avenue, New York, NY 10017

Simultaneously published in the UK
by Routledge
2 Park Square, Milton Park, Abingdon, Oxon OX14 4RN

*Routledge is an imprint of the Taylor & Francis Group, an informa
business*

First edition published by Hermagoras Press (Davis CA) 1990
Second edition published by Hermagoras, an imprint of Lawrence
Erlbaum Associates, Inc. 2001

Library of Congress Cataloging in Publication Data
   A short history of writing instruction : from ancient Greece to
   contemporary America / edited by James J. Murphy. — 3rd ed.
      p. cm.
   Includes bibliographical references and index.
   1. Authorship—Study and teaching—History.   2. Rhetoric—
   Study and teaching—History.   I. Murphy, James Jerome.
   PN181.S56 2012
   808.0071—dc23
                                                    2011046200
ISBN: 978–0–415–89746–4 (hbk)
ISBN: 978–0–415–89745–7 (pbk)
ISBN: 978–0–203–13436–8 (ebk)

Typeset in Bembo/Gill Sans
by RefineCatch Limited, Bungay, Suffolk

*The story of writing is a tale of adventure which
spans some twenty thousand years and touches every
aspect of human life.*
Albertine Gaur, *A History of Writing*

Contents

Ways to Read This Book

An Introduction

James J. Murphy

When philosopher Mortimer Adler wrote his *How to Read a Book* in 1940 it turned out that he was not really talking about books, but about readers. A book, he pointed out, was merely a silent tool waiting to be brought to life by its readers.

The makers of this book—its "authors"—have come together to examine one of the most powerful instincts of human beings, the urge to perpetuate themselves, their thoughts, and their actions through the use of visible symbols. The viewers of our inscriptions—our "readers"—have many options for vitalizing this book.

Most books are prepared with the presumption that the reader will begin at page one and march doggedly through to the last page. One reviewer of the first edition of this book complained that the graphics of its cover unfairly presumed a continuity of teaching methods over the ages, thus cheating the reader of an opportunity to make an independent judgment from the text itself. Our present cover is neutral, leaving it to the reader to decide how to exercise the options of approach.

While front-to-back reading is perhaps the preferred method for most readers, it is also possible to compare epochs/chapters, or track particular teaching methods, or look for continuities/differences, or trace the relations between sociological changes and schools' reaction to them, or work back from the Glossary of Key Terms. This book is not intended as an encyclopedia but it does cover a wide range of approaches to writing instruction. Thus it is the reader's responsibility is to decide (in Mortimer Adler's terms) how to bring the book to life.

This task is complicated by the vast variety of methods used both for the inscription and for the instruction in how to use those methods. Writing is both a physical and a mental activity, setting out thought in concrete images.

The powerful human urge to record has taken many physical forms over the ages. While we in the West rely largely on a Roman alphabet to do this recording, countless other cultures have developed sophisticated systems using everything from knotted cords to baked tablets, notched sticks, and pictographs. Even the genus "alphabet" has many species beyond the Greek and Roman ones so familiar to us—Ogham, Runic, Coptic, Etruscan, Slavonic, and Phrygian, to name a few. The point is that the urge to record, to pass on information, seems so universal that humans everywhere have struggled for thousands of years to find ways to do so. While many "oral" cultures—that is, those without a writing system—have used oral memory as a recording device for their histories and literatures, it is also true that many such cultures eventually developed a writing system that supplanted the oral.

This book, as its title indicates, is concerned with the European–American segment of this worldwide historical phenomenon. It is our belief here that we cannot understand the present state of affairs unless we also understand how that state of affairs came to be. Moreover, as the linguist Louis G. Kelly is quoted as saying at the end of Chapter 2, we can learn useful things for present use by examining what has been done before in language instruction. It is possible, for example, that a modern teacher can use in the classroom some specific methods employed in Roman, medieval, or American colonial schools.

The primary thesis of this book is that, because writing is something that needs to be taught, we owe it to ourselves to discover how people have been and are teaching this powerful human tool. In other words, we look to the history of "instruction" to learn how to write.

Our intent, then, is to trace the developments in writing instruction in Europe from ancient Greece and Rome through the Middle Ages and Renaissance, and then to follow those pedagogical patterns as they were transplanted to America. Over time, these European patterns were re-examined in America, and new forms appeared in the nineteenth and twentieth centuries. The book concludes with some observations about possible futures in writing instruction.

It is important to note at once why the term *instruction* is a key element in this history. The basic principle of the European–American tradition is that writing must be taught. For example, one of the major influences in the European phase of this history, the Roman educator Marcus Fabius Quintilianus, writing about CE 95, observes that writing, unlike speech, has to be acquired through education by someone other than the learner. A small child, he says, can acquire oral language simply by listening to and imitating those around him. But the child cannot acquire writing ability in this way. The tremendous investment of time and resources in writing instruction over many centuries would seem to reinforce Western belief in this principle.

A second major principle in the tradition is that such instruction should take place in "**schools**." We are so accustomed to schools today that we may overlook the fact that this principle was accepted in ancient times only after a major debate about whether individual tutors should teach writing in the home, as opposed to gathering students in groups for instruction by a teaching master. The debate was still going on during the first century of the Christian era, but the Roman Empire quickly moved to support schools with public money and, in fact, used the schools as a means of Latinizing their conquered lands. The acceptance of standardized teaching methods made it possible for Roman schools scattered around the world to have substantially the same classroom regimes—not because of any mandated curriculum ordered from above, but simply because the methods worked. The school tradition itself has proved so strong that even dissident or excluded groups have organized writing schools for their own purposes, from illegal "hedge schools" in occupied Ireland to mechanics' institutes in nineteenth-century England and female academies in America of the same period. The school thus serves both the established and the non-established, simply because it works.

This is not to say that every school in every place and time has done the same thing. And, as we see in Chapter 7, valiant instructional efforts have been made outside the school setting. Yet the key point is that school as mechanism has served the Western world quite well over the years, regardless of variations in detail. What is important is the continuity of writing instruction itself as a desired goal.

This book also aims to describe the various changes in writing instruction that have occurred over time. Certainly, for example, the social and cultural objectives of a Roman classroom teacher were vastly different from those of a classroom teacher in eighteenth-century Wales or an American high school teacher in the 1950s. One of the objectives of this book, therefore, is to discover whether the instructional methods differed as much as their environments did. That is why each chapter seeks to outline the dominant cultural milieu in which instruction occurred in order to measure the extent to which such forces affected the instruction. It is for this reason that the chapters are arranged chronologically—not to argue a presumptive continuity, but rather to allow readers to determine for themselves how each generation decides either to follow a traditional path or to move in some new directions.

It would not be fair, even if it were feasible, to attempt to summarize here the eight chapters that follow. Each chapter covers a unique period in human history, each with its own complexities. In the same sense that it is said that every translation is a lie, so any short summary of such intricate sub-histories would undoubtedly result in a kind of unconscious misrepresentation.

Instead, it might be worth calling attention to two themes that cut across chronological lines: power and the physical task of writing.

Writing and Power

In all the periods covered in these studies, the ability to communicate well was a source of public power. In many societies, including the ancient Greek, the cultural memory of the group was reserved originally to an elite. When writing became accessible to the non-elite in Greece, as Richard Leo Enos demonstrates in Chapter 1, a powerful force of democratization was unleashed. While we see in Chapter 2 that the paired faculties of speaking and writing were important to the Romans, each supporting the other, writing in late antiquity and the early Middle Ages became the primary transmission mode. The revolutionary decision of Benedictine monks in the sixth century to begin copying antique manuscripts preserved a vast treasury of ancient thought for later use; in turn, the need to train scribes for this purpose made writing instruction an integral part of monastic life for the next millennium. Carol Dana Lanham, in Chapter 3, describes the rise of the new *ars dictaminis*, or art of letter-writing, introducing the practical application of writing skills for the specific needs of chancery offices and other official bodies; in fact the practitioners of this art wielded great power for centuries, acting as transmitters of messages sent out by Popes, kings, and all sorts of governing bodies, especially since they dealt with the language not available to the common people—that is, Latin. In the later Middle Ages, the close study of written texts became a means of encouraging the composition of prose and poetry in both Latin and the emerging vernaculars.

With the Renaissance and its revival of Roman educational practices, the systematic pairing of the oral and the written returned as a means of upward mobility; both the English "grammar school" and the Jesuit educational program stressed careful writing, as Don Paul Abbott indicates in Chapter 5. In this same period, writing in the vernacular became increasingly popular, vastly expanding the range of readership beyond the Latinate few and thus empowering larger and larger segments of populations across Europe. The English grammar school was exported intact to colonial America. While the European model prevailed in America well into the nineteenth century, the last two chapters of this book deal with a multitude of specifically American responses to the challenges of providing writing instruction for the citizens of a democracy; these responses are predicated on the deeply ingrained presumption that writing leads to power.

One measure of writing as power is that it is independent of time and place. An oral statement is time-and-place-bound and evaporates with the last sound uttered. An oral protest, for example, can be quashed by batons and tear gas, but in written form, it can be anywhere, anytime. One of the most famous examples of this power is that of Martin Luther. When he posted his famous 95 Theses on the church door in Wittenburg on October 31, 1517, calling for a public debate about indulgences, nothing much happened. But two weeks later, when the theses were printed in pamphlet form, a wave of support sprang up. Both Latin and German vernacular versions were circulated. Scores of pamphlet writers on both sides of the issue soon entered the fray. While it is true that books were later to become the main tools of the ensuing Reformation debates throughout Europe, it was the vernacular pamphlet that informed the initial struggle for power. Often badly written and poorly printed, the pamphlet nevertheless engaged, and hence empowered, masses of lay people in an unprecedented shift of power from the clerical establishment. Suddenly, it was no longer necessary to ask ecclesiastical permission to write about religion. Both Protestant and Catholic leaders saw the urgent necessity of capturing this source of power, and it was not long before systematic educational programs emerged to serve their respective causes—Melanchthon and Sturm on the Protestant side, the Jesuits on the Catholic. It was a classic case in which recognition of power created a demand for the pedagogical means to achieve that power. Chapter 5 outlines some of the instructional consequences of that recognition.

Writing as democratizing has many other examples in the chapters that follow. They need not be detailed here, but it seems important to alert the reader to keep an eye out for the many instances that occur throughout the book.

The Physical Difficulty of Writing

Another factor that underlies most of this history is the speed of thought compared to the slowness of the writing which records that thought. The mind is fast; the hand is slow. While not every chapter cites complaints about this problem (possibly because the matter is so obvious to each generation that it hardly needs saying), the complaints that emerge from time to time indicate that it is not far from writers' minds. Consequently, it might be useful to look briefly at the technology of writing over the centuries.

Surprisingly little has been written about the sheer physical difficulty of inscribing alphabetic characters on some sort of surface. Nevertheless, until very recent times, this difficulty has been a factor in the writing process and therefore in the instructional process. This matter deserves more attention.

The earliest widely used writing surface was woven from the papyrus plant and manufactured on long sheets, which were then rolled up for storage after the writing was inscribed on one side. The *codex*, or "book" as we know it, was not developed until late antiquity; in this form, written pages were stitched together at one edge. Since it was not necessary to roll the sheets, writing could be placed on both sides.

Another surface was the scraped hide of an animal, known as *parchment* from the supposed place of its invention in Pergamum. The finest form of parchment was also known as *vellum*. A complete book could require the hides of a herd of sheep and was therefore extremely expensive. It has been estimated, for example, that the cost of a medieval parchment book of 200 pages would be the equivalent of a modern Porsche or BMW luxury automobile. The cost of parchment was important for two reasons: first, it restricted parchment writing to rich foundations, universities, or patrons, making such writing a product of elite groups; but second, it militated against classroom use for exercises or practice.

Instead, wax tablets, thin pieces of wood with a thin layer of wax, were in use in classrooms from ancient times until at least the Renaissance period. A stylus was used to scratch letters in the wax. They were commonly used in the classroom for drafts and notes. The wax could be erased by heating it with the palm of a hand and then smoothing it over. One problem with the wax was that it did not work well with cursive writing (i.e., writing using connected letters) because of wax buildup in front of the stylus after a few letters.

Paper, though extremely expensive in the beginning, was a revolutionary advance in the democratization of writing and the broadening of classroom uses. Apparently it was invented in China in the year 105 CE, but did not reach Europe until the twelfth century. The first American paper factory was set up in 1690 at Germantown near Philadelphia. Printing created a high demand for paper, which in turn encouraged the increase in the number of paper mills and a subsequent reduction in prices. By the late nineteenth century, paper was so common that it ceased to be mentioned as a factor in writing.

The instruments for inscribing on a page, however, remained a problem until very recently. Early tools were the stylus, a simple scratching rod, or the pen, a tool for laying ink on a surface. Pens were made from metal or wood, then later with quills of birds like the goose; any nonmetal pen required constant sharpening, so that a knife became a constant companion of the writer. (This is the origin of the term *pen knife*.) Note in Chapter 5 that English grammar school students are enjoined to keep sharpened pens. The fountain pen, a pen containing a reservoir of ink that is fed automatically to the nib, appeared only in the 1880s. It was prone to leakage, however, with disastrous consequences for clothing as well as the papers of students and their teachers, and many schools preferred to use regular steel pens; even after World War II, it was common to see school desks with recesses to hold ink bottles.

While wooden pencils using carbon fillers are mentioned as early as 1565 in Switzerland, the practical pencil, as we know it today, was perfected only in 1898. Very little has been written about the use of pencils in writing instruction.

The now-ubiquitous ball-point pen, using a rotating ball to draw on an interior ink supply, came into common use only as recently as 1946. It solved both the leakage problem and the inkwell problem, and its cheapness made it available at all economic levels. It has become the most democratic of writing tools.

In terms of machine writing, Mark Twain was the first major American writer to use a typewriter. (Ironically, the much-berated "QWERTYUIOP" sequence of keyboard letters was introduced initially as a way to slow down the fingers of typists who might have gone so fast that they would jam the machine.)

These technological factors are important to note because, until recently, they were limiting factors for both the would-be writer and the writing instructor. Today, when a whole class's compositions can be posted on a web site for all to see, it may be difficult for a modern generation to understand the difficulties faced by their writing forebears.

The history of punctuation is another neglected aspect of the writing process. Modern punctuation is essentially a product of the print age, when habits of rapid reading created by the flood of printed material made readers reluctant to use traditional methods of interpreting texts. Ancient Greek and Roman texts did not usually have word separations, since the reader sensitive to oral patterns could easily work out the sounds intended by the written words. In addition, it must be remembered that "reading" in ancient times (and medieval times as well) was vocalized, that is, sounded out. Note in Chapter 2 that Quintilian advises his students about the methods of reading their texts in this way. Concepts like a visual "paragraph" appeared in the Middle Ages, though first-line indentation did not, but complexities like colon/semi-colon were standardized only with printing. The quotation mark, for example, was a post-printing device, but even in sixteenth-century texts, quotation marks can be found opposite every quoted line, unlike the present practice of using them only at the beginning and the end of the quotation.

For the historian of writing instruction, then, it is critical to understand, for each period, the writing technologies and the linguistic presuppositions (e.g., punctuation) which have a bearing on teaching methods and their intended results.

Finally, the reader is warned that everyone who has ever lived has lived in what was to him or her "modern times." The following chapters, then, are not mere antiquarian curiosities looking at quaint old teaching practices, but descriptions of each age's effort to solve the problems of what to teach and how to teach it, for every person discussed in these pages considered writing to be an important human activity and therefore one worth doing well.

Chapter 1

Ancient Greek Writing Instruction and Its Oral Antecedents

Richard Leo Enos

Key Concepts

Oral culture • Memory versus writing • Tally systems • Alphabet • Writing as a craft skill • *Techne* • Stichometry • Orthography • *Abecedaria* • *Thetes* • Helots • Writing and thinking • Literacy • Women and writing • Family education and *sumposia* • *Progymnasmata* as graded composition exercises • *Paideia* • *Aoidoi* • Homeric rhapsodes • Syllabaries • Linear A and Linear B • Sophists • Logography • Ostraka • Graffiti and dipinti • *Melete* • Rhetoric • Writing in education • Plato's objections to writing • Aristotle's use of writing • Writing as an intellectual process • Isocrates's curriculum based on talent, practice and experience • *Letteraturizzazione*.

A good song, I think. The end's good—that came to me in one piece—and the rest will do. The boy will need to write it, I suppose, as well as hear it. Trusting to the pen; a disgrace, and he with his own name made. But write he will, never keep it in the place between his ears. And even then he won't get it right alone. I still do better after one hearing of something new than he can after three. I doubt he'd keep his own songs for long, if he didn't write them. So what can I do, unless I'm to be remembered only by what's carved in marble?

The opening passage by the poet-rhapsode Simonides in the
Mary Renault novel, *The Praise Singer*

Overview

Conventional approaches to understanding writing instruction in ancient Greece typically draw upon well-established literary sources. We have learned a great deal about writing instruction from the corpus of ancient writers and this work is synthesized in the present chapter. In addition, non-traditional literary sources, such as fragments of writing on durable materials and the instruments of writing, have come to light, and these primary sources also add to and refine our understanding of writing instruction. As with the previous edition, Athens is an understandable focal point of study, not only because this powerful and enduring city-state is widely regarded as the first literate community in ancient Greece and offers a substantial amount of evidence for examination, but also because new

Figure 1.1 Sitting scribe. Greek terracotta figurine from Thebes, Boeotia. 1st quarter 6th BCE. Location: Louvre, Paris, France.

(Photo Credit: Erich Lessing/Art Resource, NY)

sources of evidence have come to light in recent decades that tell us a great deal more about Athens as a literate community. Archaeological excavations in the Agora, for example, have unearthed inscriptions and related artifacts that now provide new evidence about everyday writing habits. These new resources—in the form of graffiti and dipinti—expand and deepen our knowledge of what community **literacy*** meant in ancient Athens and, correspondingly, the attendant modes of instruction that accompanied a variety of writing functions.

While the present chapter again concentrates on Athens, this chapter also includes brief perspectives on writing instruction from other prominent Greek

* Glossary terms are printed in **bold face** in their first appearance in the text.

city-states. For example, extensive study at Rhodes, Sparta and Thebes reveals not only rival manifestations of **rhetoric** but also correspondingly different approaches to the teaching of writing. Research on these city-states, unlike Athens, is at an early stage. However, what we will find when we examine the rhetorical practices of non-Athenian Hellenic rhetoric is that the approaches are driven by the specific preferences of cultures. For some, such as Athens, writing for civic and educational purposes was important. For others, such as was the case with Sparta, effective written communication in battle situations was critical. For still others, such as Rhodes, rhetoric that stressed cross-cultural issues was emphasized. Correspondingly, the instructional approaches vary in ways that correspond to the orientations of rhetoric. Of course, it would be impossible to discuss the full variety of writing instruction across the city-states of ancient Greece in one chapter, but alternate examples illustrating the diversity of writing instruction explain why certain educational approaches emphasized different features of writing in their instruction, and make clear the necessity of more field work in this area of study.

This chapter discusses not only the sites of writing instruction, but also the range of writing instruction for different groups and functions. Writing instruction, as indicated above, was wide-ranging in practice as a response to an array of socially determined needs. The hope in providing this spectrum is to illustrate the range of writing instruction in ancient Greece and to adjust long-standing (but often imprecise) views. We often assume, for example, that writing is for the privileged few. We now understand, however, that some writing was done as a functional craft practiced by artisans of the *thetes* class with instruction in the form of a labor skill. This writing instruction goes well beyond the training of scribes, who often recorded documents for religious and civic purposes. Such new evidence provides a more comprehensive view of both civic literacy and also the spectrum of writing instruction ranging from writing as an aspect of early education, writing in everyday social interaction, writing as a trade-skill, and writing at the most sophisticated and highest levels of advanced education. In a similar respect, it is important to discuss writing instruction and women in ancient Greece. The long-held belief that women were not literate needs to be reconsidered and qualified. For example, evidence examined a few years ago at the British Museum suggests that literacy was not uncommon among certain classes of Athenian women (see Figure 1.2).[1] Finally, and because ancient Greeks faced the challenge of communicating effectively, this chapter also examines writing instruction for such cross-cultural purposes as commercial transaction with Phoenicians, Carthaginians and Etruscans.

Issues of Historiography and Writing Instruction in Ancient Greece

The history of writing instruction in ancient Greece is, in one respect, a record of the discoveries of the powers of literacy and how those powers could be taught systematically. At first glance, the study of writing instruction does not appear to

---

1 Enos, Richard Leo. "The Archaeology of Women in Rhetoric: Rhetorical Sequencing as a Research Method of Historical Scholarship." *Rhetoric Society Quarterly* 32.1 (Winter 2002): 65–79.

Figure 1.2 Painter of Bologna 417 (5th century BCE). Two schoolgirls, one holding a writing tablet. Terracotta kylix (drinking cup) ca. 460–450 BCE. Location: The Metropolitan Museum of Art, New York, NY, USA.

(© The Metropolitan Museum of Art/Art Resource, NY)

seem complex, but there are issues of historiography that must be noted. If we consider "literacy" to be nothing more than acquiring the skill of how to read and write, then writing instruction would be nothing more than learning the rudiments of a recording technique that would serve as an aid to memorizing speech. *However, it is important to stress the complex, endemic relationship that existed among reading, writing and speaking in ancient Greece.* We tend to think of writing instruction as a separate category from oral instruction, but the interrelation of orality *with* literacy was much closer than our current perspectives reveal. Writing instruction was (eventually) integrated with, and became a part of, "oral" instruction, as is clearly evident when we examine Greek **declamation**.[2] From its inception in Greece, however, writing developed for reasons other than as an aid to memory for speech. Writing also served as a technology for quantitative memory and problem-solving in early mathematical accounting. In identifying and examining these methods of invention we should also acquire a more detailed understanding of the mentality of cognition and expression. In the past, insights

2 D. A. Russell, *Greek Declamation* (London and New York: Cambridge University Press, 1983).

to the cognitive processes that structure meaning have been through the study of theory and performance. An understanding of instruction will provide another critical perspective on the relationship between thought and expression in ancient Greece.

Pre-Alphabetic Influences on Writing Instruction

Before writing, of course, Greece was exclusively an oral culture. Thoughts and sentiments were preserved by long-term memory and transmitting those thoughts from mentor to **apprentice** as a form of oral instruction. While long-term memory was valued in Greek culture it was hardly a widespread trait and required considerable skill and training. Mastering the craft-techniques of oral composition and memory-training led to the guild of *aoidoi* and later to **rhapsodes**; these experts, memorizing massive amounts of language for preservation and transmission, viewed their *techne* as a specialized craft that required years of training and is often associated with the origins of rhetoric. Controlling Greek "literature" was the craft of the expert rhapsode and not a broad-based public skill. During this purely oral rhapsodic stage, heuristics for oral composition were developed and taught long before rhetoric became a discipline. Writing in pre-alphabetic Hellenic cultures was also an aid to memory but was used more for economic and mathematical functions than prose recording. Writing instructors were those who transmitted skill in using tally systems for accounting purposes.

Eventually, when scripts evolved to an alphabetic system, writing came to complement, and later replace, the need for long-term memory of oral discourse. Even at that stage, however, the ties between writing, reading and speech remained particularly strong in ancient Greece and persisted for centuries. In fact, there is very good reason to believe that most ancient Greeks never learned to read silently.[3] Of course, even from this perspective, writing instruction would be a tremendous skill if it were nothing more than simply a recording device. Yet, writing evolved into much more than an aid to memory, particularly with the evolution of the alphabet, and these changes had enormous consequences for the instruction of writing in Greece.

Alphabetic Influences on Early Writing Instruction

In one respect, writing itself is a technology and, in ancient Greece, the alphabet is the essence of that technology. By modification and adaptation of earlier Semitic scripts, ancient Greeks were able to construct a writing system that evolved to only twenty-four letters, each of which was intended to capture a discrete but essential sound of the utterances of their language. When arranged together, these discrete sounds could be echoed to reconstruct the vocal patterns of everyday speech. The alphabet was ingenious in its simplicity and monumental in its impact. Earlier pre-alphabetic writing systems were, by

---

3 W. B. Stanford, *The Sound of Greek: Studies in the Greek Theory and Practice of Euphony* (Berkeley and Los Angeles: University of California Press, 1967) 1–5; H. I. Marrou, *A History of Education in Antiquity* (Madison: University of Wisconsin Press, rpt. 1983) 195.

comparison, slow, cumbersome, complex and imprecise. The alphabet, however, could be easily learned and written—even by children—and readily remembered. It is also important to note that the alphabet made this recording device very easy to learn and to use; instruction, accordingly, moved from a specialized craft skill done for purposes of tally, accounting and computation, to a skill easily mastered by non-experts involved in public discourse. More advanced mathematical systems initially used the alphabet for computation before adopting the later Arabic system of pure numbers. Geometry, of course, is one of the exceptions that persisted (to a degree) in continued use of the Greek alphabet.

Writing could provide the conditions where not just an expert but also even an entire community—such as Athens—could be literate. Eventually, this shift would move writing instruction from a specialized craft-skill to an aspect of civic education. Writing has demonstrable benefits over "oral" techniques that are used to stimulate long-term memory far beyond tally and recording heuristics. Writing with the alphabet created the procedure used by early Greeks to capture the fleeting, momentary utterances of oral discourse. Accordingly, instruction in writing would be "democratized" in the sense that it could easily be taught to the public and move from a specialized craft-skill to a public activity and, in this sense, taught to the public as a way of facilitating civic affairs, such as the law courts and political assemblies.

In his volume, *A Study of Writing*, I. J. Gelb asserts that the Greek development of the alphabet was "the last important step in the history of writing."[4] For those of us who wish to better understand the history of writing instruction in ancient Greece, the opposite view would seem to be true. That is, the devising of the alphabet signals the beginning of widespread writing instruction in ancient Greece. If we take Gelb's remark to mean that the structure of writing was so ingeniously simplified that any child could learn to write and, therefore, any advancement would only be limited to adding or modifying letters, then we would agree with Gelb's view. *Writing instruction in ancient Greece, however, was much more than imparting directions about the arrangement of individual letters of the alphabet. With the alphabet, writing took on rhetorical functions and, in turn, the instruction of writing changed dramatically from a craft skill to also include what would eventually evolve into an art or* techne *of social power.*

Writing Instruction and Civic Power

Writing as a source of power (*dunamis*) soon became apparent to Hellenic practitioners, educators and politicians. The alphabet was the medium that both stabilized and unleashed thoughts and sentiments that were otherwise constrained when limited to oral expression. Ancient Greeks realized that writing could do much more than label and serve as an aid to memory; writing could also function as an heuristic, an aid to creating discourse and to refining patterns of thinking. Furthermore, because of strong and long-standing commercial interaction, Greeks found that the alphabet facilitated effective communication across cultures. Comparative studies of shared alphabets—especially with Phoenicians, Romans and Etruscans—reveal how writing could facilitate the sort of effective

4 I. J. Gelb, *A Study of Writing* (Chicago: University of Chicago Press, 1974) 184.

cross-cultural communication needed for trade and supply.[5] Correspondingly, from this perspective, we can see that instruction in writing was required because it was an indispensable aid in recording commercial transactions and trade agreements across cultures. Although there is no substantial body of evidence, it is likely that such instruction was done by mentor–apprentice interaction as a feature of commercial trading.

There is little doubt that writing instruction does aid oral discourse by "freezing" or stabilizing speech. Yet, stabilizing oral discourse through writing offers many more benefits than merely holding the language still and in place. Writing also facilitates not only the widespread production, but also the quality of discourse. By its very nature, the act of writing requires authors to slow down their thinking much more than is necessary in oral discourse.[6] Moreover, once written, that discourse is readily available for pondering, recall, reflection and revision. From this perspective, writing helps to stimulate abstract thought, creativity and long-term problem-solving. While these concepts seem to be contemporary concepts, they were features of writing that ancient Greeks recognized and, accordingly, assimilated into their writing instruction. The history of writing instruction in ancient Greece is much more than mastery of lockstep prescriptive methods, but rather it is the evolution of a mentality that came to understand writing itself as an heuristic for both preserving and creating new modes of thought and expression.

The Evolution of Writing Instruction from a Craft-Skill to a Public Activity

Ancient Greeks recognized the power of writing as an aid to thinking, but also that it had a social dimension. One of the most important features in the development of writing instruction in ancient Greece was that it evolved into a public activity. This social dimension to writing had an enormous impact not only on shaping writing instruction, but also in sharing the advantages of literacy beyond the individual, and often isolated, expert. Not the least of these advantages, as we will see, is that writing serves as a recording device and as an activity that facilitates widespread complex thinking. That is, a community of writers and readers could benefit from the interaction of comment and response, much like a collection of individuals can benefit from the interchange inherent in the oral dynamics of discussion. Writing instruction was done in Greece not just to train the scribe but also to enrich education by facilitating higher-level modes of thought and expression than previously had been available through oral discourse alone. Despite writing's ever-increasing social power, awareness of the cognitive benefits of writing was not immediately recognized and was the subject of considerable debate among thinkers such as Plato, as is clearly evident in both his *Gorgias* and his *Phaedrus*. To understand the evolution of writing instruction in Greece, the issues inherent in determining the place of writing instruction in

---

5 Richard Leo Enos, *Roman Rhetoric: Revolution and the Greek Influence* (Anderson SC: Parlor Press, 2008) 3–22.

6 Richard Young and Patricia Sullivan. "Why Write? A Reconsideration." *Essays on Classical Rhetoric and Modern Discourse*, ed. Robert J. Connors, Lisa S. Ede and Andrea A. Lunsford (Carbondale and Edwardsville IL: Southern Illinois University Press, 1984) 215–25.

Greek education, and its eventual impact on higher education, we must first reassess some of our presumptions about writing and its relationship to thinking, particularly writing as a technology.

As we learn more about the history of writing instruction, especially with respect to ancient Greece, we realize that many of our traditional, long-standing assumptions—such as those outlined above—are inaccurate. In this chapter we will see that "literacy" has a range of meanings, that facility in writing was not always the possession of the intellectual elite, and that writing itself undergoes a transformation as it moves from a pragmatic labor-craft to develop as an intellectual heuristic or skill for rational analysis and expression that eventually found its place in the higher education of Hellenistic Greece. By the standards of archaic Athens writing was initially learned for very functional purposes. The standards for eloquence were not written but oral expression. The impact of literacy is, in part, a change from the view of writing as a mundane recording device to the standard for artistic prose expression. The transformation of writing during this period is both caused by and reflected in the writing instruction of Athenian society. As will become apparent, our best way of seeing the evolution of writing instruction, from a labor skill to its intellectual flowering with the school of Isocrates, is to understand the social and cultural forces in operation that brought about this change. Many groups of people, entire civilizations in fact, have come and gone without any known writing system. Walter J. Ong has argued in *Orality and Literacy* that thousands of languages are known to have existed—doubtless many more have faded from memory—but only a little more than one hundred writing systems are known to have existed. Yet, the impact of those writing systems has been astounding in their facilitation of virtually every dimension of those (literate) societies: law, education, politics, and even the ways histories are recorded.[7] The relationships between these disciplines and orality and literacy are, as we shall see, also important in the development of writing instruction in ancient Greece.

Writing Instruction as a Research Topic

We should view writing instruction as a dynamic research topic, in part because we are only now beginning to understand its place and importance. Clearly, much about the history of writing instruction in ancient Greece still awaits discovery. For example, as mentioned earlier, we seek to better understand the place of women in ancient Greek writing instruction. We will say at the outset that the role of women in the history of rhetoric in general, and Greek writing instruction in particular, is under-researched and woefully incomplete. There is, however, current scholarship that provides evidence indicating that women were far more involved in Greece's literate revolution than we have suspected, and this research is thoroughly synthesized by Lois Agnew in her analysis, "Women and Classical Rhetoric."[8] Earlier scholarship by such noted researchers as Andrea

---

7 Richard Garner, *Law & Society in Classical Athens* (New York: St. Martin's Press, 1987) 138.
8 Lois Agnew, "The Classical Period." *The Present State of Scholarship in the History of Rhetoric: A Twenty-First Century Guide*, ed. Lynée Lewis Gaillet with Winifred Bryan Horner (Columbia and London: University of Missouri Press, 2010) 12–14.

Lunsford, Susan C. Jarratt, C. Jan Swearingen, Cheryl Glenn and others also has made an important contribution toward our understanding of women and their place in Greek rhetoric (e.g., *Reclaiming Rhetorica* and *Rhetoric Retold*). Although all experts agree that more research needs to be done to discover new evidence, and to develop new methods of historiography and new tools for critical analysis, current research has already revealed new insights, with evidence pointing toward the possibility of women participating in schools of rhetoric in Athens, teaching rhetoric, being involved in co-educational programs, and even establishing their own educational centers. The constraint inherent in such research, however, is that the sources and social status in Athens, and many other Greek city-states, were so heavily oriented toward male control that the quest for primary evidence about women and writing instruction remains the foremost concern before a full and detailed accounting can be made. Such scholars as those mentioned above have demonstrated that the activity and place of women in writing instruction were far greater than we have suspected. Further, **epigraphical** evidence reveals the possibility that education for women in Athens may not be representative of all of Greece. Co-educational systems were known to have existed on both Teos and Chios and, as Marrou notes, "in Hellenistic schools sexual discrimination tended to disappear."[9] All this is to say that the role of women in writing instruction in ancient Greece is a current, and very exciting, topic of inquiry. In all, the impact of writing instruction tells us much more than the nature of writing within a culture: it tells us about the culture itself.

The Homeric Tradition of Oral Education and Writing Instruction

Ancient Greeks relied on oral discourse to express thoughts and sentiments; their culture, including their educational practices, was oral. If we were to use three adjectives to characterize what we know about the earliest forms of Greek education they would be: oral, musical and athletic. The earliest known educational practices in Greece were direct and personal, often associated with family relationships. Elders of the family—both male and female—participated in educating their children personally and directly. While the earliest Greeks did not have an education that could be described as communal or systematic, the **"curriculum"** was fairly common, at least among the higher classes of citizens. The one clear exception was Sparta, whose citizens had their own mode of communal education and chose to de-emphasize literacy to the point that some Spartans even bragged about their inability to read and write.[10] In most other settings, however, the responsibility for education centered on the family. In addition to the skills necessary for managing the economy of property and (in many cases) animal husbandry, youthful citizens were "educated" by learning Homer, by engaging in athletic contests that were oriented toward military and agonistic skills, and by acquiring (to some degree) proficiency in music.

---

9 Marrou, *A History of Education in Antiquity*, 222 (esp. nn. 1 and 2).
10 Richard Leo Enos, "The Secret Composition Practices of the Ancient Spartans: A Study of 'Noncivic' Classical Rhetoric." *Renewing Rhetoric's Relation to Composition*, ed. Shane Borrowman, Stuart C. Brown and Thomas P. Miller (New York and London: Routledge, 2009) 236–47.

Such knowledge, especially at this earliest, pre-literate phase of instruction, was oral, aural and physical. At the heart of this education was the *sumposium*. That is, wisdom was imparted to youth from family elders; in the case of young boys, education passed through elder males and was seen as a means for not only imparting wisdom but also strengthening kinship bonds. Females had parallel forms of instruction, primarily directed toward learning domestic skills. In both instances, and before writing began to be introduced, the family-bound education was cemented through orality. Home-based education was strongly associated with family ties. Eventually, education would be de-centered away from the family and home in two respects. First, centers such as the gymnasium would evolve from sites of military and athletic training to include other forms of education. One of the most important aspects of this education was elementary rhetorical exercises called *progymnasmata*. Although these early exercises are most closely associated with the more formalized educational practices of the later Hellenistic and Roman periods of writing instruction, scholars such as D. A. Russell strongly argue that they were evident early in Greek education.[11] Second, instruction from the home would be extended, and correspondingly diminished, by foreign educators (*metics*), who would be attracted to Athens. In fact, many of the most famous **Sophists** were non-Athenian but saw in Athens a site that offered both the freedom and the reward for their pedagogical skills. The novelty and diversity of these educators attracted students to their schools and away from family teachers and what amounted to home schooling.

Understandably, the mode of expression that dominated these earlier forms of education was oral. Orality is apparent even in the transmission of what we know as "literature." For centuries, the transmission of this literature had been oral. Tales woven out of the *Iliad* and *Odyssey* were composed for oral performance in which virtue was lauded and vice was condemned. Homeric bards or *aoidoi*, and later rhapsodes, emerged as experts skilled in the telling and preservation of Homeric "literature." The cultural values and social standards of Homeric literature became the foundation for what ancient Greeks termed *paideia* or the virtue of intellectual excellence. Over the centuries, this Homeric heritage that served as the basis for education would be challenged and writing would be a central issue in the transformation of the concept of *paideia* or what it meant to be educated. Greek writing instruction is a study of the evolution of *paideia*, for as writing became part of the education of ancient Greeks, their notion of what *paideia* meant changed dramatically, influencing the very fabric of their society. Writing became a part of the *paideia* of Greek education when it was considered to be a pedagogical value and not merely a craft-skill. That is, writing became a means for attaining intellectual excellence. Yet, writing was not initially seen as an intellectual source of power but rather as a functional skill that served, at best, as a facilitator of the oral tradition of education.

The history of writing instruction in ancient Greece is a history of this transition from oral to oral *and* literate educational practices. Writing instruction was inextricably tied to orality. This relationship was fostered in part because of the bond that existed among reading, writing and orality. Today, when we treat the

---

11 Russell, *Greek Declamation*, 3.

language arts, we do so in terms of either orality or literacy. In the most literal sense, writing instruction in ancient Greece was oral *and* literate, one and the same. Compositions were written to be recited aloud and were meant not only to be seen but also to be heard. At its highest and most polished levels, writing instruction pointed toward compositions that were intended to be performed aloud. Writing instruction in ancient Greece, then, is more closely tied with the oral/aural than our present habits. We must also understand that to discuss writing instruction is implicitly to discuss reading instruction. Most of us see the association between writing and reading as a natural connection but, as we will discuss, the emphasis and expertise between writers and readers differed as writing was introduced and as writing/reading instruction evolved in ancient Greece. That is, some groups—and here we are speaking principally of Athenian social classes—received writing instruction for varying purposes. Some became composers as a trade; others were principally readers who learned only rudimentary skills of writing that would carry them through their daily business. In order to understand this evolution in (alphabetic) writing instruction, we must first understand its historical antecedents.

The Emergence of Pre-Alphabetic Writing Instruction in Bronze Age Greece

> *The need for permanent records for numbers of things must have arisen very early in the history of mankind.*
>
> Graham Flegg, *Numbers: Their History and Meaning*, p. 41

The Origins of Writing Instruction: Economics and Mathematics

The temptation to romanticize writing instruction in ancient Greece is strong and is nurtured by Victorian characterizations of scholarly men sitting in a circle in rapt attention to intellectuals such as Isocrates. In many ways, however, the characterization of Isocrates and his school, where writing instruction played a central role in advanced education, is not the beginning of writing instruction in ancient Greece but the culmination of writing instruction at its pinnacle. The origins of writing instruction in Greece are not found in the classroom or on leisurely peripatetic strolls through the peristyles of a stoa. Rather, the writing that we imagine at the highest levels of literacy in Athens, for example, was a consequence of an evolution that is dimly understood. The beginnings of writing instruction are mundane and functional rather than artistic and intellectual. While there is no doubt that writing instruction did come to play a central role in Isocrates' notion of *paideia*, the origins of writing instruction in ancient Greece were anything but ideal. Writing did not come into existence as an art (*techne*) in the Greek world, but rather emerged as a functional craft-skill, the consequence of an evolutionary process driven by economic and cultural needs. Writing came into existence by and because of technology. It served to facilitate primary orality by supplying the benefits that are lacking in orality: stabilization of meaning, a prompt for acoustics, and an extension of memory.

The earliest evidence of writing in Greece comes in the form of pictographs, ideographs and **syllabaries** during the Bronze Age. That is, writing was composed through drawings that represented visual images (pictographs), concepts or ideas (ideographs), and symbols that are cluster-units of sounds composed into groupings of consonants and vowels (syllabaries). These syllabaries, as will be discussed later, are especially important for the study of writing instruction in Greece, for they begin to show the effort to reduce characters into phonetic units that, when articulated orally, are prompts to the reader/auditor of how the scratch markings are to be pronounced.[12] From this perspective, syllabaries are a transition in writing leading to the refinement of sound units in their most discrete units, the alphabet. Before, and for a period of time after the Bronze Age, even this limited evidence of writing disappeared to the extent that scholars characterize these periods as the "dark age"—a time when Greece "sunk" back into orality. Such sweeping historical characterizations by nineteenth- and twentieth-century scholars have enormous implications for understanding writing instruction in ancient Greece. These macroscopic generalizations by modern scholars of rhetoric's history are based on the erroneous presumption that writing is categorically different than oral composition and, therefore, that writing instruction is separate from instruction in oral composition. Quite the opposite is the case. Nascent systems of understanding and sharing meaning grew out of oral composition since writing has its roots in orality. That is, early writing was done for recording not only the memory of events and items but also for recording the acoustic elements of speech. When "viewed" by auditors, writing provided cues to orality so that meaning could be sounded out.

We would think that the earliest forms of writing in Greece would be for the purpose of preserving Homeric tales and other legends of obvious cultural value. At this pre-alphabetic stage, however, such recordings were still done orally, primarily, we may assume, because the technology of writing instruction was at the nascent stage of representing empirically acoustic data. That is, early, pre-alphabetic writing systems had not yet been developed to express thoughts, sentiments, wishes and values embodied in Homeric tales. Rather, the earliest systems of writing that we have show a strong tie with mathematics.[13] Michael Ventris and John Chadwick, in the process of revealing their decipherment of the pre-alphabetic Greek script, Linear B, have demonstrated the dominant functions of such writings to be pictographs, ideograms and syllabaries used for the purpose of recording personnel lists, tallies of livestock and agricultural produce, land ownership and function, tribute and ritual offerings, the accounting of various textiles, vessels and furniture, and the recording of metals and military equipment.[14] In sum, writing's function is for the empirical purpose of recording, accounting and computation. Doing such tally recordings and descriptive accounting orally has inherent limitations. Even today, the need for

---

12 John Chadwick, *The Decipherment of Linear B*, 2nd ed. (Cambridge: Cambridge University Press, 1970) 42.

13 Denise Schmandt-Besserat, "Chirographic Culture," *The Cambridge Encyclopedia of Language Sciences*, ed. Patrick Colm Hogan (Cambridge: Cambridge University Press, 2011) 156.

14 Michael Ventris and John Chadwick, eds., *Documents in Mycenaean Greek*. Eds., 2nd ed. (Cambridge: Cambridge University Press, 1973).

technology—writing out math problems or using calculators—reveals the inherent limitations in remembering tallies and in performing computations when done solely "in our heads."

Externalizing our computations by recording them removes the need for sustained memory and stabilizes the concepts into fixed symbolic meaning. For example, Denise Schmandt-Besserat has demonstrated that semetic tally systems in Bronze Age were done as an aid to memory, primarily to keep track of goods, livestock and other units of quality in basic social functions both at home and in social transactions.[15] Early examples of Greek scripts, such as Linear B, show the importance of inventories for basic economic (in Greek, literally "household") purposes. Making these tallies symbolic—scratching them on durable material—preserved an accurate record. Driven by orality and the desire for efficiency, these symbolic systems evolved from pictographic/ideographic markings to symbols of oral pronunciation, and the earliest writing in Greece reveals a syllabary that was intended to capture vocal characterizations of articulated meaning. In fact, if we consider writing instruction as existing in pre-alphabetic Greece, then a strong argument could be made that the origins of writing instruction in ancient Greece are not in prose but rather in economics and mathematics. Economics is used here in its original sense of "house-keeping" accounts; that is, writing was used as a recording device for keeping tallies and other forms of non-discursive accounting.

Teaching a symbolic system of recorded empirical referents for utterances facilitated, but also enabled, writing to stabilize other parts of speech than nouns. That is, moving from pictographs and ideographs to syllabaries and (eventually) to alphabets meant that parts of speech other than nouns could also be visualized through writing. The technology of writing began to record symbolically expressed actions of feelings and moods, and (eventually) to do so in the full range of oral communication: tense, mood, voice, person and number. Further refining the stabilization of writing evolved into an alphabet, a simple but ingenious system where the full range of human expression—and the ultimate in precise meaning normally associated with orality—could now be expressed and taught literally. Rooted in orality, writing instruction could enable the full range of the parts of speech to be inscribed and could express the agent/auditor. The value of such a technology would be apparent to all, and the demand to learn nurtured the teachers who would provide instruction.

Writing Instruction for Cross-Cultural Communication

A Study of Stichometry and Orthography

As indicated above, the origins of writing instruction cannot be separated from orality, and grew out of the pragmatic necessity of a craft-skill that would eventually be specialized. Part of the inherent benefits of writing is apparent from the aid-to-memory and the aid-to-speech discussed above. Another benefit,

15 See the list of some of her publications in the Suggested Readings section at the end of the chapter.

Figure 1.3 Linear A. Arthur Evans' original reproduction of an oblong tablet that is "ruled" at intervals for the convenience of the scribes, as it appeared in *The Athenaeum*.

(Courtesy of The American School of Classical Studies: Agora Excavations)

however, that stimulated writing and its instruction was in communicating across cultures. Fragments of pottery, remnants of precious minerals and the discovery of artifacts far removed from their locale all indicate the extensive commercial activity evident as early as the Bronze Age in Greece.[16] The widespread opportunities of commerce were fueled by the environs of Greece, where sea travel became the natural mode of transportation, and where exploration reaped benefits in commodities as well as eventual colonies. Literary accounts, such as the *Iliad* and the *Odyssey*, although mythological in origin, nonetheless reveal the inherent diversity of culture and how that diversity was exposed through sea travel. Given these conditions, there is little wonder why city-states such as Athens, that dominated through a thalassocracy, would rise to power in

16 Emily Vermeule, *Greece in the Bronze Age* (Chicago and London: University of Chicago Press, 1964).

the Greek world. At the same time, however, such activity meant exposure to a variety of dialects and languages. Exposure to such ethnic diversity in commercial activity required language proficiency across cultures, so that transactions could be understood and shared. From this perspective, there is little wonder why the Phoenicians—the Biblical "Sea People"—were experts in the development of writing and the transmitters of a nascent form of the alphabet to the Greeks. In fact, every culture in the Bronze Age that is either Greek or known to have interacted with Greeks in commercial activity had created or borrowed some form of alphabetic writing system.

Our knowledge of the writing instruction that went on in these early periods is only a point of speculation, but there are reasonable inferences that can be advanced. We do know that early methods of oral composition were passed down from mentor to apprentice. Along with the transmission of this body of material, techniques for developing memory were also known to have been taught, since memory was the "technology" for recording and preserving knowledge. It is reasonable to think that the earliest forms of writing instruction would be taught in a similar manner. That is, writing would be acquired as an on-the-job-skill and then transmitted as a craft-skill from mentor to apprentice. From this view, it is easy to imagine that such writing would not only be refined but also specialized to the extent that "experts" in writing would emerge as a sort of "guild' in the way that Homeric rhapsodes from Chios, or Homeridae, asserted their identity, or as artisans are known to have emerged later from the *thetes* class in Athens as engravers and recorders of public matter, and as "chancellory" scribes developed as recorders of religious matters. From this perspective we can speculate with some degree of confidence that the earliest forms of writing instruction were likely pragmatic and task-driven. Moreover, such tasks were basic labor skills driven by the need to be effective, efficient and understandable to others, both to those who shared a dialect as well as to those who came from different languages where a shared meaning across cultures had to be created.

The (R)evolution of Writing Instruction During the Archaic Period

The impact of writing instruction was so dramatic that some scholars have characterized it as a "literate revolution." That is, we are tempted to think of the introduction of writing and its instruction as a startling and immediate "event," something akin to a society being invaded and taken over by an alien force. The more accurate representation, as the discussion in the chapter to this point reveals, is that writing instruction was an evolution and that the impact of literacy—which did flower in the late fifth and early fourth centuries BCE—began centuries earlier. To understand the nature and impact of this literate revolution, we must understand first the "(r)evolution" of writing instruction.

As with some other groups, early (pre-alphabetic) Greeks both developed and borrowed symbols to transcribe and therefore "freeze" ideas. These symbols were both descriptive and representational. That is, the earliest Greek scripts—writing well before the alphabet was invented—captured meaning through pictures (presentational symbols) and symbols to represent sounds (phonetic symbols). Influenced by contact with other groups of people, particularly the sea-faring

Phoenicians, early Greeks evolved their (pre-alphabetic) writing systems into syllabaries, systems for pronouncing based on clusters of sounds in the prosody of the language. For example, a syllabic writing system would have three signs approximating the vocalization for each cluster of sounds in the word "*in-struc-tion*." The two most famous of these early Greek writing systems emerged during the Bronze Age and are known as Linear A and Linear B. At this early level, however, any sort of writing instruction was idiosyncratic and learned because of the pragmatic utility of the symbols, principally for commercial and economic reasons. That is, early manifestations of writing were helpful for the economic concerns of counting, recording and remembering. These early, crude systems were not writing systems as we think of them today. They were not used to record long prose narratives or to help in the explication of complex modes of reasoning. Rather, these syllabaries were **shorthand** methods for recording that served as aids-to-memory, such as in recording jars of oil or the number of oxen. In the twentieth century, office secretaries and courtroom recorders developed task-specific shorthand systems that enabled them to accurately capture oral dictation and legal testimony.

Although these early Greek writing systems had pragmatic functions, they were nonetheless difficult to learn, making instruction all the more selective. Early Greek syllabaries normally comprised scores of characters, requiring no small degree of commitment to learn. There is, moreover, no direct evidence of how this earliest Greek writing instruction was actually taught. The prevailing belief, however, is that writing instruction paralleled the normal patterns of early Greek instruction, particularly the habits for acquiring oral compositional techniques. Most likely, these complex systems were taught by mentor to apprentice and sustained by individuals who saw the benefits of recording economic data and possessions and had the resources to utilize it. These early Greek writing systems, the forerunners to the alphabet, helped to stabilize a system of expression that would be refined into the alphabetic script.

As mentioned earlier, what Gelb means by the last great invention—the development of the alphabet—is the finalization of a system that could be learned simply and used widely. The alphabet could be learned by children without great difficulty and, as ancient Greeks discovered, was useful in ways that extended far

Figure 1.4 Abortive *abecedarium.*

(Courtesy of The American School of Classical Studies: Agora Excavations)

beyond counting and chronicling. The elegant simplicity of the alphabet made instruction much easier as well. That is, the "expert" did not need to know the scores of characters that were required by Greece's earlier syllabaries but a comparatively few number of characters with distinct phonetic equivalents. From this perspective we can understand why earlier, pre-alphabetic writing instruction was a craft-tool used for the employment of economic concerns and not artistic production or educational development. The possibilities for the alphabet, however, were enormous, extending the benefits across society and making the system of writing so simple that it could be learned only a few years after birth.

Not the least of the alphabet's public consequences was that the need for a scribe became less essential. This type of **"craft" literacy**—such as the scribe necessary for mastering the intricacies of Egyptian hieroglyphics—diminished to largely civic and administrative functions. Yet, the increased dissemination of writing brought into existence another kind of craft literacy: the need for artisans who could inscribe and engrave this new writing for widespread public dissemination. In this respect, Gelb's last phase of writing—the emergence of the alphabet—is the solidification of a system that would begin an evolution toward public literacy. The progress of that evolution is the progress and refinement of writing instruction. It is for these reasons that, while earlier Greek writing systems existed, the attention to the development of writing instruction starts—not ends as Gelb implies—with the emergence of the alphabet in Greece around 800 BCE. The technological ease of the alphabet meant that writing skill could be acquired publicly. The potential of the Greek alphabet, as has been mentioned, meant that not only was communal literacy possible but also that writing instruction could be systematized for civic, non-expert instruction.

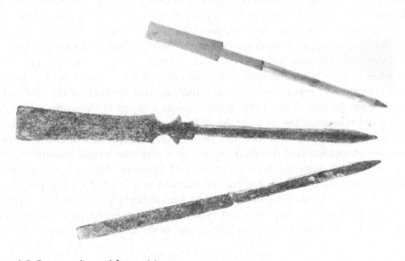

Figure 1.5 Bone styli used for writing.

(Courtesy of The American School of Classical Studies: Agora Excavations)

Early Writing and Specialized Instruction: Artists and Artisans

The evolution of literacy in ancient Greece took several hundred years. As indicated above, alphabetic writing existed around 800 BCE and was probably in existence quite some time prior to that date. Knowledge of alphabetic writing and its widespread instruction, however, are two different matters. During this early period, the ninth and eighth centuries BCE, Greece was in a transitional phase known as "pre-literacy." Alphabetic writing had some use and its familiarity was spreading—doubtless due to its utility in trade and commerce—but was not widely employed. In brief, writing is apparent throughout Greece but there is little evidence that most people knew how to read and write to any extent that widespread, public literacy could be claimed. In this respect, writing instruction was in a transitional period, evolving from a specialized craft into what would later become a public skill. By the Archaic Period (late seventh century to early fifth century BCE) early manifestations of writing instruction as a craft are apparent in two dominant groups. The first group of (written) composers was the Homeric rhapsodes who were mentioned earlier. These bards were the artists who orally transmitted the tales of Homer and other forms of poetry. As the etymology of their Greek name implies, they were "stitchers of odes" who wove their compositions into tales. Rhapsodes evolved into a specialized guild out of the early Homeric *aoidoi*, the earliest balladeers that appear within the works of Homer.[17] As the singers of Homeric tales, rhapsodes took pride in being the linguistic guardians of the "proper" pronunciation of Homeric Greek, acquiring their reputations from their ability to orally chant recitations of Homeric "literature" and to do so in a tongue that was becoming increasingly distant from the numerous, evolving dialects of Greece.

Homeric rhapsodes began a system of writing instruction that was designed to preserve the words—which also meant the oral quality—of the Homeric tongue. In an effort to record, and thereby preserve Homer, as well as capture the euphony of the Homeric tongue, many rhapsodes began to use writing as an aid-to-memory and soon saw writing instruction as a part of their craft. Rhapsodes transmitted their thesaurus of Homeric literature from mentor to apprentice and it is doubtless that through this process writing was taught. Such a form of writing instruction, however, was far from public. Rhapsodic composition was more akin to the specialized craft-skill mentioned earlier, an orthographic system used to preserve the oral features of epic poetry. Accounts indicate that the texts of the *Iliad* and the *Odyssey* that we have today came about because a group of rhapsodes gathered to codify and transcribe the spoken tales of Homer, thus stabilizing and establishing the inscribed text. Unlike the function of earlier, pre-alphabetic syllabaries, however, rhapsodes used this craft literacy in a way that would become a part of their art (*techne*). Instruction in the writing of Homeric discourse was pragmatic but, as evidenced by Plato's *Ion*, this instruction was learned for the purposes of preserving semi-divine (oral) literature. The *Ion* further helps to reveal the mentality of rhapsodes toward composing and writing instruction, because the dialogue-character Ion believes that his abilities come from divine inspiration.[18] Hellenic

---

17 For a Homeric example of an *aoidos*, see the early passage of *Odyssey* IX.
18 Plato, *Ion* 533D–535A.

rhapsodes are among the first Greeks to show expert ability in writing and its instruction as a group. Their educational practices, however, were not directed to the public but rather to other apprentice rhapsodes, who learned reading and writing as a technology to help sustain Homeric oral features.

The second major group of individuals to demonstrate any sort of expertise in writing that required specialized instruction was the artisans of the Archaic Period, the public workers or *demiourgoi* of the *thetes* (labor) class.[19] A few inscriptions, possibly dating back to the Homeric period, have been discovered on objects that have words and phrases scratched on the surface. As we move through the Archaic Period, however, this form of writing becomes much more stylized and even a part of the art itself. In one example, an urn portrays a Homeric rhapsode and words from Homer are "spoken" from the figure's mouth. As Greek plastic art evolved, writing became a common trait and was associated with physical features of artistic expression. In short, the sort of prestige of stylized writing associated with earlier Egyptian hieroglyphics or later medieval calligraphy became (to a limited degree) part of the art of ancient Greece. Names of gods and heroes were included on pottery and artisans dedicated objects of art—probably at the request of their patrons—to beneficiaries of these precious gifts.

The association of writing with fine art applies also to architecture. Existing monuments and public structures reveal that artisans inscribed buildings; lists of individuals and chronicles of events label important structures throughout Greece.[20] The ever-increasing occurrence and popularity of this form of public writing makes it apparent that artisans, coming from the *thetes* or labor class, learned to write first as a part of their building trade and later as a trade in its own right. Thus, in two specialized occupations that seem somewhat distant from each other—the Homeric rhapsode and the common labors of the *thetes* artisans—writing was learned as a craft literacy.

The writings of Homeric artists and common artisans provided material that nurtured public literacy and more popular forms of writing instruction. The proliferation of writing was directed more and more toward public readers; while writing was done by craft experts for defined tasks, the reading was directed toward larger audiences. There should be little question about the connection between these early forms of writing instruction and the spread of literacy. Yet, even here, we should be cautious about making generalizations about instruction. While the presence of writing is a sign of some sort of instruction, it is not a basis for inferring that such instruction was widespread or systematic, just as we cannot infer widespread literacy because some evidence of writing is known and discovered to be "public" at various sites throughout archaic Greece. These two forms of specialized literacy, however, should compel us to ask questions about the increasing spread of literacy, for while these two forms of writing comprise the bulk of our evidence, it is clear that there was some sort of ever-increasing

19 Kevin Robb, *Literacy and Paideia in Ancient Greece* (New York and Oxford: Oxford University Press, 1994) 129, 200.
20 See, e.g., James Fredal, *Rhetorical Action in Ancient Athens: Persuasive Artistry form Solon to Demosthenes* (Carbondale IL: Southern Illinois University Press, 2006).

literate public who were the beneficiaries. That is, the rhapsodes and artisans were the "composers" but they were composing for listeners and readers.

What writing we do have from "non-expert" writers during the Archaic Period is little more than child-like scratch marks (e.g., Figure 1.4). There is some evidence of **abecedaria**—fragments of the alphabet written out for practice—that has been excavated this century from the Athenian Agora, which shows that the learning of "letters" did begin to have a place in the *sumposium* education of Athenian citizens. It is likely, however, that this education could better be classified as reading rather than writing instruction, for, with the exception of short, pithy phrases of dedication and brief messages, the literacy instruction of most Athenians was undertaken to benefit from what was written by the two groups of experts: the artists and the artisans of the Archaic Period. By degree of emphasis, writing was being composed and produced as a craft of a select group with reading being the emphasis for the remaining citizenry.

The Classical Period: Writing Instruction in the Service of Orality

As Athens moved from the Archaic and into the Classical Period of the fifth and fourth centuries BCE, the nature of writing instruction, and even its purposes and benefits, altered dramatically. We have seen that writing during the Archaic Period was little more than a recording device learned as a trade in the service of

Figure 1.6 A fourth-century BCE shopping list.

(Courtesy of The American School of Classical Studies: Agora Excavations)

the upper classes. The wealthier and more aristocratic classes of Athens did, as we have discussed, learn to write. During this early period, however, these classes learned writing as an aid in carrying out the routine and mundane tasks of the day. The emphasis in literacy for these upper-class Athenians was more in reading, and there is some anecdotal evidence to support the belief that reading knowledge was fairly widespread during the Classical Period, such as the labeling of voting disks by *deme* and the naming of individuals on ostraka (e.g., Figure 1.7).

The Classical Period, however, ushered in significant changes in writing and, accordingly, altered its instruction dramatically. While it is accurate to state that writing-in-order-to-read was still (by degree) the orientation of the upper classes, that emphasis was shifting during the Classical Period. During the Archaic Period, writing was done to stabilize texts for their permanence. Hence the works of Homer, the chronicling of historical events, and the finalization of laws dominated the more formal craft-skills of artisan writers. The Classical Period continued to utilize artisan writers but newer, more specialized writing tasks developed and with them more specialized writers emerged. The distinguishing feature of this emerging form of writing instruction is that it was done in the service of orality. The *progymnasmata* mentioned earlier provided elementary drills and exercises. In these sessions students typically developed skills in composing narratives, fables, rudimentary issues and points of law, and argumentation. What is persistent in the exercises of *progymnasmata* is the close ties between oral and written composition. Later we will discuss how this close association between oral and written composition would be extended into the more sophisticated and advanced educational exercises that Greeks called **melete** and Romans called *declamatio*.

Athens offers the most explicit example of writing in the service of orality. As democracy stabilized political procedures in Athens, the need for writers to record specific events of oral and civic functions increased. Writing was helpful in recording the oral deliberations necessary in the operations of the *polis*. That is, writing was used to record events that had more immediate and pragmatic impact. For example, during this period the **hupogrammateus** emerged as a secretary charged with the responsibility of recording oral transactions of civic deliberation. Such recordings were, on occasion, subject to time constraints since orators were limited by the *klepsydra* (or water-clock) and, correspondingly, so were those who had to transcribe their speeches.[21]

The new conditions of writing in the service of orality modified the nature of writing instruction, at least writing instruction done for these specialized tasks. The momentary and fleeting discourse that is the nature of speech prompted the *hupogrammateus* to develop shorthand systems of writing called tachygraphy. Diogenes Laertius claimed that Xenophon was the first Athenian to use shorthand symbols.[22] Unfortunately, we have no extant evidence of Xenophon's

---

21 Richard Leo Enos, "Inventional Constraints on the Technographers of Ancient Athens: A Study of *Kairos.*" *Rhetoric and Kairos: Essays in History, Theory, and Praxis.* Ed. Phillip Sipiora and James S. Baumlin (Albany NY: State University of New York Press, 2002) 77–88.
22 Diogenes Laertius, *Xenophon* 2.48.

Figure 1.7 Ostraka used in fifth-century BCE voting.

(Courtesy of The American School of Classical Studies: Agora Excavations)

work—or any direct examples of systematic tachygraphy—until the early Christian centuries.[23] Even these artifacts, unfortunately, come from Egypt not Athens. If the account of Diogenes Laertius is accurate, however, we have a very important piece of evidence about the (r)evolutionary emphasis of writing moving into the upper classes. Xenophon was from an old and established aristocratic family. The fact that he would "create" a writing heuristic to aid orality provides an instance of the diminishing stereotype of writing as a lower-class craft while, at the same time, demonstrating its use by a member of the upper classes of Athenian society.

There is, however, other, more abundant evidence of writing in the service of orality and its ever-increasing emphasis among the upper classes of Athens during the Classical Period. Much of the credit for integrating higher-level writing functions goes to the Sophists. One of the most important aspects of this advanced, foreign education is that many of these Sophists readily assimilated writing into the course of advanced studies, thereby encouraging the view that writing was a part of advanced instruction. Practice in compositions for the law courts, public and ceremonial occasions and the writing of history all revealed more sophisticated dimensions (and benefits) of the writing process. These educators, concentrating on advanced studies, encouraged extending education into young adulthood.

Logography is one illustration of how a long-established pragmatic skill evolved into a higher-level study of writing in the service of orality. The concept of "logography" existed during the Archaic Period as a specialized skill to record accounts of important events. In this respect, early chroniclers and even Herodotus—called the father of historians—would be considered "logographers." Here too, however, this form of specialized writing would alter during

23 Eunapius, *Vitae Sophistarum* 489.

the Classical Period because it was applied to the immediate constraints of orality. During the Classical Period logography evolved to become a profession in which individuals would compose speeches for others, normally during legal proceedings where each male citizen was compelled to speak for himself. Logographers wrote these speeches for a price and instructed clients in their "readings," that is, in the preparation for their oral performance before courts. Our evidence is that the most successful of logographers, such as Lysias, and quite possibly Isocrates, were popular because they composed oral arguments well for others. At least some of these logographers, such as the two mentioned above, came from the upper classes but, due to their own financial misfortunes, had to use these writing skills to earn a living. The success of logographers began to alter the perception of writing, which came to be viewed more and more as part of an intellectual process. Eric Havelock has done much research that reveals the importance of writing in the service of orality. One of Havelock's most important (but debated) claims is that such writing served to facilitate abstract thought. That is, writing speeches helped to stabilize oral arguments by shaping and molding words that would otherwise be thought of as "winged" if left to the fleeting notions of oral discourse and memory alone.[24]

There are other arenas that illustrate the impact of writing in the service of orality during the Classical Period of Athens. One such kind of writing might best be considered as "composing for the gods." Most of our attention to writing instruction has been oriented toward the more civic functions typical of Athenian rhetoric, that is, writing used in the orally based activities of the *Ekklesia*, or public assembly, and the courts. Our current view of writing instruction for epideictic discourse—rhetoric that is often ceremonial and occasional—has been limited and narrow, with the exception of Donovan J. Ochs' *Consolatory Rhetoric*. If, however, we extend our notion of epideictic rhetoric to other ceremonial functions, we can begin to see better the pervasive influence of writing in the service of orality.

The best examples of writing instruction for the arts of expression are Hellenic literary festivals. The Olympic Games are, of course, the most famous of all Greek festivals. There were, however, other religiously rooted festivals, such as the Isthmian Games of Corinth and the games held at Delphi. These games included athletic contests, but often literary and oratorical contests as well. Although many of these major games were held every four years, other smaller games were held annually. All this is to say that literary and oratorical contests for Athenian citizens were widely available and, based on epigraphical evidence, regularly attended by Athenians as both spectators and participants.[25]

Contest winners from these literary games were recorded on marble and other durable material, often listing not only events but also the names and origins of victors. The games held at the Amphiareion at Oropos, a site approximately thirty miles from Athens, show that Athenians regularly participated in these contests, which included such events as satire, comedy, rhapsodic odes and

24 Stacia Dunn Neeley, D. B. Magee and Richard Leo Enos. "The Very Rhetorical Mr. Havelock: A Re-View Essay." *Rhetoric Review* 17 (Fall 1998): 194–204.

25 Enos, *Roman Rhetoric*, 152–63.

tragedy. It is reasonable to infer that these Athenians, as well as contestants from throughout Greece, would have used writing to aid in the preparation and recording of their literary performances. This sort of composing, done to honor the gods at various religious festivals, reveals that the processes of writing were becoming a part of the creative process. Although these festivals never lost their oral emphasis, it is also reasonable to assume that instruction in poetry and the fine arts would have increasingly incorporated writing into its preparation. Other types of physical evidence lend support to the claim that writing was becoming integrated into artistic expression and education in general. Vase paintings, for example, depict youths practicing their musical instruments, reciting aloud and learning their letters—all within the same scene (e.g., Douris "school" cup, Staatliche Museen [2283], Berlin). Writing instruction was becoming a part of the arts of expression.

Writing Instruction in Ancient Athens after 450 BCE and the *Ratio Isocratea*

More and more, writing was becoming a part of daily life at all class levels. Recent archaeological evidence, excavated just last century at Athens' Agora, demonstrates the pervasiveness of everyday writing as we move through the Archaic and into the Classical Period. Personal notes of affection appear on pottery. Such personal possessions as spear-butts are labeled for ownership. Shopping lists for parties have been scratched on pottery fragments (e.g., Figure 1.6). As mentioned above, several *abecedaria*, lists of the alphabet made as writing practice, have also been unearthed. The majority of this writing is not sophisticated and certainly does not match some of the elegant inscriptions of the artisans mentioned earlier. What it does demonstrate, however, is that writing, while still used for functional purposes, is much more widely used by Athenian citizens.[26]

Our most complete sources of this functional writing come from Athens, but it is clear, primarily through the efforts of such epigraphists as L. H. Jeffery, that such writing occurs throughout Greece. This evidence tells us that writing was studied increasingly for its everyday use and demonstrates a level of widespread literacy that we could only speculate on earlier. During the fifth century BCE, however, Athenian education underwent significant changes. As advanced levels of education assimilated writing, its importance shifted from a functional tool to an heuristic for advanced thought. The upper levels of Athenian society began to complement their ever-increasing emphasis on reading with writing to clarify and record advanced intellectual problems.

The Classical Period of Greece (the fifth and fourth centuries BCE) is famous for the flowering of Athenian democracy, the emergence of intellectual luminaries, and the stabilization of higher education, particularly in Athens. Many historians of rhetoric believe that writing played a part in these achievements of the Classical Period. As mentioned earlier, operations of government and the systematization of legal procedure, both of which remained

---

26 Richard Leo Enos, "Writing Without Paper: A Study of Functional Rhetoric in Ancient Athens." *On the Blunt Edge: An Introduction to Technology in Our Pedagogy and History.* Ed. Shane Borrowman et al. (Anderson SC: Parlor Press, forthcoming).

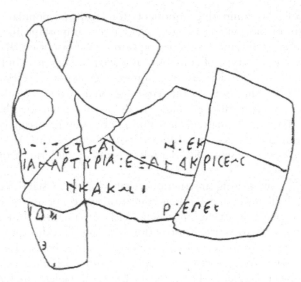

Figure 1.8 Lid of a pot used to hold copies of written evidence, fourth century BCE.
(Courtesy of The American School of Classical Studies: Agora Excavations)

predominantly oral, included writing as a way of recording and disseminating deliberative and forensic activities. Prominent thinkers and artists, moving away from a strictly oral tradition, included writing as a feature of work ranging from philosophy to history to theatrical composition. In short, by widespread practice, writing was manifested throughout Athenian society. For the purposes of our inquiry, it is important to see how this popularity relates to instruction.

By the Classical Period the traditional, Homeric form of education was being replaced. Music lost emphasis and writing gained increasing status. This influence of writing instruction, which flowered during the subsequent Hellenistic Period, grew into the **paideia** of Greek education, eventually reaching all levels. The small child (*paidion*) learned letters necessary for reading and writing from the grammatist (*grammatistes*) at the primary level. As an older child (*pais*), more advanced levels in reading and writing were taught by the grammarian (*grammatikos*). This secondary emphasis, for children ranging from 7 to 14 years of age, covered the more sophisticated levels of exposition, interpretation and criticism. The culmination of the grammarian's curriculum was instruction in *krisis*, or arguing for an evaluative judgment. From the ages of 15 to 20 males underwent military education as *epheboi*. In Athens, this form of education was formalized in an Ephebic College. Finally, and normally after required military service, an adolescent male (*meirakion*) could elect to study rhetoric with a Sophist. It should be understood that this latter phase altered and upset the traditional form of education and faced resistance.

As mentioned earlier, the traditional oral features of education were being complemented by writing instruction at all levels. Preliminary exercises in rhetoric, *progymnasmata*, were introduced that extended the earlier training of grammarians by integrating oral and written assignments that ranged from the analysis of fables to composing arguments for legal and popular debate. The advanced form of these exercises, *melete*, had a very important impact not only on writing instruction but also the perception of rhetoric itself. Russell argues that instruction in this type of composition played "a large part in the development of literature."[27] Proficiency in complex declamatory exercises became a feature of higher education in the Greco-Roman world. Writing, brought into existence to aid in the pragmatic needs of functional speech, became in effect an art. That is, the mastery of technique became increasingly valued not only for its functional effect but also for its aesthetic merits. *Melete*, and later Roman *declamatio*, represents, for Russell, a shift of rhetoric "from discourse to literature."[28]

The changes in writing instructions that would be stabilized and fully integrated in Hellenistic and Roman education were not assimilated without resistance. Conservative citizens, those who wished to preserve the long-standing modes of education, saw writing instruction by Sophists as disrupting the strong family-oriented bonds of education associated with the *sumposium*. Others doubtless continued to see writing as a form of manual labor associated with the trades of the lower *thetes* class. If we understand these underlying tensions about writing, and the uneasiness that some established families had over having their sons taught by non-Athenians, we can gain a much more sensitive understanding of Plato's objections to writing instruction and sophistic rhetoric in general, as well as Aristotle's cryptic but critical views of "technographers" in the opening passages of his *Rhetoric*.

Plato expressed great concern about writing because he felt that it destroyed the dynamic and interactive exchange that took place in the (necessarily) oral deliberations of dialectic. The assimilation of writing into the highest forms of education can be credited in large part to the Sophists. Many Sophists, most in fact, were not Athenian citizens but **metics**, non-Athenian Greeks who came to Athens to teach for a price. Some of these Sophists were famous orators and others were logographers. Many Sophists recognized the benefits of writing in higher levels of education and actively promoted the use of writing among their aristocratic Athenian students. As mentioned earlier, the *sumposium* methods of Athenian education were both oral and family-centered. Sophists ruptured this traditional *paideia* both as foreigners and as non-family teachers of writing. Socrates' views against writing instruction are well expressed through the dialogues of his student Plato, particularly in the *Gorgias* and the *Phaedrus*. Plato viewed writing as a constraint because it mediated the essential function of primary, direct, oral interaction between thinkers. Plato valued memory and believed that writing would limit and devalue the important role that memory has in internalizing knowledge. Plato further believed that writing instruction by Sophists was not an instrument for knowledge but rather a technical skill and should be seen as such.[29]

Plato's criticism of writing instruction as taught by the Sophists was echoed by his student Aristotle, who clearly believed that these "technographers"

27 Russell, *Greek Declamation* 3.
28 Russell, *Greek Declamation* 15.
29 Plato, *Protagoras* 236C, D.

emphasized "supplements" and missed the heuristic potential for rhetoric. In the opening passages of his *Rhetoric*, Aristotle criticizes "technographers" who taught and practiced only the surface techniques of their craft and did not understand rhetoric as an "art," that is, a *techne* for creating rational proofs.[30] Our understanding of the emergence of writing instruction in higher education through the Sophists helps us to understand Aristotle's views. At the time that Aristotle wrote his *Rhetoric*, writing was shifting in emphasis from an aid to **oratory** to an art unto itself. The revolution of literacy, however, was not so much that more and more people could read and write—although that appears to be the case. The actual "revolution," as recognized by thinkers such as Aristotle, was that writing instruction could be a system for enhancing more complex patterns of thought and expression. It is important to recognize that Aristotle clearly sees writing as an important feature in his *Rhetoric* and treats it as a part of the process of thought and expression. In a rarely cited passage of the *Rhetoric*, Aristotle explicitly comments on how the exactness of writing composition (*akribestate*) aids in stylistic precision.[31] Moreover, Aristotle later comments on how epideictic rhetoric is especially suited to writing, since it is intended to be read.[32] Aristotle's observation complements Russell's belief that *progymnasmata* and *melete* were forms of writing instruction that aided the development of literature. It is also significant to note the reason why Aristotle claims he wrote the *Rhetoric*. Aristotle asserts in the beginning of his *Rhetoric* that he wishes his work to be a corrective for the current Sophistic practices. Given the views of Aristotle discussed above it is clear that he believed that the Sophists did not fully realize the potential (*dunamis*) for writing as an heuristic for complex discourse. There is strong reason to believe, in addition and more specifically, that Aristotle was contesting the views of Isocrates, whose instruction he associated with the Sophists.

The advancement of writing instruction in ancient Greece came with Isocrates and his important school of rhetoric. Enormous changes took place in writing instruction from the Archaic into the Classical Periods. Writing instruction moved from a labor skill to an intellectual process. This ultimate phase of its development, however, only became apparent with Isocrates and his school, which Friedrich Solmsen has called the *Ratio Isocratea*.[33] Isocrates' views on writing are best understood by contrasting his mode of instruction with the practices of his contemporaries. During the Classical Period, writing was used increasingly in higher education for the more aristocratic citizens. Sophists, in fact, saw writing as a feature of higher education, often incorporating writing instruction into the educational practices of their oldest and most distinguished students. By all our accounts, however, Sophists did not fully recognize the heuristic potential of writing. Yet, where the Sophists valued the functional features of writing, Plato viewed writing and its instruction as a necessary evil at best, while Aristotle saw writing's potential as unrealized by the educators of his

---

30 Aristotle, *Rhetoric*, 1354a–55b.
31 Aristotle, *Rhetoric*, 1413b.
32 Aristotle, *Rhetoric*, 1414a.
33 Friedrich Solmsen, "The Aristotelian Tradition in Ancient Rhetoric." *American Journal of Philology* 62 (1941): 190.

day. Plato had strong reservations about writing because it was a poor alternative to the dynamics of primary, direct oral interaction. Aristotle saw the Sophists—and in that group he unfairly included Isocrates—as embracing the technical features of transcription and recording. Aristotle clearly saw advantages to writing and said so in his *Rhetoric*, but his recognition of writing as a dynamic heuristic process is nowhere as apparent as it is within the writings of Isocrates.

Isocrates' distinguished career as an educator is well chronicled both by his contemporaries and by our current scholarship. Yet, it is only recently that we have come to understand how important his view of writing instruction is in education and how it modified the concept of *paideia*. For Isocrates, writing instruction is an integral part of intellectual growth. Two of Isocrates' treatises are especially valuable in revealing his views on writing instruction. Isocrates' *Against the Sophists* was composed fairly early in his career. Isocrates wished to distance himself from the Sophists, to illustrate that his mode of instruction was based on his own version of philosophy. Attacking the pretentiousness of the Sophists, Isocrates sought to demonstrate his genuine concern for the worth of the individual. At the same time, however, Isocrates also distanced himself from Plato. Isocrates' notions of "philosophy" and "truth" were not based on, or even derived from, Plato's belief that knowledge is predicated on universals. Nor did Isocrates believe that the apparatus for securing such knowledge was through dialectic. Isocrates had his own philosophy and in *Against the Sophists* he reveals how this knowledge is derived from a study of people and cultures, how social knowledge and normative values are a type of knowledge which, when applied, can help to promote justice and wise choices about human affairs, social conduct and ethics. For scholars such as Werner Jaeger, Isocrates is the father of the humanities, principally because Isocrates' theory of knowledge and the grounding for action centers on, and is derived from, social and communal standards.

In many respects, the ideas that Isocrates presented in *Against the Sophists* are elaborated on in his later work, *Antidosis*. Written at the age of 82, and thus several decades after *Against the Sophists*, Isocrates' *Antidosis* is the statement of an educator whose reputation was secure. The *Antidosis* provides a much more detailed explanation of his views on education and the place of writing. For Isocrates, writing is a way of coming to understand. Yet, as he points out, his writings are not the writings of the sycophants of legal logographers but rather speeches composed with the intent of resolving social issues. His ideas about education are a synthesis of all that we associate with classical education: the conditioning of the body with the development of the mind; the orchestration of talent, practice and experience; the harmony that comes from self-knowledge and self-restraint. All of these ideas are, for Isocrates, "composed" through writing, for it is through writing, Isocrates believes, that we can unite wisdom and eloquence in the pursuit of virtue (*arete*) and justice (*dike*). If we fail to be impressed by Isocrates' pan-Hellenic motives, we should be impressed by the seriousness of his beliefs. So complex was Isocrates' curriculum that, as he points out in the *Antidosis*, some of his students studied for three to four years. In short, writing was not, for Isocrates, a skill mastered as a technical craft nor merely a technique one masters as a child. For Isocrates, writing is a central part of a process of social knowledge and language interaction that can only be mastered—when it is mastered—at the pinnacle of one's education and only with the most rigorous training of the best minds. A reading of these two treatises of Isocrates will not only make apparent why the *Ratio Isocratea* was a mainstay of classical education, but also why writing had emerged as one of its central features.

While Isocrates provides us with the particulars of his writing instruction in his *Antidosis*, we also can thank ancient authorities such as Plutarch, and modern scholars such as R. C. Jebb, H. I. Marrou and R. Johnson, for synthesizing and expanding on Isocrates' own comments. As mentioned above, Isocrates stressed relationships in his educational philosophy. He believed that mind and body should complement each other, and that education was based on talent, practice and experience.[34] Marrou calls Isocrates' education the development of "mental culture."[35] Isocrates believed in a broadly based education that included such subjects as history, political science, poetry, ethics, geography, literary studies, mathematics and oral and written rhetoric. In fact, rhetoric was at the core of all of these subjects and composition was at the heart of his literary rhetoric. As Johnson points out, Isocrates' curriculum "is centered on rhetorical composition."[36] Isocrates' writing instruction prepared students by developing writing as a source of civic power. As Jebb argues, writing was "recognized as a mode of influencing public opinion on the affairs of the day."[37] In fact, if we were to condense Isocrates' educational philosophy it would be that he considered writing instruction to be the art of expressing good judgments to others about civic matters.

Athens is well known for moving from an oral culture to an oral *and* literate culture. Some contemporary scholars, such as Eric Havelock, consider this shift as nothing less than a "revolution." Isocrates' methods of writing instruction reveal his revolutionary mode of literary rhetoric. Although Isocrates taught many students over his own distinguished career, he instructed small numbers of students at a time, probably no more than eight. Study by imitation was important but Isocrates also sharpened critical thinking by debate exercises, pitting students against one another in agonistic verbal warfare. There is also evidence that Isocrates encouraged his students to discuss and evaluate in groups, so that they would have comments coming not only from him but from peers as well. He taught excellence in writing through exercises that bonded oral with literary composition. Isocrates' students declaimed from written speeches and doubtless his own experiences as a logographer grounded his writing instruction.

In terms of writing instruction, Isocrates is the educator behind Athens' literate revolution, the educator who established the importance of writing in the classical curriculum. Of all the educators of the Classical Period, Isocrates is credited as the first to realize the full potential for writing instruction. That is, writing instruction as a part of higher education was a method for facilitating thought and expression. Marrou considers Isocrates to be the first literate rhetorician.[38] Isocrates, himself an excellent and prolific writer, encouraged writing among his students, many of whom rank among the most respected of Athenian

---

34 Isocrates, *Antidosis* 187.
35 Marrou, *A History of Education in Antiquity* 83.
36 R. Johnson, "Isocrates' Method of Teaching," *American Journal of Philology* 80 (1959): 31.
37 R. C. Jebb, *The Attic Orators from Antiphon to Isaeos*, Vol. 2 (New York: Russell & Russell, 1875, repr. 1962) 47.
38 Marrou, *A History of Education in Antiquity*, 79–89.

citizens. In his writings, Isocrates makes it clear that education directed toward human concerns and immediate social issues is noble and a philosophical orientation in its own right, albeit a more pragmatic and directed one than Plato's or Aristotle's. If we judge educators by the merits of their students, we begin to see the merits of Isocrates' mode of instruction. His school produced not only leading politicians but also historians and educators. Isocrates established writing as endemic to the highest, most complex and most serviceable of all levels of education. It is not too much to say, and significant to note, that no great thinker or statesman emerged in Athens after Isocrates who is not also known for his literate ability. Marrou has called Isocrates and Plato the two pillars upon which classical education was built. Although we can see profound differences between Isocrates and Plato, especially in their views on writing instruction, there is also no doubt that both were highly literate and that it was through their respective accomplishments in writing, and the writings of their students, that we measure their importance and impact.

Rival Illustrations of Greek Writing Instruction

As mentioned at the beginning of this chapter, there is a need for greater fieldwork in order to discover the practices and methods of writing instructions in sites other than Athens. What little has been done, however, shows potential for reconstructing a more complete representation of writing instruction across ancient Greece than currently exists. Two examples have already demonstrated the value of such inquiry. For many years, historians of rhetoric operated under the assumption that Sparta was, for all practical purposes, non-literate. As a consequence, little or nothing could be said about writing instruction, although the education of Spartans did indeed value writing, but the value that they saw in writing was culture-specific. Spartans emphasized an education that stressed military preparedness. This emphasis was understandable since the Spartan slaves (*helots*) not only vastly outnumbered Spartan citizens, but the Spartans felt the need to be ready for threats from outside of their own city. Correspondingly, it is understandable why interest in teaching writing would be oriented toward basic civic affairs and the use of writing in battle situations.[39]

In a similar respect, Rhodes emphasized writing education that also was suited to her particular orientation.[40] A center for commercial trade, Rhodes constantly interacted with a variety of city-states and non-Hellenic cultures. The political delicacies of Rhodes' attractive strategic location prompted sensitivity to diplomacy and cross-cultural communication. Schools at Rhodes, beginning with Aeschines' famous school of rhetoric, taught oral and written rhetoric in a manner that stressed effective communication across cultures. This orientation toward instruction not only gained fame among other Greek city-states, but

39 Richard Leo Enos, "The Secret Composition Practices of the Ancient Spartans: A Study of 'Noncivic' Classical Rhetoric." *Renewing Rhetoric's Relation to Composition.* Ed. Shane Borrowman, Stuart C. Brown and Thomas P. Miller (New York and London: Routledge, 2009) 236–47.
40 Richard Leo Enos, "The Art of Rhetoric at Rhodes: An Eastern Rival to the Athenian Representation of Classical Rhetoric." *Rhetoric Before and Beyond the Greeks.* Ed. Carol S. Lipson and Roberta A. Binkley (Albany NY: State University of New York Press, 2004) 183–96.

eventually became an educational center for Romans. In fact, Rhodes became so popular that Romans not only traveled to Rhodes for their rhetorical education, but also invited Rhodian educators to come to Rome and offer their services to wealthy and powerful patrons.

Preliminary work at Thebes, although now in its nascent stages, is again revealing the same pattern for writing instruction. That is, akin to Sparta and Rhodes, early work at Thebes shows that their modes of instruction are responsive to the cultural demands of not only their own city but (albeit eventually) the external forces of such powerful patrons as Rome.[41] Again, these examples are not intended to imply that we now have a full representation of the range of writing instruction in ancient Greece. Yet, even our limited knowledge of writing instruction in these areas reveals that continuing study will provide a better understanding of how Greeks interacted with other ancient groups, such as Phoenicians, Etruscans and Romans.[42] From this perspective, such examples as those mentioned here are intended to serve as illustrations of how a fuller understanding of writing instruction across Greece and with other cultures waits on, and beckons for, further research.

Conclusion

How can we best understand how the "(r)evolution" of writing could come about so quickly? How can we explain how thinkers such as Plato, Isocrates and Aristotle—who exhibit such control over writing that they became the standards of literacy for their culture—seem to spring into existence so quickly? What we witness with such individuals as Plato, Isocrates and Aristotle is a phenomenon of rhetoric that normally is discussed only with reference to macroscopic views of cultures and societies: the phenomenon of *letteraturizza-zione*. George Kennedy's treatment of *letteraturizzazione*—first introduced to readers of English in his 1980 edition of *Classical Rhetoric and Its Christian and Secular Tradition from Ancient to Modern Times*—is a concept that is meant to explain what happens when literacy is introduced into oral cultures. *Letteraturizzazione* explains the process by which features of oral rhetoric are appropriated and applied to writing. The analogy to this concept would be akin to the principles of typing being transferred and applied to word-processing on the computer. Early versions of personal computers borrowed heavily from the systems invented for manual typewriters. Over time, however, certain techniques that were helpful remained while those techniques of typing that were not useful were removed or replaced with a more "user-friendly" approach. Personal computing evolved into its own system but the residue of some of the principles of mechanical typing can still be found. For our purposes, written rhetoric appropriated some of the techniques of oral rhetoric, discarded others, and created new heuristics that were unique to writing. As with personal computing, written rhetoric

---

41 Richard Leo Enos, "Finding the 'Good' in Nero: The Emperor as Performer and Patron of Rhetorical Contests." *Contested Writings.* Ed. Mary R. Lamb. Under review.

42 Richard Leo Enos, "Scriptura Etrusca: A Prolegomenon to Roman Rhetoric." *Rhetoric in the Rest of the West.* Ed. Shane Borrowman, Robert L. Lively and Marcia Kmetz (Newcastle upon Tyne UK: Cambridge Scholars Publishing, 2010) 35–60.

still has the residue of some of its primary oral antecedents, such as a writer's "tone" and "voice."[43]

This overview of writing instruction in ancient Greece reveals the evidence of the dynamic power of writing which, when realized, facilitates stunning intellectual advancements. What we see with individuals such as Plato, Isocrates and Aristotle is the phenomenon of *letteraturizzazione* manifested on a personal level. That is, all three of these individuals were so highly literate that they were able to apply writing as a heuristic for problem-solving. Each manifested his power of advanced proficiency in writing in very different but dynamic ways. For Plato, writing was an aid to abstract concepts of ontology that refined his philosophy. For Isocrates, writing in terms of political issues and history helped to explain, account and interpret social activity and human conduct. For Aristotle, writing was an essential heuristic in his quest to provide taxonomical systems that enabled him to analyze and synthesize in order to organize phenomena for better understanding. Studying in the respective schools of these three thinkers meant not only studying their orientations but also how writing facilitated thought and expression in each of their domains of inquiry. The evolution of writing—much like a plane taxiing on a runway—builds speed until the moment that it is airborne. For these three thinkers, writing moved beyond a recording device to become an instrument that freed them and their students into the higher levels of abstract thought and expression.

The luxury of history is that we can retrospectively see that those educators who did incorporate writing instruction into the highest levels of education flourished. Isocrates, considered the first of the literate rhetoricians, established educational practices that became the cornerstone of Hellenistic education. In this respect, the school of Isocrates is a pivot between the culmination of classical education and the entry into the zenith of Greek education, the Hellenistic Period. The evolutionary role of writing into and throughout the *paideia* of Greek education is the marker for such change. Perhaps we should modify Marrou's analogy of Plato and Isocrates being the classical pillars upon which Hellenistic and Roman education was built. Our discussion of writing instruction would reconfigure Marrou's image into a tripod, for Aristotle also helped to bring writing instruction into the foundation of the classical curriculum.

This perspective, of course, does not conclude our understanding of the critical importance of writing instruction, but rather opens new and exciting possibilities for rhetoric's history. This notion of the personal level of *letteraturizzazione*, for example, provides a heuristic that helps us to better realize the wide-reaching power of literacy. Understanding the breadth of writing instruction will, for instance, be a great help in securing a better understanding of the literate power of women in ancient Greece. Thanks to the nascent efforts of scholars such as those mentioned in this chapter, we already have begun to identify prominent women who warrant inclusion in the history of rhetoric. Through our study of writing instruction, we can extend that group by considering the possibility of

---

43 For a full discussion of the oral residue in writing, see: Walter J. Ong, *Orality and Literacy: The Technologizing of the Word* (London and New York: Methuen, 1982) *passim*.

everyday literacy among women and the implications that such a phenomenon holds for writing instruction in ancient Greece. By re-examining the place of women—as well as other previously overlooked groups—we will extend both the knowledge of our own discipline and the very concept of *paideia* itself by having a more thorough appreciation of the art of intellectual excellence in ancient Greece than currently exists from the conventional methods, approaches and topics of the history of our discipline.

Suggested Readings and References

No specific editions are presented for classical sources since the citation method is standard and universal. All translations of classical works, unless otherwise stated, were done by the author. The Loeb Classical Library Series of Harvard University Press provides excellent editions of classical works with English translations appearing on opposite pages.

Agnew, Lois. "The Classical Period." *The Present State of Scholarship in the History of Rhetoric: A Twenty-First Century Guide.* Ed. Lynée Lewis Gaillet with Winifred Bryan Horner. Columbia and London: University of Missouri Press, 2010: esp. 12–14. Print.

Aristotle. *Rhetoric.*

The Athenian Agora. American School of Classical Studies at Athens. 4th edition. Princeton NJ: Institute for Advanced Study, 1990. Print.

Chadwick, John. *The Decipherment of Linear B.* 2nd edition. Cambridge: Cambridge University Press, 1970. Print.

Diogenes Laertius. *Xenophon.*

Documents in Mycenaean Greek. Eds., 1st edition, Michael Ventris and John Chadwick; ed., 2nd edition., John Chadwick. Cambridge: Cambridge University Press, 1973. Print.

Enos, Richard Leo. "The Archaeology of Women in Rhetoric: Rhetorical Sequencing as a Research Method of Historical Scholarship." *Rhetoric Society Quarterly* 32.1 (Winter 2002): 65–79. Print.

——. "The Art of Rhetoric at Rhodes: An Eastern Rival to the Athenian Representation of Classical Rhetoric." *Rhetoric Before and Beyond the Greeks.* Ed. Carol S. Lipson and Roberta A. Binkley. Albany NY: State University of New York Press, 2004: 183–96. Print.

——."Finding the 'Good' in Nero: The Emperor as Performer and Patron of Rhetorical Contests." *Contested Writings.* Ed. Mary R. Lamb. Under review. Print.

——. *Greek Rhetoric Before Aristotle.* Revised and expanded edition. Anderson SC: Parlor Press (forthcoming). Print.

——. "Inventional Constraints on the Technographers of Ancient Athens: A Study of Kairos." *Rhetoric and Kairos: Essays in History, Theory, and Praxis.* Ed. Phillip Sipiora and James S. Baumlin. Albany NY: State University of New York Press, 2002: 77–88. Print.

——. *Roman Rhetoric: Revolution and the Greek Influence.* Revised and expanded edition. Anderson SC: Parlor Press, 2008. Print.

——. "Scriptura Etrusca: A Prolegomenon to Roman Rhetoric." *Rhetoric in the Rest of the West.* Ed. Shane Borrowman, Robert L. Lively and Marcia Kmetz. Newcastle upon Tyne UK: Cambridge Scholars Publishing, 2010: 35–60. Print.

——. "The Secret Composition Practices of the Ancient Spartans: A Study of 'Noncivic' Classical Rhetoric." *Renewing Rhetoric's Relation to Composition.* Ed. Shane Borrowman, Stuart C. Brown and Thomas P. Miller. New York and London: Routledge, 2009: 236–47. Print.

——. "Writing Without Paper: A Study of Functional Rhetoric in Ancient Athens." *On the Blunt Edge: An Introduction to Technology in Our Pedagogy and History.* Ed. Shane Borrowman et al. Anderson SC: Parlor Press (forthcoming). Print.

Eunapius. *Vitae Sophistarum.*

Flegg, Graham. *Numbers: Their History and Meaning.* New York: Schocken Books, 1983. Print.

Fredal, James. *Rhetorical Action in Ancient Athens: Persuasive Artistry form Solon to Demosthenes.* Carbondale IL: Southern Illinois University Press, 2006. Print.

Garner, Richard. *Law and Society in Classical Athens.* New York: St. Martin's Press, 1987. Print.

Gelb, I. J. *A Study of Writing.* Chicago: University of Chicago Press, 1974. Print.

Glenn, Cheryl. *Rhetoric Retold: Regendering the Tradition from Antiquity Through the Renaissance.* Carbondale and Edwardsville IL: Southern Illinois University Press, 1997. Print.

Harris, William V. *Ancient Literacy.* Cambridge MA: Harvard University Press, 1989. Print.

Harvey, David. "Greeks and Romans Learn to Write." *Communication Arts in the Ancient World.* Ed. Eric A. Havelock and Jackson P. Hershbell. Humanistic Studies in the Communication Arts. New York: Hastings House Publishers, 1978: 63–80. Print.

Havelock, Eric A. *The Literate Revolution in Greece and Its Cultural Consequences.* Princeton NJ: Princeton University Press, 1982. Print.

——. *Preface to Plato.* Cambridge MA: The Belknap Press of Harvard University Press, 1963. Print.

Homer. *Iliad.*

——. *Odyssey.*

Isocrates. *Against the Sophists.*

——. *Antidosis.*

Jaeger, Werner. "The Rhetoric of Isocrates and Its Cultural Ideal." *Landmark Essays on Classical Greek Rhetoric.* Ed. Edward Schiappa. Davis CA: Hermagoras Press, 1994: 119–41. Print.

Jebb, R. C. *The Attic Orators from Antiphon to Isaeos.* Volume 2. New York: Russell & Russell, 1875 (reprinted in 1962). Print.

Jeffery, L. H. *The Local Scripts of Archaic Greece.* Revised edition. Oxford: Clarendon Press, 1990. Print.

Johnson, R. "Isocrates' Method of Teaching." *American Journal of Philology* 80 (1959): 25–36. Print.

Kennedy, George A. *Classical Rhetoric and Its Christian and Secular Tradition from Ancient to Modern Times.* 2nd edition. Chapel Hill and London: University of North Carolina Press, 1999. Print.

Lang, Mabel. *The Athenian Agora, Volume 21, Graffiti and Dipinti.* Princeton NJ: The American School of Classical Studies at Athens, 1976. Print.

——. *Graffiti in the Athenian Agora.* Excavations of the Athenian Agora: 14. Princeton NJ: American School of Classical Studies at Athens, 1974. Print.

Lentz, Tony M. "Writing as Sophistry: From Preservation to Persuasion." *Quarterly Journal of Speech* 68 (February 1982): 60–68. Print.

Lord, Albert B. *The Singer of Tales.* New York: Athenaeum, 1976. Print.

Lunsford, Andrea A. (ed.) *Reclaiming Rhetorica: Women in the Rhetorical Tradition.* Pittsburgh and London: University of Pittsburgh Press, 1995. Print.

Marrou, H. I. *A History of Education in Antiquity.* Trans. George Lamb. Madison WI: University of Wisconsin Press, 1956 (reprinted in 1983). Print.

Neeley, Stacia Dunn, D. B. Magee, and Richard Leo Enos. "The Very Rhetorical Mr. Havelock: A Re-View Essay." *Rhetoric Review* 17 (Fall 1998): 194–204. Print.

Ochs, Donovan J. *Consolatory Rhetoric: Grief, Symbol, and Ritual in the Greco-Roman Era.* Columbia SC: University of South Carolina Press, 1993. Print.

Ong, Walter, J. *Orality and Literacy: The Technologizing of the Word.* London and New York: Methuen, 1982. Print.

Plato. *Gorgias.*

——. *Ion.*

——. *Phaedrus.*

——. *Protagoras.*

Plutarch. *Moralia: Vitae Decem Oratorum: Isocrates.*

Renault, Mary. *The Praise Singer.* New York: Pantheon Books, 1978. Print.

Robb, Kevin. *Literacy and Paideia in Ancient Greece.* New York and Oxford: Oxford University Press, 1994. Print.

Russell, D. A. *Greek Declamation.* London and New York: Cambridge University Press, 1983. Print.

Schmandt-Besserat, Denise. "Accounting in the Prehistoric Middle East." *Archeomaterials* 4.1 (Winter 1990): 15–23. Print.

——. "Chirographic Culture." *The Cambridge Encyclopedia of Language Sciences.* Ed. Patrick Colm Hogan. Cambridge: Cambridge University Press, 2011: 154–57. Print.

——. "The Earliest Precursor of Writing." *Scientific American* 238.6 (June 1978): 50–59, 160. Print.

——. "The Envelopes That Bear the First Writing." *Technology and Culture: The International Quarterly of the Society for the History of Technology* 21.3 (July 1980). Chicago: University of Chicago Press: 357–85. Print.

——. "The Invention of Writing." *Discovery: Research and Scholarship at The University of Texas at Austin* 1.4 (June 1977): 4–7. Print.

——. "Tokens and Counting." *Biblical Archaeologist* (Spring 1983): 117–20. Print.

——. "Two Precursors of Writing: Plain and Complex Tokens." *The Origins of Writing.* Ed. Wayne M. Senner. Lincoln and London: University of Nebraska Press, 1989: 27–39. Print.

Solmsen, Friedrich. "The Aristotelian Tradition in Ancient Rhetoric." *American Journal of Philology* 62 (1941): 35–50, 169–90. Print.

Stanford, W. B. *The Sound of Greek: Studies in the Greek Theory and Practice of Euphony.* Sather Classical Lectures: Volume 38. Berkeley and Los Angeles: University of California Press, 1967. Print.

Vermeule, Emily. *Greece in the Bronze Age.* Chicago and London: University of Chicago Press, 1964. Print.

Young, Richard, and Patricia Sullivan. "Why Write? A Reconsideration." *Essays on Classical Rhetoric and Modern Discourse.* Ed. Robert J. Connors, Lisa S. Ede and Andrea A. Lunsford. Carbondale and Edwardsville IL: Southern Illinois University Press, 1984: 215–25. Print.

Yunis, Harvey (ed.) *Written Texts and the Rise of Literate Culture in Ancient Greece.* Cambridge: Cambridge University Press, 2003. Print.

Chapter 2

Roman Writing Instruction as Described by Quintilian

James J. Murphy

Key Concepts

Habit (*hexis*) Roman education as a system • Public schools • Concept of curriculum • Writing and oral language • Quintilian • Facility (*facilitas*) • Tutorial teaching • Isocrates' influence • Male-centered education • Five parts of Latin rhetoric • Cicero as model • Theory and practice • Triad of precept, imitation, practice • Inheritance from Greek pedagogy • *Grammaticus* • *Rhetor* • Grammar and rhetoric as precept • Seven steps of imitation • Form preceding free expression • Graded composition exercises (*progymnasmata*) • Hermogenes and Aphthonius • Declamation • Sequencing • Modern criticisms of the system.

In writing are the roots, in writing are the foundations of eloquence.
Marcus Fabius Quintilianus, *Institutio oratoria*, X.3.1

Every educational program has a cultural rationale behind it, even when instruction is on a one-to-one basis. The Masai warrior teaching his son how to use a spear to kill a lion is preparing him for life in the bush, just as a merchant might make sure that his son knows the rudiments of accounting to ensure that he can manage the money that is the heartline of his business. On the level of whole societies, however, it may be more difficult to identify the relation between the needs of a whole community and the specific instructional devices used to achieve those goals.

In the previous chapter we have seen how Greek society gradually moved from a purely oral community to one in which writing played an important role. The free citizen came to depend on his communication skills in both speaking and writing. Nevertheless, there was no public consensus about the best way to ensure that the citizens and their children acquired that communicative ability so necessary to the democracy. Isocrates, as we have seen in the preceding chapter, developed a fairly systematic curriculum based on his triad of Talent, Education, and Practice; yet it was a personalized program built around the skill of one person; he had influence partly because he lived a very long time and thus taught many students over his lifetime. Other Sophists had programs of their own, but again in a personalized way depending on the skill of the individuals involved. There was a rough homogeneity among approaches in the various city-states, but hardly a unified approach to education.

We will never know how the Greeks might eventually have solved that problem, because there were even greater forces at work to put a stop to the great experiment in democracy—every man speaking and voting for himself—in the form of military invaders from the west. The Roman armies stamped out Greek democracy—in 146 BCE Macedonia became one of eight Roman provinces, and by 127 BCE all the Greek city-states were organized into the province of Achaea.

This Roman society was vastly different from the Greek one it conquered. Neither the Greek nor the Roman society was an egalitarian one. Both depended on masses of slaves who made it possible for their male elites to take part in civic life. But the Romans cultivated an efficiency remarkable in the ancient world. They were, if anything, a systematic and structured people. The examples are well known. They built aqueducts relying on gravity to bring water to their cities, sometimes from hundreds of miles away. They built four-level, tapered roads so well constructed that some of them have survived to this day. They pioneered city planning. They standardized military tactics and armor to create a logistical system that was the wonder of their age. For example, they constructed chariots of identical parts that could be stored and re-assembled easily; these chariots were exactly three feet wide, so that the standard eight-foot Roman roads could be constructed to allow space for chariots to pass each other.

They were social engineers as well. They hammered out a constitution for their Republic so effective that thousands of years later it was one of the models used by American revolutionaries in setting up their own state after breaking with the British. The Republic included an executive branch—two Consuls to deter dictatorship—an elected Senate, a graded system of courts, and a growing panoply of laws, all built around an elective process which demanded a high level of communicative skill from its citizens. Like the Greeks, they recognized the societal need for enhancing the communicative skills of citizens to make the system work. But they worked out a solution radically different from their predecessors.

It should not be surprising, then, to find that instruction in writing and speaking in Rome should have become as systematic as other elements in the society. How the change from Greek generality to Roman efficiency came about is the subject of the following section.

Social Engineering in the Classroom

The remarkable thing about Roman education is that it took the comparatively loose ideas of Greek educators and molded them into a coherent system, which instilled in its students a **habit** (*hexis*) of effective expression. Moreover, the Romans embedded the system in a network of "public" schools (i.e., classrooms of numerous students, each under one master), which used a common curriculum throughout the Roman world.

Virtually every individual element found in the Roman education pattern was inherited from the Greeks. What was not inherited, however, was the deftly designed correlation of these elements into a learning system that could be replicated worldwide as a tool of Roman public policy equal in geopolitical value to the legions of soldiers and the tax collectors in making the world Roman.

The basic principle of this system is that students can be habituated into both skill and virtue. Skill of language comes from the adroit use of **precept**,

imitation, and practice in the classroom, while moral and political virtues are absorbed through the contents of the texts and orations studied there.

To understand the unique qualities of this Roman educational program, then, it will be useful to examine not only the role of writing but the manner in which the full system came to supplant the old private, **tutorial** method, which had been the practice in the early days of the Republic. (And, as we have seen in the previous chapter, such changes bring opposition.)

It is clear that writing and oral language go hand in hand in the Roman educational program. If oral eloquence was the desired product of the schools, writing was a major means to that end. "In writing are the roots, in writing are the foundations of eloquence." This judgment, written in CE 95 by Marcus Fabius Quintilianus in his *Institutio oratoria*,[1] was not unique to him. It was an idea already pervasive in Roman culture. Quintilian quotes Marcus Tullius Cicero as saying a century and a half earlier that the pen is "the best modeler and teacher of eloquence." It was to be a long-lasting concept, as Carol Dana Lanham points out in the next chapter. Three centuries after Quintilian, the young Aurelius Augustinus, a teacher of rhetoric later to be a Christian bishop and one of the four Latin Fathers of the Church, describes in his *Confessions* his own efforts to teach oral and written composition to the unruly young in North Africa. The Christian encyclopedists of the sixth and seventh centuries still insist on the same point.

The Roman educational system—and indeed it was truly a "system"—had rhetorical efficiency as its primary goal. Quintilian's term for this objective is **Facility** (*facilitas*), or the habitual capacity to produce appropriate and effective language in any situation. This result was to be achieved by a carefully coordinated program of reading, writing, speaking, and listening. The process carried boys from beginning alphabet exercises at age 6 or 7 through a dozen years of **interactive classroom** activities designed to produce an adult capable of public improvisation under any circumstances.

Writing was an integral part of this process, inseparable from the other elements. As Quintilian notes:

> I know that it is often asked whether more is contributed by writing, by reading, or by speaking. This question we should have to examine with careful attention if in fact we could confine ourselves to any one of these activities; but in truth they are all so connected, so inseparably linked with one another, that if any one of them is neglected, we labor in vain in the other two—for our speech will never become forcible and energetic unless it acquires strength from great practice in writing; and the labor of writing,

1   *Institutio oratoria* X.3.1. Quotations from Books One, Two, and Ten are from *Quintilian on the Teaching of Speaking and Writing: Translations from Books One, Two, and Ten of the Institutio oratoria*, ed. James J. Murphy (Carbondale: Southern Illinois University Press, 1987). Quotations from other books will be from *Quintilian: The Orator's Education*, ed. and trans. Donald A. Russell, 5 vols. (Loeb Classical Library: Cambridge MA: Harvard University Press, 2001). The standard Latin edition is that of Michael Winterbottom (Oxford University Press, 1970). Winterbottom and Tobias Reinhardt have re-edited Book Two (Oxford University Press, 2006) with extensive commentary on each of the 21 chapters in the book including detailed analyses of Quintilian's sources; they suggest that Quintilian may have had available to him a Greek work by Theon ("or someone like Theon") which affected his ordering of student exercises.

if left destitute of models from reading, passes away without effect, as having no director; while he who knows how everything ought to be said, will, if he has not his eloquence in readiness and prepared for all emergencies, merely brood, as it were, over locked-up treasure.

(*Institutio* X.1.1)

Since Roman writing instruction was so firmly embedded in such a complex process, then, the modern reader needs to understand all the elements of the system itself in order to appreciate the role played by writing. Consequently, the following section describes the manner in which rhetorical education supplanted the "**Old Education**" in Rome during the first century before Christ. The next sections discuss that educational process as described in Quintilian's *Institutio oratoria*, followed by a brief analysis of the advantages and disadvantages of the Roman educational pattern.

The Roman Transition to Systematic Rhetorical Education

The first century before Christ was the turning point in the Roman transition from the Old Education of the conservative Republic to the more systematic rhetorical program, which dominated European practice for the next two millennia.

The change was from a native Latin, tutorial process to a Greek-originated "school" system. In a real sense it was a triumph of Isocratean educational principles over a familial approach that had emphasized private tutors and apprenticeship. The historian Cornelius Tacitus, writing later in the middle of the first Christian century, looks back fondly on "the good old days" before there were "professors of Rhetoric":

Well then, in the good old days the young man who was destined for the oratory of the bar, after receiving the rudiments of a sound training at home, and storing his mind with liberal culture, was taken by his father, or his relations, and placed under the care of some orator who held a leading position at Rome. The youth had to get the habit of following his patron about, of escorting him in public, of supporting him at all his appearances as a speaker, whether in the law courts or on the platform, hearing also his word-combats at first hand, standing by him in his duellings, and learning, as it were, to fight in the fighting-line. It was a method that secured at once for the young students a considerable amount of experience, great self-possession, and a goodly store of sound judgment: for they carried on their studies in the light of open day, and amid the very shock of battle, under conditions in which any stupid or ill-advised statement brings prompt retribution in the shape of the judge's disapproval, taunting criticism from your opponent—yes, and from your own supporters' expressions of dissatisfaction. So it was a genuine and unadulterated eloquence that they were initiated in from the very first; and though they attached themselves to a single speaker, yet they got to know all the contemporary members of the bar in a great variety of both civil and criminal cases. Moreover a public meeting gave them the opportunity of noting marked divergences of taste, so that they could easily detect what commended itself in the case of each individual speaker, and what on the other hand failed to please.[2]

Thus in this older, conservative program, there were three levels of education: home training, military service, then apprenticeship to some prominent orator to learn the practical ways of the world. The process could be confusing. For instance, the father of Marcus Tullius Cicero—destined to become one of Rome's most famous speakers—placed him with Q. Mucius Scaevola Augur; the young boy first had to learn rhetoric but advisers had earlier warned him away from the new-fangled Latin rhetorician L. Plotius Gallus, and Cicero went off instead to Rhodes to study Greek rhetoric there before coming home to take up his apprenticeship with the Roman orator.

If Roman education was male-centered, it was because the society was male-centered. Women had little status under the law, and children—even adult sons with their own careers—were regarded as subjects of their fathers in many circumstances. This was not so much a conscious social decision as it was a continuation of assumptions common to many ancient societies, including the Greek and the Judaic. It is important therefore for a modern reader, even while deploring this situation, to look beyond that feeling to assess the teaching methods actually employed. Plutarch tells us how the elder Cato (234–149 BCE) taught his own son two centuries before Christ:

> When his son was born, no duty (save perhaps some public function) was so pressing as to prevent him from being present when his wife bathed the child and wrapped it in its swaddling clothes. His wife suckled the child with her own milk, and would often give her breast to the children of her slaves, so as to gain their affection for her son by treating them as his brothers. As soon as the boy was able to learn, Cato took him personally in charge and taught him his letters, although he owned an accomplished slave, named Chilon, who was a schoolmaster and gave lessons to many boys. But Cato, to use his own words, would not have a slave abuse his son nor perhaps pull his ears for being slow at his lessons; nor would he have his boy owe a slave so precious a gift as learning. So he made himself the boy's schoolmaster, just as he taught him the laws of Rome and bodily exercises; not merely to throw the javelin, to fight in armour or to ride, but also to use his fists in boxing, to bear heat and cold, and to swim against the currents and eddies of a river. And he tells us himself that he wrote books of history with his own hand, and in large characters, so that his son might be able even at home to become acquainted with his country's past; that he was as careful to avoid all indecent conversation in his son's presence as he would have been in presence of the Vestal virgins; and that he never bathed with him. This last point seems to have been a Roman custom, for even fathers-in-law were careful not to bathe with their sons-in-law to avoid the necessity of stripping naked before them.[3]

---

2 *Cornelius Tacitus, A Dialogue on Oratory*, trans. Sir William Peterson (Cambridge: Harvard University Press, 1946) 105–06.

3 Quoted in Aubrey Gwynn S. J., *Roman Education from Cicero to Quintilian* (Oxford: Clarendon Press, 1926; New York: Columbia Teachers Coll., n.d.) 19.

Significantly, the resident schoolmaster Chilon was both Greek and a slave. The militant Romans had conquered Greece, so that many educated Greeks were brought back to Rome as slaves. During the republican period, then, most teachers had a very low social status since they were enslaved members of a conquered class. Matters Greek were thus to be despised in that period. Despite a popular visit to Rome in 168 BCE by the grammarian and literary scholar, Crates of Malos, there was general resentment against Greek philosophy and against certain Greek practices such as nudity in athletics. In 161 BCE, the Roman Senate passed a decree enabling the Praetor to expel all Greek teachers of philosophy and rhetoric.

The first clear evidence of a Latin, as opposed to Greek, teacher of rhetoric comes from 93 BCE. In that year, L. Plotius Gallus began teaching in Latin, but was stopped almost at once. In 92 the two Censors, Cn. Domitius Aenobarbus and L. Licinius Crassus, issued the following edict, which was aimed not only at Plotius Gallus but at other unnamed teachers:

> A report has been made to us that certain men have begun a new kind of teaching, and that young men are going regularly to their school; that they have taken the name of teachers of Latin rhetoric (*Latini rhetores*): and that our young men are wasting their whole days with them. Our ancestors ordained what lessons their children were to learn, and what schools they were to frequent. These new schools are contrary to our customs and ancestral traditions (*mos maiorum*), and we consider them undesirable and improper. Wherefore we have decided to publish, both to those who keep these schools and to those who are accustomed to go there, our judgment that we consider them undesirable.[4]

The tone of this decree would make it appear that the phenomenon of Latinized rhetoric was a recent and even sporadic or unusual occurrence. Yet two almost simultaneous publications, both issued shortly after the decree, show instead that there already existed a well-organized and comprehensive system of Latin rhetoric which included provisions not only for theory but for teaching.

Since the study of that rhetoric was such an integral part of the Roman educational system, it may be useful to describe that subject briefly before turning to the role of writing in the whole pedagogical process.

It is not known exactly how a rather generalized rhetoric from the time of Aristotle (d. 322 BCE) became a specifically organized and standardized five-part system by about 100 BCE. The names of some Greek teachers, especially those on the island of Rhodes, are known, as well as some lost treatises like that of Hermagoras of Temnos, mentioned by both Cicero and Quintilian. Of the precise transition to the five-part theory of rhetoric, however, comparatively little was known until fairly recently.

One thing known is that a young Roman, Marcus Tullius Cicero, wrote a rhetorical treatise circa 89 BCE titled *On Invention* (*De inventione*).[5] Cicero was

---

4 Quoted in Gwynn, *Roman Education*, 61.
5 Cicero, *De inventione. De optimo genere oratorem. Topica*, trans. H. M. Hubbell (Loeb Classical Library: Harvard University Press, 1968). Cicero was only seventeen when he wrote the *De inventione*. For an account of the backgrounds leading to the rhetorical theory embedded in these two works, see Robert N. Gaines, "Roman Rhetorical Handbooks," in *A Companion to Roman Rhetoric*, ed. William Dominik and Jon Hall (Oxford: Blackwell Publishing, 2007) 163–80.

only 17 years old, so it is clear that he is still relying heavily on his teachers. In it, Cicero declares that rhetoric is divided into five "parts": Invention, Arrangement, Style, Memory, and Delivery. Cicero discusses only the first of these five, promising to write later about the other four; he never carried out the promise, however.

What is also known is that an anonymous author (Cornificius?) published a book circa 86 BCE which treated all five parts named by Cicero. Since the book is addressed to one Gaius Herennius, it has traditionally been titled the *Rhetorica ad Herennium* (*The Book of Rhetoric Addressed to Herennius*).[6] Its full treatment of the five parts makes the *Rhetorica ad Herennium* the first complete Latin rhetoric. It is a rigorously practical manual. The author says he will treat only what is pertinent to speaking: "That is why I have omitted to treat those topics which, for the sake of futile self-assertion, Greek writers have adopted." Moreover, he uses only his own Latin examples throughout the book (as he explains in IV.6.9–10).

The remarkable correspondence between these two books suggests the prior existence of a standardized theory of rhetorical education, dating perhaps to 100 BCE or even earlier. The adolescent Cicero is clearly reporting only what he had been taught some time earlier, while the older author of the *Ad Herennium* not only admits the influence of "my teacher" and refers to students studying in schools (*utuntur igitur studiosi*), but specifically declares that rhetorical skill is to be attained through the three means of Precept, Imitation, and Exercise (I.2.3).

Rhetoric, then was the "Precept" portion of the Roman educational triad. As such, it was embedded in a consciously organized program designed to translate the "rules" into activities that would transform the students into rhetorical men. In fact the author of the *Ad Herennium* says that the five parts of rhetoric are what should be "in the orator" (*in oratore*), a phrase Harry Caplan translates as "faculties." In other words, the whole apparatus aimed at practical ability rather than mere knowledge. This ability was to be "in" the person, not in his books. The striking homogeneity of Roman rhetorical theory at this early period may be seen clearly in the similar definitions of the five parts as given by Cicero and the author of the *Ad Herennium:*

Cicero, *De inventione*	*Rhetorica ad Herennium*
Invention is the discovery of valid or seemingly valid arguments to render one's cause plausible.	Invention is the devising of matter, true or plausible that would make the case convincing.
Arrangement is the distribution of arguments thus discovered into the proper order.	Arrangement is the ordering and distribution of the matter making clear the place to which each thing is to be assigned.
Expression is the fitting of the proper language to the invented matter.	Style is the adaptation of suitable words and sentences to the matter devised.

---

6 [Cicero], *Ad C. Herennium De ratione dicendi (Rhetorica ad Herennium),* trans. Harry Caplan (Loeb Classical Library: Harvard University Press, 1954). Caplan's Introduction (especially xxi–xxxii) has interesting notes on the possible author of the book and its possible relation to the *De inventione* of Cicero.

Memory is the firm mental grasp of matter and words.	Memory is the firm retention in the mind of the matter, words, and arrangement.
Delivery is the control of the voice and body in a manner suitable to the dignity of the subject matter and the style.	Delivery is the graceful regulation of the voice, countenance, and gesture.

Both books accept Aristotle's view that speeches are of three kinds: Forensic, dealing with legal accusation and defense; Deliberative or Political, dealing with public policy; and Epideictic, dealing with praise or blame. The similarity of the two books is so great that, during the Middle Ages and early Renaissance, it was commonly assumed that Cicero was the author of both. Medieval writers called the *De inventione* Cicero's "First Rhetoric" (*Rhetorica prima*) or "Old Rhetoric" (*Rhetorica vetus*), relying on Cicero's statement that he planned to write on all five parts of rhetoric; these same writers believed that the *Rhetorica ad Herennium* was Cicero's carrying out of this promise, terming it his "Second Rhetoric" (*Rhetorica secunda*) or, more frequently, his "New Rhetoric" (*Rhetorica nova*). It was only in the late fifteenth century that humanists like Raffaele Regio began to question Cicero's authorship of the *Ad Herennium*.[7]

Though there are some differences between the books (e.g., the *Ad Herennium* offers two methods of Arrangement whereas Cicero proposes only one), the basic doctrines are substantially similar. These rhetorical precepts remained standard for antiquity, the Middle Ages, and the Renaissance, and had currency well into the eighteenth century. It is fair to say that there is such an entity as "Roman Rhetoric," characterized by the five-part division of the subject and by standard treatments of each of the parts.

This standardization was achieved by a resolute rejection of eclecticism after about 100 BCE. The *Ad Herennium* draws on a number of Greek sources ranging from pre-Aristotelian to contemporary Rhodean ideas. But this "synthesis of various teachings" (to use translator Caplan's term) petrifies the chosen ideas into a lasting framework. Cicero simply assumes that the five-part plan is standard, "as most authorities have stated" (I.6.9). The basic theoretical proposal of this Roman rhetoric is that the speaking process involves four chronologically arranged interior steps, followed by one exterior step. The speaker finds ("invents") ideas, then arranges them in an order, then puts words to them, then remembers all of this; finally, the exterior expression ("delivery") occurs through vocal sound, facial expression, and bodily gesture. By analogy the writing process is almost the same, with the physical handwriting (*orthographia*) replacing oral delivery as the final step.

---

7 For an account of the medieval reception of the book, see James J. Murphy, *Rhetoric in the Middle Ages: A History of Rhetorical Theory from Saint Augustine to the Renaissance* (University of California Press, 1974) 106–14. Interestingly, the book was virtually unknown until late antiquity. For an account of Regio's argument against Cicero's authorship, see James J. Murphy and Michael Winterbottom, "Raffaele Regio's 1492 *Quaestio* doubting Cicero's authorship of the *Rhetorica ad Herennium*: Introduction and Text," *Rhetorica* 17 (1999): 77–87.

Invention was accomplished through two major processes. One was the use of "status" or "issue" questions, which could be asked in any controversy. "Every subject which contains in itself a controversy to be resolved by speech and debate," Cicero says, "involves a question about a fact, or about a definition, or about the nature of an act, or about legal process" (I.8.10). The other method was to discover ideas through the use of "**topics**" or "**commonplaces**" such as Division, Consequence, Cause, Effect, or Definition; each of these was considered a "region of an argument," a mental pathway that could lead the mind to find a useful line of argument. So important was this method that Cicero wrote a separate book (*Topica*) on the subject.

Arrangement specified six parts of an oration: Exordium or introduction, Narration or statement of facts, Division or the outline to be followed, Confirmation or proof, Refutation or attack on the opposition's arguments, and Peroration or conclusion.

Style included both general discussion of desirable wording and a very specific treatment of "figures" like Synecdoche, Metaphor, Antithesis, and Isocolon. The fourth book of the *Rhetorica ad Herennium*, in fact, presents the first systematic treatment of Style in Latin, with the first discussion of 64 figures (*exornationes*) which give "distinction" (*dignitas*) to language. Declaring that there are three levels of style (Plain, Middle, and Grand), the author says that good style should have the three qualities of Taste, Artistic Composition, and Distinction. This Distinction is achieved by two kinds of figures: To confer distinction upon style is to render it ornate, embellishing it by variety. The divisions under Distinction are the Figures of Diction and the Figures of Thought. It is a figure of diction if the adornment is comprised in the fine polish of the language itself. A figure of thought derives a certain distinction from the idea, not from the words (IV.13.18). Then follow definitions and examples for 45 figures of speech (diction) and 19 figures of thought; the treatment of the figures occupies more than a fourth of the total length of the book, primarily because of the extensive examples the author feels necessary to make his definitions clear. It is interesting to note that this particular set of figures, not particularly well organized and not always mutually exclusive, became a sort of canon for writers as late as the sixteenth century. The figures became an accepted part of Style for Roman rhetoricians from Cicero onwards, and Quintilian regards them as so important that he devotes two entire books (Eight and Nine) of his *Institutio oratoria* to their analysis.

Memory, "the storehouse of invention," was described as being either natural or artificial. The natural memory could be improved by exercise, just like a bodily muscle. The artificial or artistic memory employed a mnemonic system of "images" and "backgrounds," in which the mind could store symbols (images) set in a visualized neutral space (background). Here too the *Rhetorica ad Herennium* is the first to describe the image–background system, though the theory may well have been commonly known.

Delivery, the final exteriorization, involved detailed consideration of vocal tones, facial expressions, and body movements, including the management of posture, arms, and fingers.

This five-part division of rhetoric had the virtue of being analytic, permitting further study of the individual parts without neglecting their relation to the whole. Cicero, as it has already been demonstrated, could write an entire book dealing only with Invention, and, within that area another book treating only the Topics. Quite naturally there were technical debates about subpoints, for instance, the question whether there were really four issues in Invention or as few as three or as many as five. Nevertheless, the main framework held steady for centuries. Perhaps it was the logicality of the process description, the theory that idea-collection precedes arrangement which precedes style and memory. As a working hypothesis for speech preparation, it seems to have had a recognized value for a very long time.

At the same time, the written treatises had the defect of being schematic at best and mechanical at worst. The technical could, and did, become hypertechnical at times. When Cicero grew older, he began to react against what he saw as an over-technical approach he had favored in his youthful *De inventione*. His dialogue, *De oratore*,[8] written in 55 BCE, argues that a liberal education is more important for the orator than "rules"; while Cicero's spokesman Crassus accepts the familiar doctrines of Roman rhetoric, he also declares that "the prize must go to the orator who possesses learning" (III.35.14). The character Crassus in *De oratore* is the same historical personage, Crassus, who was one of the censors prohibiting the Latin teachers of rhetoric from operating their schools in 92 BCE, and Cicero has him explain his motives for the act; Crassus replies that they had no sense of the humanities and "so far as I could see these new masters had no capacity to teach anything except audacity" (III.24.94). In a sense, Cicero's *De oratore*, with its plea for a broad general education, is the last major objection against a well-organized, discourse-centered teaching program which was clearly already well rooted in Roman society.

Clearly, any modern student of Roman instruction must keep in mind the nature of the "precepts" taught to the students. Yet the treatises of *praecepta* were only a part of the picture. The *Rhetorica ad Herennium* concludes with an insistence on *exercitatio*: "All these faculties we shall attain if we supplement the rules of theory with diligent practice (*diligentia . . . exercitationis*)" (IV.56.69).

What, then, does *exercitatio* mean in this context? What is the nature of the system in which rhetoric is embedded? The evidence indicates that the system was as standardized as its rhetorical precepts.

The Roman Educational System as Described by Quintilian: The Search for Future Language

The most complete description of the Roman educational system appears in a work published in 95 CE, almost a century and a half after the death of Cicero but reflecting a process already under way during Cicero's lifetime; it was destined to continue in substantially unchanged form throughout antiquity, to survive the barbarian invasions of late antiquity, and to become a major force in medieval and Renaissance education. What makes Quintilian's *Institutio oratoria* so valuable as a source of our understanding is that it was written by Rome's acknowledged master teacher, based both on twenty years of classroom

---

8 Cicero, *De oratore*, trans. E. W. Sutton and H. Rackham, 2 vols. (Cambridge MA: Harvard University Press, 1967).

experience and on years of courtroom practice.[9] Moreover, because it is Quintilian's method not only to discuss his own methods but to compare other approaches and to analyze the advantages and disadvantages of each, the book offers a wide-ranging treatment of educational issues in addition to its specific descriptions of the Roman process.

Quintilian was born about 35 CE in Callaguris (modern Calahorra) in Spain.[10] When he was about sixteen he went to Rome, attaching himself, as was the custom, to a famous orator, Domitius Afer. At sixteen he would already have finished his formal education in Spain and taken on the toga of an adult. When Domitius Afer died in 59, Quintilian returned to Spain. He must have taken up a career as a pleader and orator with some success, for he was among those who went to Rome in 68 with the governor of Spain, Galba, who became emperor in January 69.

Quintilian was both teacher and pleader in Rome. He mentions (IV.1.19) that he once pleaded a case before Queen Berenice, sister of the King Agrippa who questioned Saint Paul in Caesarea before the apostle was sent to Rome for trial. He also says (IV.2.86) that in many trials "the duty of setting forth the case was generally entrusted to me"—certainly a mark of his peers' respect for his oratorical abilities. He says (VII.2.24) that he published one of his courtroom speeches; however, the text has been lost.

His reputation as a teacher, however, was even greater. He was among the rhetoricians provided an annual subsidy from the public treasury in 72 by the Emperor Vespasian. A famous epigram by Martial a few years later, in 84, is evidence of his continuing reputation:

> Quintiliane, vagae moderator summe iuventae,
> Gloria Romanae, Quintiliane, togae.
> O Quintilian, supreme guide of unsettled youth,
> Glory of the Roman toga, O Quintilian.
> *Epigrams* 2.90.1–2

Even the satirist Juvenal remarked on Quintilian's good influence on the young, while his pupils included such famous figures as Pliny the Younger and perhaps the historians Tacitus and Suetonius. The Emperor Domitian entrusted the education of his two grandnephews to Quintilian even after he had retired from teaching. His career was financially successful, as he himself notes (VI.

---

9   "The Empire's greatest professor of rhetoric," according to Brother E. Patrick Parks F.S.C. in *The Roman Rhetorical Schools as a Preparation for the Courts Under the Early Empire* (Baltimore: Johns Hopkins University Press, 1945) 98.

10 For biography, see George A. Kennedy, *Quintilian* (New York: Twayne, 1969). There is, of course, a considerable bibliography. For a select bibliography see Murphy (ed.), *Quintilian On the Teaching of Speaking and Writing* xlix–li. Keith V. Erickson has published a listing of about one thousand items in "Quintilian's *Institutio oratoria* and Pseudo-*Declamationes*," *Rhetoric Society Quarterly* 11 (1981): 78–90. See also George A. Kennedy, *The Art of Rhetoric in the Roman World* (Princeton: Princeton University Press, 1972) 45–62. Kennedy has since amalgamated several of his rhetorical histories as *A New History of Classical Rhetoric; An Extensive Revision and Abridgment of The Art of Persuasion in Greece, the Art of Rhetoric in the Roman World, and Greek Rhetoric Under Christian Emperors, with an Additional Discussion of Late Latin Rhetoric* (Princeton: Princeton University Press, 1994).

Preface 4); on the other hand, as he laments in the same section, he suffered
the loss of a beloved son, then his young wife, and finally a second son. Upon
his retirement about the year 90, the Emperor Domitian granted him consular
rank, a remarkable honor at that time for a rhetorician. There is no record of
Quintilian after the murder of Domitian in 96, and Kennedy suggests that
he may have died within a year or two of the publication of his *Institutio oratoria*,
in 95.

Quintilian says that he spent two years of his retirement preparing to
write the *Institutio*, after refusing for a while the requests of his friends that he
write a book on the "art of speaking." In his Preface, addressed to Marcellus
Victorius, he charges that other books on the subject have failed to recognize that
such an art depends on the educational foundation of the orator; he says that
a visible eloquence depends on an invisible preparation, "as the pinnacles of
buildings are seen, while the foundations are hid." Hence his program is a
comprehensive one:

> For myself, I consider that nothing is unnecessary to the art of oratory,
> without which it must be confessed that an orator cannot be formed, and
> that there is no possibility of arriving at the summit in any subject without
> previous initiatory efforts: therefore, I shall not shrink from stooping to
> those lesser matters, the neglect of which leaves no room for the greater, and
> shall proceed to regulate the studies of the orator from infancy, just as if he
> were entrusted to me to be brought up.
>
> (Preface 5)

The result is a work, divided into twelve books, which proposes an educational
process beginning in the cradle and lasting into retirement from public life. It
starts with what we would call **language acquisition** and ends with a discussion
of honorable leisure in old age. Quintilian includes a detailed description of
elementary and secondary education (Books One and Two), with a book (Ten)
on adult self-education, and a lengthy treatment of the five parts of rhetoric. The
final book, Twelve, discusses the ideal orator as "a good man speaking well."
Charles E. Little describes the *Institutio* as four books blended into one: a treatise
on education, a manual of rhetoric, a reader's guide to the best authors, and a
handbook on the moral duties of the orator.[11] Quintilian's own description
includes the moral flavor permeating the work:

> The first book, therefore, will contain those particulars which are ante-
> cedent to the duties of the teacher of rhetoric. In the second book we shall
> consider the first elements of instruction under the hands of the professor of
> rhetoric and the questions which are asked concerning the subject of rhet-
> oric itself. The next five will be devoted to invention (for under this head
> will also be included arrangement); and the four following, to elocution,
> within the scope of which fall memory and pronunciation. One will be

11 Charles E. Little, *Quintilian the Schoolmaster*, vol. 2 (Nashville: George Peabody College for
Teachers, 1951).

added, in which the orator himself will be completely formed by us, since we shall consider, as far as our weakness shall be able, what his morals ought to be, what should be his practice in undertaking, studying, and pleading causes, what should be his style of eloquence, what termination there should be to his pleading, and what may be his employments after its termination.

(I. Preface 21–22)

What then of the subject of rhetoric itself? Quintilian follows this passage with the statement that rhetoric will be taught throughout the whole program, where suitable:

Among all these discussions shall be introduced, as occasion shall require, the art of speaking, which will not only instruct students in the knowledge of those things to which alone some have given the name of art, and interpret (so to express myself) the law of rhetoric, but may serve (also) to nourish the faculty of speech, and strengthen the power of eloquence; for in general, these bare treatises on art, through too much affectation of subtlety, break and cut down whatever is noble in eloquence, drink up, as it were, all the blood of thought, and lay bare the bones, which while they ought to exist and be united by their ligaments, ought still to be covered with flesh.

(I. Preface 23–24)

In other words, Quintilian provides an integrated approach in which a major subject, rhetoric, is shown in its proper setting. The author of the *Rhetorica ad Herennium* specifies that the three elements of Precept, Imitation, and Exercise are necessary to the art, but leaves unspecified what he means by Imitation and Exercise. It is quite possible that he felt it unnecessary to do so for his contemporary readers, who would know, from their own experience, what went on in the schools. (As a matter of fact he does remind his readers [II.24.38] of the way "students in rhetorical schools" are taught to use Dilemma in argument.) As already shown, Quintilian complains that previous books on rhetoric ignored the fact that the subject is embedded in a total learning process; but his great book fastens on the person learning, not merely on the subject itself. The subject of rhetoric, important though it may be, is but one of the tools in that learning process. Quintilian's title is "The Education of the Orator" (*Institutio oratoria*), not "A Book of Rhetoric" (*De rhetorica*).

As Aldo Scaglione has observed, what we today call "composition" had no equivalent in ancient and medieval literary theory.[12] Instead, the movement from silent voice or empty page to fully fashioned appropriate language was the province of rhetoric as assisted by its ancillary, **grammar**. The oralness or writtenness of the language was regarded as less important than its wholeness in fitting the situation at hand; that is why there is no separate "art of letter-writing" in Roman antiquity (as there is in the Middle Ages), no separate "art of

---

12 Aldo Scaglione, *The Classical Theory of Composition from Its Origins to the Present: A Historical Survey*, University of North Carolina Studies in Comparative Literature 53 (Chapel Hill: University of North Carolina Press, 1972) 3.

historiography" or separate "art of poetry-writing."[13] The movement toward future language is the concern of an entire educational program built around rhetoric in its broadest sense but including much more than rhetoric itself.

The objective of the program is the shaping of an adaptive man of discretion, with an ingrained "habit" of adjusting his language to suit any subject or occasion. This sort of schooling does not attempt to lay down "rules":

> But let no man require from me such a system of precepts as is laid down by most authors of books of rules, a system in which I should have to make certain laws, fixed by immutable necessity, for all students of eloquence . . . for rhetoric would be a very easy and small matter, if it could be included in a short body of rules; but rules must generally be altered to suit the nature of each individual case, the time, the occasion, and necessity itself. Consequently, one great quality in an orator is discretion, because he must turn his thoughts in various directions, according to the various bearings of his subject.
>
> (II.13.1–2)

Nevertheless, even if Quintilian disdains reliance on "rules," he describes a systematic, programmatic educational program. However, it is possible that a modern reader, untrained in the technical processes of Roman education, may well overlook the architectonic framework lying behind Quintilian's readable style and sensible advice.

It has been noted that, if there is an art that conceals art, Quintilian has an art which conceals method. His Latin style makes extensive use of periodic sentences, with frequent parallel structures, sometimes quite complex by modern standards. (A good example may be found in the passage just quoted or in the preceding quotation on the role of rhetoric in the teaching program.) Also, since he usually presents various viewpoints before declaring his own judgment on each point, only the most careful reader will be able to track his main threads of thought through such discussions. His highly personalized accounts of his own teaching methods may also mislead an unwary reader into believing falsely that the *Institutio* is more of an autobiography than an exposition. All of this makes Quintilian extremely difficult to summarize.

Roman Teaching Methods

Virtually every individual element found in the program described by Quintilian was inherited from the Greeks, and especially from Isocrates. The Romans accepted Isocrates' principle that three key elements are required in successful education: Talent, Education, and Practice. What was not inherited, however,

---

13 For the close correspondence between Horace's *Ars poetica* and the standard rhetorical lore of the day, see George Converse Fiske and Mary A. Grant, *Cicero's De oratore and Horace's Ars poetica*, University of Wisconsin Studies in Language and Literature 27 (Madison: University of Wisconsin Press, 1929). There was, of course, a separate art of verse-writing in the Middle Ages; see Martin Camargo and Marjorie Curry Woods in Chapter 4 of this volume, and Murphy, *Rhetoric in the Middle Ages*, 135–193.

was the deftly designed correlation of these elements into a "system."[14] As a system the process could be—and was—replicated over time and space. As a system it could be promoted worldwide as a tool of public policy equal in geo-political value to the legions and the tax collectors in making the world Roman. As the television commentator Alistair Cooke once remarked, "Language is a dialect with an army and a navy," and history does in fact tell us that for more than half a millennium, the Latin language and its schools served as a kind of social cement throughout the Western world.[15]

Quintilian is not the inventor of this system; he is merely describing a process already familiar to Romans for almost two centuries. However, he is one of our best sources for both its philosophy and its details. Donald A. Russell suggested that Quintilian could even be used as a guide to understanding earlier Greek developments:

> The conservatism of rhetorical teaching over such a long period makes it possible to give an account of it as a system, based on the late textbooks which survive, without feeling that one's conclusions are likely to be funda-mentally wrong for the earlier period. Quintilian is undoubtedly the best guide.[16]

Some modern critics have argued that Quintilian is presenting an idealized or even wistfully utopian view of education. They point to his insistence on morality as a reaction to the decadence he saw around him, noting that many of his examples hearken back to the presumably more virtuous days of the pre-Imperial Republic. Yet he says that he bases the *Institutio oratoria* on his own teaching experience in a career that won the approbation of at least two Emperors, Vespasian and Domitian, and attracted the plaudits of writers like Juvenal and Martial. What is more important, though, is that what Quintilian describes is consistent with other evidence about Roman education from the time of Cicero up to the fall of Rome to the barbarians in the fifth Christian century. It is also generally consistent with the evidence about the early Middle Ages, up to the late twelfth century at least. Obviously not every student went all the way through the course, just as today there are many "dropouts" in even the best of schools. The poor sent their children to school for only the most elementary education with the *ludi magister* for grammar or the *calculator* for

---

14 For a schematic overview of the five elements of the Roman teaching methods, see the Appendix at the end of this chapter.

15 Robert Pattison offers a useful analysis of the power of the Latin language "in the service of authority" in his book, *On Literacy: The Politics of the Word from Homer to the Age of Rock* (Oxford: Oxford University Press, 1982): "As it began its expansion, Rome also began to develop formal, written Latin for the business of the Empire. The soldier and the grammarian proceeded in lockstep to spread the Roman way, one by conquering the world, the other by providing it with correct Latin as a medium of organization," 67.

16 Donald A. Russell, *Criticism in Antiquity* (University of California Press, 1981) 25. S. F. Bonner also stresses the systematic, devoting 162 pages of his *Education in Ancient Rome from the Elder Cato to the Younger Pliny* (Berkeley: University of California Press, 1977) to a section titled "The Standard Teaching Programme."

basic numbers.[17] No doubt many students had to content themselves with the instruction in grammar without ever proceeding to more advanced studies with a rhetorician. Nor did every teacher have the mastery of a Quintilian; Seneca tells the story of the Spanish schoolmaster Porcius Latro, who could declaim brilliantly before his pupils but was paralyzed with fright when called upon to speak in public.[18]

If nothing else, the homogeneous longevity of the system proves its efficiency. Pierre Riché remarks that even in the sixth Christian century teachers of grammar, rhetoric, and law were still listed in the public budget under "barbarians" like Theodoric and his successor Athalaric. "When we look inside the schools of the grammarian and the rhetor," Riché adds, "we can observe that the program and methods of instruction also had not changed."[19] The ever-practical Romans surely did not continue the system out of any philosophical regard for "liberal arts"—Cicero's *De oratore* in 44 BCE was apparently the last major Roman stand on that issue—but rather for the quite pragmatic reason that it worked. It provided literacy for many, competence for some, excellence for a few. The dividing line separating these three levels of accomplishment probably was based on the length of time the student could spend in the program.

What Quintilian demonstrates, then, is the complete system. Whether this or that student benefited fully from it depended more on socioeconomic factors than on the integrity of the system itself. Consequently, it would seem useful to examine in a bit more detail the actual methods designed to produce what Quintilian calls *facilitas*, the ability to produce appropriate language on any subject in any situation. This examination covers Precept (Rhetoric and Grammar), Imitation, the two exercise programs of *Progymnasmata* and Declamation, and **Sequencing**.

Precept

Both grammar and rhetoric are included here. The *Rhetorica ad Herennium*, as has been shown, defines *praecepta* as "a set of rules that provide a definite method and system of speaking." Cicero's *De inventione* defines Eloquence as speaking based on "rules of art." Quintilian, as seen from his Preface, cautions that such "rules" should be not followed slavishly, and he adds in another place that "these rules have not the formal authority of laws or decrees of the plebs, but are, with all they contain, the children of expediency (*utilitas*)" (II.13.6). For him they serve as guides rather than commandments. No doubt this attitude was that of the best rhetors, though we can imagine the worst masters, just as today, driven to a helpless reliance on the rules because they do not know their subject well enough to be flexible.

---

17 The most comprehensive account of ancient education is that of Henri I. Marrou, *A History of Education in Antiquity*, trans. George Lamb (New York: Sheed, 1956). He discusses Roman education in chapters 4 through 7 (265–313). For a discussion of terms like *calculator*, see E. W. Bower, "Some Technical Terms in Roman Education," *Hermes* 89 (1961): 462–77. Now also see Yun Lee Too (ed.), *Education in Greek and Roman Antiquity* (Leiden: Brill, 2001).

18 Cited in Gwynn, *Roman Education*, 67.

19 Pierre Riché, *Education and Culture in the Barbarian West Sixth through Eighth Centuries*, trans. John J. Contreni (Columbia: University of South Carolina Press, 1976) 40.

The exact Roman method of teaching rhetoric as precept is not clear. Quintilian suggests that the precepts were offered throughout the program; this could mean either that the master introduced precepts at each stage or that separate times were set aside for them. The *Institutio oratoria* does not describe any separate segment for teaching precepts, though it would seem logical that the older students preparing for Declamation would have to know the principles of at least deliberative and forensic rhetoric, the major fields covered in the imaginary cases students were asked to plead.

The Roman boy's educational progress was divided into three main steps: the acquisition of the most basic language skills, especially reading and writing; then a period of exercises with the *grammaticus*; then, when he was ready, training under the teacher of rhetoric (the *rhetor*). Book Two of the *Institutio* covers the teaching done by the rhetorician. One might expect a discussion of *praecepta* at this point. Yet what Quintilian describes is not a systematic instruction in rhetorical precepts, but instead a more advanced version of the same types of classroom exercises already handled under the *grammaticus*. In fact, Quintilian declares that the exercises are more important than the precepts: "I will venture to say that this sort of diligent exercise will contribute more to the improvement of students than all the precepts of all the rhetoricians that ever wrote" (II.5.14). When he does come to a treatment of rhetoric in Book Two, he adds another caution about the relation of precept to exercise:

> For the present I will only say that I do not want young men to think their education complete when they have mastered one of the small text-books of which so many are in circulation, or to ascribe a talismanic value to the arbitrary decrees of theorists. The art of speaking can only be attained by hard work and assiduity of study, by a variety of exercises and repeated trial, the highest prudence and unfailing quickness of judgment.
>
> (II.13.15)

Since his discussion of rhetoric occupies eight of the twelve books of the *Institutio*, however, it is clear that he regards the subject as important. Yet, Quintilian's whole approach is to teach students, not subjects. The most likely explanation is that rhetorical precept was not taught in a block, all at once or even on assigned days; rather, individual concepts must have been introduced whenever they suited the exercise at hand. When Quintilian discusses Narration of histories under the teacher of rhetoric (II.4.3–19), for example, he outlines the qualities of good narration and then refers to his later treatment of the subject under Judicial Oratory in his rhetoric section. Quintilian's recurrent principle for the assignment of individual exercises to the student is "When he is ready." He criticizes grammarians (II.1.2) for taking upon themselves some aspects of rhetorical instruction for which the boys will not yet be ready.

One thing is certain. The rhetoric treatise was not a student "textbook" in the modern sense of the word, with each student having a copy to study. The "textbook" in our sense of the word is a product of the printing age, when books became cheap enough to distribute in a classroom. In any case, Roman rhetoric was so homogeneous that any reasonably well-educated teacher could master and transmit the principles orally without much difficulty. There were rhetoric texts available for study (they apparently sold well), even if public libraries were comparatively rare.

No doubt students were asked to **memorize** some materials. For example, the "commonplaces" (topics) would be useful for students to have ready to hand. Certainly it is known that they were obliged to memorize poetry and prose for the process of Imitation, and in fact Quintilian prefers this over having them memorize their own writing, even if doting parents preferred to hear their sons recite their own compositions from memory for public presentations. His argument is that they might as well memorize the best authors rather than perpetuating their own errors. But he makes no mention of memorizing precepts.

Grammar was another matter. Although Quintilian refers to "those rules which are published in the little manuals of professors" (I.5.7), the subject of grammar was not nearly as well developed in his day as rhetoric had already been for more than two centuries. There was no standard treatise on the subject. As a consequence, Quintilian feels obliged to devote a significant portion of Book One (chapters 4 to 7) to such matters as "word," analogy, usage, spellings, barbarisms, solecisms, vocal tones, and the differences between Greek and Latin. Chapter 7 deals with Orthography, the art of writing words correctly on the page. He justifies this attention to apparently minor matters by arguing that correct language is the basis for every good use of language. "These studies," he says, "are injurious, not to those who pass through them, but only to those who dwell immoderately on them" (I.7.35).

Grammar is regarded as so foundational that students must be taught its precepts directly, especially in the earliest stages. And in the exercise of Imitation, the fine points of grammar are noted carefully in meticulous critiques of the models being studied. These two types of instruction are pointed out in his definition of the subject. Quintilian defines grammar in what was already a traditional way: "the art of speaking correctly, and the interpretation of the poets" (I.4.2). Thus it includes what we would today call the "rules" of correctness, and also the study of what we would call "literature."

(Later Roman teachers had access to a standard textbook on grammar. By the fourth Christian century, a widely accepted manual of basic Latin grammar, the brief *Ars minor* of Aelius Donatus fl. 350 CE[20] was available. This book petrified for later centuries the concept of "**eight parts of speech**"; another work, his larger *Ars grammatica* (*Ars maior*), not only treats the eight parts of speech in greater detail but includes a section dealing with *schemes* [figures of speech] and *tropes*, which would ordinarily have been treated by the rhetor rather than the grammarian. It was another two centuries before the appearance of what was to become the standard advanced Latin grammar text for more than a thousand years, that is, the *Ars grammatica* of Priscian fl. 500 CE, who was a teacher of Latin grammar in the Greek-speaking city of Constantinople. This work contains eighteen books, the last two dealing with "construction" [syntax], or the elements of composition.[21])

---

20 It has been translated by W. J. Chase in *The Ars Minor of Donatus*, University of Wisconsin Studies in the Social Sciences and History 36 (Madison: University of Wisconsin Press, 1926). The Latin text is in Henry Keil (ed.), *Grammatici Latini*, 7 vols. (Leipzig, 1864) 4, 355–66.

21 Text in Keil, *Grammatica Latini* 4, 367–402. Priscian was the first Latin grammarian to discuss syntax.

Even without such books in the earlier periods of Roman history, however, all the evidence indicates a consistency of grammatical instruction in the schools. The *grammaticus*, after all, received a young boy who had only the rudiments of reading and writing skills; the exigencies of standard-setting through all the complex classroom exercises provided ample opportunity for the grammarian not only to teach the rules themselves but to insist on their proper application in both writing and speaking.

What is to be remembered, above all, about the role of Precept in the Roman schools is that it was only a part of an integrated system designed to produce not merely knowledge but ability. Quintilian reminds his readers of this fact in Book Ten: "But these precepts of being eloquent, though necessary to be known, are not sufficient to produce the full power of eloquence unless there be united to them a certain Facility, which among the Greeks is called *hexis*, 'habit'" (X.1.1). This facility is resident in the psyche of the person, not merely in his knowledge.

To comprehend how the Romans produced this habit in young men, it is necessary to understand the precise role played in the schools by Imitation, and by the graded composition exercises known as *Progymnasmata*.

Imitation

The concept of *Imitatio* (*Mimesis*) is much misunderstood today. On one hand, it could mean the artistic re-creation of reality by a poet or artist; on the other, it could mean the deliberate modeling of an existing artifact or text.[22] Actually it was for the Romans the second of these, a carefully plotted sequence of interpretive and re-creational activities using preexisting texts to teach students how to create their own original texts. Each phase in the sequence has its own purpose, but takes its value from its place in the sequence. It would be a mistake, therefore, for a modern reader to assume that each of the parts is independent of the others or to think that the set of compositional activities is a kind of smorgasbord to be picked up and used at random. It is not mere eclecticism.

The concept is certainly an ancient one. Plato has Protagoras say that when schoolboys memorize the great poets they imbibe not only the poetry but the moral qualities of the great men described in the poems (*Protagoras* 325–26). Isocrates makes it a key teaching tool (*Antidosis* 276–77). Aristotle begins his discussion of drama with a statement of principle: "Imitation is natural to man" (*Poetics* 1148b). The *Rhetorica ad Herennium*, as we have seen, begins and ends with the injunction to use Imitation as well as Exercise to learn the art of speaking. Cicero, the object of fervid imitation during the Renaissance,[23] opens the second book of his *De inventione* with the statement that he has taken the best from many sources, just as the painter Zeuxis of Heraclea chose the five most beautiful girls from Croton as models for a painting of Helen the city had commissioned for its Temple of Juno. The continuity of Imitation was so strong

---

22 There is a good brief survey of ancient views in Russell, *Criticism in Antiquity*, 99–113.

23 See Izora Scott, *Controversies Over the Imitation of Cicero as a Model for Style and Some Phases of Their Influence on the Schools of the Renaissance* (Davis CA: Hermagoras Press, 1991). It is important to note, however, that some Renaissance discussions of Imitation deal with adults deciding which authors to imitate in their own literary works, while others do deal with Imitation in educating the young.

throughout the Roman period that the first Christian rhetorician, Saint Augustine, writing in 426 CE, declares in his *De doctrina Christiana* (IV.3) that Imitation is more important than Precept for the newcomer to rhetoric.

The Roman school system perfected a seven-step process of Imitation, with writing or the analysis of written texts being coupled to oral performance by the students before master and peers in the classroom. What today would be called peer criticism is an integral part of the scheme; in the Roman interactive class-room the student-critic shapes his own critical judgment by assessing publicly what he hears and reads. The teacher is not merely to tell the students what to think, Quintilian says, "but frequently to ask questions upon them, and try the judgment of his pupils" (II.5.13). A brief explanation of these seven steps may show how Imitation works in the Roman classroom.[24]

A. Reading Aloud (lectio)

Either the master or one of the students could **read a text aloud**. Models are to be carefully chosen for their linguistic virtues, though occasional faulty ones may be used to illustrate how defects may occur. In the later stages when speeches become the texts for study, the master may declaim a speech or even declaim one of his own (though Quintilian prefers that the master use an acknowledged orator like Cicero rather than his own work). Quintilian introduces implicitly a major educational principle at this point, namely, that no exercise should be conducted for a single purpose only. The students hear not only the form of a text, including its rhythmical or other sonic patterns, but also take in uncon-sciously its subject matter and moral tone. Hence the insistence on histories as well as poems, as offering salutary models of conduct.

B. Analysis of the Text (praelectio)

This is the beginning of the application of judgment. The master literally dissects the text. The immediate intent is to show the students how the author made good or bad choices in wording, in organization, in the use of figures, and the like; the long-range objective is to accustom the student to what today we could call a "close reading" of texts. Since it is a written text done orally, the exercise also trains the "ear" of the student for later exercises in analyzing the oral argu-ments used in orations. Both good models and bad models are to be presented. Quintilian's brief summary in Book Two of the *Institutio* seems straightforward enough; in the following passage he is explaining the method in respect to analyzing an oration, though the method is exactly the same for a poem or a history (as he points out in I.8.13–21):

> The master, after calling for silence, should appoint some one pupil to read (and it will be best that this duty should be imposed on them by turns), so

---

24 A useful account of Imitation may be found in Donald Lemen Clark, *Rhetoric in Greco-Roman Education* (New York: Columbia University Press, 1957) 144–76. Clark's account may be particularly inter-esting to readers concerned with teaching method, since he consistently analyzes the rationale for the exercises more clearly than other historians like Marrou or Bonner.

that they may thus accustom themselves to clear pronunciation. Then, after explaining the cause for which the oration was composed (so that what is said will be better understood), he should leave nothing unnoticed which is important to be remarked, either in the thought or the language: he should observe what method is adopted in the Exordium for conciliating the judge; what clearness, brevity, and apparent sincerity is displayed in the statement of facts; what design there is in certain passages, and what well-concealed artifice (for that is the only true art in pleading which cannot be perceived except by a skilful pleader); what judgment appears in the division of the matter; how subtle and urgent is the argumentation; with what force the speaker excites, with what amenity he soothes; what severity is shown in his invectives, what urbanity in his jests; how he commands the feelings, forces a way into the understanding, and makes the opinions of the judges coincide with what he asserts. In regard to the style, too, he should notice any expression that is peculiarly appropriate, elegant, metaphorical, what figures of speech are used; what part of the composition is smooth and polished, and yet manly and vigorous. Nor is it without advantage, indeed, that inelegant and faulty speeches—yet such as many, from depravity of taste, would admire—should be read before boys, and that it should be shown how many expressions in them are inappropriate, obscure, timid, low, mean, affected, or effeminate.

(II.5.6–10)

When Quintilian and his colleagues say that they will "leave nothing unnoticed," they mean exactly that. The dissection of the text is intended to be microscopic. While a reader may cover whole sections with a sweep of the eye, the composing writer/speaker must commit himself to one word or even one syllable at a time as he creates a text. Hence the truly analytic reader needs to reach back through the wholeness of paragraph or argument to identify the microcosmic decisions made by the composer.

An excellent example of this Roman micro-analysis may be found in a later work written by the grammarian Priscian about 500 CE. Priscian's *Analyses of the First Lines of the Twelve Books of Virgil's Aeneid* is an extremely meticulous work, occupying fifty-four pages in the standard edition of Henry Keil. The beginning section provides a good example of the method:

Scan the line *Arma virumque cano Troiae qui primus ab oris.*

How many caesurae are there?

Two.

What are they?

The penthemimera and the hephthemimera [*semiquinaria, semiseptenaria,* Priscian says in his barbarous Latin]. Which is which?

The penthemimera is *Arma virumque cano,* and the hephthemimera *Arma virumque cano Troiae.*

How many "figures" has it?

Ten.

Why has it got ten?

Because it is made up of three dactyls and two spondees.

[Priscianus takes no notice of the final spondee.]

How many words ["parts of speech"] are there?

Nine.

How many nouns?

Six—*Arma, virum, Troiae, qui* [sic], *primus, oris.*

How many verbs?

One—*cano.*

How many prepositions?

One—*ab.*

How many conjunctions?

One—*que.*

Study each word in turn. Let us begin with *Arma.* What part of speech is it?

A noun.

What is its quality?

Appellative.

What kind is it?

General.

What gender?

Neuter.

How do you know?

All nouns ending in -*a* in the plural are neuter.

Why is *Arma* not used in the singular?

Because it means many different things.[25]

This kind of methodical treatment, carried on over all kinds of texts for ten or a dozen years, must surely have promoted a high degree of linguistic sensitivity in the students. It must be remembered, too, that the same treatment was given to the students' own compositions.

On the other hand, the mere analysis of others' texts could produce a sort of compositional paralysis, with the writer fearing his inability to do as well as the

25 Quoted in Marrou. *History of Education in Antiquity,* 279–80.

models. Quintilian is quite aware of what we would call "writer's block." He tells the story of a young man named Secundus, whose uncle, Julius Florus, found him in a dejected state one day; Secundus told his uncle that he had been trying for three days to write an introduction to a subject he had to write upon for school. Florus responded smilingly, "Do you wish to write better than you can?" (X.3.14). For improvement, Quintilian adds, there is need of application, but not of vexation with ourselves.

The close analysis of texts was of course not the only method used. It took its value from its place in the system. The next steps called upon the student to apply his own energies.

C. Memorization of Models

Quintilian is convinced that memorization of models not only strengthens the memory in the way that physical exercise strengthens a muscle but also provides the student with "an abundance of the best words, phrases, and figures" for possible use later on (II.7.4). Memorization is especially useful for the very young, who do not yet have the capacity for intellectual analysis of their texts. "The chief symptom of ability in children," he says, "is memory" (II.3.1). (He says the same thing about teaching a foreign language to the very young.) He is quite adamant about the virtue of memorizing good models rather than one's own writing, and in fact says that such memorization will equip the student better to recall his own compositions when necessary. As usual, though, he has a keen eye for the pedagogical opportunity: a student may be allowed to recite his own work from memory only as a reward, when he has produced "something more polished than ordinary" (II.7.5). The problem he sees is that otherwise the student may end up perpetuating his faults if he memorizes his own work.[26]

D. Paraphrase of Models

The re-telling of something in the students' own words begins at the earliest stages of the program—for example, with first an oral and then a written **paraphrase** of a fable of Aesop (I.9.2)—but continues throughout the instruction of both the *grammaticus* and the *rhetor*. The more advanced students deal with more complex types of narrations such as plots of comedies or the accounts found in histories (II.4.2); here Quintilian refers to the concepts of narration to be found in rhetorical doctrine, though he expressly reminds the reader that the exercise is a continuation of that begun earlier under the *grammaticus*. (Here too is another example of the way in which formal rhetorical precepts are fed into the system as the need arises.)

The ultimate purposes of paraphrase are two: to accustom students to fastening on the structure of the model rather than its words, and to begin the development of a personal style in narration. "It is a service to boys at an early age," he says, "when their speech is but just commenced, to repeat what they have heard

---

26 There is a brief analysis of Quintilian's view of memory in Frances A. Yates, *The Art of Memory* (Chicago: Chicago University Press, 1966) 21–26.

in order to improve their faculty of speaking. Let them accordingly be made, and with good reason, to go over their stories again, and to pursue them from the middle, either backward or forward" (II.4.15).

It is in this section, dealing with the first efforts of the students to compose in their own terms, that Quintilian lays down his principles of classroom **correction**. The students should be shown the faults in their writing and speaking, but should also be praised for whatever they have accomplished. If the performance is so bad that the student is asked to write again on the same subject, he should be told that he can indeed do better, "since study is cheered by nothing more than hope" (II.4.13). Quintilian applauds exuberance in compositions by the young, if it is made clear that later on a more sophisticated standard will be demanded. He comments that "the remedy for exuberance is easy, but barrenness is incurable by any labor" (II.4.6). Elsewhere he refers to an ancient aphorism that "it is easier to prune a tree than to grow one" (II.8.9). Accordingly he urges the master to promote freedom of invention in the early stages of the student's development, tolerating (though noting) some stylistic faults which can be corrected as the student becomes more adept in language.

E. Transliteration of Models

There is no precise English term for the Roman exercises in text re-casting. The process could take several forms: direct **translation** of the text from Greek to Latin or Latin to Greek; re-casting of Latin prose to Latin verse; re-casting of Latin prose to Greek verse, or vice versa; making the model shorter, or longer, whether in verse or prose; altering the style from plain to grand or vice versa. **Transliteration** could be an extremely sophisticated assignment, demanding precise knowledge of verse forms and prose rhythms as well as an extensive vocabulary. Indeed, Quintilian notes, the difficulty of the exercise makes it valuable for teaching a keen awareness of language. A sure knowledge of the model is a prerequisite. As for critics of this method, he points out agreement on the principle: "About the utility of turning poetry into prose, I suppose no one has any doubt" (X.5.4). Once the principle of usefulness for re-casting is established, he implies, there is no reason to shy away from other modes of accomplishing the same end. (A monolingual culture like the American, in which knowledge of foreign languages is severely limited, might be hard put to use some translative forms of the method, but other forms—e.g., verse–prose or prose–verse, or plain style–grand style—might well be considered today as classroom tools.)

F. Recitation of Paraphrase or Transliteration

The oral–written relationship is so strong in Roman educational practice that even Quintilian does not always make explicit what he clearly expects everyone to take for granted. This relationship is spelled out at the very beginning of his discussion of teaching methods: "Not only is the art of writing combined with that of speaking, but correct reading also precedes illustration" (I.4.3). The student, having "read" his text analytically, writes his own paraphrase or transliteration of it, and then brings his own work into the public classroom for oral presentation. Sometimes it will be recited from memory, sometimes read aloud.

G. Correction of Paraphrase or Transliteration

The admonitions of the master concerning this performance are shared with all who hear, thus raising the standards of everyone. Quintilian argues that this is the prime advantage of public over private tutorial education:

> At home he can learn only what is taught himself; at school, even what is taught others. He will daily hear many things commended, many things corrected; the idleness of a fellow student, when reproved, will be a warning to him; the industry of anyone, when commended, will be a stimulus; emulation will be excited by praise; and he will think it a disgrace to yield to his equals in age, and an honor to surpass his seniors. All these matters excite the mind; and though ambition itself be a vice, yet it is often the parent of virtues.
>
> (II.2.21–22)

This "exercise of judgment," as Quintilian calls it, could also enroll the students themselves as critics. Not only was the Roman schoolroom interactive between master and students, but between students and students as well. Quintilian is quite explicit about this for the older boys doing formal declamations or practice orations: "Shall a pupil, if he commits faults in declaiming, be corrected before the rest, and will it not be more serviceable to him to correct the speech of another? Indubitably" (II.5.16). Even though he does not make the same kind of statement about the earlier stages of the program, the whole tone of the book, especially chapter 2 of Book One on the virtues of the public classroom, argues for what he continually refers to as "activity of the mind" among the students. There is no reason to believe that this would exclude what we call "peer criticism." Perhaps Quintilian intends only the older boys to comment on each others' work, but everything else he says throughout the book is at least consistent with the possibility that he encourages student criticisms at every stage.

Two principles govern his use of correction. The first is that oral correction should be tailored to the capacities of the student involved; however, since correction is public, the master must keep in mind the other hearers in the classroom, "who will think that whatever the master has not amended is right" (II.6.4). The second is that some early faults can be tolerated, as part of the student's natural development of a particular skill. For the adult practitioner he discusses in Book Ten, there is another kind of **self-correction** involved in the practice of writing. This involves personal decisions about what to add, to take away, or to alter (X.5.1), rather than the public pronouncements in a classroom about something just recited. Even so, it is logical to assume that Quintilian would ask the adult writer to analyze his own written text with the same methods used earlier in the classroom process of Imitation. He proposes lifetime use of methods learned in school.[27]

The process of Imitation, then, is for Quintilian and other Romans a specific sequence of learning activities for students from the youngest to the oldest. The

---

27 Accordingly, Quintilian includes in Book Ten a lengthy section (X.1.37–2.26) analyzing a wide range of authors and orators worthy of imitation by the adult learner. He concludes the section by saying that "we should do well to keep a number of different excellences before our eyes."

method remains the same over time, the only change being in the models imitated. The young lad who begins with a simple fable of Aesop ends up years later as a young adult doing the same thing with a complex speech of Demosthenes or Cicero. The student learns political science, history, morals, and literature by a kind of intelligent osmosis. His attention is focused on the style and structure of the particular text, but he cannot escape an awareness of historical circumstances or ethical problems as he moves through the various steps.

The objective, of course, is to enable the student eventually to compose his own texts: "For what object have we in teaching them, but that they may not always require to be taught?" (II.5.13). Free composition must be based on knowledge of the options available to the writer, and this knowledge comes only from Imitation. Imitation is thus a life-long pursuit. Quintilian remarks early in the *Institutio* that a child learns spoken language easily through natural imitation, so that even a two-year-old can speak and understand what is said to him. Writing, however, must be taught to him. The boy follows the forms of the letters of the alphabet before he is allowed to write them for himself, tracing indented patterns with his stylus to accustom his hand kinesthetically to the form of a letter before he writes it freely. "By following these sure traces rapidly and frequently, he will form his hand, and not require the assistance of a person to guide his hand with his own hand placed over it" (I.1.27). This kind of tactile Imitation is based on exactly the same principles as the school exercises and the self-learning activity recommended in Book Ten for adults to continue even into retirement. To put it into abstract terms, form precedes freedom. The writer who knows only one mode of writing is not free, but is bound for ever to that one mode.

As valuable as Imitation is, however, it too is but one part of the total educational system. The Roman student also underwent a parallel program of specific writing/speaking exercises (*Progymnasmata*).

Progymnasmata (*Graded Composition Exercises*)

This is one area of methodology in which Quintilian is less than thorough, perhaps because of what he calls "this haste of mine" (II.1.12). In the opening chapter of Book Two he discusses the proper spheres of *grammaticus* and *rhetor*, arguing that the teacher of rhetoric (as well as the teacher of grammar) "should not shrink from the earliest duties of his profession" (II.1.8). What he means is that both should teach the "little exercises" that ultimately prepare the boy to be an adept user of language. Then he rapidly lists nine exercises: **narration**, praise, blame, **thesis**, **commonplaces**, statement of facts, eulogy, invective, and refutation; then, in chapter 4, he discusses some of these exercises and adds three more: **comparison**, cause and effect (which he calls a *chreia*), and praise or censure of laws. Earlier (I.8.3), he had named *prosopopoeiae* in connection with proper oral reading. This makes thirteen altogether. He concludes chapter 4 with this observation: "On such subjects did the ancients, for the most part, exercise the faculty of eloquence" (II.4.41). In other words, he is simply listing rapidly a number of exercises long known and undoubtedly familiar to his readers—hence his brevity.[28]

---

28 Ronald F. Hock and Edward N. O'Neill, *The Chreia in Ancient Rhetoric, Vol. 1, The Progymnasmata* (Atlanta: Scholars Press 1986) 10–22.

What he writes about here is a set of graded composition exercises which had long since come to be called *progymnasmata* (though he himself does not use that term). The name comes from the function of the exercises: if the highest forms of school training are the Declamations or fictitious speeches (*gymnasmata* in Greek), so that which prepares for them is Pre-Declamation (*progymnasmata*). Even though the term itself is Greek, and the major ancient writers of textbooks on the subject were Greek, it is clear from Quintilian's account that the use of the exercises is already solidly entrenched in Latin schools.

The earliest surviving textbook defining and illustrating the exercises is that by Aelius Theon of Alexandria, writing probably in the latter half of the first Christian century—a contemporary of Quintilian though probably unknown to him. Two of the most popular Greek textbooks come long after Quintilian, written by Hermogenes of Tarsus[29] (second century) and Aphthonius of Antioch[30] (fourth century). Both these books had impact well beyond antiquity. Hermogenes' treatise was translated into Latin as *Praeexercitamenta* by the Latin grammarian Priscian around 500 CE, and had use during the Middle Ages and Renaissance. Aphthonius, however, eclipsed Hermogenes in antiquity by far, mainly because he included useful examples, and his work became a standard Byzantine textbook as well; when introduced to the Latin West during the fifteenth century, it achieved a new popularity extending even to colonial America.

Quintilian's concern with the proper role of the grammarian proved to be a prophetic one. It was not a question of whether the *progymnasmata* should be taught, but rather a question of who should teach them. Quintilian urges the rhetorician to keep some control, even if it means taking up "the earliest duties of his profession" by working with very young students just beginning narrations of fables. History tells us that the grammarians eventually won out in Roman schools, taking over these exercises for themselves. As a practical matter, this development may have meant little to the boys who came through the system, since they received the instruction in any case.

We see in Quintilian, then, a comparatively early stage in which these exercises still fall under the purview of both masters. It is true, nevertheless, that his brief account can show us their relation to the schools' objectives. Specifically, he argues that the exercises train students in the exact functions needed in the real world:

> But what is there among those exercises, of which I have just now spoken, that does not relate both to other matters peculiar to rhetoricians, and, indisputably, to the sort of causes pleaded in courts of justice? Have we not to make statements of facts in the forum? I know not whether that department of rhetoric is not most of all in demand there. Are not eulogy and invective often introduced in those disputations? Do not commonplaces, both those which are leveled against vice (such as were composed, we read, by Cicero), and those in which questions are discussed generally (such as were published by Quintus Hortensius, as, "Ought we to trust to light proofs?" and "For witnesses and against witnesses"), mix themselves with the inmost substance

29 Translated by Charles S. Baldwin, *Medieval Rhetoric and Poetic* (New York: Macmillan, 1928) 23–38.
30 Translated by Ray Nadeau, *Speech Monographs* 19 (1952): 264–85.

of causes? These weapons are in some degree to be prepared, so that we may use them whenever circumstances require. He who shall suppose that these matters do not concern the orator, will think that a statue is not begun when its limbs are cast.

(II.1.10–12)

This argument is coupled with the proposal that the *grammaticus* continue to teach the students part of the time even after they join the *rhetor*. This, he says, will show the students the continuity of their instruction while providing them with variety in their masters. "Nor need there be any fear," he adds, "that the boy will be overburdened with the lessons of two masters. His labor will not be increased, but that which was mixed together under one master will be divided. Each tutor will thus be more efficient in his own province" (II.1.13). Perhaps the futility of his argument lay in the fact that both masters used the same methods anyway, with the exception of Declamation belonging clearly to the *rhetor*.

In any case, Quintilian does not define or illustrate most of the terms he uses for the exercises, so we must look elsewhere. The *Progymnasmata* of Hermogenes of Tarsus is as good a source as any, since it transmitted the well-accepted definitions which even the more popular Aphthonius used later as the basis for his own book. Even though Hermogenes is writing in the second Christian century, he reflects a tradition found not only in Quintilian but going well back before the time of Cicero.

Donald Lemen Clark has an incisive statement about the educational value of the *progymnasmata* as found in Hermogenes and his successors:

They all give patterns for the boys to follow. They present a graded series of exercises in writing and speaking themes which proceed from the easy to the more difficult; they build each exercise on what the boys have learned from previous exercises . . . yet each exercise adds something new.[31]

The key term here is "graded." Like other elements of the Roman system, the *progymnasmata* are taught not for themselves but for habit-building in the mind of the student. With each accomplishment of the student, there comes a new and more difficult challenge, just as Imitation moves by steps from the oral reading through model-based writing to the final free composition of the student. The "how" is carefully spelled out at each stage.

Hermogenes presents twelve *progymnasmata*: **fable**, **tales**, *chreia*, **proverb**, **refutation and confirmation**, **commonplace**, **encomium**, comparison, **impersonation** (*prosopopoeia*), **description**, **thesis**, and **laws**. (Aphthonius makes these into fourteen by separating refutation and confirmation, and by making censure the opposite of encomium; Quintilian, as we have seen, adds cause and effect.)

The twelve can be divided according to the three types of rhetoric:

---

31 Clark, *Rhetoric*, 181. For a modern adaptation of this idea, see John Hagaman, "Modern Use of the Progymnasmata in Teaching Rhetorical Invention," *Rhetoric Review* 5 (1986): 22–29.

- Deliberative rhetoric: fable, tale, *chreia*, proverb, thesis, laws.
- Judicial rhetoric: confirmation and refutation, commonplace.
- Epideictic rhetoric: encomium, impersonation, comparison, description.

However apt this kind of division might be in terms of future usefulness to the student, though, it does not represent the order in which the *progymnasmata* were taught. (Indeed the concept of "three genera of speeches," introduced by Aristotle and followed by the Romans, was always more theoretical than practical in terms of speeches made in the real world; any one oration might require elements of all three genera, as Cicero's performances have shown.) The exercises were taught in a certain order, for the good reason that they naturally succeeded each other.

The following abstract of the twelve *progymnasmata* of Hermogenes is necessarily brief, since the inclusion of overnumerous examples would produce an account as long as the book itself; examples are provided only in those cases (e.g., the *chreia*) which might otherwise be difficult for a modern reader to understand.[32]

I. Fable

The first exercise is the retelling of fables from Aesop. The retelling may be either more concise than the original, or expanded beyond it with invented dialogue or additional actions to enhance the tale.

2. Tales

This is the recounting of something that happened (a history) or of something as if it had happened (an epic, a tragedy, a comedy, a poem). Hermogenes names five modes: direct declarative, indirect declarative, interrogative, enumerative, comparative.

3. Chreia

This is an exercise in **amplification**, dealing with what a person said or did. Hermogenes says there are three types of *chreia* to be used in this way:

> Of words only: "Isocrates said that education's root is bitter, its fruit is sweet" (*Chreia* 43).

> Of actions only: "Crates, having met with an ignorant boy, beat the boy's tutor" (Quintilian I.9.5).

> Mixed, with both words and actions: "Diogenes, on seeing a youth misbehaving, beat his tutor and said, 'Why are you teaching such things?'" (*Chreia* 26).

Hermogenes notes that a *chreia* differs from a maxim in three ways: a maxim has no character speaking, does not involve actions, and does not have an implicit question and answer.

---

32 The following account is based largely on Clark.

The main point, of course, is the amplification asked of the student. Hermogenes suggests a sequence of eight methods to write about a *chreia*: praise of the speaker quoted, an expanded restatement of the *chreia*, its rationale, a statement of the opposite view, a statement from analogy, a statement from example, a statement from authority, and an exhortation to follow the advice of the speaker.

Ronald F. Hock and Edward N. O'Neill have recently published translations of the *chreia* of seven ancient authors including Quintilian; an appendix listing 68 *chreia* shows a remarkable similarity among the various collections, whether the "speaker" named is Demosthenes, Diogenes, or Plato.[33] This is not surprising, since the books are written for teachers rather than students; and utility not variety is the standard.

4. Proverb

This is an exercise in amplification of an aphorism (*sententia*). It is not radically different from the preceding exercise, but is intended as incremental repetition. Hermogenes suggests methods similar to those for the *chreia*, though of course without praise for a speaker or an action. The *Rhetorica ad Herennium* (IV.43.56–58) cites the Proverb as an element of a figure of speech called Dwelling On One Point (*expolitio*); seven means of amplification are offered for the proverb "Often one who does not wish to perish for the republic must perish with the republic."

5. Refutation and Confirmation

This involves disproving or proving a narrative. Quintilian (II.4.18–19) makes credibility the main heading to be considered. Hermogenes, however, says that the elements of Destructive Analysis are obscurity, incredibility, impossibility, inconsistency, unfittingness, and inexpediency. Constructive analysis takes the opposite of these.

6. Commonplace

This exercise asks the student to "color," that is, to cast either a favorable or an unfavorable light upon an established fact, a thing which has been admitted. Aphthonius says the Commonplace is practice in arousing the emotions of an audience in the face of an established fact—for example, the discovery of a temple robber:

> Begin with the contrary, analyzing it, not to inform, for the facts are assumed, but to incite and exasperate the auditors. Then introduce a comparison to heighten as much as possible the point you are making. After that introduce a proverb, upbraiding and calumniating the doer of the deed. Then a digression, introducing a defamatory conjecture as to the past life of the accused; then a repudiation of pity. Conclude the exercise with the final considerations of legality, justice, expediency, possibility, decency, and the consequences of the action.[34]

---

33 See note 28.
34 Quoted in Clark, *Rhetoric*, 194.

This treatment is called a Commonplace, he says, because it can be applied commonly to any temple robber or other miscreant.

7. Encomium

This is an exercise in praise of virtue and dispraise of vice, either in a thing or in a person. (Aphthonius makes the positive [Encomium] and negative sides [Vituperation] of this exercise into two separate items, but most others keep them as one.) Since praise and blame are the function of Epideictic oratory, the exercise of Encomium could draw upon all the lore of that section of rhetorical theory. Theon is reported to have developed the topics of Encomium in 36 divisions and subdivisions. Hermogenes contents himself with ten ways to praise a person: marvelous events at his birth, his nurture, his education, the nature of his soul, the nature of his body, his deeds, his external resources, how long he lived, the manner of his end, and the events after his death. Quintilian praises this exercise both because "the mind is thus employed about a multiplicity and variety of matters" (II.4.20), and because it furnishes the students with many examples for later use.

8. Comparison

This exercise builds on the preceding one of Encomium by doubling the subjects to be treated in one composition. The same methods are to be used.

9. Impersonation

Here the student is asked to compose an imaginary monologue that would fit an assigned person in certain circumstances. The task is to make the language appropriate not only to the person (age, background, and emotional state) but to the circumstances in which he speaks. For example, what might Achilles say to the dead Patroclus, or what might Niobe say over the bodies of her dead children? There were three standard divisions: Ethopoeia is the imaginary statement of a known person; Prosopopoeia is the imaginary statement of an imaginary person; and Eidolopoeia are lines written for the dead to speak. Despite these theoretical divisions of the textbooks, the term "Prosopopoeia" (as in Quintilian) is often used to denote the whole range of impersonative exercises.

10. Description

The exercise in vivid description (ecphrasis) asks the student to write and speak so that he is "bringing before the eyes what is to be shown"—a phrase used by Theon, Hermogenes, and Aphthonius as well as Quintilian. Quintilian discusses this kind of imaging in Book Eight under Ornateness; the figure enargeia (Vivid Illustration), he says, portrays persons, things, and actions in lively colors, so that they seem to be seen as well as heard (VIII.3.61). Clark (203) uses the term "Epideictic word-painting" for ecphrasis, and quotes Hermogenes as saying that "The virtues of the ecphrasis are clearness and visibility." It requires a careful attention to detail, and here the ecphrasis builds on the earlier exercises of

Commonplace and Encomium. The student does not simply say a wall is large, but describes its stones, its height, its thickness, its circumference, its battlements— dilation of detail until the reader/hearer can "see" it in his mind.

II. Thesis

This advanced exercise asks the student to write an answer to a "General Question" (*quaestio infinita*)—that is, a question not involving individuals. Cicero states in his *De inventione* (I.6.8) that rhetoric does not deal with such general questions, but only with those involving individuals. Quintilian too notes that a general question can be made into a persuasive subject if names are added (II.4.25). That is, a Thesis would pose a general question such as "Should a man marry?" or "Should one fortify a city?" (A Special Question on the other hand would be "Should Marcus marry Livia?" or "Should Athens spend money to build a defensive wall?") Hermogenes distinguishes the Thesis from the Commonplace by declaring that the Commonplace amplifies a subject already admitted, while the Thesis is an inquiry into a matter still in doubt. Since both negative and positive answers may be supported, the exercise calls on the student to marshal arguments, using his rhetorical skills on the chosen side; as a consequence both Hermogenes and Aphthonius recommend the same structure that is used in orations.

12. Laws (Legislation)

This final exercise asks the pupil to compose arguments for or against a law. Quintilian regards this as the most advanced of the set of exercises: "The praise or censure of laws requires more mature powers, such as may almost suffice for the very highest efforts" (II.4.33). That is, it requires almost as much skill as the most advanced student activity, the Declamation. He says that the chief topics to be considered are whether the law is proper or expedient; under "proper" he includes consistency with justice, piety, religion or similar virtues; the "expedient" is determined by the nature of the law, by its circumstances, or by its enforceability. Quintilian also complains that some teachers make too many divisions of the two topics he discusses; as a matter of fact Hermogenes lists the six topics of evident, just, legal, possible, expedient, and proper.

The *progymnasmata*, then, offered Roman teachers a systematic yet flexible tool for incremental development of student abilities. The young writer/speaker is led step-by-step into increasingly complex compositional tasks, his freedom of expression depending, almost paradoxically, on his ability to follow the form or pattern set by his master. At the same time he absorbs ideas of morality and virtuous public service from the subjects discussed, and from their recommended amplifications on themes of justice, expediency, and the like. By the time he reaches the exercise of Laws he has long since learned to see both sides of a question. He has also amassed a store of examples, aphorisms, narratives, and historical incidents which he can use later outside the school.

The student is, in short, ready to take on the most complex of all the Roman school's learning experiences—the Declamation (*declamatio*), or fictitious speech. Declamation is the cap, the culmination of the whole process.

Declamation

The Declamation is a rhetorical exercise designed to develop skill in deliberative (political) and forensic (judicial) oratory.[35] The two main types, in fact, are the *suasoria*, in which the speaker urges an assembly or person either to act or not to act, and the *controversia*, in which the speaker prosecutes or defends a person in a given legal case. Here again the Romans adapt for the schools a Greek practice apparently in use well before the time of Aristotle. The earliest Latin rhetorical treatises take it for granted. The author of the *Rhetorica ad Herennium* describes several deliberative exercises he finds useful; for example, one finds Hannibal debating with himself whether to return to Carthage or stay in Italy (III.2.2). Cicero says in his *De oratore* that every day he made up fictitious cases and made practice orations on them.

Besides the school practice sessions there was a public form of declamation, first among friends for mutual edification and entertainment (as in the time of Cicero), then under the Empire as a regular type of public display or even competition—the Emperor Nero himself "won" such a competition on one occasion. Later, under the period of oratorical virtuosity known as "The Second Sophistic," the public declaimers attracted crowds and wealth which today only a rock star could command.[36]

Declamation thus has a curious history. Obviously any would-be orator would want to practice, and there is the famous story of Demosthenes delivering a practice oration on shore against the sound of the breakers to improve his speaking voice. No doubt speakers since the very earliest days have practiced their skills in made-up controversies, and it would not be surprising to find Greek teachers like Gorgias or Isocrates putting their students through such drills.

The great virtue of Declamation for the Roman schoolmaster, though, was that the whole technical apparatus of rhetorical theory was available as resource for the classroom activity of the oration. All that was needed was a set of subjects on which to deliver speeches. It is significant that Quintilian, after devoting most of the first two books of the *Institutio* to the early education of the student, turns briefly to Declamation (II.10.1–15) and then begins the detailed exposition of rhetoric which occupies eight of the ten remaining books. Once Declamation is reached, in other words, rhetoric becomes the master's concern. The complete oration, even in the classroom, demands a full appreciation of the five parts of rhetoric: Invention, Arrangement, Style, Memory, and Delivery. Heretofore, rhetoric has been used piecemeal in the preliminary exercises, the precepts being introduced wherever useful. Now every skill of the student has to be harnessed toward one goal. The student facing an audience of colleagues and master, and

35 S. F. Bonner, *Roman Declamation in the Late Republic and the Early Empire* (Liverpool: University Press of Liverpool, 1949). For pre-Roman declamation, see D. A. Russell, *Greek Declamation* (Oxford: Oxford University Press, 1983). Clark has an account in *Rhetoric*, 213–61. There are shorter descriptions in Gwynn, Marrou, Parks, and Kennedy.

36 See, for instance, Eunapius's account of the declamation which Prohaeresius delivered in Athens in the third century as part of his candidacy for the highly paid position of *rhetor* in that city; the crowds were so great that soldiers had to be used to control the situation. Prohaeresius started his extempore speech on one side of a difficult theme, then switched to the opposite side—then challenged the shorthand reporters to check his accuracy as he repeated both impromptu speeches word for word! The story is in Eunapius, *Lives of the Philosophers*, in Philostratuus and Eunapius, *Lives of the Sophists*, trans. Wilmer C. Wright (Cambridge MA: Harvard University Press, 1922) 495–97.

often facing a student opponent as well, had rhetorical problems similar to those in the outside world. Quintilian has high expectations for Declamation, rather sarcastically answering critics who see no value in it:

> For, if it is no preparation for the forum, it is merely like theatrical ostentation, or insane raving. To what purpose is it to instruct a judge who has no existence? To state a case that all know to be fictitious? To bring proofs on a point on which no man will pronounce sentence? This is nothing more than trifling; but how ridiculous is it to excite our feelings, and to work upon an audience with eagerness and sorrow, unless we are indeed preparing ourselves, by imitations of battle, for serious contests and a regular field?
>
> (II.10.8)

These "imitations of battle" take a standard format in the Roman schools. The master assigns a problem ("theme") to one or more students; they prepare and deliver an oration before the class in reply to the problem posed in the theme; the master delivers an oral comment on the orations, perhaps adding to it a declamation of his own to show how it might be done better. Quintilian in fact proposes that the master ask the students to evaluate his own declamation as a means of sharpening their critical skills (II.2.13). An easy variation involves matching two students against each other, especially in the forensic declamations (*controversiae*).

Typically the Declamation is divided into the four parts of proem, narration, proofs, and peroration (i.e., conclusion). A division after the narration could lay out the overall plan the speaker intends to follow; for example he might divide his remarks into Letter of the Law (*ius*) versus Spirit of the Law (*aequitas*). Classroom practice encouraged amplification as a means of testing the students' powers, particularly in the use of weighty statements (*sententiae*) or in the devising of novel approaches (*colores*). To go into greater detail here about the methodology of the Declamation would be to rehearse the entirety of rhetorical theory. This is of course not our main concern.

What part did writing play in the exercise of Declamation? The answer is not clear. Quintilian does not specifically mention writing, though he does say of Declamation that "it comprehends within itself all those exercises of which I have been treating, and presents us with a very close resemblance to reality" (II. 10.2). Certainly writing plays a major part in Imitation and in the *progymnasmata* which go before. Quintilian mentions the practice of providing written outlines for students to follow in their declamations (II.6.2). Given Quintilian's whole orientation toward the relation of speaking and writing, it would not be surprising to find various written forms behind the oral performance. For one thing, his constant admonitions about storing examples for future use imply written record as well as strong memory. And what he says in Book Ten about the writing orator (e.g., X.3.10) seems to imply that at least some of the oral was first the written. The Declamation itself was of course purely oral, but we are not yet sure how much writing lies behind it.

However, Quintilian's advice to adults about writing may well indicate his attitude toward writing for the young. Certainly Quintilian urges the adult speaker to use writing both as a general preparation and as a tool for shaping certain parts of a speech in advance of its delivery: "By writing we speak with greater accuracy and by speaking we write with greater ease" (X.7.29). He makes this remark, one of his most famous aphorisms, in discussing the value of meditation as compared to the value of writing:

> As to writing, we must certainly never write more than when we have to speak much extempore; for by the use of the pen a weightiness will be preserved in our matter, and that light facility of language, which swims as it were on the surface, will be compressed into a body as husbandmen cut off the upper roots of the vine (which elevate it to the surface of the soil) in order that the lower roots may be strengthened by striking deeper. And I know not whether both exercises, when we perform them with care and assiduity, are not reciprocally beneficial, as it appears that by writing we speak with greater accuracy, and by speaking we write with greater ease. We must write, therefore, as often as we have opportunity; if opportunity is not allowed us, we must meditate; if we are precluded from both, we must nevertheless endeavor that the orator may not seem to be caught at fault, nor the client left destitute of aid. But it is the general practice among pleaders who have much occupation, to write only the most essential parts, and especially the commencements, of their speeches; to fix the other portions that they bring from home in their memory by meditation: and to meet any unforeseen attacks with extemporaneous replies.
>
> (X.7.28–30)

Quintilian adds (X.7.30–31) that Cicero and many other orators used written memoranda as aids in preparing their speeches.[37] His personal recommendation is to use short notes and small memorandum-books which may be held in the hand while speaking. In his discussion of Memory in Book Eleven there are constant references to written texts of orations for which the memory must be used (esp. XI.2.25–49). If the adult speaker is urged to use writing, it certainly seems likely that the young student preparing to be an orator would have been given the same instructions.

There have been many critics of the Declamation, both ancient and modern. Tacitus complains in his *Dialogue on Oratory* (85 CE) about "the training merely of tongue and voice in imaginary debates which have no point of contact with real life."[38] Quintilian himself says that "The practice, however, has so degenerated through the fault of the teachers, that the license and ignorance of the declaimers have been among the chief causes that have corrupted eloquence" (II.10.3). To this, however, he immediately has a positive reply: "But of that which is good by nature we may surely make a good use."

---

37 For a discussion of the role played by writing in Cicero's oratory, see Richard Leo Enos, *The Literate Mode of Cicero's Legal Rhetoric* (Carbondale: Southern Illinois University Press, 1988). Orthography— the physical task of writing—is important to Quintilian; he urges writers to use wax tablets for drafts to speed up composition without breaking the pattern by having to dip a pen in ink (X.3.31–33). For a brief history of the wax tablet, see Richard and Mary Rouse, "Wax Tablets," *Language and Communication* 9 (1989): 175–91. See also Albertine Gaur, *A History of Writing*. Revised edition (London: The British Library, 1992); the illustration of pens and a stylus on p. 52 may help illuminate Quintilian's remarks noted above.

38 Tacitus, *Dialogue*, ed. Peterson, 31.

Many of the criticisms concern the subjects chosen for classroom use.[39] Manifestly such subjects must be difficult enough to challenge the capacities of the students, yet generalizable enough to permit the students to work on them without vast research. As a consequence a large array of fantastic or even incredible topics came to be associated with Declamation, and especially with the forensic type. They feature pirates, seducers, wronged heirs, poison cups, cruel husbands, contradictory laws, cures for the blind, shipwrecks, and a host of other calamities and dilemmas calculated to present the student orator with difficulty. The deliberative type was generally more staid ("Cato deliberates whether to take a wife"), but the Romans always considered the forensic the more difficult and therefore exercised more ingenuity in posing its problems. One example from the collection of Seneca the Elder may suffice to show the level of complexity which was employed:

The Daughter of the Pirate Chief

A young man captured by pirates writes his father for ransom. He is not ransomed. The daughter of the pirate chief urges him to swear that he will marry her if he escapes. He swears. Leaving her father, she follows the young man, who, upon his return to his home, takes her to wife. A well-to-do orphan appears on the scene. The father orders his son to divorce the daughter of the pirate chief and marry the orphan. When the son refuses to obey, the father disowns him.

(*Controversiae* I.6.6)[40]

S. E. Bonner, one of the most perceptive modern students of the Declamation, defends such classroom subjects on the very grounds that critics use to attack them. The subjects are deliberately more complex than real life, he says, as a test of the student's powers: "they were deliberately designed to provide an almost, but not quite, impossible hurdle."[41]

The public circulation of declamatory texts also shows a public interest in the topics and their treatment. While the published *Progymnasmata* of Hermogenes and Aphthonius were for the use of teachers, the sets of declamations published by the elder Seneca and by the Pseudo-Quintilian[42] were intended for a general reader. Such works were successful enough that someone wrote two collections

---

39 "The world of the declamation was a fantastic and melodramatic one," writes Martin Lowther Clarke, "and for that reason perhaps popular in a humdrum age." He makes the remark in *Rhetoric at Rome: A Historical Survey* (London: Cohen, 1953) 91.
40 Quoted in Clarke, *Rhetoric*, 231.
41 Bonner, *Roman Declamation*, 83.
42 See Seneca the Elder, *Controversiae. Suasoriae*, ed. and trans. Michael Winterbottom, 2 vols. (Cambridge MA: Harvard University Press, 1974). Seneca says he wrote the declamations for his sons, but the work had a more general circulation anyway. Michael Winterbottom has edited the *Minor Declamations Attributed to Quintilian* (New York: Walter de Gruyter, 1984), with a commentary which includes treatment of the subject of possible authorship of the collection. See also Lewis A. Sussman, *The Declamations of Calpurnius Flaccus: Text, Translation, and Commentary* (Leiden: Brill, 1994); George A. Kennedy, *Progymnasmata: Greek Textbooks of Prose Composition and Rhetoric.* Writings from the Greco-Roman World 10 (Atlanta: Society of Biblical Literature, 2005); and Robert J. Penalla et al. (eds.), *Rhetorical Exercises from Late Antiquity: A Translation of Choricius of Gaza's Preliminary Talks and Declamations, with an Epilogue of Choricius' Reception in Byzantium* (Cambridge: Cambridge University Press, 2009).

to which Quintilian's name became attached. The reason, of course, is that there were popular public declamations put on by adult orators to demonstrate their rhetorical virtuosity; the throngs attending such displays of extempore eloquence might well treasure a written form of what they had heard, just as sports fans today read eagerly the newspaper account of a game seen the day before.

In any case, history shows that the Declamation served the Roman schools for many centuries—again, a case in which the very longevity of the practice demonstrates its perceived value. The Declamation is the remote ancestor of the *disputatio* of the medieval university, and of scholastic debate beginning in colonial American colleges and lasting into the present time. Like the *Progymnasmata* and Imitation, Declamation may well have had far-reaching influences in Western culture not yet completely recognized by modern scholars.

Sequencing

The systematic ordering of classroom activities in Roman schools was to accomplish two goals: Movement, from the simple to the more complex; and Reinforcement, by reiterating each element of preceding exercises as each new one appears. To these can be added another principle: no exercise should be done for just a single purpose.

It is these principles which lead to the constant interrelating of writing, speaking, reading, and listening. Writing is a solitary activity, Quintilian notes, but recitation of the written is a public one. What is written by one student is heard by another when recited. What is read—and we must remember that even private reading in ancient times is generally vocalized, and therefore "heard" by the reader—becomes the model for the written. Writing makes speaking precise, Quintilian says, just as speaking makes writing easy. Listening prepares the student for analysis of the oral arguments he will later hear his opponent raise against him in forum or courtroom. Everything fits: there are no random activities in the Roman schoolroom.

The "Good Man Speaking Well"

Quintilian concludes the *Institutio oratoria* with a book devoted to the character of the perfect orator—the "Good Man Speaking Well," as Cato the Censor named him centuries earlier—so perfect that no one, not even Cicero, has yet met that standard. His Book Twelve is no longer technique-based, but is instead a sketch of the ideal human product of the whole system described in the previous eleven books. He draws on Stoic concepts of virtue, but argues that philosophy alone is not enough for the orator destined to act publicly. Nevertheless, the orator needs to know ethics and the law to do his job well. His concluding sentence is a telling reminder of the purpose of the whole work:

> This, then, Marcus Vitorius, is the best contribution I think I can personally make to the teaching of oratory; the knowledge of it, even if it fails to give the young student much practical help, will at least—and this is more important to me—give him good intentions.

(XII.11.31)

Conclusion

Habituation is the key to success in the Roman school. For example, a dozen years of re-telling stories, from simple Aesop to complex Demosthenes, make narrative skill second nature by adulthood. Likewise the analytic phases of Imitation make critical reading the norm. The step-by-step progression through the *progymnasmata* equips the student with powerful tools of amplification, just as the Declamation prepares him to see instinctively the two sides to any controversy. Quintilian declares Habit (*hexis*) to be the ultimate goal of the program. What he means is something a bit different from the modern idea of habit as something fixed and somewhat out of our control. His "habit" means a deep-rooted capacity (his word is *facilitas*) to employ language wherever needed, on whatever subject, in whatever circumstances. His meaning is close to Aristotle's, who defines rhetoric as a "faculty" of observing the available means of persuasion in a given case; this "faculty" for Aristotle is seen as virtually a part of the personality (*ethos*) of the *rhetor*. In a sense, for both men, the person *becomes* rhetorical. And if he absorbs what he reads and hears for all those years, he can be a moral person as well.

It is for this reason that Quintilian and other Roman masters are willing to set up this grueling sequence of sometimes petty and dull exercises. The goal is no less than the perfect orator, whose molding is worth every effort. Quintilian would probably say that the way to train an architect is to start him as a boy on building bricks; the child need not know what a wall is, when he begins to make bricks, but later he can be taught how to make small brick piles, then walls, then houses, then palaces, and then even cities. This is just the way Roman schools approach language use. The master envisages word-cities even from the time the child begins to trace letters with his stylus, and then leads him incrementally through a nicely coordinated sequence of learning experiences which make efficient language use virtually a part of his personality. The letter of the alphabet becomes years later a stirring oration in the Roman Senate. The whole enterprise is a search for future language.

Many of these individual exercises can be used profitably today, of course, since each is largely self-explanatory. Nevertheless, a modern reader should understand that the full power of their use resides in their interrelation to each other, and in their place in a proven sequence.[43]

It was an efficient system, producing a habit of language use designed to last a lifetime. As the next four chapters demonstrate, the core concepts of the Roman educational program lasted in a recognizable fashion through late antiquity, the Middle Ages, the Renaissance, and into colonial America. And later chapters show the massive social and cultural changes in Western society which eroded the coherence of the system even while fragments of its teaching methods continue in use, often unrecognized, to this day.

It is a story of system and continuity. It seems inconceivable that any human activity of such longevity could be valueless. This is not to say that the enterprise was perfect or without fault. Its very longevity has provided ample opportunity

---

43 For a comment on modern use of the system, see James J. Murphy, "The Modern Value of Roman Methods of Teaching Writing, with Answers to Twelve Current Fallacies," *Writing On the Edge* 1 (1989): 28–37.

for criticism, from Cicero and Tacitus to modern detractors like Martin Lowther Clarke, who notes that "The Romans had administrative capacity in their bones, and it could survive even the follies of the lesser rhetoricians."[44] He complains that the schools fostered a cult of ornateness; that the system of Imitation and Invention by Topics prevented students from thinking for themselves; that truth was made less important than imagination; that directness in speech was discouraged; and that the same educational labor could well have been spent on something better. He concludes with the observation that Pliny is narrower than Cicero, and Fronto is narrower than Pliny. Others complain that the education was purely literary (word-centered), thus training declaimers rather than orators. Still others maintain that the student was given no real sense of history, no training in philosophy except for a scattering of ethical commonplaces, no unifying picture of society or government; another criticism is that as an elitist mechanism the schools merely perpetuated the order of a ruling class.[45]

At the same time its pedagogical values surely seem worth studying. It might be well to conclude this chapter with an observation from a modern historian of language, Louis G. Kelly:

> Nobody really knows what is new or old in present-day language teaching procedures. There has been a vague feeling that modern experts have spent their time in discovering what other men have forgotten; but as most of the key documents are in Latin, moderns find it difficult to go to original sources. In any case, much that is being claimed as revolutionary in this century is merely a rethinking and renaming of earlier ideas and procedures.[46]

44 Clarke, *Rhetoric*, 162.
45 For a succinct array of charges against the system, see Robert A. Kaster, *Guardians of Language: The Grammarian and Society in Late Antiquity* (Berkeley: University of California Press, 1988) 12–13. Kaster also provides (*Guardians*, 231–440) demographic records of hundreds of teachers for the period 250–440 CE.
46 Louis G. Kelly, *25 Centuries of Language Teaching. An Inquiry into the Science, Art, and Development of Language Teaching Methodology 500 BCE–1969* (Rowley: Newbury, 1969) ix.

Appendix
Overview of Roman Teaching Methods Described
in the *Institutio oratoria*

They fall into five categories: (1) Precept, (2) Imitation, (3) Composition exercises (*progymnasmata*), (4) Declamation, and (5) Sequencing.

1. Precept: "a set of rules that provide a definite method and system of speaking." Grammar as precept deals with "the art of speaking correctly, and the interpretation of the poets." Rhetoric as precept occupies eight of the twelve books of the *Institutio oratoria:*

a.   Invention
b.   Arrangement
c.   Style
d.   Memory
e.   Delivery

2. Imitation: the use of models to learn how others have used language. Specific exercises include:

a.   Reading aloud (*lectio*)
b.   Master's detailed analysis of a text (*praelectio*)
c.   Memorization of models
d.   Paraphrase of models
e.   Transliteration (prose/verse and/or Latin/Greek)
f.   Recitation of paraphrase or transliteration
g.   Correction of paraphrase or transliteration

3. Composition exercises (*progymnasmata* or *praeexercitamenta*): a graded series of exercises in writing and speaking themes. Each succeeding exercise is more difficult and incorporates what has been learned in preceding ones. The following twelve were common by Cicero's time:

a.   Retelling a fable
b.   Retelling an episode from a poet or a historian
c.   *Chreia*, or amplification of a moral theme
d.   Amplification of an aphorism (*sententia*) or proverb
e.   Refutation or confirmation of an allegation
f.   Commonplace, or confirmation of a thing admitted
g.   Encomium, or eulogy (or dispraise) of a person or thing
h.   Comparison of things or persons
i.   Impersonation (*prosopopeia*), or speaking or writing in the character of a given person
j.   Description (*ecphrasis*), or vivid presentation of details
k.   Thesis, or argument for/against an answer to a general question (*quaestio infinita*) not involving individuals
l.   Laws, or arguments for or against a law

4. Declamation (*declamatio*), or fictitious speeches, in two types:

a.   *Suasoria*, or deliberative (political) speech arguing that an action be taken or
not taken
b.   *Controversia*, or forensic (legal) speech prosecuting or defending a fictitious
or historical person in a law case

5. Sequencing, or the systematic ordering of classroom activities to accomplish
two goals:

a.   Movement, from the simple to the more complex
b.   Reinforcement, by reiterating each element of preceding exercises as each
new one appears

Perhaps the most important aspect of these methods is their coordination into a
single instructional program. Each is important for itself, but takes greater
importance from its place within the whole.

Chapter 3

Writing Instruction from Late Antiquity to the Twelfth Century*

Carol Dana Lanham

Key Concepts

Latin as dominant language • Continuity of content and method • Role of Christianity • Types of sources • School leading texts • Grammar • Rhetoric • *Progymnasmata* • Glossaries, *differentiae*, scholia • *Sententiae* • *Exempla* • Colloquies • Formula and letter collections • Teaching anthologies and manuals • Narrative sources • Writing instruction • *Lectio divina* • Influence of poetry on prose • Style and diction • Rhythm • *Progymnasmata* and prose composition • Imitation, paraphrase, variation • *Compilatio* • *Dispositio* • *Ars dictaminis*, the art of letter-writing • *Progymnasmata* and epistolography.

Since in school exercises nothing is more useful than to practice what should be accomplished in the art, his scholars wrote daily in prose and verse, and proved themselves in discussions.

John of Salisbury (1159) on Bernard of Chartres

The Social, Cultural, and Political Background

Quintilian described an educational program created for a small, homogeneous population of Latin-speaking males free to concentrate on a single purpose: becoming eloquent public speakers and political leaders who could guide the civic life of Rome and the cities of her empire. It was a brief moment of comparative tranquility before the illusory unity expressed by "Romania" yielded to the ethnic and linguistic patchwork of nations now known as Europe.

From the late second century onward, all across the lands that correspond, more or less, to modern Europe and North Africa, Germanic tribes—"barbarians"—migrating westward in search of land and food provoked wars, devastation, and movements of displaced people. The first wave of great invasions reached its peak after the middle of the fifth century. (Long before then, the Roman Empire had split into two main parts; the eastern, Greek-speaking part would have a longer but hardly more tranquil existence as the Byzantine Empire.) Meanwhile, the new Christian religion had spread steadily, provoking other

---

* This chapter is reprinted with the permission of Richard Lanham

kinds of turmoil and sporadic persecutions even after the Emperor Constantine declared it the official religion of the empire in 323 CE.

Remarkably, the essence of Quintilian's educational program survived the fragmentation and decay of civic life and the painful transition to a multiplicity of Christian societies in which the imperial system of publicly supported schools and teachers deteriorated and in some places apparently disappeared altogether. For a time, classical learning hung by a frayed thread. At its lowest point, perhaps in the first half of the seventh century, education seems to have been available only within monasteries or from scattered private tutors.

Whatever education did take place was conveyed in Latin. The teaching of Latin had spread early to Rome's provinces,[1] where it would evolve into the Romance languages, and Latin remained the dominant language for centuries, overwhelming local vernaculars as the universal medium of instruction, worship, and public discourse. The first references to the need to communicate in a language other than Latin appear early in the ninth century, by which time Latin was a second language for everyone. How did teachers educate the increasing numbers of non-Romance speakers for whom Latin was totally foreign?

Instruction to a minimal level of what is now called functional literacy cannot begin to account for the sustained explosion of literary creativity that accompanied the spread of Christianity across Europe from the fourth century on. The Anglo-Saxon, Irish, and Germanic peoples had to devote great effort—more than the French, Spanish, and Italians—to learning the forms and syntax and vocabulary of Latin, but they all were apt pupils and were soon displaying their accomplishments abundantly in writing. Although it may be going too far to claim that it was principally the Bible that gave sixth- and seventh-century Merovingian scribes the "possibility" of expressing themselves in Latin,[2] there is no denying that the heritage of classical Latin literature was vastly enlarged and enriched by Christian Latin.

As a religion of the book, Christianity brought new words, concepts, and imagery to the Latin language, new purposes to education, and renewed vigor to rhetoric. Christian grammar teachers recognized the suitability of the classical education's analytic methods for penetrating the Bible's linguistic mysteries and embraced them readily—at the cost of including their pagan content—and added Christian poetry to their pupils' reading. Pagan rhetoric was a harder sell. Christians long remained uneasy about using rhetoric's arsenal of persuasive techniques, even though they acknowledged the need for able speakers and writers to explain and interpret Scripture and to debate controversial theological issues. St. Augustine, by showing in his *De doctrina christiana* (completed in 427) how to redeploy rhetoric for the purposes of Christian oratory and writing, made possible a Christian theory of rhetoric[3]—and, by his own voluminous writings, encouraged an ever-growing flood of treatises arguing points of Christian teaching.

---

1 Suetonius, *De grammatibus et rhetoribus* §3.0.

2 Alf Uddholm, *Formulae Marculfi: Etudes sur la longue et le style* (thesis, Uppsala, 1953) 209.

3 See Averil Cameron, *Christianity and the Rhetoric of Empire: The Development of Christian Discourse* (Berkeley: University of California Press, 1991); Michael Roberts, *Biblical Epic and Rhetorical Paraphrase in Late Antiquity*, ARCA Classical and Medieval Texts, Papers and Monographs 16 (Liverpool: Francis Cairns, 1985) 62–63.

Thanks in part to a sea change in the quality of Latin writing starting after the middle of the eighth century, the ninth century is often called the Carolingian renaissance. Charlemagne sought not only to vanquish his political foes and enlarge the territories under his rule but also, by ordering the founding of schools, to improve the education of clerics and the Latinity of documents produced in his realm. The copying of manuscripts in monastic scriptoria exploded, and interest in secular classical Latin literature reawakened. Although internecine warfare resumed not long after Charlemagne's death, secure foundations had been laid for a lasting revival of schools and education.

By the twelfth century, the landscape of Europe had changed dramatically. Increasing commerce and trade stimulated the growth of towns and cities in the tenth and eleventh centuries. Urban cathedral schools appeared, and students traveled far to study under famous teachers. From Rome, a powerful papal bureaucracy directed the parish and episcopal structures that had grown into a Europe-wide network. Secular and ecclesiastical powers alike needed educated chancery clerks and lawyers; the study of Roman law and canon law revived, and the first universities were founded.

This chapter in the history of writing instruction must attempt to survey more than a thousand years of European history—centuries marred by loss and destruction and by marvels of preservation and achievement, centuries that can be called "dark ages" only in the sense that too much about them is still obscure. To borrow a topos of medieval Latin prefaces, it is a vast and turbulent sea, and my vessel is but a frail coracle. It would be misleading if not impossible to attempt a linear chronological account of writing instruction over this vast space and time. The fundamental **continuity** of content and method from Roman times onward is clear, however, and strikingly confirmed by the far better documented curriculum of the sixteenth-century English grammar school—still taught in Latin— that Don Paul Abbott describes in Chapter 5. Looking backward, Quintilian's *Institutio oratoria*, with its wealth of precious and vivid detail, supplies an essential foundation for my survey of this later period, and, to minimize repetition, I shall assume that the reader has digested James J. Murphy's account in Chapter 2. Because they are so various, and likely to be unfamiliar, I begin by cataloging the several kinds of extant original source materials that can shed light on how writing was taught in the early Middle Ages. Although I occasionally refer to Greek sources, it is only instruction given in Latin that I discuss.

A Survey of the Sources

Two generalizations can be made about the history of education in the thousand years or so after Quintilian's death: relevant source materials are hard to find, and most of the documentation is indirect and therefore subject to differing interpretations. For every kind of primary source, scholars are at the mercy of manuscript transmission, and considering how much has been lost, we must be doubly grateful for what survives.[4] Since most teaching was oral, the numerous grammar

---

4 In *Scribes and Scholars: A Guide to the Transmission of Greek and Latin Literature*, 3rd ed. (Oxford: Clarendon Press, 1991), L. D. Reynolds and N. G. Wilson tell with marvelous clarity the epic story of how "classical literature has been transmitted from the ancient world to the present day" (1). As they say, "The history of texts cannot be separated from the history of education and scholarship" (v).

and rhetoric textbooks that do survive (chiefly from the fourth century and later) tell us almost nothing about how, or indeed if, they were actually used in the classroom. Of the preserved Greek and Latin papyri and wax tablets that represent students' classroom notebooks, nearly all contain only grammar and penmanship exercises.

In what follows, I attempt to identify and briefly describe the various late antique and early medieval source-types that pertain to writing instruction. I have arranged them on a rough sliding scale from direct evidence to indirect; some kinds of sources, such as glossed manuscripts, can reside in either category. In this section, I concentrate on describing content; in the following sections, I draw further from these materials to suggest how they were used to teach writing.

Two caveats should always be kept in mind when dealing with medieval Latin texts. First, a particular danger lurks in judging postclassical and medieval Latin writing not on its own terms but by comparing it to the "golden age" styles represented by Cicero and Virgil.[5] Second, medieval Latin authors often borrowed older material and turned it to their own purposes without giving any indication of the original source, leaving it to modern editors to play detective. Writing three centuries after Quintilian, St. Jerome appropriated his advice for teaching a child to read and write (ep. 107.4, 9, 12); but he concentrated on her reading program in the Bible and Christian authors, and—perhaps because the child in question was a girl?—said nothing about how she might use the ability to write. Whole pages of Julius Victor's *Ars rhetorica* (fourth century?) would disintegrate if his borrowings from Cicero's *De inventione* and Quintilian were removed. Martianus Capella took his sections on rhetorical figures from Aquila, who had gotten them from a Greek text. Cassiodorus stitched together his rhetoric section (*Institutiones* 2.2) from *De inventione* and Fortunatianus, and Isidore in turn relied chiefly on Cassiodorus for his compendium of rhetoric in *Etymologies*, Book 2.[6]

School Textbooks

After learning how to read and write the alphabet, a Roman child went to the school of the *grammaticus*, or teacher of literature, whose job (according to Quintilian 1.4.2) was to teach "the art of speaking correctly and the interpretation of the poets." Probably only the teacher had access to any textbooks, and lectured or dictated to pupils from them. This pattern continued at least until the rise of universities in the thirteenth century.

1. Grammar

Fairly complete Latin grammar texts are extant from the third century on. Most popular by far, throughout the Middle Ages, was the little introductory grammar

---

5 Michael Roberts argues forcefully for the more open-minded approach to late Latin literature in the introduction to his *The Jeweled Style: Poetry and Poetics in Late Antiquity* (Ithaca: Cornell University Press, 1989).

6 For my caveat about such borrowings, see footnote 68. The "borrowing" texts mentioned are edited by Karl Halm, *Rhetores latini minores* (Leipzig: Teubner, 1863). On Isidore's sources in Book 2, see the edition edited by Peter K. Marshall (Paris: Les Belles Lettres, 1983) 5–7.

in question-and-answer format by St. Jerome's teacher Donatus; in the eighth and ninth centuries it attracted numerous commentaries, chiefly by Irish and Anglo-Saxon scholars for whom Latin was a totally foreign language. The educational reforms initiated by Charlemagne to improve the level of literacy among the clergy also stimulated keen interest in grammar: about thirty manuscripts written in the late eighth century and the first third of the ninth are collections of grammatical texts, most dating from the fourth and fifth centuries, and together they represent about three-fourths of the Roman and early medieval grammars extant.[7] Their core is uniformly the eight parts of speech (the brief *Ars minor* of Donatus contains nothing else); their method, to explicate at dizzying length pronunciation, syllable and word formation, declension, and conjugation. Some grammars also address the special requirements of poetry by cataloging the complex rules of word accent and metrics. Priscian's monumental advanced grammar, written early in the sixth century, did not come into widespread use until the ninth; the last two of its eighteen books, treating syntax, then sometimes circulated separately. Grammatical theory developed much more slowly than rhetorical theory, and we cannot discern any real theory of Latin grammar before the twelfth century.[8]

In addition to teaching correct speech, the grammar teacher was responsible for instilling correctness in writing. He began with the faults (*vitia*) to be avoided, divided into barbarisms (faults within a single word, e.g., a misspelling or mispronunciation) and solecisms (faults involving two or more words, e.g., lack of agreement between subject and verb). His second main task, "interpretation of the poets," naturally included introducing students to the ornaments of style, the figures or *colores*. Book 3 of Donatus's larger *Ars maior*, which often circulated separately under the title *Barbarismus*, briefly describes the *vitia* and defines a modest selection of figures (*metaplasmi, schemata, tropi*) found in literature.

2. Verse Composition

From antiquity until the tenth century, reading at the grammar school level consisted almost entirely of poetry. A number of self-contained texts on metrics, often associated in manuscripts with grammars, describe the many meters of classical poetry (as with grammatical terms, Latin borrowed both meters and terminology from Greek). Vast quantities of Latin poetry, both good and bad, survive; some of it is almost certainly student exercises on set themes. Because there is nowhere any explicit discussion of how pupils learned to compose poetry, some scholars maintain—with, I think, excessive caution—that no school instruction was given in this complicated subject, at least not in antiquity.

---

7 Bernhard Bischoff, "Libraries and Schools in the Carolingian Revival of Learning," in *Manuscripts and Libraries in the Age of Charlemagne*, trans. Michael Gorman (Cambridge: Cambridge University Press, 1994) 99. The major grammar texts are edited by Heinrich Keil, *Grammatici latini* (hereafter *GL*), 7 vols. plus suppl. (Leipzig: Teubner, 1857–80). For an overview of Latin grammar from its beginnings through Priscian, see "Grammar, grammarians, Latin" in the *Oxford Classical Dictionary*, 3rd ed. (1996).

8 James J. Murphy, *Rhetoric in the Middle Ages: A History of Rhetorical Theory from Saint Augustine to the Renaissance* (Berkeley: University of California Press, 1974) 140–46, 152–56.

3. Progymnasmata

Murphy has outlined, in Chapter 2, the graded composition exercises subsumed under this name and has noted the significant amount of extant material in Greek. In Latin, the only complete set known is Priscian's *Praeexercitamina*, a translation and adaptation of a work traditionally attributed to Hermogenes, a second-century Greek rhetorician. Since at least twenty-four manuscripts from the late eighth through the twelfth century survive, it seems to have been widely used for a long time.[9] From one Emporius (sixth century?), we have *progymnasmata* sections on *ethopoeia*, commonplaces, and encomium. Book 1 of Isidore's *Etymologies*, on grammar, ends with sections on fable and history (1.40–44), and Book 2, on rhetoric, includes sections on *sententia*, confirmation and refutation, *prosopopoeia*, and *ethopoeia* (2.11–14).

Probably the most famous witness to the practice of these exercises is St. Augustine, who describes being made to impersonate an angry goddess Juno in an exercise of *ethopoeia* as he paraphrased the poet's words in prose (*Confessions* 1.17). Augustine also mentions the exercise of encomium, *laus*, and lists several possible subjects for praise, ranging from heaven to a rose.[10] The extremes to which the latter exercise could be carried—only hinted at by Augustine— appear in two fragmentary letters of Fronto (died c. 166) as encomia of smoke and negligence.[11]

4. Rhetoric

A number of postclassical rhetoric texts, most stemming from the fourth and fifth centuries, were edited by Karl Halm in *Rhetores latini minores*. As his source notes make clear, their authors made much use of Cicero's speeches and his *De inventione* (indeed, the longest work in the book is Victorinus's commentary on the latter), and of Quintilian, but not of the *Ad Herennium*. That work, which was attributed to Cicero throughout the Middle Ages, is first cited by St. Jerome; then there is almost total silence until the tenth century, when the number of manuscripts multiplies rapidly. Although Cicero's reputation as master of eloquence never faltered, it was not until the twelfth century that new commentaries on his rhetorical works began to appear.[12] In the interval, rhetorical figures attracted much interest; Halm includes several brief treatises devoted to rhetorical figures, and many more are lost (Quintilian mentions some).

9 Halm, 551–60; Maria Passalacqua, ed., *Prisciani Caesariensis opuscula.* vol. 1: *De figuris numerorum, De metris Terentii, Praeexercitamina* (Rome: Edizione di Storia e Letteratura, 1987) n. 43; trans. Joseph Miller in *Readings in Medieval Rhetoric*, ed. Joseph H. Miller, Michael H. Prosser, and Thomas W. Benson (Bloomington: Indiana University Press, 1973) 52–68.

10 In *Ps.* 144.7, quoted by Roberts, 64.

11 *The Correspondence of Marcus Cornelius Fronto*, ed. and trans. C. R. Haines, Loeb Classical Library, 1.39–49 (Cambridge MA: Harvard University Press, 1928).

12 For *the Ad Herennium*, see Harry Caplan's introduction to his Loeb Classical Library edition, xxxiv–xxxv (Cambridge MA: Harvard University Press, 1954); and *Texts and Transmission: A Survey of the Latin Classics*, ed. L. D. Reynolds (Oxford: Clarendon Press, 1983) 98–100. The Ciceronian commentary tradition is exhaustively treated by John O. Ward in *Ciceronian Rhetoric in Treatise, Scholion and Commentary*, Typologie des sources du Moyen Age occidental 58 (Turnhout: Brepols, 1995); see especially Chapter 2, "Evolution of the Genre."

Occasional fragments from unidentified rhetorical works offer tantalizing glimpses of other losses: Julius Victor's *Ars rhetorica*, after drawing heavily throughout on Cicero and Quintilian, ends with two remarkable sections from unknown sources, offering rules for conversation (*sermo-cinatio*) and letters (*epistolae*); an important late eighth-century manuscript of school texts includes a substantial paragraph of untraceable epistolary theory.[13]

Auxiliary Instructional Materials and Reference Works

To help students understand what they read, the teacher discussed the meanings of words and their etymologies, explained syntactical difficulties and mythological and historical allusions, and pointed out rhetorical figures. Surviving collections of such words and of notes that are arranged by letter of the alphabet or by lemmas taken in sequence from a literary work must have originated as teaching or reference books. Longer independent texts, such as collections of historical anecdotes, could be read for their intrinsic interest or used as sourcebooks for composition topics. Did students have direct access to such reference books? It is not known for certain, but probably they did not.

I. Glossaries

A *gloss*, in its simplest form, represents an effort to explain an unusual or unknown word by a common, familiar one. Numerous surviving glossaries, Greek–Latin, Latin–Latin, and Latin–vernacular, are traceable from about the sixth century, but some contain material that may be centuries older.[14] Although interest in etymology and rare words goes back at least to Varro, a prodigious Roman scholar of the first century BCE, what we think of as dictionaries did not begin to develop until after the middle of the eleventh century, as an outgrowth of glossaries. Michael Lapidge describes a glossary's stages of growth:

> [F]irst, various (perhaps random) interpretations or *interpretamenta* are copied into a manuscript above or alongside particular difficult words (or *lemmata*); secondly, the various *lemmata* and their accompanying *interpretamenta* are collected and copied out separately in the order in which they occur in the text (we refer to these as *glossae collectae*); thirdly, the various *glossae collectae* are sorted roughly into alphabetical order, with all items beginning with the same letter being grouped together (*a*-order); finally, the entries under each letter are resorted into more precise alphabetical order, taking account of the first two letters of each lemma (*ab*-order). A surviving glossary may (and usually does) include materials or batches of words treated in any of these ways, though it will be obvious that when one is trying to identify the text on which the glosses were based, *glossae collectae* offer the clearest evidence.[15]

---

13 Halm, 446–48, 589. I describe the contents of the eighth-century manuscript on p. 103 ("The *Progymnasmata* and Prose Composition").

14 For a brief overview and bibliography, see the entry "Glossa, Glossary" in the *Oxford Classical Dictionary*, 3rd ed. (1996).

15 Michael Lapidge, "The School of Theodore and Hadrian," *Anglo-Saxon England* 15 (1986) 53–54.

The first stage represents the teacher's writing into his copy of the work being studied a brief note—which might concern meaning, etymology, pronunciation, or syntax—about a word or words in the text under study, as an *aide-mémoire* for his oral explication of the text; additional bits of information tended naturally to accumulate. Modern historians of education are extracting valuable information about curriculum and teaching methods from glosses attached to texts in manuscripts and from the collections of glosses abstracted from manuscripts and organized into glossaries.[16]

2. Differentiae

Common from the fourth century on, these collections (which may also be titled, misleadingly, *De orthographia*) take their name from semantic distinctions between partial synonyms, but also may include spelling and pronunciation notes and what might be called usage notes—all, of course, aimed at teaching correct speech and writing.[17] One such compilation, Bede's *De orthographia*, has been felicitously compared to Fowler's *Modern English Usage*;[18] here are two examples of *differentiae* from it:

> *Accidunt* mala, *contingunt* bona, *eveniunt* utraque. (Bad things *befall* one, good things *come to pass*, both *happen*.)

> *Incredibile* quod credi non potest, *incredulus* qui credere non vult. (*Incredible* of what cannot be believed, *incredulous* of one who does not want to believe.)

The same impulse to differentiate produced *Exempla elocutionum*, an alphabetized collection made by the grammarian Arusianus Messius around 400. He used the works of four standard school authors (two poets, Virgil and Terence, and two prose writers, Cicero and Sallust) to illustrate words that have more than one grammatical construction.[19] Cassiodorus cites it (*Institutiones* 1.15.7) as an authority under the title *Quadriga* (literally, 'a team of four horses') and Priscian uses some of the same examples in Book 18.

16 See, for example, Suzanne Reynolds, *Medieval Reading: Grammar, Rhetoric and the Classical Text* (Cambridge: Cambridge University Press, 1996); and Gernot R. Wieland's work on glossed manuscripts in Anglo-Saxon England: "The Glossed Manuscript: Classbook or Library Book?" *Anglo-Saxon England* 14 (1985) 153–73, and *The Latin Glosses on Arator and Prudentius in Cambridge University Library MS GG. 5.35* (Toronto: Pontifical Inst. of Mediaeval Studies, 1983).

17 Carmen Codoñer surveys the genre in "Les plus anciens compilations de Differentiae. Formation et évolution d'un genre littéraire grammatical," *Revue de philologie* 59 (1985) 201–19.

18 By Helmut Gneuss, "The Study of Language in Anglo-Saxon England," *Bulletin of John Rylands University Library of Manchester* 72 (1990) 9–10. For the second example quoted, compare Theodore M. Bernstein, *The Careful Writer: A Modern Guide to English Usage* (New York: Atheneum, 1977) 231: "INCREDIBLE, INCREDULOUS: *Incredible* means unbelievable; *incredulous* means unbelieving, skeptical. From these definitions the error in the following not uncommon misuse should be obvious: 'The incredulously rude Khrushchev. . . .' " I quote Bede's text from Keil, *GL* 7.264.20, 275.25.

19 Text in Keil, *GL* 7.449–514. According to *Texts and Transmission* 54, he quotes most of Cicero's extant speeches as well as four lost ones.

3. Scholia and Commentaries

The grammar teacher's task included, in addition to *enarratio poetarum* (explication of the literary work in all its aspects), *indicium* or critical evaluation. Scholia are isolated bits of explanatory or critical comment found in medieval manuscripts; free-standing commentaries that move sequentially through a work provide the best picture of how this kind of classroom instruction probably proceeded. One of the largest and most important such commentaries is that of Servius (c. 400) on the works of Vergil. It was clearly designed for use in teaching and was quarried in later centuries for the same purpose. Servius marches "word by word and line by line through the text, remarking on punctuation, meter, uncertain readings, myth or other *Realien*, and especially on the language."[20] A few examples show Servius at work:

> (on *Aeneid* 3.16) *litore curvo* 'the curved shore': "curved" is the constant epithet of shores; for when he says in the sixth book, "then he is borne straight along the shore [*recto . . . litore*] to the harbor of Caieta," it means that he sailed in such a way as not to leave the shore.

> (on *Aeneid* 4.582, of the speed with which Aeneas's men obeyed his command to board their ships and leave Carthage): *litora deseruere* 'they deserted the shore', a wonderful description of haste.

> (on *Aeneid* 4.638, when Dido declares her plan to sacrifice to Jove) *Iovi Stygio* 'to Stygian Jove': that is, to Pluto. You should know that the Stoics say that god is one being whose names vary according to his acts and duties. This is also why the divinities are said to be of dual sex, so that when they are in action they are males, but females when they have the nature of being passive . . .[21]

Explication of the text was early transferred to the Bible and other Christian works, but since the text of the Bible was considered divinely inspired its quality was not subject to criticism. An outstanding example of biblical commentary is that of Cassiodorus on the Psalms (mid-sixth century). He made a significant addition to the usual format: a set of thirteen marginal reference marks designating specific topics discussed, such as scriptural idioms, interpretations of names, and rhetorical figures, as well as arithmetic and music.[22]

4. Sententiae

Latin literature abounds with proverbial sayings and moral maxims. The briefest, used to teach children to read, are the two- to four-word injunctions found in

---

20 Robert A. Kaster, *Guardians of Language: The Grammarian and Society in Late Antiquity* (Berkeley: University of California Press, 1988) 170; chapter 5 is devoted to Servius.

21 Quoted from vol. 3 of the "Harvard Servius," *Servianorum in Vergilii carmina commentariorum*, ed. A. F. Stocker, A. H. Travis, et al. (Oxford: Oxford University Press, 1965).

22 James J. O'Donnell, *Cassiodorus* (Berkeley: University of California Press, 1979) 160; James W. Halporn, "Methods of Reference in Cassiodorus," *Journal of Library History* 16 (1981) 71–91.

the first section of the ancient *Dicta Catonis*, such as *Mundus esto* 'Be tidy' and *Alienum noli concupiscere* 'Do not covet what is another's.' An alphabetically arranged anthology that derives from Publilius Syrus, a mid-first-century BCE mime, contains longer sayings, such as *Homo semper aliud, Fortuna aliud cogitat* 'Man's plans and Fortune's are ever at variance.' The *Liber scintillarum*, a large collection drawn from the Bible and Christian writers, was assembled around 700 by a monk named Defensor. Its contents are arranged under 81 headings (e.g., humility, justice, lying, pity, drunkenness, etc.), and the extracts range from a few words to several sentences in length. Its topical arrangement would have made the *Liber scintillarum* very useful (especially for preachers?) and surely contributed to its great popularity: at least 361 manuscripts are known. All of these adages could serve as commonplaces for writing exercises or to ornament longer compositions.[23]

5. Exempla

Latin literature is filled with illustrative anecdotes drawn from mythology or history, used to point out a moral. The animal fables that supplied children's earliest extended reading and writing exercises are self-contained *exempla* about behavior, good and bad. The handbook *Memorable Deeds and Sayings*, composed on an equally condensed scale in the first century CE by Valerius Maximus, supplied to the Middle Ages nine books' worth of canned Roman history and sententious observations, conveniently arranged under such perennially useful headings as chastity and bravery. As with the *Liber scintillarum*, its topical arrangement marks it as a potential sourcebook for speakers and writers.[24]

6. Colloquies

Colloquies, or dialogues, were used to teach the vocabulary and grammar of a foreign language. They normally concentrate on daily life, including the routines of dressing, meals, and school, and perhaps sections on various trades or other subjects. The earliest one known was written for Greeks learning Latin, and the latest Latin colloquies were composed by Erasmus for English schoolboys; all are fascinating and often amusing for modern readers.[25]

What might be called a monologic variation on the colloquy form is Isidore of Seville's *Synonyma*. This curious (and popular) work in two books later lent its

---

23 Both the *Dicta Catonis* and Publilius Syrus are in *Minor Latin Poets*, trans. J. W. Duff and A. M. Duff, Loeb Classical Library, 585ff. and 15ff. respectively (Cambridge MA: Harvard University Press, 1935). *Liber scintillarum*, ed. H. M. Rochais, 117, Corpus Christianorum Ser. latina (Turnhout: Brepols, 1957).

24 For a study of the work's original purposes and intended audience, see W. Martin Bloomer, *Valerius Maximus and the Rhetoric of the New Nobility* (Chapel Hill: University of North Carolina Press, 1992).

25 A good overview of the form, with an edition of a very interesting fourth-century colloquy plus translation and commentary, is A. C. Dionisotti, "From Ausonius' Schooldays? A Schoolbook and Its Relatives," *Journal of Roman Studies* 72 (1982) 83–125. See also Scott Gwara, ed., *Anglo-Saxon Conversations: The Colloquies of Ælfric Bata*, trans, with intro. by David W. Porter (Woodbridge, Eng.: Boydell, 1997). A fully annotated translation of Erasmus's *Colloquies* appeared in 1997 as volumes 39 and 40 in the *Collected Works of Erasmus*, University of Toronto Press.

name to *the stilus Isidorianus*, one of four writing styles first described and named in the twelfth century.[26] It is in essence an extended set of variations arranged into a narrative sequence. Scholars still debate whether Isidore (died 636) wrote it for educational purposes or for private meditation and spiritual edification. At least one teacher, the eleventh-century Englishman Ælfric Bata, used it for educational purposes in a colloquy.[27] His colloquy (which has an interlinear Anglo-Saxon version) proceeds in the usual way, until the stylistic register changes abruptly at the climax of a scene between the master and a wayward pupil who is being flogged by his fellow pupils at the master's command. Begging for mercy (*Iam moriturus sum* 'I'm about to die'), the student breaks out into a page-long variation on *Synonyma* 1.5–21 in which he laments his wretched state: surrounded by evils, scorned and hated by all, it would be better to die, and so on. It must be intended as a demonstration of how to vary and expand an existing text; I quote parallel sections below when discussing the compositional techniques of paraphrase and imitation.

7. Formula and Letter Collections

Earlier I mentioned traces of epistolary theory in the fourth-century rhetoric of Julius Victor, and I return to the theory of letter-writing later. Latin letters are a phenomenally rich resource for study and were during the Middle Ages as well. Collections of real letters by the hundreds were formed and published from Cicero onward, by their authors and by others, and were copied and imitated even centuries later.[28] Late in the tenth century, Gerbert modeled his epistolary style on that of Symmachus (fourth century), and letters of Symmachus turn up in twelfth-century handbooks of letter-writing instruction, the *artes dictaminis*.

A related category is the so-called formula collections, most of which were assembled in the eighth and ninth centuries. Various kinds of legal documents (such as wills and donations) predominate, but they also include real letters and model letter salutations, and are characterized by having *Ille* or *N.*, the equivalent of "So-and-so," in place of proper names. One early formula collection, the mid-seventh-century *Formulae Marculfi*, was made specifically for purposes of instruction, according to the author's own preface.[29]

Teaching Manuals and Anthologies: Manuscript Transmission

Gernot Wieland (see note 16) has sought to develop criteria by which to distinguish manuscripts used for actual classroom teaching from library reference

---

26 See Douglas Kelly, *The Arts of Poetry and Prose*, Typologie des sources du Moyen Age occidental 59 (Turnhout: Brepols, 1991) 83–84, with bibliography.

27 Scott Gwara, ed., *Latin Colloquies from Pre-Conquest Britain*, Toronto Medieval Latin Texts (Toronto: Pontifical Inst. of Mediaeval Studies, 1996) 15–16.

28 For an excellent overview of the genre, see Giles Constable, *Letters and Letter-Collections*, Typologie des sources du Moyen Age occidental 17 (Turnhout: Brepols, 1976). For Gerbert and Symmachus: Jean-Pierre Callu, "Gerbert et Symmaque," *Haut Moyen Age: Culture, éducation et société; Etudes offerts à Pieire Riché*, ed. Claude Lepelley et al. (La Garenne-Colombes: Erasme, 1990) 517–28.

29 *Marculfi formularum libri duo*, ed. Alf Uddholm (Uppsala: Eranos Frlag, 1962) 10: "Sed ego non pro talibus viris [i.e., rethores et ad dictandum peritos], sed ad exercenda initia puerorum, ut potui, aperte et simpliciter scripsi."

books, for example, patterns and content of glossing within related manuscripts, accent marks for reading aloud, and "Why this?" notations for oral questioning. Or the collective contents of a medieval manuscript may mark it as a teaching manual: typically, such a manuscript brings together works on grammar, metrics, and rhetorical figures; perhaps works related to numerical calculation, calendar-reckoning, and weights and measures; and sometimes exemplary texts as well. *Florilegia*, or anthologies of literary texts (often, extracts), provide yet another kind of evidence for what was studied in schools and thought worthy of imitation.

Analysis of the manuscript transmission of classical Latin literary works yields information about their changing popularity and use in the Middle Ages. Birger Munk Olsen has published several studies on this topic, concentrating on the period before the twelfth century.[30] In one article, for example, he examines classical texts preserved in more than five manuscripts that were copied in the tenth century. Most such manuscripts seem to have been school texts: they contain interlinear and marginal glosses, lives of the authors, and introductory or explanatory notes. Although works in prose were still the exception among these school texts, a growing interest in history—Livy and Sallust—suggests that prose was moving into the curriculum.[31] This kind of careful quantitative analysis confirms that the "renaissance of the twelfth century," marked by a revival of classical Latin literature, was rather a gradual growth with its roots in the tenth century if not the ninth.

Narrative Sources and Incidental Testimonia

Inevitably, there is an "et cetera" category. For this period, it forms a large haystack, from which the occasional needle can be recovered, but one must work hard to find it and often fall back on speculation.

Incidental remarks in unexpected places may yield significant information. Toward the end of the seventh century, Julian of Toledo wrote an *ars grammatica* based on Donatus. In two separate places, he uses letters to illustrate a point of grammar:

> [On the adverb] Name an adverb that comes from a pronoun. *Meatim, tuatim.* How is it used? For example, if I am composing a letter, and you compose one like it, I say, "You did it my way"; if another boy composes a letter like yours, "he did it your way."

> [On metonymy] Likewise, the agent for the effect, as we say "a happy letter" to mean the happiness of those whom the reading of it makes happy.[32]

---

30 Birger Munk Olsen, *L'Etude des auteurs classiques latins aux XIe et XIIe siècles* (Paris: CNRS, 1982–87); "La popularité des textes classiques entre le IX et le XII siècle," *Revue d'histoire des textes* 14–15 (1984–85) 169–81; "Les classiques latins dans les florilèges médiévaux antérieurs au XIIIe siècle," *Revue d'histoire des textes* 9 (1979) 47–121 and 10 (1980) 47–172.

31 Birger Munk Olsen, "Les classiques au Xe siècle," *Mittellateinisches Jahrbuch* 24–25 (1989–90) 341–47.

32 *Ars Iuliani Toletani Episcopi: Una gramática latina de la España visigoda*, ed. Maria A. H. Maestre Yenes, Publicaciones del Instituto Provincial de Investigaciones y Estudios Toledanos Ser. II: Vestigios del Pasado 5 (Toledo 1973) 80.37–39 and 206.116–18.

How vivid the scene of two boys comparing their wax tablets on which each has laboriously composed his own version of, say, an abbot's letter of recommendation for a monk who must travel abroad: "You did it my way!" Because Julian uses letters so casually to make his points, we can infer that practice in letter-writing took place in his schoolroom.

Biographies of saints were immensely popular with medieval readers and writers, and *Vitae* by the hundreds survive. Their format tends to be stereotyped; the saint's education, for instance, is usually passed over with "He was steeped in letters as a child."[33] More interesting for my present purpose, many early *Lives* later came to be viewed as factually or stylistically inadequate, and were rewritten, prefaced by criticism of the version being replaced. I think it likely that this kind of revision was also done as a school exercise to practice paraphrase, narrative, and *ethopoeia*; the topic certainly deserves study.

Information about schools and teaching is more likely to surface in secular biographies, letters, and histories, but it rarely includes details about techniques of instruction. Richer's history of France, written at the end of the tenth century, describes the education of his own teacher, Gerbert of Reims (later Pope Sylvester II), and the liberal arts curriculum Gerbert designed. At first sight it looks promising for this topic, as Richer enumerates the texts Gerbert assigned for study of dialectic and the classical poets—but after mentioning rhetoric as next in the sequence, he skips right over it with *qua instructis* 'after they had been instructed in it'!

John of Salisbury wrote his *Metalogicon* (1159) as a defense of the arts of the trivium. After relaying with approval Quintilian's advice to grammar teachers, John describes how the famous teacher Bernard of Chartres taught grammar in the early twelfth century. Since his portrait stands almost alone in its wealth of detail, it is worth quoting at length.

> This method was followed by Bernard of Chartres. By citations from the authors he showed what was simple and regular; he brought into relief the grammatical figures, the rhetorical colours, the artifices of sophistry, and pointed out how the text in hand bore upon other studies; not that he sought to teach everything in a single session, for he kept in mind the capacity of his audience. He inculcated correctness and propriety of diction, and a fitting use of congruous figures. Realizing that practise strengthens memory and sharpens faculty, he urged his pupils to imitate what they had heard, inciting some by admonitions, others by whipping and penalties. Each pupil recited the next day something from what he had heard on the preceding. The evening exercise, called the *declinatio*, was filled with such an abundance of grammar that anyone, of fair intelligence, by attending it for a year, would have at his fingers' ends the art of writing and speaking, and would know the meaning of all words in common use. But since no day and no school ought to be vacant of religion, Bernard would select for study a subject edifying to

---

33 See Martin Heinzelmann, "Studia sanctorum: Education, milieux d'instruction et valeurs éducatives dans l'hagiographie en Gaule jusqu'à la fin de l'époque mérovingienne," in *Haut Moyen Age* 105–38 at 108–12 and 133–34: early hagiographers, distrusting secular education, often suppressed or downplayed information about a saint's secular education—as indeed did such prominent religious figures as Gregory of Tours concerning their own education.

faith and morals. The closing part of this *declinatio*, or rather philosophical recitation, was stamped with piety: the souls of the dead were commended, a penitential Psalm was recited, and the Lord's Prayer.

For those boys who had to write exercises in prose or verse, he selected the poets and orators, and showed how they should be imitated in the linking of words and the elegant ending of passages. If anyone sewed another's cloth into his garment, he was reproved for the theft, but usually was not punished. Yet Bernard gently pointed out to awkward borrowers that whoever imitated the ancients (*maiores*) should himself become worthy of imitation by posterity. He impressed upon his pupils the virtue of economy and the values of things and words: he explained where a meagreness and tenuity of diction was fitting, and where copiousness or even excess should be allowed, and the advantage of due measure everywhere. He admonished them to go through the histories and poems with diligence, and daily to fix passages in their memory. He advised them, in reading, to avoid the superfluous, and confine themselves to the works of distinguished authors [. . .]. But since in school exercises nothing is more useful than to practise what should be accomplished by the art, his scholars wrote daily in prose and verse, and proved themselves in discussions.[34]

Several of these points are echoed in two letters that St. Anselm wrote to his nephew, for whose education he was responsible, at about the same time. In both, he urges the youth to study *grammatica* diligently and to practice writing, especially in prose; the second letter, written a year or two later, advises him in more specific detail to develop the habit of daily writing practice (*dictate cotidie assuesce*) and not to write in a complicated, elaborate style but in a straightforward, "reasonable" style.[35] Anselm's letters nicely illustrate how evidence from one kind of source can corroborate that from another, very different kind—in this case, private, personal letters not intended for publication confirm the portrait drawn in a very public, formal document.

Writing Instruction: Structure, Content, and Methods

As John of Salisbury's account suggests, most features of the Roman educational program outlined by Quintilian and analyzed in Chapter 2 by Murphy lived on in the Middle Ages: "microscopic" analysis of texts studied; for each kind of

---

34 Trans. Henry Osborn Taylor, *The Medieval Mind*, 4th ed., 2 vols. (Cambridge MA: Harvard University Press, 1949) 2.157—58 (more fluent and readable than Daniel McGarry's *The Metalogicon of John of Salisbury: A Twelfth-Century Defense of the Verbal and Logical Arts of the Trivium* [Berkeley: University of California Press, 1962] 67–70).

35 The first letter also mentions *declinatio*, which according to Gillian Evans, "implies the systematic parsing and analyzing of passages of exemplary writing": "St. Anselm's Technical Terms of Grammar," *Latomus* 38 (1979) 413–21. Anselm's letters are edited by F. S. Schmitt, O.S.B., in vols. 3–5 of *S. Anselmi, Cantuariensis Archiepiscopi, Opera omnia* (Edinburgh 1946–51), ep. 290 and 328 (dated 1103 and 1104–05 respectively). It is clear from John's description and from how Anselm uses forms of *declinare* elsewhere (ep. 64, ed. Schmitt 3. 180) that it does not mean the grammatical exercise of changing the construction of a *chreia* to vary the cases of the nouns it contains (Diomedes gives samples of this type: Keil, *GL* 1.310). It sounds rather like the kind of microscopic analysis performed in Priscian's *Partitiones* (see next section, "Creating the Child's Mind-Set").

speaking and writing exercise, sequencing by length and by degree of difficulty; imitation, paraphrase, and transliteration of what was read; and, from the beginning, memorization—of syllables, adages, fables and myths, reams of poetry (especially Virgil), the Psalms—to an extent that we can scarcely imagine. Of these processes I need only add some medieval examples. Certain other features, and some changes of emphasis, call for closer inspection.

Creating the Child's Mind-Set

First, consider how this kind of education in the verbal arts established the child's "mind-set," which ever after would inform how he or she read and wrote. Of its earliest stage, E. J. Kenney says:

> The methods used [. . .] were slow, thorough, and relentlessly pedantic. Under his elementary schoolmaster (*litterator, magister ludi litterarii*), from about the age of seven, the child practised writing and reciting the letters of the alphabet in every possible combination before repeating the procedure with syllables and then complete words. No short cuts were permitted. "There is no short way with syllables," says Quintilian. "They must be learned thoroughly, and the difficult ones must not (as usually happens) be left until they are encountered in actual words" (1.1.30). That is to say, attention to form is to precede attention to sense . . .[36]

Even a brief extract from a Latin grammar text on syllables will suggest the deadening force of this approach, which one is tempted to call mindless. To begin his treatment of the noun, Sacerdos (late third/early fourth century) proceeds through the entire alphabet by last letter of the nominative singular and, within that scheme, through all possible combinations of letters into syllables, whether or not such combinations are actually found in any Latin nouns. His treatment of nouns whose nominative singular ends in -*r* covers seven printed pages; it begins thus (I have abbreviated slightly):

> Many nouns end in the letter -*r*. They are of all three genders; neuters belong only to the third declension. Nouns ending in plain [i.e. unbound] -*ar*, none. In plain -*er*, masculine nouns of the second declension, feminine nouns of the third. In plain -*ir*, one, indeclinable, contrary to the rule I just gave that neuter nouns ending in -*r* belong to the third declension and have their genitive in -*is*. In plain -*or*, masculine and feminine nouns of the third declension with the genitive in -*ris*, the -*o*- being short in the nominative and long in the genitive. I have found no noun ending in plain -*ur*.

He then starts over with three-letter syllables: -*bar*, -*ber*, -*bir* (none), -*bor*, -*bur*; -*car* . . . all the way through the null sets of -*xur*, -*zar*, -*zer*, -*zir*, -*zor*, and -*zur*.[37]

---

36 E. J. Kenney, "Books and Readers in the Roman World," in *The Cambridge History of Classical Literature: Latin Literature* (Cambridge: Cambridge University Press, 1982) 6. The process is well described by Stanley F. Bonner, *Education in Ancient Rome* (Berkeley: University of California Press, 1977) 165–77.

37 Quoted from Keil, *GL* 4.1 1 ff. (attributed by the text to Probus, but see Kaster, 348–50 and 352–53).

All this—which is confirmed by written exercises preserved in papyri and wax tablets—before the child ever experienced the thrill of learning to read and write whole words, not to mention the two-word sentences of the *Dicta Catonis*! (Martianus Capella hints at its mind-numbing nature in *De nuptiis Philologiae et Mercurii*, Book 3: the goddess Minerva cuts off Lady Grammar's presentation of her topic at about this point, just as she is really warming to her task, because the gods have become bored!)[38] This fatigue-march progression from letters to syllables to words to short sentences persisted for centuries; these four distinct stages of grammar study are named by St. Ambrose and St. Jerome and in the ninth century by Remigius of Auxerre.[39]

What Paul Saenger calls the physiology of reading Latin makes this early focus on syllables and words more comprehensible.[40] The lack of a fixed word order and the absence of word separation and punctuation in written texts made reading a matter of decoding, even for the experienced reader. (The beginnings of fixed word order, which would be generalized in Latin's Romance descendants, are visible by about the second century, first in texts that reflect spoken Latin; Jerome introduced the arrangement of text by sense units—*per cola et commata*—in his Vulgate Bible translations; word separation and punctuation in manuscripts spread gradually from the ninth century on.) Harry Gamble prints five lines of a familiar biblical text with no word separation, and comments, "If a familiar text is surprisingly difficult, an unfamiliar one would present a far greater challenge. The relentless march of characters across the lines and down the columns required the reader to deconstruct the text into its discrete verbal and syntactical components."[41] Even the small surface area and clumsiness of the waxed tablets normally used for drafting compositions must have encouraged thinking in small sense units.[42]

Earlier I quoted samples of Servius's commentary on Virgil's *Aeneid*, and in the same vein Murphy cites what is surely the best example of the "micro-analysis" practiced in *praelectio* and *enarratio poetarum*: Priscian's *Partitiones* on the first line of each book of the *Aeneid*. From it, Murphy quotes the first six questions on the first word of the poem, *Arma*; in fact, the commentary inspired by this one word consumes three full pages in print, and the commentary on the first line alone covers ten-and-a-half pages.[43] None of it concerns the line's content or significance, such as its echoing the first line of the *Iliad*.

---

38 *Martianus Capella and the Seven Liberal Arts*. vol. 2: *The Marriage of Philology and Mercury*, trans. W. H. Stahl and Richard Johnson (New York: Columbia University Press, 1977) 105.

39 François Dolbeau, "Deux manuels latins de morale élémentaire," in *Haut Moyen Âge* 195, and Pierre Riché, "Apprendre à lire et à écrire dans le haut Moyen Age," *Bulletin de la Société nationale des Antiquaires de France*, 1978–79, 195; and, referring to poetry, Marjorie Curry Woods. "Medieval Progymnasmata: Basic Texts, Basic Techniques," paper read at March 1995 meeting of the 4Cs.

40 Paul Saenger, "Physiologie de la lecture et séparation des mots," *Annales E.S.C.* 44/4 (1989) 939–52, and "The Separation of Words and the Order of Words: The Genesis of Medieval Reading," *Scrittura e civiltà* 14 (1990) 49–74. See now his *Space Between Words: The Origins of Silent Reading* (Stanford: Stanford University Press, 1997).

41 Harry Y. Gamble, *Books and Readers in the Early Church: A History of Early Christian Texts* (New Haven: Yale University Press, 1995) 203.

42 A preference for the small unit of composition was still lively in the twelfth-century *artes poetriae*: Franz Quadlbauer called it a "Tendenz zur kleinen Einheit " (cited by Kelly, 38–39 and 85–88).

43 Keil, *GL* 3.459.23–169.12.

This approach to literature mapped neatly onto the Christian ideal of *lectio divina*. By a process called *meditatio* or *ruminatio*, patristic exegetes sought to peel back from the divinely inspired biblical text every layer of its significance: factual, metaphorical, allegorical, tropological. The blending of secular and religious methods of analysis can be seen in Cassiodorus's commentary on the Psalms; it is clearest, though, in a commentary on a nonbiblical religious text such as the *Benedictine Rule*, the rule book for Benedictine monasteries that all Benedictine monks learned by heart and from which they heard daily readings: a ninth-century commentary on the Rule (whose author was or had been a teacher) takes eighty pages to explicate its prologue and chapter 1, which comprise about four modest pages in print. Isidore's *Synonyma* offers another kind of *ruminatio*, with its catena of variations slowly drawing the reader on through a finely calibrated sequence of thoughts.

Quintilian's stricture about memorizing all possible syllables, at one extreme, and Christian *meditatio* at the other, reflect a second fundamental aspect of what I have called the mind-set inculcated by Roman education and its medieval heirs: the role of memory. An educated Christian, one raised on adages, Aesop, and the *Aeneid*, who spent years memorizing and reciting the Bible, meditating on its layers of meaning, paraphrasing its stories, had acquired the "habit," the *copia* that Quintilian wished the finished orator to have ready to supply the words for any occasion. Allusions, paraphrases, and quotations from the Bible and the Fathers of the Church inhabit most medieval texts, and few medieval writers do not at least occasionally betray their early acquaintance with classical literature as well.

Perhaps an "ordinary" person of no literary renown can exemplify this routine use of memory best. In the mid-ninth century, a Gallic noblewoman named Dhuoda wrote a handbook of moral instruction for her teenage son. Dhuoda was a well-educated, deeply religious layperson. Except for Donatus and other elementary school texts (e.g., glossaries, computus), she cites only religious writings, often adapting them to her own context: all but about a dozen of the 150 Psalms, Augustine, Gregory the Great, Isidore's *Synonyma*, and a few Christian poets.[44] Although it seems unlikely that she had received any instruction in rhetorical theory, she strives (with no great success) for elegant effects. How did she learn to construct sentences, paragraphs, whole compositions; to choose a suitable style, apply appropriate ornaments? The obvious answers are "from the Bible" and "by imitation." She would have been hearing and memorizing those 150 Psalms orally and absorbing their style, even before she learned to read. And it may well have been her readings in Augustine that impelled her to reach for his eloquence by stringing together five gerunds in a row.

Classical and Medieval Verse Composition

Because the principles that governed the writing of Latin verse, though complex, are easier to trace in operation than those for prose, I touch just briefly on poetry. Some modern scholars argue, *ex silentio*, that formal instruction in verse

---

44 Pierre Riché, ed., *Dhuoda, Manuel pour mon fils*, Sources chrétiennes 225 (Paris 1975) 32–37.

composition was not part of the ancient Roman school curriculum but rather was a medieval development.[45] This seems to me highly improbable, given the widespread evidence that poetry formed the heart of the grammar curriculum. Students certainly had to learn how to scan and read the various meters of quantitative verse correctly, and their composition exercises likely included verse paraphrases of poetry.[46] The inclusion of metrical material in grammars and the association of grammar and metrics texts in manuscripts strengthen the assumption, as does the unbroken practice of writing quantitative verse in the Middle Ages and the discussion in twelfth-century *artes poetriae* of metrical and rhythmic versification.[47]

The interplay between Latin syllable formation, word accent, and the meters of classical Latin poetry is not easy to grasp.[48] First, we as speakers of English with its strong stress accent lack sensitivity to the metrical considerations that shaped both Latin poetry and artistic word order in Latin prose. Second, poets borrowed their meters from Greek, which had a different linguistic structure from Latin. Third, because Latin writers on pronunciation and metrics also adopted their terminology from Greek, their analyses are sometimes opaque.

Briefly, then, spoken Latin had a stress accent, the position of which was determined by the length (*weight* is Allen's better term) of each word's penultimate syllable. In order to compose quantitative verse correctly, it was not enough to know which syllables carried the stress accent: you had to know the quantity, or weight, of every syllable (here is the justification for memorizing every possible combination of letters into syllables).[49] A "short" syllable equaled one beat; a "long" syllable, two beats. Gradually, classical poets met the challenge of fitting Latin words into the quantitative Greek metrical forms; the general tendency, brilliantly represented by Ovid, was to make the metrical accent, or *ictus*, coincide with the word accent.

Awareness of syllable length was fading by St. Augustine's lifetime, however, and new stress-based rhythmic verse forms were emerging, to exist in great variety side-by-side with the ancient quantitative meters throughout the Middle Ages.[50] A twelfth-century tour de force is Bernard of Cluny's poem *De contemptu mundi*, some 3,000 lines of strongly rhythmic "leonine" dactylic hexameters, with internal and end-rhyme throughout. It begins:

45 E.g., M. L. Clarke, "Quintilian on Education," in *Empire and Aftermath: Silver Latin II*, ed. T. A. Dorey (London: Routledge & Kegan Paul, 1975) 111; and Roberts, 70–71.
46 One example is a third/fourth-century papyrus line-for-line verse paraphrase of *Aeneid* 1.477–493; Roberts, 52, cites it, but only to illustrate paraphrase, rather than as new composition for which knowledge of metrical principles was required.
47 Kelly, 82–85.
48 Highly recommended, as a brief, clear, and sensible introduction: W. Sidney Allen, *Vox Latina: A Guide to the Pronunciation of Classical Latin*, 2nd ed. (Cambridge: Cambridge University Press, 1978).
49 Diane Warne Anderson has prepared a detailed diachronic survey of medieval texts for teaching syllable quantities, to appear in a volume of essays I am editing on Latin grammar and rhetoric.
50 The basic handbook is Dag Norberg, *Introduction à l'étude de la versification latine médiévale* (Stockholm: Almqvist & Wiksell, 1958). Janet Martin surveys the production of both kinds of poetry (as well as prose) in the twelfth century, "Classicism and Style in Latin Literature," in *Renaissance and Renewal in the Twelfth Century*, ed. Robert L. Benson and Giles Constable (Cambridge MA: Harvard University Press, 1982) 537–68.

Hóra novíssima, témpora péssima súnt, vigilémus. . . .

The principle of fitting stress-based rhythms into originally quantitative metrical forms is familiar to us from Shakespeare's accentual iambic pentameters:

The quá | li tíe | of mér | cy ís | not stráined;

It dróp | peth ás | the gén | tle ráin | from heáv'n . . .

The Influence of Poetry on Prose

Given the central position of poetry in schooling, it is not surprising to find widespread traces of poetic forms and practices in Latin prose, from the classical period on. What may surprise, given the equally central emphasis on the close study of language, is that Latin writers, Cicero excepted, show little interest in exploring the defining differences between poetry and prose.

I. Rhythm

Prose was often defined negatively by the absence of meter, as *oratio soluta*, speech freed from the constraints of meter, and the use of rhythm in each form is the single area to attract close analysis. Cicero wrote in thoughtful detail about the nature and long history—reaching back to Gorgias and Isocrates—of rhythm in oratorical prose (especially *Orator* §168 ff.). Aristotle, he says (§172), "forbids the use of verse *in oratione* [*oratio* can mean 'prose' as well as 'oration'], but requires rhythm," *numerus*. Nevertheless, as he demonstrates, poetry and prose share the same metrical patterns. The trick in prose is to keep them from turning into verse.

Quintilian deals with rhythm in the context of *compositio* (the technical term for sentence-level composition) and periodic structure (9.4.1–147). Although he twice declares that the three essentials for artistic *compositio* are *ordo, iunctura, numerus* 'order, connection, rhythm' (9.4.22, 9.4.147), for him the three are not equal: considerations of rhythm govern decisions about order and connection. As the translator notes at the beginning of this discussion (506), "*Compositio* in its widest sense means 'artistic structure.' But in much of what follows it virtually equals 'rhythm.'" Like Cicero, Quintilian discusses metrical feet appropriate for use in prose.

There is ample evidence that later writers and audiences remained sensitive to rhythm in prose, if not to syllable length. St. Augustine, a keen observer of early fifth-century linguistic change, contrasts people's diligence in observing "the rules of letters and syllables received from former speakers" with their neglect of God's covenants of salvation (*Confessions* 1.18); pondering the nature of time, he notes that a long syllable takes longer to say than a short one (*Confessions* 11.22, 23). Rufinus (late fifth century?), writing "on word arrangement and the rhythms of orators," takes Cicero as his chief authority and also quotes approvingly another grammarian's scornful observation that some fools think prose should not use metrical feet, that is, be rhythmical.[51]

---

51 Keil, *GL* 6.572.18–23; trans. Ian Thomson in Miller, *Readings*, 45. For his date, see Raster no. 130.

By the early sixth century, the characteristic forms of the medieval accentual *cursus*, rhythmical patterns of clause and sentence endings, are visible in Latin prose texts; these are the "elegant ending of passages" that John of Salisbury says Bernard of Chartres recommended to his pupils. By the twelfth century, the overwhelmingly dominant cursus forms would be (using English mnemonics to indicate preferred word divisions):

planus	méns wear | de párt ment
tardus	(a) góv ern ment | súb si dy
	(b)mód ern | phi lós o phy
velox	líb er al | éd u cá tion

Not all medieval writers employ *cursus*, and modern scholars looking for it in medieval texts sometimes disagree about what they have found; it is particularly risky to use the results of *cursus* analysis to identify an anonymously transmitted text as having been written by an author whose characteristic *cursus* patterns have been established.[52]

2. Diction and Style

If prose too used rhythm, we may ask again, what distinguished poetry from prose? Cicero, after noting that "It once seemed to be a matter of rhythm and verse, but now rhythm has become common in oratory" (*Orator* §66–68), says merely that poets are both constrained by meter and freer to form and arrange words. Quintilian writes at length in Book 1, and again in Book 8, about correctness in choice and arrangement of words, but offers no systematic discussion of differences between poetic and prosaic diction; he says only that, because the poet is the servant of his meter, "poetic license" excuses in poetry what would be faults in prose (1.5.11–13, 6.2, 8.14). Surveying rhetorical figures in Books 8 and 9 (in which he draws his examples of stylistic ornament from both poetry and prose), he observes of nine figures that poets have greater freedom to use them: simile, metaphor, synecdoche, metonymy, antonomasia, catachresis, epithet, periphrasis, and tmesis.[53] In Book 10.1.27–29, discussing the kinds of reading that contribute most to maintaining and improving the finished orator's skills (he recommends poetry, but with reservations), he repeats that poets enjoy greater freedom of language and use of figures and explains that metrical necessity compels them to use circumlocutions and to substitute, lengthen, shorten, or transpose words. Other writers on style make similar remarks, often using "poetic license" or "metrical necessity" as a kind of shorthand for whatever characteristics of poetic diction they have in mind.

At the same time, in the first century CE, literary fashions were changing to favor, among other things, greater use of those rhetorical *colores* recorded

---

52 The literature on *cursus* is enormous, difficult, and sometimes contentious. For a general introduction, see the index to Murphy. The period of transition is well explained by Harald Hagendahl, *La correspondance de Ruricius* (Göteborg: Wettergren & Kerbers Förlag, 1952). In *Prose Rhythm in Medieval Latin from the 9th to the 13th Century* (Stockholm: Almqvist & Wiksell, 1975), Tore Janson developed statistical methods of cursus analysis that have been widely adopted.

53 Roberts, 72 n. 42.

as especially poetic by Quintilian. "The adornment of the poet is demanded nowadays also in the orator," says the "modernist" Aper in the *Dialogue on Oratory* (§20) by Quintilian's contemporary Tacitus, the dramatic date of which is about 75 CE. Whatever distinctions had once separated prose and verse diction and stylistic conventions were fading rapidly, and many prose texts acquired a poetic coloring. An egregious example of this bland statement is Apuleius's romance *Metamorphoses* (after c. 160 CE), the florid style of which does full justice to its picaresque contents.[54]

The tendency continued in the next few centuries, aided unwittingly by the effort to reduce Latin grammar to a system, because Donatus and other grammarians who discuss rhetorical figures took their examples almost entirely from poetry, chiefly Virgil. The confusion of diction and stylistic levels is especially noticeable in Insular (Anglo-Saxon and Irish) writers and those influenced by them, to whom all classical Latin words and texts were equally foreign and who thought that Donatus, *the* authority on Latin, was not merely classifying but also commending.[55] A modern Latin dictionary, in contrast, can tell us by its citations whether a given word was used exclusively in prose, or label it as, for example, "poetic and post-Augustan prose." Possibly some collections of *differentiae* attempted something similar. Although the *Exempla elocutionum* of Arusianus Messius illustrates syntactical constructions from two poets and two prose authors, it makes no perceptible distinctions between prose and verse usage.

In short, I know of no ancient or medieval Latin treatment comparable to Axelson's *Unpoetische Wörter*,[56] which (among other things) reminds us that many Latin words were excluded from quantitative verse simply by their metrical structure, their sequence of long and short syllables. We are left to assume that when students were introduced to prose texts, their teachers may have pointed out various ways in which prose differed from the poetry they were used to studying.

The Progymnasmata *and* Prose Composition

To put it very crudely, in the Roman education of Quintilian's time, poetry was grammar's domain, and prose was rhetoric's. But if reading in the grammar school consisted entirely of poetry, how, and when, did pupils learn to write prose? It was in the *progymnasmata*, the series of graded exercises originally designed to introduce students to rhetoric, that any study of prose writers and instruction in prose composition took place. The classical curriculum made no provision for the systematic study of prose genres outside the *progymnasmata*.

Scholars have sometimes portrayed the *progymnasmata* as a self-contained intermediate stage, a preprofessional curriculum for future orators and advocates studying with a special rhetoric teacher. We should rather understand the *progymnasmata* as a general introduction to rhetoric, for even the most elementary

---

54 Known to St. Augustine *(De civ. Dei* 18.18) and ever since as *The Golden Ass*: P. G. Walsh, *The Roman Novel* (Cambridge: Cambridge University Press, 1970) 143 n. 1.

55 Michael Winterbottom, "The Style of Aethelweard," *Medium Aevum* 36 (1967) 114–15.

56 Bertil Axelson, *Unpoetische Wörter. Ein Beitrag zur Kenntnis der lateinischen Dichtersprache* (Lund: Gleerup, 1945).

exercises could teach the basic techniques of invention, arrangement, and style that are applicable to any kind of planned discourse, oral or written. It seems obvious that lower-school teachers of language and literature, the *grammatici*, would invoke these principles when teaching poetry: surely they could not be postponed until the advanced course in rhetoric, when the students analyzed famous speeches and practiced declamation. And indeed, Quintilian indicates (2.1–3, 4) that by his time the rhetoric teachers had abandoned most or even all of the *progymnasmata* to the *grammatici*. Responsibility for teaching the rhetorical figures was also assumed by grammar teachers, the division between figures of speech (grammar) and figures of thought (rhetoric) being impossible to maintain in practice.[57]

While grammar teaching continued to emphasize poetry, then, it is clear that the formal study of prose at the elementary level had begun to expand in Quintilian's time or shortly after. Already in place, that is, were the outlines of the "grammar school" curriculum that would live on into the British six-form structure. When new Latin translations of Aphthonius's *progymnasmata* appear in sixteenth-century Europe, they are used in the grammar school.[58]

That structural change originated within the schools. From without, powerful forces of social, political, and religious upheaval that would eventually break up the Roman Empire reinforced it. First, the nature of deliberative and forensic oratory was changing—again, by Quintilian's time—under an increasingly bureaucratic imperial government that favored technical legal skills, streamlined procedural exactitude, and written documents over extended oral presentation.[59] The new atmosphere is palpable in Tacitus's *Dialogue on Oratory*; contrasting the expansive, leisurely style of the Ciceronian era with the modern courtroom, the speaker says:

> [W]hat we need is novel and choice methods of eloquence, by employing which the speaker may avoid boring his hearers, especially when addressing a court which decides issues, not according to the letter of the law, but by virtue of its own inherent authority, not allowing the speaker to take his own time, but telling him how long he may have, and not waiting patiently for him to come to the point, but often going so far as to give him a warning, or call him back from a digression and protest that it has no time to spare.[60]

---

57 Louis Holtz, "Grammairiens et rhéteurs romains en concurrence pour l'enseignement des figures de rhétorique," in *La rhétorique à Rome*, Calliope I (Paris, 1979) 207–20; Marc Baratin and Françoise Desbordes, "La 'troisième partie' de l'*ars grammatica*," *Historiographia linguistica* 13.2/3 (1986) 215–40.

58 See Chapter 5 by Don Paul Abbott in this volume. The translation of Aphthonius by Ray Nadeau in *Speech Monographs* 19 (1952) 264–85 has been revised by Patricia P. Matsen, *Readings from Classical Rhetoric*, ed. Patricia P. Matsen, Philip Rollinson, and Marion Sousa (Carbondale: Southern Illinois University Press, 1990) 266–88.

59 Michael C. Leff (following John Ward's suggestion), "The Material of the Art in the Latin Handbooks of the Fourth Century A.D.," in *Rhetoric Revalued*, ed. Brian Vickers, Medieval & Renaissance Texts & Studies 19 (Binghamton, NY: Center for Medieval & Early Renaissance Studies, 1982) 75–76.

60 Tacitus, *Dialogus* §19, trans. William Peterson, 65, Loeb Classical Library (Cambridge MA: Harvard University Press, 1914).

Second, public oratory did not, as is sometimes assumed, decay or die out in late antiquity. Although Quintilian deplored the current excesses of declamation (2.10), it long remained popular, together with panegyric—both public show-pieces of epideictic speechmaking. Two Greek treatises on panegyric and other forms of epideictic, probably from the late third or early fourth century, have parallels in extant Latin speeches as late as the sixth century (the last recorded Latin panegyric was delivered by Cassiodorus in 536).[61] Long before then, however, a new Christian public had emerged, to provide eager audiences for other kinds of speakers and writers.

It fell to grammar, strengthened by the additional tasks it had already taken over from the rhetoric curriculum, to construct a new rhetoric curriculum: one that would be less single-mindedly devoted to litigation and display, and flexible enough to meet the new needs of new kinds of societies. Nearly all of the rhetor-ical *progymnasmata* would be not merely useful but essential for educated persons participating in a culture increasingly dependent on writing. What more natural stimulus for Priscian—*Priscianus grammaticus*, a teacher of Latin grammar and literature, not a rhetorician—to translate a Greek *progymnasmata* text into Latin, early in the sixth century?

Other evidence for the survival of Latin *progymnasmata* is easy to overlook, because their content duplicates (or rather, prefigures) that of rhetoric proper. Certain texts usually seen as rhetorics are, or incorporate, *progymnasmata* collections. The thirteen pages in Halm's *Rhetores latini minores* of Emporius, a shadowy figure perhaps contemporary with Priscian, come from a *progymnasmata* text. Book 1 of Isidore's *Etymologies*, on grammar, ends with transitional sections on *fabula* and *historia*, and the epitome of rhetoric that opens Book 2 contains four sections of *progymnasmata* exercises, including *ethopoeia*. On a larger scale, I have already alluded to an impor-tant manuscript of school texts written at the end of the eighth century that reflects the new curriculum in its choice and arrangement of texts:[62] after 250 folia containing texts devoted to metrics, grammar, and rhetoric, there comes a group of excerpts from various sources that together form a *progymnasmata* sequence. They include anonymous paragraphs on encomium and epistolary theory and the partial text of Emporius (which starts in the middle, with *prosopopoeia*), followed by Priscian's *Praeexercitamina*. Then—most revealing, from the perspective of the later *artes dictaminis*—come rules for composing *litterae formatae*, the coded letters issued by episcopal chanceries: many dictaminal texts, starting with Alberic of Monte Cassino's *Breviarium*, contain similar instructions. (The final ten texts in this manu-script are a miscellany of dialectic, *computus*, calendar reckoning, glosses, etc.)

Techniques of Prose Composition

Writing somewhat later than Priscian, Cassiodorus defined grammar thus:

---

61 For the Greek treatises, see *Menander Rhetor,* ed. and trans. D. A. Russell and N. G. Wilson (Oxford: Clarendon Press, 1981) xi. On the popularity of panegyric in the West, see Sabine MacCormack, "Latin Prose Panegyrics: Tradition and Discontinuity in the Later Roman Empire," *Revue des études augustiniennes* 22 (1976) 29–77 (for the speech of Cassiodorus, 73 n. 173).

62 Louis Holtz, "Le Parisinus Latinus 7530, synthèse cassinienne des arts libéraux," *Studi medievali* 3rd ser. 16 (1975) 97–152. I follow Holtz's analysis and numbering of the manuscript's contents.

> Grammar is the knowledge of speaking attractively [*pulchre loquendi*], gath-
> ered from distinguished poets and authors; its duty is to teach faultless
> composition [*sine vitio dictionem*] in prose and verse; its end, to give pleasure
> through flawless skill in refined speech or writing.
>
> (*Inst.* 2.1.1)

Note that grammar has by now, the sixth century, explicitly assumed the task of
teaching composition in both poetry and prose. While "faultless" and "flawless"
refer to basic grammatical correctness, the mention of attractiveness and pleasure
implies the addition of rhetorical considerations, especially style. (Cassiodorus
defines rhetoric in the following section simply as speaking persuasively in civil
cases.) Priscian's *progymnasmata* address the first two parts of rhetoric, invention
or content and arrangement—each exercise contains a definition and at least one
sketchy example of how to construct it—but ignore that fountain of pleasure,
style and rhetorical ornament. Where did the students find the matter for their
compositions, and learn how to organize and ornament it?

I. Imitation, Paraphrase, and Variation

Reading and learning to compose proceeded hand in hand from grammar school
on. Murphy has analyzed above how imitation, "the deliberate modeling of an
existing artifact or text," informed the entire Roman educational program—
practiced from the child's first efforts at learning the shapes of the letters through the
most advanced composition exercises of the *progymnasmata*. St. Augustine even
upheld the power of imitation alone to teach eloquence (*De doct. chr.* 4.3.5). Paraphrase
too was thought to have sovereign powers: Michael Roberts similarly extends its
reach in his invaluable survey of classical and late antique paraphrase, observing, "In
a sense, then, the *progymnasmata* could be subsumed under the genus paraphrase,
since they all involved the stylistic elaboration of a predetermined subject."[63]

    Paraphrase at the level of word and sentence is *variatio*, and its practice was
encouraged by the microanalytic approach to literature, by the glossaries and
differentiae, by the catalogs of rhetorical figures, by such masters of Latin style as
St. Augustine, and perhaps even by Isidore of Seville's paradigmatic *Synonyma*.
To teach vocabulary, one of the Anglo-Saxon colloquies offers five ways to say
"What do you want?": *O frater! Quid vis? Quicquid queris? Quid aspicis? Quid
cupis? Quid optas?* Aethelweard, writing a chronicle early in the eleventh century,
found several different ways to express the passage of time (as his subject repeatedly required him to do) beyond a simple *post annum* 'after a year', such as *post
decursum anni unius* and *impleta serie anni unius*, and similarly varied ways to express
victory in battle.[64] Aethelweard's technique was not novel; in fact, it pales beside
the fourth-century historian Ammianus Marcellinus (a Greek writing in Latin),
who invented 29 expressions for dying, 35 for daybreak, and 16 for a river flowing
into the sea or another river.[65] (The all-time champion of *variatio* is Erasmus, who

---

63 Roberts, 23.
64 Winterbottom, 115–16.
65 Harald Hagendahl, *Studia Ammianea* (Uppsala Universitets Årsskrift, 1921) 100–103; the first two are
    cited by Roberts, 151 n. 116.

in *De copia* produced 147 variations on "Your letter pleased me very much," and 203 variations on "Always, as long as I live, I shall remember you.")[66]

A spectacularly extended example of all three practices—imitation, paraphrase, and variation—occurs in the eleventh-century colloquy by Ælfric Bata mentioned earlier. A brief excerpt highlighting the parallels will show how the speaker in the colloquy, a schoolboy being punished, weaves in and out of his source, Isidore's *Synonyma*, like a modern jazz musician:

Isidore, *Synonyma*:

> *Nullus mihi protectionem praebet,* nullus *defensionem* adhibet, *nullus adminiculum tribuit, nullus malis meis succurrit, desertus sum ab omnibus* hominibus; *quicunque me aspiciunt, aut fugiunt, aut* fortasse *me persequuntur,* intuentur me quasi infelicem, et nescio quae *loquuntur mihi in dolo verbis pacificis; occultam* malitiam *blandis sermonibus* ornant, et *aliud ore promunt, aliud corde volutant.* (1.7)

Ælfric Bata's colloquy:

> *Nullus mihi protectionem prebet* nec *defensionem* prestat, *nullus adminiculum tribuit, nullus malis meis succurrit. Desertus sum ab omnibus* amicis meis et proximis et notis et propinquis. *Quicumque me aspiciunt aut fugiunt aut me* ubique *persequuntur,* et non quiescunt falsa testimonia contra me preparare et dicere [this clause is taken from three paragraphs further on in the *Synonyma*]. *Loquuntur mihi in dolo uerbis pacificis* et nequitiam *occultant* suam *blandis sermonibus. Aliud ore promunt, aliud corde uolutant* (id est cogitant).[67]

2. Compilatio

To modern eyes, this kind of "variation" looks more like rampant plagiarism. It is, however, endemic among late antique and medieval Latin authors, even though some paid lip service to the modern concept of intellectual property (copyright, of course, did not exist).[68] The usual attitude is expressed by Symmachus, writing to a friend who had reproached him for circulating the friend's poem to others: "Once the poem left you, you lost all rights over it; a work that has been made public is a free object [*Oratio publicata res libera est*]."[69] Once published, a literary work became common property, available for imitation, paraphrase, and appropriation by subsequent writers.

"Adaptive reuse" of another's work can be detected in any number of medieval Latin works, sometimes simply because the borrowing is inept, or the adaptation

---

66 Thomas O. Sloane, "Schoolbooks and Rhetoric: Erasmus's *Copia*," *Rhetorica* 9.2 (1991) 119.

67 Gwara, *Latin Colloquies,* 15–16 and 86–87 lines 66–74. "(id est cogitant)" 'i.e., they think' is a gloss on *volutant* that has crept over [*volutant*] another in their heart."

68 See the informative survey by Neil Hathaway, "Compilatio: From Plagiarism to Compiling," *Viator* 20 (1989) 19–44.

69 Ep. 1.31.2, cited by Harald Hagendahl, "Methods of Citation in Post-Classical Latin Prose," *Eranos* 45 (1947) 118.

unsuited to the new context. Bernard of Chartres surely would have reproved for theft the late eighth-century letter-writer who inserted into his different context several phrases taken, in order, from two letters of St. Jerome (himself a notorious borrower) and attributed to the Old Testament prophet Malachi a quotation he had stitched together from three biblical sources, *not* including the book of Malachi; the equivalent but unattributed quotation in Jerome's letter in turn echoes a letter of Cyprian.[70] Did the author of this letter learn his compositional technique in the classroom? Impossible to say, but he had plenty of distinguished company in the practice.

3. Compositio (Structure)

For the grammar teacher, *compositio* meant chiefly considerations of correctness in word choice, order, arrangement, and syntactical construction within the sentence. Priscian is the first Latin grammarian to treat syntax, in the final two books (*De constructione*) of his magisterial grammar; he includes helpful comments about semantics and usage along the way (for instance, the difference in meaning between the demonstrative pronouns *hoc, iste*, and *ille*, 17.58).

The rhetoric teacher moved beyond the basics of speaking correctly at the sentence level to consider artistic structure—how to speak *well*—and the characteristics of different sentence styles and their appropriate use. Quintilian discussed grammatical *compositio* in Book 1. In Book 9, his rhetorical treatment, he identifies two kinds of sentence style: one is markedly hypotactic, "closely welded and woven together [*vincta atque contexta*], while the other is of a looser texture [*soluta*]" (9.4.19). (Some rhetorics add a third, paratactic style, *oratio perpetua*.) The first is what we know as the periodic style, "composed of three elements: the *comma*, or as we call it *incisum*, the *colon*, or in Latin *membrum*, and the *period*" (9.4.22).

The third-century rhetor Aquila Romanus included a segment on these styles (three, for him) and their use in his handbook on the figures of speech and thought (Halm 27–28), and Martianus Capella took it over for his survey of rhetoric in Book 5 (sections 526–29; trans. Stahl and Johnson 198–99). *Oratio soluta*, which does not require rhythm or hypotaxis, is used for ordinary speech and for letters, and in judicial speeches when one wants to adopt a conversational tone. *Oratio perpetua* connects clauses paratactically in the normal sequence of thought, and is appropriate for history and narrative. Aquila gives examples of a period and its parts, but does not indicate what kind of writing it is best suited for. He concludes by declaring that a mixture of all three styles is best, because any one alone becomes tiresome. Augustine makes the same point in analyzing biblical examples of periodic structures (*De doct. chr.* 4.7.11ff.).

As its terminology indicates, the theory of the period is Greek, first formulated by Aristotle.[71] It is essentially a theory of prose rhythm, and the centrality of

---

70 Bernhard Bischoff, ed., *Salzburger Formelbücher und Briefe aus Tassilonischer und Karolingischer Zeit*, Sitzungsberichte d. Bayerische Akademie d. Wissenschaften, Phil.-hist. Kl., 1973 Heft 4 (Munich 1973) 56. I have studied these letters in "Formulaic Parallels and Epistolary Style," part 2 of an article published jointly with Bengt Löfstedt under the title "Zu den neugefundenen Salzburger Formelbüchern und Briefen," *Eranos* 63 (1975) 69–100 at 83ff.

71 See George Kennedy, *The Art of Persuasion in Greece* (Princeton: Princeton University Press, 1963) 109–11.

rhythm to Latin prose guaranteed its continued vitality through the development of the cursus and into the High Middle Ages of Latin literature.

4. Dispositio *(Arrangement)*

Rhetoric texts analyzed the sources of arguments and methods of handling them under invention, the first part of rhetoric. *Dispositio*, the second part, covers the arrangement within each part of the work and of the work as a whole. When discussing it in Book 7, Quintilian declines to generalize: he says, in effect, that you must learn by doing, by working on one case at a time, because the circumstances of each individual law case will determine the best arrangement of your material. Therefore, his precepts (which are in any case specific to litigation) are not transferable to instruction in composition.

Two very different kinds of rhetorical practice documents display one aspect of how arrangement was taught. The 145 "Minor Declamations" attributed to Quintilian are (if not actually by him) "fragments . . . from a practising teacher's workshop," and each speech is carefully signposted to make its divisions and succession of arguments clear. "It is just the same impulse, to make the shape of the speech intelligible *in advance*, that causes the frequent use of such phrases as 'postea videbo' [afterwards I shall see], answered by 'interim . . .' [meanwhile]."[72] I found exactly the same impulse at work in Merovingian and Carolingian formula collections comprising students' practice letters: sentence is linked to sentence by *and so, therefore, hence, for this reason*, and so on; larger divisions are set off by *in the first place, next, finally*. Aristotle laid down the principle of using connecting words between sentences (*Rhetorica* 1407a19), and medieval *artes dictandi* advise letter-writers to mark off the divisions of the letter with appropriate introductory words.[73]

Ars Dictaminis: The Medieval Art of Letter-Writing

The Progymnasmata *and Epistolography*

From Cicero's time onward, letters were a major literary genre. Thousands of Latin letters survive (and thousands more in Greek), evincing every conceivable subject and style. For Christians, the genre carried special significance: as George Kustas notes, "Christianity had introduced itself to the world in the form of a letter; most of the earliest Christian documents are letters."[74] Christian writers quickly recognized a chief advantage of the format: "The great variety of types and functions of early Christian letters illustrates the flexibility of the genre."[75] I believe that, as part of the centuries-long shift from an oral culture to one dependent on writing, the written letter replaced the spoken declamation of classical antiquity as the primary vehicle for practice in prose composition.

---

72 Michael Winterbottom, "Schoolroom and Courtroom," in *Rhetoric Revalued*, 64, 66.
73 Carol Dana Lanham, *"Salutatio" Formulas in Latin Letters to 1200: Syntax, Style, and Theory*, Münchener Beiträge zur Mediävistik und Renaissance-Forschung 22 (Munich: Arbeo-Gesellschaft, 1975) 60–63.
74 George L. Kustas, "The Function and Evolution of Byzantine Rhetoric," *Viator* 1 (1970) 59.
75 Gamble, 37.

Letters were the only form of elementary composition that was, by definition, written. An ancient, partly traceable theory of **letter-writing** illuminates epistolary practice and suggests that the letter provided an excellent framework for teaching prose composition.[76] A letter was viewed as half of a conversation, intended to represent the spoken word and the character of the writer, and, therefore, simple vocabulary and an informal style were considered appropriate. Beginners could manage the informal diction, akin to that of ordinary speech, which was recommended for letters. Letters were supposed to be brief; "epistolary brevity" is often invoked to end a medieval letter. Best of all, letters had no fixed subject matter. The letter format was therefore ideal for schoolroom practice on circumscribed themes, and yet, for a mature writer, the genre was elastic and accommodating, even inviting. This broad applicability of the letter form, and its informal and elastic nature, made it an attractive vehicle for teaching the *progymnasmata* exercises in rhetoric.

But where is the link between epistolography and *progymnasmata*? Kustas again: "From the point of view of rhetorical theory, it [epistolography] falls under the heading of *ethopoeia*, the progymnasma par excellence which gave the freest scope to the expression of personality traits"; he cites an anonymous scholion on Aphthonius that *ethopoeia* is the perfect kind of *progymnasma*.[77] This exercise, the speech in character, was considered to be among the more difficult, and many examples of it survive, especially of the type using figures from poetry or history that students would have read. St. Augustine recalled having as a schoolboy to deliver a version of Juno's speech in the *Aeneid* (*Confessions* 1.17), and the works of Ennodius (early sixth century) offer several examples, such as what Thetis said when she saw her son Achilles dead, or what Menelaus said when he saw Troy burning. The larger rhetorical principle being stressed in this exercise is *decorum*, suiting one's words to the speaker's age, rank, and fortune, as well as to the situation.

Establishing an authorial voice, an *ethos*, is a central task for any speaker or writer, but character portrayal addresses the very essence of the letter, which is, after all, a substitute for one's physical presence. Two Greek *progymnasmata* texts mention letter-writing in their treatment of *ethopoeia*. Theon (thought to be approximately contemporary with Quintilian) observes that this exercise is useful not only for panegyric and protreptic oratory but also for letters; he explains that a young man should speak differently from an old man, a farmer from a soldier, and so on. Nicolaus (fifth century) recommends practicing the exercise of *ethopoeia* in letter form because one must take into account the character (*ethos* again) of both the sender and the recipient of the letter. Priscian does not mention letters under this exercise, which he calls *allocutio*, but his treatment is otherwise similar.

Splendid literary examples of fictional letters created in accordance with the rhetorical rules for *ethopoeia* are Ovid's *Heroides* and, in Greek, the second- and third-century letters of courtesans, fishermen, and farmers by Aelian and

---

76 I argue this point in detail in "Freshman Composition in the Early Middle Ages: Epistolography and Rhetoric before the *ars dictaminis*," *Viator* 23 (1992) 115–34.

77 Kustas, 59.

Alciphron. The fourth-century invented correspondence between Seneca and St. Paul is best explained as a classroom exercise in style and characterization; constructed as an exchange between a pagan philosopher and a Christian, the letters also had to employ simple argumentative techniques of confirmation and refutation. Its example suggests an image of schoolboys, perhaps even working in pairs, composing such letters as a variation on the orally delivered speech in character—like the students Julian of Toledo used to illustrate the adverbs *meatim* and *tuatim*.

One might also look for evidence of other *progymnasmata* exercises in letters, singly or in combination with *ethopoeia*. The equally important exercise of *narratio*, for example, was begun early in the sequence. The principles of judicial rhetoric required that the narrative section of a speech should normally be composed in a plain style, akin to that of ordinary conversation; it should be brief; and it should be clear (see, for example, *Ad Herennium* 1.9). Exactly the same prescriptions of clarity, brevity, and simplicity governed letter style, and so an assignment that combined *narratio* with *ethopoeia* can be readily envisioned. Again, moral maxims abound in letters, accompanied by paraphrase and exegesis; likewise for commonplaces. Neither is it hard to find set-piece descriptions (*ecphrases*) in letters.

To turn the question around, what other forms besides the letter might the study and practice of prose take? A clue is found in Book 1 of Isidore's *Etymologies*, where he sketches a grammar curriculum that includes the study of narrative prose of all kinds. Starting with Donatus and his eight parts of speech, Isidore discusses thirty components of *ars grammatica* (1.5). The last four have no analogue either in Donatus or (according to Jacques Fontaine) in any grammar text before Isidore: they are *prosa, metra, fabulae*, and *historiae*.[78] Fontaine calls this "the central addition of Isidorian grammar."[79] Isidore treats all four at length before turning to rhetoric with Book 2. He associates *fabula* with *res fictae*, and *historia* with *res factae*—fiction and fact, in modern terms, a distinction made by the classical rhetoric texts in discussing *narratio* (e.g., Cicero, *De inventione* 1.19.27; *Ad Herennium* 1.8).[80] In short, although Quintilian thought that the *progymnasmata* exercise of *narratio* should be the first one taught by the rhetoric teacher (2.4.1), in Isidore's scheme, grammar has effectively claimed *narratio* from rhetoric, and with it *fabula* and *historia*, the practice of artistic prose of all kinds.

There is some evidence that by the ninth century "epistola" could mean simply "prose." Writing to a bishop, Alcuin recommends dividing the pupils in an episcopal school into three levels: the first group learns the elements of Latin morphology and grammar, the most advanced students study Scripture, and the middle group reads *epistolas et parvos libellos* 'letters and little books'.[81] *Libelli* must represent the standard fare of poetic texts customarily read at the grammar school level; by 800, this included not only the *Disticha Catonis*, moralized fables in verse, and Virgil, but also Christian poets such as Juvencus and Prudentius.

---

78 Jacques Fontaine, *Isidore de Séville et la culture classique dans l'Espagne wisigothique*, 2 vols. (Paris: Etudes Augustiniennes, 1959; rev. ed. 3 vols. 1983) 1.54.

79 Fontaine, 1.56.

80 Fontaine, 1.174–85.

81 Alcuin, ep. 161, MGH Epistolae 4, ed. Ernst Dümmler (Hanover 1895) 260.13–15.

Alcuin's letter specifies where in the curriculum the study of letters/prose occurred, but does not confirm that the pupils practiced composing letters (or anything else, for that matter) themselves. That can be glimpsed in Notker's *Life of Charlemagne* when the emperor, returned to the palace after a long stint on the battlefield, summons the boys he had entrusted to the Irish teacher Clemens, so that they might show him *epistulas et carmina sua* 'their letters and poems'.

The Life of Burchard, bishop of Worms 1000–1025, describes his teaching methods at the cathedral school in similar terms:

> In addition, he firmly instructed each pupil, according to his ability, to present to him every day a carefully prepared recitation or written work. Then indeed, because they saw that the servant of God was devoted to study and learned in the pages of holy Scripture and filled with the wisdom of God, they were not afraid to offer him their speeches and letters and various [written] questions (*sermones et epistolas quaestiunculasque varias*).[82]

The passage continues with an example of a *quaestiuncula*, which may have been a specific kind of prose composition exercise: in the mid–1060s, Alberic of Monte Cassino, apparently as a novice monk, addressed at least two sets of *quaestiunculae* on scriptural topics to Peter Damiani in letter form (only Peter's answers are preserved).[83] Later, *artes dictandi* often begin by dividing *dictamen* into verse and prose composition and then specifying letters as a subdivision of prose. An early one warns, "There is a great difference between *prosa* and *epistola*, although one is very often put for the other";[84] Conrad of Mure (c. 1275) even declares that all artistic prose is either *sermo* (spoken face-to-face) or *epistola* (written to absent persons).[85]

The Worms letter collection (dated to the second quarter of the eleventh century, just after Burchard's tenure as bishop) contains numerous exchanges between students and teachers; others sound like school exercises on a set theme. One pair (ep. 20–21) offers an excellent example of letter-writing instruction carried on in letter form. A student has written to the cathedral schoolmaster seeking career advice; the master's reply contains an extended rhetorical analysis of the student's letter, beginning with its salutation. Significantly, the teacher observes that the student has employed a rhetorical *captatio benivolentiae* in his salutation, even though he has not yet studied that subject, that is, rhetoric.

The Rise of Ars Dictaminis

With the better schools and renewed interest in classical literature that characterize the Carolingian era, the study of rhetoric began to revive in the eighth and

---

82   Walther Bulst, ed., *Die ältere Wormser Briefsammlung*, MGH Briefe der deutschen Kaiserzeit 3 (Weimar 1949) 5.

83   *Die Briefe des Petrus Damiani*, ed. Kurt Reindel, MGH Briefe der deutschen Kaiserzeit 4, vol. 3 (Munich 1989), nos. 126, 127 (= PL 145.621–34).

84   Franz Josef Worstbrock, "Die Anfänge der mittelalterlichen Ars dictandi," *Frühmittelalterliche Studien* 23 (1989) 34.

85   *Die Summa de arte prosandi des Konrad von Mure*, ed. Walter Kronbichler (Zurich, 1968) 30.

ninth centuries. Toward the end of the tenth century, Gerbert included dialectic and rhetoric in his curriculum at Reims, and new treatises on rhetorical figures appeared in the eleventh century. Worms was almost certainly not the only cathedral school in which letter-writing was taught early in the eleventh century; at exactly the same time, Fulbert of Chartres—to name but one of several outstanding figures—an influential teacher, a leader in the church, and a fine literary stylist, was writing letters that would be collected and used as school models by the second half of the century.[86] If it is true that the letter form had, at some earlier point, become the primary vehicle for instruction in prose composition, it is hardly surprising that the eleventh and twelfth centuries were a great age of Latin letter-writing, in both quantity and quality.

I. S. Robinson, arguing that "The letter was the form of composition *par excellence* in which eleventh-century scholars could display their training in the *artes*,"[87] has shown what rich opportunities the second half of the century gave them to do so. Long-festering problems within the church, including its relations with secular powers, produced a widespread reform movement that culminated in the investiture contest between papal and imperial factions, sparked by the election of Pope Gregory VII in 1073. Polemical tracts flew around Europe. Regardless of their length and the complexity of their contents, they were cast in the form of letters, with conventional epistolary formulas of salutation and closing; "epistolary brevity" was sometimes adduced to excuse omitting even more argumentation. The twelfth century would, in turn, collect these polemical works and use them as models of style.

Although the verb *dictare* and the noun *dictamen* have the general sense "to compose, composition" and so designate any kind of writing, the *ars dictaminis* 'art of composition' that began to blossom after 1100 concerns only letter-writing.[88] Scholars used to ignore the traces of epistolary theory that antedate the appearance of *dictamen*. They explained the rather swift rise of the new specialized art as a response to the growth of bureaucracy in the eleventh century: royal and ecclesiastical chanceries needed trained scribes to handle their increasingly large and complex correspondence, for which the old formula collections, dating from the sixth century to the ninth, no longer sufficed.[89] There were indeed new markets for instruction in epistolary technique, but, as the scholarly work of the last few decades has shown, they grew out of a much more organic and widespread process of development.[90]

Dictaminal manuals typically begin by distinguishing prose from verse and then subdivide prose into two or more kinds, one of which is *epistolae* 'letters', before declaring that they will treat only letters. Since the medieval letter

86 A. Clerval, *Les écoles de Chartres au Moyen Age, du Ve au XVIe siècle* (Paris, 189S; rpt. Frankfurt am M. 1965) 114.

87 I. S. Robinson, "The 'Colores Rhetorici' in the Investiture Contest," *Traditio* 32 (1976) 231.

88 Martin Camargo gives a concise but thorough introduction to *ars dictaminis*, with rich bibliography, in *Ars dictaminis, ars dictandi*, Typologie des sources du Moyen Age occidental 60 (Turnhout: Brepols, 1991).

89 See, for example, E. R. Curtius, *European Literature and the Latin Middle Ages*, trans. Willard R. Trask, Bollingen Ser. 36 (New York: Pantheon, 1953) 75–76.

90 William D. Patt, "The Early 'ars dictaminis' as Response to a Changing Society," *Viator* 9 (1978) 133–55, with additional bibliography.

permitted a great variety of form and content, however, the restriction is more apparent than real. As Martin Camargo concludes, "The *ars dictaminis*, then, may be defined as that department of medieval rhetoric which taught the rules for composing letters and other prose documents."[91]

The manuals devote vastly disproportionate attention to the salutation—the only part peculiar to the letter form. To it they apply the classical rhetorical theory of the exordium, emphasizing its function of *captatio benivolentiae*. Numerous sample salutations, arranged by rank of addressee, are usually included. Adjectives and phrases appropriate to various categories of sender and addressee (abbot, bishop, king, pope, etc.) and the relationship between them are offered, sometimes in great numbers. In modern America, one rarely encounters a formal letter salutation other than "Dear So-and-so," to which the simple *salutem* of Cicero's letters is comparable. By the twelfth century, however, a continuous tendency to elaborate the opening greeting had so overloaded it that theorists divided salutation and *captatio benivolentiae* into separate components.

A second important task of dictaminal manuals is to define the parts and proper organization of the letter, and classical *dispositio* is found to govern the letter's organization, just as it did that of the speech. In the body of the letter, the narrative receives the most attention, probably because it shared with the letter form brevity and simplicity as defining characteristics. Advice about *elocutio* 'style' is sprinkled throughout, together with examples of ornamentation; rules for *cursus* are given, and various kinds of letters may be defined and exemplified. Epistolary brevity is almost certain to be mentioned. A collection of model letters, real or invented or both and (like the sample salutations) arranged by rank of addressee, concludes the handbook; some such collections also circulated independently.

For a sense of the (mostly hidden) tradition of epistolary theory that underlay the *ars dictaminis*, compare the following extracts from (1) the section of epistolary theory at the end of Julius Victor's rhetoric (fourth century); (2) an anonymous paragraph of epistolary theory in the late eighth-century collection of school texts I described earlier; and (3) the *Flores rhetorici* (alternatively titled *Radii dictaminum*) by Alberic of Monte Cassino, written about 1075:[92]

> (1) If you are writing to a superior, your letter should not be facetious; if to an equal, it should not be discourteous; if to an inferior, not haughty. Do not write carelessly to a learned man, nor negligently to one who is uneducated [. . .]. The openings and closings of letters should be reckoned with an eye to differences in friendship or rank—after taking account of customary usage.
>
> (Halm, 448)

---

91 Camargo, 20.

92 *Alberici Casinensis Flores Rhetorici*, ed. M. Inguanez and H. M. Willard, Miscellanea Cassinese 14 (Monte Cassino, 1938); trans. Joseph M. Miller (unreliable and misleading) in Miller et al., 131–61. I say "about 1075" simply for convenience: nothing in the *Flores* or in what is known about Alberic's life permits a more precise dating. The passage quoted as (3) below is found in Inguanez and Willard 38; my translation.

(2) In letters one must consider who is writing to whom and about what. With regard to who is writing to whom, the attributes of the persons must be noted. These are ten: birth, sex, age, upbringing, education, profession, character, disposition, reputation, and rank. For it makes a great difference whether we are writing to a nobleman, an old man, a magistrate, to a father or a friend, to one who is prospering or one who is sad, and so forth.

(Halm, 589)

(3) The first consideration should be the nature of the sender and that of the person to whom [the letter] is sent: whether, that is, he is of high rank or low, a friend or an enemy, and finally, what his background and situation are [. . .]. If he is of high rank, it should be written in an elevated style; if humble, in a simple style [. . .]. If a learned man writes to one who is of middling or no learning, you will adapt the words to the powers of the recipient. You will represent a prelate in one way, a subordinate in another.

All three passages assume a knowledge of rhetorical *ethopoeia* and *decorum*, of how to suit one's words and style to sender and recipient and to the occasion. And all three antedate the earliest dictaminal texts. (But anyone who has studied *dictamen* will recognize in each its characteristic preoccupation with the minute differentiation of rank and social position that were of paramount importance in constructing twelfth-century letter salutations.)[93]

Alberic of Monte Cassino was a pivotal figure. In the *Flores rhetorici*, he discusses letter-writing in considerable detail, but in the larger context of rhetoric. He begins by treating the parts and structure of a speech and of a letter in exactly parallel fashion and then offers five sample salutations and three model letters before devoting the largest part of the work to rhetorical figures, *colores*. Significantly, he says that people are eager for instruction in how to write letters. A second, longer (and less coherent) work called the *Breviarium* contains not only "letter-specific" material (sample salutations, instructions for and models of papal and imperial letters, including *litterae formatae*) but also material appropriate for general instruction in writing: on synonyms and *variatio*, figurative ways to express praise and blame, ornate ways to express simple thoughts, proverbial expressions, and so on. (Alberic's own style ran to the ornate, and so it was child's play for him to convert "Have you eaten?" into "Has your collector [*exactor*, usually 'tax collector'] received his daily debt today?" or "Have you paid the collector his daily debt?" or "Have the rumblings of your gut been extinguished by a sufficient abundance?") Since neither of Alberic's works concentrates exclusively on letters, neither is yet a true *ars dictandi*; but both contain the necessary ingredients.

A rivulet of dictaminal manuals began to appear about 1115, first in northern Italy, and soon swelled to a flood. By the last quarter of the twelfth century the

---

93 See especially Giles Constable, "The Structure of Medieval Society According to the *Dictatores* of the Twelfth Century," in *Law, Church, and Society: Essays in Honor of Stephan Kuttner*, ed. Kenneth Pennington and Robert Somerville (Philadelphia: University of Pennsylvania Press, 1977) 253–67.

art had spread to France, whence it traveled to England.[94] Hundreds of *artes* are extant, in some 3,000 manuscripts and early printed books from the twelfth through fifteenth centuries, but the enormous task of identifying, cataloging, describing, and editing them is far from finished.[95] Handbooks of letter-writing instruction and model letters in the vernacular continued to appear throughout Europe for centuries—and indeed, the genre lives on even today, both in print and in computer software offering hundreds of instantly customizable model letters "for all occasions!"

Conclusion

The five parts of rhetoric were codified in Hellenistic times as invention, arrangement, style, memory, and delivery; its goal was to speak persuasively. By the end of the first century CE, the grammar curriculum included stylistic ornament (i.e., the study of rhetorical figures) as well as grammatical correctness, and at least some of the *progymnasmata* exercises in composition. Writing exercises required invention and arrangement even when the goal was merely paraphrase of a given subject; memory training was an integral part of all education, and students learned the basics of delivery through presenting their composition exercises orally. (Surely the youthful Augustine was expected to do more than "Stand up straight!" and "Don't mumble!" when he delivered his speech in the persona of the goddess Juno.) Already, that is, the dividing line between grammar and rhetoric had shifted to enlarge grammar's mandate very substantially.

Quintilian could almost be said to have outlined in his Book 10 (summarized in Chapter 2 of this volume) what I have ventured to call a new grammar school curriculum, already taking shape in his own time. There, he advised the now-trained orator how to keep his speaking skills honed by assiduous practice in reading, writing, and speaking. Wide reading, including a certain amount of poetry, history, and philosophy, will, by furnishing one with a rich stock of words and phrases, a variety of figures, and a method of composition *(copia verborum, varietas figurarum, componendi ratio,* 2.1), instill the ability to imitate, which forms a large part of art. One will practice writing, for "It is in writing that eloquence has its roots and foundation" (3.3). One should write slowly and critically at first, revising often. But what to write? For subjects, Quintilian refers the reader back to the sequence of studies prescribed in Books 1.9 and 2.4; now, concerned only with acquiring copiousness and the habit or facility

---

94 Martin Camargo has recently edited five English *artes*, with introductions: *Medieval Rhetorics of Prose Composition: Five English "Artes Dictandi" and Their Tradition* (Binghamton, NY: Medieval & Renaissance Texts & Studies, 1995).

95 Volume 1, *Von den Anfängen bis um 1200,* of a *Repertorium der Artes dictandi des Mittelalters,* prepared by Franz Josef Worstbrock, Monika Klaes, and Jutta Lütten was published in 1992 (Munich: Wilhelm Fink Verlag), and two more volumes are planned. Emil J. Polak has published two of a projected four volumes recording dictaminal manuscripts in libraries worldwide: *Medieval and Renaissance Letter Treatises and Form Letters,* vol. 1: *A Census of Manuscripts Found in Eastern Europe and the Former USSR;* vol. 2: *A Census of Manuscripts Found in Part of Western Europe, Japan and the United States of America,* Davis Medieval Texts and Studies 8, 9 (Leiden: Brill, 1993, 1994). Camargo, *Ars dictaminis* (n. 88 above), records many printed editions both in his notes and in chapter 5, "Editions," but comments, "A large proportion of those printed [. . .] are in need of new, modern editions" (51).

(*facilitas*, Greek *hexis*), he recommends translation from Greek, paraphrase of various kinds, theses, proofs and refutations, commonplaces, declamations, history, dialogues, and even (for amusement) verse. Composition teachers should enjoy Quintilian's comments on the writing and revision process (10.3.19–33), which include sensible remarks on the environmental conditions conducive to concentration and the recommendation to write on wax tablets because it is easier to erase.

Since Quintilian's program of education and lifelong practice was designed for professional public speakers, the last two chapters of Book 10 are strictly confined to speaking skills. He could not know that classical rhetoric's classical purpose would change with the times. By the fourth century, rhetorical theory had begun to divide into specialized subsets that favored written discourse over oral, and the *ars dictaminis* would later be one of these subsets. After analyzing how the fourth-century rhetorical handbooks "depart from the conceptual framework of earlier Latin theory," Michael Leff describes a trajectory linking them in kind to the rise of *ars dictaminis* some seven hundred years later:

> [W]e have reason to believe that some of the characteristics of medieval rhetorical theory already begin to surface as early as the fourth century, e.g.: the shift in focus from oral to written discourse, the decline of a holistic conception of the art in favor of a loose borrowing of particular elements of the classical system, and an implicit assumption that rhetoric is something to be used for specialized purposes, that it is not the main organizing force in the liberal education of a citizen. By the fifth and sixth centuries, we can recognize conscious attempts to redefine the subject of rhetoric. Augustine, for example, rejects the civil issue entirely [. . .]. The Middle Ages dispersed the elements of rhetoric into a vast number of learned and practical disciplines, and subsequent attempts to reestablish its integrity have stressed the unity of the art as process, not as substance.[96]

For a diachronic study such as this one, where some of the dots are missing from the lines to be connected and one must rely on drawing inferences, the retarding weight of tradition is a helpful ally. When change comes with glacial slowness, we can safely extrapolate from the known to the unknown. Two examples from letter-writing practice can suffice.

Certain topoi and formulaic expressions, such as the language of conversation and the theme of friendship, recur century after century in real letters and then reappear in the *artes dictandi*. A very common epistolary motif, expressing the essence of the letter's purpose, is *absens praesens* 'absent [in body], present [in spirit]'. This is blended with the biblical injunction (Matt. 19.6, Mark 10.9), "Whom God has joined, let not man separate" to produce "Although a great distance separates us, we are nevertheless joined in spirit." When we then encounter this topos in a model letter in an early twelfth-century *ars dictandi*, the dots almost connect themselves.[97]

---

96 Leff, 74, 76. Leff's article is followed in the same volume by R. R. Bolgar's highly condensed (Seven pages) but masterly survey of "The Teaching of Rhetoric in the Middle Ages."
97 Lanham, "Freshman Composition," 132–33.

Almost miraculously, throughout all those turbulent centuries, the exchange of letters connected and reassured friends and religious communities separated by vast distances. I believe that the enormous popularity of letters and letter collections and the existence of a theory of letter-writing prompted the introduction of school instruction in letter-writing, perhaps even before the fourth century. Hundreds, even thousands, of late antique and early medieval letters preserved in collections reflect acquaintance with traditional epistolary topoi and instruction in proper letter-writing practice. Many such letters read very much like practice compositions, and the extant ninth-century collections of salutation formulas were certainly made for instructional purposes.

Similarly, the link between the study of proverbs in school and their use in letters is established; it remains to find *artes dictandi* recommending the use of proverbs, and indeed they do. I noted earlier that Latin literature is filled with adages and moral *sententiae*, which, gathered into collections, supplied children with their first reading (the *Dicta Catonis*) and writers with material (Publilius Syrus, the *Liber scintillarum*). One *progymnasmata* exercise was to elaborate on a proverb, and it was common in the twelfth century to use a proverb or similar sententious saying to begin a letter, as a way of announcing its theme. John of Garland's *Parisiana Poetria de arte prosaica, metrica, et rithmica* (c. 1220–1235) is an unusual and very interesting work that attempts, as its title indicates, to combine *ars dictaminis* with *ars poetriae* into a universal art of composition.[98] Under the heading of invention, John offers a collection of about sixty *sententiae* suitable for various epistolary situations (12–19); some of his topical headings, and many more of the sayings, echo those in the *Liber scintillarum*. Further on, he instructs how to begin a letter by announcing its theme with a proverb.

Of late medieval England, Camargo points out that:

> the teachers of grammar in both the universities and the lower schools shared many pedagogical methods with the professional *dictatores*, including the composition of models for letters, the most important prose form. Nicholas Orme quotes from the 1309 statutes of St. Albans School, for example, the requirement that those who wished to attain the dignity of Bachelor "take a proverb from the master and compose verses, model letters and a *rithmus* on the subject [i.e., exercises in the three types of *dictamen*], as well as carrying on a disputation in the school."[99]

We know that a new Latin translation of Aphthonius's *progymnasmata* became very popular in Europe from early in the sixteenth century. If my reconstruction of the early medieval grammar curriculum to include rhetorical instruction in the *progymnasmata* and letter-writing is correct, the continuity from Quintilian to the Tudor grammar school curriculum, described by Don Paul Abbott in Chapter 5 of this volume, is seamless. The one missing ingredient was the

---

98 Traugott Lawler, ed. and trans., *The "Parisiana Poetria" of John of Garland* (New Haven: Yale University Press, 1974) xvi–xvii.

99 Camargo, *Medieval Rhetorics of Prose Composition*, 29, quoting Nicholas Orme, *English Schools in the Middle Ages* (London 1973) 101. Camargo notes ad loc that lists of proverbs occur in association with several *artes dictandi*, including John of Garland.

declamation, the pinnacle of the classical rhetorical curriculum. The humanist scholars of Renaissance Italy restored the oration to popularity, and thence it was imported into the Tudor curriculum, for a (temporary) return to dominance of an oral rhetoric.

Finally, then, what had changed by the end of the eleventh century? Coloring all else, ever since the disintegration of the Roman public schools in the fifth or sixth century, education had been in the hands of a church that sought to spread the Word of God. Second, since about the eighth century, Latin had been a second language for everybody, to be learned systematically in school (by those who went to school) and usually in preparation for a clerical career. For the rest, the content of education changed remarkably little before the twelfth century, except in the early structural shift which transferred some of rhetoric's traditional tasks to grammar. The heritage of classical (i.e., profane or secular) Latin literary texts survived, however precariously (some in a single manuscript), to be recopied for new readers and imitators during the Carolingian renaissance and later, and the secular content of schooling began to increase. Slow but insistent pressures of social, political, and religious change created a demand for specialized bureaucracies—and what bureaucracy has not needed professional, trained personnel: clerks, letter-writers, document processors? The *ars dictaminis* was the first big change, a pragmatic creation that answered a specific need. As the next chapter of this volume shows, more general innovations in writing instruction were on the way.[100]

Parts of this chapter appeared in different form in "Freshman Composition in the Early Middle Ages: Epistolography and Rhetoric before the Ars dictaminis," Viator 23 (1992) 115–34. Translations are my own unless noted otherwise.

---

100 James J. Murphy discusses the implications for instruction of Latin's "second language" status in the twelfth century, in "The Teaching of Latin as a Second Language in the 12th Century," *Historiographia linguistica* 7.1/2 (1980) 159–75.

Chapter 4

Writing Instruction in Late Medieval Europe

Martin Camargo and Marjorie Curry Woods

Key Concepts

Arts of composition • The medieval and modern classroom • *Facilitas, proprietas, auctoritas* • Teaching a foreign language • Arts of poetry and prose • *Poetria nova* • *Tria sunt* • Medieval students' exercises • Variation • Transposition • Expansion and abbreviation • Initiation • Proverbs and Exempla • Derivation • Impersonation • Contestation • Contemporary applications • Medieval and modern writing exercises.

The material to be moulded, like the moulding of wax, is at first hard to the touch. If intense concentration enkindle native ability, the material is soon made pliant by the mind's fire, and submits to the hand in whatever way it requires, malleable to any form.

Geoffrey of Vinsauf

Setting the Stage

Between the late eleventh and the early thirteenth centuries, far-reaching changes took place in the way that knowledge was organized and expressed in Western Europe. In the history of writing instruction, this so-called Renaissance of the Twelfth Century is known especially for producing new varieties of textbooks that summarized and rationalized teaching practices that had been evolving for centuries. By the early thirteenth century, at least three distinct genres of medieval composition textbook had developed, and all three continued to be used by teachers throughout Western Europe for the remainder of the Middle Ages.[1] Two of these genres offered instruction in specific, culturally significant

---

1 The origins and development of these three varieties of textbook are a central concern of James J. Murphy's *Rhetoric in the Middle Ages: A History of Rhetorical Theory from Saint Augustine to the Renaissance* (Berkeley and Los Angeles: University of California Press, 1974; rpt. Tempe: Arizona Center for Medieval and Renaissance Studies, 2001). Byzantine tradition is still mostly unexplored, but see Robert Browning, "Teachers," in *The Byzantines*, ed. Guglielmo Cavallo, trans. Thomas Dunlap, Teresa Lavender Fagan, and Charles Lambert (Chicago: University of Chicago Press, 1997) 95–116; Vessela Valiavitcharska, "Figure, Argument, and Performance in the Byzantine Classroom," *Rhetoric Society Quarterly* 41.1 (2011) 19–40; and the works cited in these essays. Of related interest is Federica Ciccolella, *Donati graeci: Learning Greek in the Renaissance*, Columbia Studies in the Classical Tradition 32 (Leiden: Brill, 2008).

forms of discourse: the *artes dictandi* (arts of composing) distilled the rules for composing letters and quasi-epistolary documents, and the *artes praedicandi* (arts of preaching), those for sermons, especially the variety known as "university sermons." The third genre of textbook is not tied to any particular variety of text. These are often called *artes poetriae* (arts of poetry) or *artes versificandi* (arts of versifying) but are in fact "arts of poetry and prose" that teach the fundamental rules for composing all types of texts, including rules that concern the features of letters and sermons that are not restricted to those forms.[2]

The arts of poetry and prose are the clearest window into medieval writing pedagogy for several reasons. Because they provide general instruction, they foreground the basic principles that underlie all composition. In the more specialized textbooks, these basic principles are understood to apply but need not be spelled out explicitly, since the person studying letter writing or sermon writing can be assumed to have already received training in general composition. Because the arts of poetry and prose are addressed to elementary students—including grammar-school boys—and their teachers, they also devote more space to classroom exercises than the treatises on composing letters and sermons typically do. Again, there is evidence that the teachers of the more specialized courses used some of the same exercises in their instruction, but the arts of poetry and prose describe a broader spectrum of such exercises in greater detail and thus provide the further benefit of suggesting how the full ensemble of composition exercises might have been organized into a coherent curriculum. Especially when supplemented by examples of school compositions, whether those of actual students or illustrative models prepared by their teachers, descriptions of writing exercises are more effective than lists of definitions and rules in bringing the medieval writing classroom to life and recapturing the goals of the activities that structured it.

Examples of medieval exercises are rare, not because students did not compose, but because there was no cheap yet relatively permanent method of recording their compositions. We have no medieval trash heaps of papyrus like those in Egypt that have furnished us with evidence of late antique school exercises,[3] and paper did not become widely available in Western Europe until the later Middle Ages. Then we do find it used by students, but primarily for taking down their own copies of standard school texts and teachers' commentaries (a practice that lasted well into the early modern period in some areas of Europe).[4] Students did have access to wax tablets as aids in composing, but these leave no permanent record, and writing a text on parchment was a complex and time-consuming practice demanding special skills and resources.[5] Yet these constraints and

---

2 The term is Douglas Kelly's; see *The Arts of Poetry and Prose*, Typologie des sources du moyen âge occidental 59 (Turnhout: Brepols, 1991).

3 For what these remnants reveal, see the works of Raffaella Cribiore and also Jeffrey Walker's study, *The Genuine Teachers of This Art: Rhetorical Education in Antiquity* (Columbia: University of South Carolina Press, 2011).

4 Dilwyn Knox, "Order, Reason and Oratory: Rhetoric in Protestant Latin Schools," in Peter Mack, ed., *Renaissance Rhetoric* (New York: St. Martin's Press, 1994), p. 67.

5 See Christopher de Hamel, *Scribes and Illuminators* (Toronto: University of Toronto Press, 1992), for a detailed and delightful description of the physical demands of all aspects of preparing and using parchment and paper, quills and inks, and brushes and paints.

seeming limitations may offer a fruitful parallel to the changing circumstances of contemporary writing instruction in our own classrooms.

The cost of writing materials and the complex technology of medieval textual production meant that composition was often carried out in one's head and delivered orally. Thus, despite the distinction between oral and written culture made much of by many medievalists, most composition practices, even in Latin by students studying to be *litterati*, were highly oral in character.[6] There were students at different levels in the same classroom—a situation that can occur in modern universities as well, especially in first-year courses, because of disparities in student backgrounds and prior education. Medieval teachers thought of their task as training students' creative muscles to take on any kind of composition assignment, and they focused on exercises that could work no matter what level of student was being taught. Similar kinds of exercises (rewriting, moving from prose to verse, expanding or contracting) were used to teach prose as well as poetry, and letters as well as narratives.

Goals

As a framework for our discussion of the different kinds of composition exercises used by medieval teachers during this period, let us first consider the goals that they wanted to achieve by assigning them. When they reflected on the shape of their instruction, medieval writing teachers favored the number three. For example, one of the treatises highlighted later in this chapter, the anonymous *Tria sunt*, opens like one of its most important sources by declaring that a composition teacher is concerned with the three parts of any formal text, the beginning, the middle (or continuation), and the end.[7] Many other such triads can be found in the textbooks, some of them borrowed from prestigious authorities,[8] others tailor-made by a particular teacher.[9] If we were to reduce to three broad categories the qualities that medieval teachers strove to instill in the writing of their students, we might label those categories with the Latin terms *facilitas, proprietas*, and *auctoritas*. These three concepts are usefully distinct, even though an individual composition exercise might apply more than one of them at once, as we will see below.

6 See the famous description of the teaching methods and exercises of Bernard of Chartres (partially quoted below): *Ioannis Saresberiensis Metalogicon*, ed. J. B. Hall, Corpus Christianorum: Continuatio Mediaevalis 98 (Turnhout: Brepols, 1991), pp. 51–55 (I.24); trans. Daniel D. McGarry, *The Metalogicon of John of Salisbury: A Twelfth-Century Defense of the Verbal and Logical Arts of the Trivium* (Berkeley and Los Angeles: University of California Press, 1962), pp. 65–71.

7 Geoffrey of Vinsauf, *Documentum de modo et arte dictandi et versificandi*, ed. Edmond Faral, *Les arts poétiques du XIIe et du XIIIe siècle. Recherches et documents sur la technique littéraire du moyen âge* (Paris, Honoré Champion, 1924; rpt. 1962), pp. 265–320, at p. 265. Cf. also Matthew of Vendôme's *Ars versificatoria*, which begins by discussing how to begin and ends by discussing how to end. See *Mathei Vindocinensis Opera*, vol. 3: *Ars versificatoria*, ed. Franco Munari, Storia e Letteratura: Racolti di studi e testi, 171 (Rome: Storia e Letteratura, 1988), pp. 43–55 and 217–21.

8 E.g., the qualities of accomplished style: *elegantia* (taste), *conpositio* (artistic composition), and *dignitas* (distinction): *Rhetorica ad Herennium* IV.xii.17–xiii.18.

9 E.g., Gervase of Melkley's classification of the methods for producing eloquent discourse as *idemptitas* (identity), *similitudo* (similarity), and *contrarietas* (opposition): *Gervais von Melkley: Ars Poetica*, ed. Hans-Jürgen Gräbener, Forschungen zur romanischen Philologie 17 (Münster: Aschendorff, 1965) p. 6.8–9.

Facilitas, the ability to compose artful discourse easily, was acquired above all through practicing techniques that generate *copia* (abundance). Even though the latter term has come to be associated especially with Erasmus because his textbook *De copia* (first edition 1512) was so incredibly popular, its application to rhetoric already was well established in classical antiquity.[10] In medieval schools great emphasis was placed on exercises that developed a student's ability to say the same thing in a multitude of ways. The epigraph at the beginning of this chapter evokes the almost physical nature of this manipulating and reshaping of language that is at the basis of medieval composition training. The many exercises devised to impart skill in variation of expression include techniques that focus on small units of discourse, such as a phrase or sentence, a single line of verse, or even individual words. Exercises in amplification and **abbreviation** also belong to this category, as do exercises that require an entire text to be rewritten in alternative forms. No medieval (or modern) student who mastered such techniques would ever face writer's block.

Proprietas, in the sense of suitability or decorum, was an essential feature of effective writing in a stratified, hierarchical society. Medieval students were trained to adjust their style and argumentative strategies according to Ciceronian rhetorical categories called attributes and circumstances, especially the kinds and rank of persons or characters involved and the nature of the subject matter treated. The medieval *doctor universalis*, Alan of Lille, summarizes the attributes of persons according to Cicero as follows: "name, nature, way of life, and fortune (who displays changeable faces), habit, feeling, deceitful counsel, interest, accident, speech, [and] accomplishment."[11] Exercises in praising and blaming, physical and moral description, use of proper epithets, and differentiated levels of style (high, middle, low) were among the most common means of inculcating skill in writerly decorum.[12] Similar exercises are a focus of modern creative writing texts, and the medieval versions are also a useful tool for analyzing pre-modern literature from a then-contemporary point of view.

Auctoritas (authority) is both a means and an end in medieval compositions. An effective writer or speaker had to command a broad spectrum of materials—ranging from traditional proverbs and anecdotes (*exempla*) to scholarly treatises, from classical poetry to the Bible and patristic commentary on it—and a full array of techniques with which to treat them. This knowledge was applied and refined in exercises in which authoritative texts were manipulated or recast, selected and marshaled as means of proof, or employed as catalysts for generating new texts. A text that made effective use of such "authorities" would achieve "authority" of its own.[13]

---

10 *Copia* is a classical term whose meaning with regard to language was "The ability to express oneself well and fully . . ." (*OLD*, sv. *copia* 6 [rhet.]). During the Middle Ages, the term had both its "original meaning of abundance, plentiful supply" as well as the specific meaning of 'copy' from 1274 onwards . . ." (Mariken Teeuwen, *The Vocabulary of Intellectual Life in the Middle Ages* [Turnhout: Brepols, 2003], p. 198). For a discussion of the renaissance meanings of *copia* and the importance of Erasmus's treatment of it, see Don Paul Abbott's chapter following this one.

11 *Anticlaudianus* 3.216–18, qtd. in *TS* 12.2.

12 Cf. Martin Camargo, "Latin Composition Textbooks and *Ad Herennium* Glossing: the Missing Link?" in Virginia Cox and John O. Ward, eds., *The Rhetoric of Cicero in Its Medieval and Early Renaissance Commentary Tradition* (Leiden: Brill, 2006), pp. 267–88, at pp. 277–80.

13 See also the discussion of *auctoritas* and related terms in Teeuwen, *Vocabulary*, 222–23.

Medieval composition teachers consistently had their students create *copia* by working with—imitating, modifying, adapting—existing texts, often canonical texts fraught with *auctoritas*, much like the academic texts with which contemporary composition teachers confront their own students and with which those students will have to engage in their academic writing. The *facilitas* that students acquired by manipulating the words of others, in the process making them their own, enabled them to join privileged speech communities and eventually to make their own contributions to shaping the discourse that defined those communities.

For medieval composition students, especially in the early stages of their training, ideas followed words rather than summoning them. Those medieval students were learning to compose in Latin. Even for students whose native language was one of the Latin-based Romance vernaculars, Latin, especially the learned Latin they had to master in school, was a highly artificial language whose proper use was carefully coded to create the desired level and kind of *proprietas*.[14] For students in England or Germany, Latin was a completely foreign language. At first glance this fact would seem to mark an important distinction between medieval and modern writing instruction, but in the end it actually points to a similarity. At least at the university level, modern students learning to master the codes and conventions of academic English often feel as if they are grappling with a foreign language. The techniques developed to impart skill in the medieval language of learning, including practice in speaking as well as writing that language, may well prove effective in producing mastery of our own language(s) of learning.

Texts and Exercises

In the rest of this chapter we attempt to give a synoptic view of writing instruction from the thirteenth through the fifteenth centuries, with a special emphasis on medieval classroom exercises that can be used effectively by contemporary teachers. We draw on the whole spectrum of the surviving evidence, but we make special use of three sources. Two of these are medieval writing textbooks, both composed in England, one dating from the very beginning and the other from near the end of the period encompassed by this chapter. The first two appendices at the end outline the techniques and exercises taken from these two related *artes poetriae* or arts of poetry and prose. The third source is a rich collection of materials for writing instruction compiled in England near the beginning of the period in question.

I. Poetria nova

The exercises in the most popular medieval rhetorical treatise, the *Poetria nova* of Geoffrey of Vinsauf (written ca. 1200–1215), are listed in Appendix A.[15] This work survives in over two hundred manuscripts and was taught all over Europe

---

14 See Dante, *De vulgari eloquentia.*
15 We have used the translation of the *Poetria nova* of Geoffrey of Vinsauf by Margaret F. Nims, revised by Martin Camargo (Toronto: Pontifical Institute of Medieval Studies, 2010). The Latin text is edited by Faral, *Les arts poétiques,* pp. 197–262.

for several centuries.[16] It weaves together verse precepts and verse examples in a text of more than two thousand Latin hexameters that continued to be recognized as a significant poem long after it stopped being used in the schools. The *Poetria nova* is organized along aesthetic and rhetorical as well as pedagogical lines: it was analyzed in classrooms as both a rhetorical treatise and a rhetorical argument in verse. As the *accessus* or academic introduction to the *Early Commentary* on the *Poetria nova* puts it,

> [T]he book principally consists of the five parts of rhetoric. . . . These are the parts: Invention, Arrangement, Style, Memory, and Delivery. . . . The instrument of this art is the discourse, which has six parts, namely the Introduction, the Narration, the Division or Distribution, the Proof, the Rebuttal or Refutation, and the Conclusion. And these parts of a discourse are the parts of invention . . . .
>
> (*EC, accessus* 3–5, 17–18)[17]

The Early Commentator's emphasis on invention in all parts of the *Poetria nova* reinforces the generative aspect of medieval writing instruction. This text was especially important for showing an author performing what he taught. Geoffrey uses all of the resources of verse composition, including fanciful descriptions of techniques that encode them as well (e.g., metaphorical descriptions of metaphor), to create a memorable text in and of itself. One of the most notable aspects of this text was the inclusion of long, virtuoso set pieces, such as the series of apostrophes on the death of Richard Lionheart, which Geoffrey probably composed earlier, and whose popularity may have been the inspiration for the composition of the *Poetria nova*.[18] He also includes passages that appear to question authority and that offer parodies or other reworkings of known stories that made the *Poetria nova*'s poetry, as well as its precepts, memorable. Teachers used it as a book of composition doctrine combined with rhetorical examples all by a single author and arranged in a specific sequence for particular effects. They admired Geoffrey as a writer.

2. Tria sunt

Our second source, the late fourteenth-century *Tria sunt*, is a much later work with a more specific geographical significance; it is preserved in more than a dozen English manuscripts of the fifteenth century, when it was the chief composition textbook employed in the schools of Oxford.[19] But rather than a text that performs what it teaches, like the *Poetria nova*, the *Tria sunt* is structured

---

16 See Marjorie Curry Woods, *Classroom Commentaries: Teaching the* Poetria nova *across Medieval and Renaissance Europe* (Columbus: Ohio State University Press, 2010).

17 *An Early Commentary on the* Poetria nova *of Geoffrey of Vinsauf*, ed. [and trans.] Marjorie Curry Woods (New York: Garland Publishing, 1985); hereafter *EC*.

18 See Martin Camargo, "From *Liber versuum* to *Poetria nova*: The Evolution of Geoffrey of Vinsauf's Masterpiece," *Journal of Medieval Latin* 21 (in press).

19 See Martin Camargo, "*Tria sunt*: The Long and the Short of Geoffrey of Vinsauf's *Documentum de modo et arte dictandi et versificandi*," *Speculum* 74 (1999): 935–55. One of its main sources is another work by Geoffrey of Vinsauf, the *Documentum de modo et arte dictandi et versificandi*, and for a long time it was considered Geoffrey's own revision of that work.

more like a practical syllabus for a late-medieval composition course. It is an eclectic combination of prose instruction with examples in both verse and prose drawn from a broad range of the classical and medieval authors that were taught in the classroom. Its author-compiler brings together instruction and examples from several of the earlier arts of poetry (including the *Poetria nova*), as well as quoting and commenting on advice and providing exercises based on one of the major classical sourcebooks of those works, the Roman poet Horace's *Ars poetica*. The author of the *Tria sunt* summarizes its contents at the work's end.

> In this book is contained virtually everything useful that Horace provides in his *Ars poetica*. And it contains the sixteen chapters that follow:
>
>> The first chapter is about natural and artificial beginnings and the eight methods for artificial beginnings. The second is about the continuation of the subject matter and transitional expressions. The third is about the eight ways of generating and lengthening the subject matter and about the technique for composing letters. The fourth is about the seven ways of shortening the subject matter and about how to decide which verbal ornaments to use in adorning a given subject matter. The fifth is about the ten kinds of "transumption" (metaphoric language), by means of which one produces "ornamented difficulty" and reveals the weightiness of what one has written. The sixth is about matters that concern all verbal ornamentation and about the words that provide the best ornamentation. The seventh is about "ornamented facility" (non-metaphorical figures) and about "determination" (qualifying one word with another), which is the principal seasoning of style, and about the colors of words and thoughts. The eighth is about the functional categories into which all of the colors can be sorted and about how the "figures" correspond to the "colors." The ninth is about the art of discovering ornamented words that enable one to beautify every uncouth expression with "fresh flowers." The tenth is about developing an original subject matter. The eleventh is about developing a familiar subject matter. The twelfth is about the attributes of persons and actions, by means of which one provides the characteristic details that are suited to a particular subject matter. The thirteenth is about the "poetic" and the "modern" styles and their characteristics. The fourteenth is about the six chief faults to be avoided in any kind of composition. The fifteenth is about the genres of discourse and the varieties of poetic compositions. The sixteenth and last is about conclusions and how they should be produced. (*TS* 16.9)[20]

These subjects are arranged in a "natural" order for teaching composition, very different from the "artificial" or "artistic" medieval arrangement of the *Poetria*

---

20 Martin Camargo has published a number of articles on the *Tria sunt* and is editing and translating it for the Dumbarton Oaks Medieval Library, a new series published by Harvard University Press. An excerpt from his translation has appeared in "*Tria sunt* (after 1256, before 1400)," in *Medieval Grammar and Rhetoric: Language Arts and Literary Theory, CE 300–1475*, ed. Rita Copeland and Ineke Sluider (Oxford: Oxford University Press, 2009), pp. 670–81.

nova according to the parts of rhetoric and the parts of a rhetorical discourse.[21] The author moves through the parts of a composition step by step (beginning, transition to body, body of text, and conclusion), treating each in detail and with examples taken from a variety of sources, including the *Poetria nova*. There is coverage of a number of other aspects of composition also ignored by the author of the *Poetria nova*, such as letter writing, original and familiar subject matter, the attributes of persons and actions, and the levels and categories of styles. The author of the *Tria sunt* provides a comprehensive, step-by-step approach to composition, bringing in the best writers on the subject that are known to him. This kind of composition manual creates trust in the author's expertise and comprehensive knowledge. It makes composition a straightforward matter that is teachable and learnable.

Yet the basic set of exercises is the same in each, as Appendices A and B listing these exercises make clear (with the sections identified by letter to make comparison between them easier). Each text encourages the *copia* that produces *facilitas* by emphasizing the ways to create and vary compositions (ranging from a single word to a whole narrative, but in the opposite order in the *Poetria nova*), *proprietas* by addressing characters of various types and social stations, and *auctoritas* either by reworking known stories in the *Poetria nova* or by citing a range of authors in *Tria sunt*. Both texts include a wide range of rhetorical examples, and they are shaped around a rhetorical core based on the Ciceronian tradition. Thus, taken together, the *Poetria nova* and the *Tria sunt* reveal both what remains constant in composition teaching during this period as well as the various ways in which such instruction could be deployed.

3. Hunterian Manuscript V.8.14

Our third featured source provides additional context for the use of such textbooks in medieval schools, as well as a rich assortment of the verse compositions that would have resulted from the exercises assigned by medieval writing teachers. The early thirteenth-century English manuscript Glasgow University Library, MS. Hunterian V.8.14 (formerly 511), is a major source for our knowledge of medieval composition practices.[22] This famous collection of rhetorical poetry also contains all the arts of poetry and prose written up to this point: Matthew of Vendôme's *Ars versificatoria*, Geoffrey of Vinsauf's early *Summa de coloribus rhetoricis* and his *Documentum de modo et arte dictandi et versificandi*, as well as his popular *Poetria nova*, and Gervase of Melkley's *De arte versificatoria et modo dictandi*. In addition to the exercises within these treatises, the manuscript contains a number of separate poems that we take to be student compositions,[23] some of which may be verse exercises composed by the authors of the *artes poetriae* when they themselves were students.

---

21 On artificial order in the *Poetria nova* itself, see *EC* 1588.4–12; discussed also in Woods, *Classroom Commentaries*, pp. 85–87.

22 For studies of this manuscript see Edmond Faral, "Le manuscrit 511 du 'Hunterian Museum' de Glasgow," *Studi medievali*, n.s. 9 (1936): 18–119; and Bruce Harbert, ed., *A Thirteenth-Century Anthology of Rhetorical Poems: Glasgow MS. Hunterian V.8.14* (Toronto: Pontifical Institute of Mediaeval Studies, 1975). Numbers preceded by # in the notes below refer to item numbers in Harbert's edition.

23 See Harbert's Introduction, especially p. 4.

At first glance, these verse exercises may look like a hodgepodge of forms and (cross-)purposes:

1. a letter in elegiac verse from a student to his mother bewailing (*heu!*) his financial situation and complaining that his friends are leaving him because of his lack of funds. This exercise may possibly be an early example of a common later exercise in which a letter in prose is recast in verse (sometimes more than one type of verse). Prose letters asking parents for money were a staple of medieval letter-writing collections taught along with the *artes dictandi*.[24]

2. Two versions of a poem in praise of King Henry II and his victory over a rebellion led by (among others) his wife Eleanor of Aquitaine and three of their sons; the second poem is an amplification of the first.[25]

3. Two verse fables, one long ("The Clerks and the Farmer") and one short ("The Snake, the Man, and the Wolf"), rewritten from prose fables in *Disciplina clericalis* by Petrus Alphonsus.[26] The author of the *Tria sunt* distinguishes among three genres of discourse (dramatic, hermeneutic, and didactic [*TS* 15.1]), and teachers may have assigned exercises in transposing material from one to the other, resulting in a composition like the first of these fables, which converts "hermeneutic" discourse into "dramatic" discourse. The second is copied among the character delineations that follow.

4. A number of character delineations, mainly from classical mythology and probably based on Ovid's *Metamorphoses*, of Paris; Io, Tiresias, Jupiter, Asterie, Arachne, and Myrrha grouped together; and two of Niobe.[27] The longer of the two Niobe poems, forty-two lines long, uses twenty-one of the thirty-five figures of words.[28] The first three distichs, or couplets, demonstrate the first three figures: *repetitio*, repetition of the first words of successive phrases or clauses; *conversio*, repetition of the last words of successive phrases or clauses; and *complexio*, repetition of the first and last words of successive phrases or clauses:

> **How** stupid, **how** insane, **how** wicked it is to vex the gods, you teach by your cry, O Daughter of Tantalus.

> You are in heart **swollen**, in speech **swollen**, in deed **swollen** as you prepare to surpass Latona's progeny with your own.

> **Why** do you do **this? Why** do you affect **this? Why** do you believe that you can profit in **this?**[29]

---

24 Harbert #2; Harbert attributes this poem to Matthew of Vendôme (p. 9). Matthew produced a collection of verse epistles, many on standard school topics such as this one, and he retains in the *Ars versificatoria* some of his own student compositions. On the subjects of student letters, see Charles Homer Haskins' landmark study, *The Renaissance of the Twelfth Century* (Cambridge, MA: Harvard University Press, 1927), pp. 144–46.

25 Harbert #11–13; Harbert edits these as three separate poems, rather than one long and one short one, and attributes them to Geoffrey of Vinsauf (p. 18); see also Martin Camargo, "Geoffrey of Vinsauf's Memorial Verses" (forthcoming).

26 Harbert #14 and 17.

27 Harbert #6, 15–16, 18–21, 24–25.

28 Faral, "Le manuscrit 511," pp. 34–36.

29 Unpublished translation by Cheryl Eve Salisbury and Wilma Wierega quoted with permission (emphasis ours).

The companion piece to this poem, only three distichs long, emphasizes in abbreviated form the emotional and dramatic aspects of Niobe's self-absorption:

> Famous Niobe—prolific, powerful, generous—scatters wealth, rejoices in offspring, recounts her ancestors.

> With her husband a king, with her face a dowry, with her stock from the gods, she holds herself better than her people because of her offspring, and she swells with pride.

> Her husband Amphion begins to swell just like the progenitor of his ancestors on the genealogical tree—she the granddaughter, he the son of Jove.[30]

Although both poems are relatively short, as is appropriate for student composition assignments, Edmond Faral notes that they are complementary in length as well as focus and treatment. They constitute a set pair of examples of school exercises in amplification and abbreviation, with appropriately different techniques and approaches.[31]

The second verse fable and all the character delineations except the shorter Niobe poem are composed of four elegiac distichs (each composed of a hexameter verse followed by a pentameter verse) in which, as with modern couplets, the sense is completed at the end of each two-line element. Several distichs may have been a common format for a composition assignment, especially one retelling a known narrative or focusing on a known character. The popularity of the distich for such exercises may well have to do with the widespread use of the so-called *Distichs of Cato* as an elementary textbook in medieval schools. Such exercises are another means of adapting fabulous material, as well as imitating *auctoritates* (canonical texts and authors) and practicing the use of the attributes, or *proprietates*, of characterization (elaborated in some detail in *TS* 11 and 12).

5. Two epitaphs, one for a man named *Clarus* (also an adjective meaning "famous") based on a text by the twelfth-century poet Peter Riga, and one for a hunter.[32] Epitaphs, too, seem to have been a popular exercise, with potential for both abbreviation and amplification. Geoffrey of Vinsauf is supposed to have composed the highly compressed (one distich) epitaph that was inscribed on Henry II's tomb at Fontevraud ("The tomb is enough for one for whom the whole world had not been enough: / a small thing is vast for one for whom the vast was small"),[33] and his sixty-three-line lament for Richard I, included in the *Poetria nova* (lines 368–430) as an example of amplification by means of apostrophe, was the most famous contemporary epitaph for Henry's son and heir.[34]

---

30 Unpublished translation by Asa Gopal of Harbert 25.1–6, quoted with permission.
31 Faral, "Le manuscrit 511," p. 36.
32 Harbert #27–28, 34.
33 The text and attribution are from Geoffrey of Vinsauf's English contemporary and fellow composition teacher Gervase of Melkley. See *Gervais von Melkley: Ars Poetica*, ed. Gräbener, p. 171.19–21.
34 See Camargo, "Memorial Verses."

6. Descriptions, one of the Greek army setting out for Troy and one of a fertile valley, possibly exercises in amplification.[35] Although Homer's *Iliad* was not available in Latin translation during the Middle Ages in the west, there were a number of school texts and other works that presented some of the same material.[36] The story was well known, as we can see from the discussion of the story of Troy as a "common topic" of composition in the *Tria sunt*:

> In developing a common subject matter let us be careful to observe the five methods that Horace assigns us in his *Poetics*. For Horace says that it is more praiseworthy and more artful to treat common subject matter in one's own way than to treat original subject matter. For it is more difficult and more artful to rehearse becomingly the war of Ilium, that is, of Troy, than a new subject matter that has not been heard by everybody. . . . But though it be difficult to treat a common subject matter well, it is nonetheless possible . . . if we observe the five methods.
>
> The first method is that we do not pause where others make a pause, but where they make a pause we move on. And we should understand this pause as having to do with digressions, descriptions or such like, since in a common subject matter, if they digress to something or describe something in such a way that they create a pause in the subject matter, we should not pause in the same place but briefly pass over that place in the subject matter.
>
> (TS 11.1–2)[37]

Despite the seeming randomness of the student exercises in the Hunterian manuscript, they display the students' growing knowledge of *facilitas*, *proprietas*, and *auctoritas*. With regard to developing *facilitas* through *copia*, the students are learning to say the same thing in different ways or with different degrees of elaboration and to translate from one form into another (exercises 1, 2, 3, and 4); with regard to *proprietas*, the students have learned how to evoke status, character, and accomplishment, often with the specific aim of praise or blame (2, 4, and 5); and in terms of *auctoritas*, they have learned to command a knowledge of canonical texts and to use this knowledge effectively in new ways (3, 4, 5, 6). Most of the exercises, like those described in the arts of poetry and prose also found in the manuscript, involve presenting the same or similar material in different lengths of treatment. These are usually recastings of a known source, often a text read in school but originally written for adults.[38] Such exercises are particularly applicable to modern courses in which academic content plays a significant part in the syllabus.

---

35 Harbert #22–23.

36 See A. G. Rigg, *History of Anglo-Latin Literature, 1066–1422* (Cambridge: Cambridge University Press, 1992; rpt. 1996), especially pp. 99–102; Kathryn L. McKinley, "The Medieval Homer: The *Ilias Latina*," *Allegorica* 19 (1998): 3–61; and, of course, Book 2 of the *Aeneid*.

37 For the other four methods see Appendix B (K).

38 Even the texts that were most often used to teach reading and formed the most basic part of the curriculum were not composed as school texts: the Psalms, biblical excerpts comprising Books of Hours, Cato's *Distichs*, the *Eclogue of Theodulus*, *Peniteas Cito*, etc.

Medieval and Modern Instruction

In the remainder of the chapter we outline the kinds of instruction used most widely, giving special attention to those exercises that can be reproduced easily and productively in the modern classroom.[39] They offer cumulative training in rhetorical skills, and all but the first are extant in versions of increasing complexity. The first one is the easiest to adapt, and the last, while it takes up much more classroom time and energy, has become increasingly recognized as an effective teaching tool in the academy. Exercises 1 through 3 focus the student's attention on working with a given verbal unit provided by the teacher, whether a word, a sentence, or a narrative; exercises 4 through 7 use structures or formats provided by the instructor to teach the student how to create new kinds of texts, some very lengthy and elaborate, that produce specific desired effects.

I. Variation: Words, Words, Words

Very small-scale, elementary exercises, such as "conversions" from one part of speech or one case to another and metaphorical substitutions of a phrase for a single word, allowed medieval students to focus on the smallest variations and details of expression. For modern students as well, these exercises offer a chance to concentrate on words or even parts of words rather than big ideas or structures. This practice generates a sense of competence and (later) the cumulative importance of detail in verbal artistry.

At the most basic level, any text is a collection of words, and each of those words can be modified to change the effect of the text as a whole. Most medieval teachers identify certain types of words as more productive of such variations than others, and many of them devote considerable space to techniques for expanding a student's mastery of such words. In the second chapter of his *Ars versificatoria* (before ca. 1175), Matthew of Vendôme provides long lists of adjectives and verbs that can be used to elegant effect in lines of verse, as he illustrates for each one.[40] Likewise, Geoffrey of Vinsauf, in his earliest textbook, the *Summa de coloribus rhetoricis*, offers his own list of verbs that are especially suitable for metaphoric use and then, for each verb in his list, demonstrates that use in three brief metrical examples.[41] It is likely that both Matthew and Geoffrey had their students use the same words to compose their own examples in verse (and perhaps also in prose) and in the process expand their vocabulary and thus their ability to say the same thing in a number of different ways.

Many of the words these teachers recommend are derived from Greek roots or are exotic in other ways, and students often are encouraged, on the authority of Horace's *Ars poetica* (lines 46–72), to expand their vocabulary still further by

---

39 See also Alex Mueller, "The Medieval Writing Workshop," especially the section on "Medieval Pedagogy in the Postmodern Classroom," available at http://www.teamsmedieval.org/ofc/F08/writing.php (accessed November 10, 2011).

40 *Ars versificatoria*, ed. Munari, pp. 139–59. The best English translation of this treatise is by Aubrey E. Galyon: Matthew of Vendôme, *The Art of Versification* (Ames: Iowa State University Press, 1980); the relevant passage is on pp. 66–84.

41 Edmond Faral does not print the full text of this (by far the longest) part of the treatise, but he does list the verbs whose use Geoffrey recommends and illustrates: *Les arts poétiques*, p. 325.

coining new words.[42] Matthew of Vendôme organized his lists of adjectives by endings and Geoffrey of Vinsauf arranged his list of verbs in alphabetical order. In the *Parisiana Poetria* (ca. 1220; revised 1231–1235), John of Garland made it still easier for his students to memorize and use new vocabulary by placing parallel terms classified by level of style (high, middle, and low) into the three compartments of a circular diagram that he called Virgil's Wheel.[43] His schema would have been especially helpful for substitution exercises that required an entire text to be transposed rather than a single word to be replaced.

Many of the exercises that single out an individual word that is to be replaced by its equivalent involve amplification as well as substitution. Periphrasis or circumlocution is a good example. In fact, since a circumlocution that takes the form of a roundabout phrase is always longer than the simple word that it "talks around," the *Poetria nova* and, following it, the *Tria sunt* classify periphrasis among the eight methods of amplification (*PN* 226–40; *TS* 3.A.3–6). Because periphrasis is a form of substitution, however, the *Tria sunt* also treats it as one of the five "lighter" varieties of transumption, or metaphorical discourse (*TS* 5.31–35).[44] When describing strategies for generating circumlocutions in the classroom, the author of the *Tria sunt* emphasizes two distinct functions of periphrastic substitution: either to render what is brief and colorless more vivid through expansion or to render what is prolix more concise and concentrated through abbreviation. In still another context, the author of the *Tria sunt* values periphrasis for its ability to veil unpleasant topics (euphemism), an important aspect of *proprietas* in the sense of decorum (*TS* 9.3). Given the many different purposes that periphrasis serves, no wonder the anonymous teacher believes that "This color is the best for teaching boys" (*TS* 5.32).

"Conversion" in its simplest form, where the same word is retained but its form and its function in a sentence are changed, is a surprisingly practical exercise that arises today in writing applications, letters of recommendation, or any other kind of text in which a request is made or a course of action is advocated. How to write extended discourse asking for money or a job in which every sentence contains a reference to oneself but does not begin with "I" is a skill not to be sneezed at. Geoffrey of Vinsauf's treatment of this exercise in the *Poetria nova* (lines 1588–1760) was excerpted, imitated, and augmented by later teachers with a frequency that testifies to its pedagogical usefulness.

His first example illustrates the basic technique. The verb "I am grieving" (*doleo*) is converted into the noun "grief" (*dolor*), which is then converted in turn through each of its grammatical cases:

> Precept may be clarified here by example; take the following brief theme: ***I am grieving*** *over this matter.* Now apply the principle just established: *From this fountain* **grief** [*dolor*: nominative case] *flows over me. Hence the root* (or *the*

---

42 See especially Gervase of Melkley, ed. Gräbener, pp. 90–104, and *Tria sunt* 5.10–21.

43 John of Garland, *Parisiana poetria*, ed. and trans. Traugott Lawler, pp. 36/37–40/41. The connection with Virgil is through his three major poetic works, each of which was thought to illustrate a different level of style: the *Aeneid* (high), the *Georgics* (middle), and the *Eclogues* (low).

44 Geoffrey of Vinsauf says that he will treat ten varieties of transumption (*PN* 959) but actually treats only nine; periphrasis is the one he omits, perhaps because he treated it earlier under amplification.

seed, or *the fount,* or *the source*) **of grief** [*doloris:* genitive case] *rises within me. This affair is matter and cause* **for grief** [*dolori:* dative case]. *It sows* (or *gives birth to,* or *piles up*) **grief** [*dolorem:* accusative case]. **O** **tormenting grief** [*dolor anxie:* vocative case], *you rage against me with cruel wounds. My mind, as it were, lies prostrate, injured and ill* **with grief** [*dolore:* ablative case].

(*PN* 1622–29)[45]

Each of the seven sentences in the example says the same thing as the others, literally, but does so with a subtly different emphasis and connotation. What is more, as the options added to most of the sentences indicate, in practice there is no limit to the number of substitutions one can employ in a given sentence. As Geoffrey goes on to observe, the technique of conversion allows one to generate multiple sequences like the one above by replacing the original verb with other verbs of related meaning—such as "I sigh" (*suspiro*), "I complain" (*queror*), "I groan" (*gemo*), and "I weep" (*lacrimor*)—and then converting each to a noun that can be run through all of its cases. The more this process of grammatical substitution elaborates on and extrapolates from the literal original, the more it shades into the semantic substitution of metaphor (*PN* 1633–46). By repeating such techniques of substitution, whether applied to a single word or to multiple words in the same sentence, one quickly generates abundance and variety (*copia*). In its characteristic and complementary forms of grammatical *conversio* and metaphorical *transumptio,* the principle of synonymy or substitution was fundamental to medieval training in writerly *facilitas.*

Exercises in transumption or metaphorical discourse occupy major sections of both the *Poetria nova* and *Tria sunt,* where their ten varieties are grouped under the heading "Difficult Ornament" (*PN* 765–1093; *TS* 5.1–54). The amount of space devoted to them is due not only to their importance but also to the fact that such exercises are chiefly based on imitation of examples, which are provided in abundance and often at some length. The same is true of the figures classified under "Easy Ornament," namely the thirty-five non-metaphorical figures of words, which achieve their effect chiefly through sound rather than sense, and the nineteen figures of thought, which structure somewhat larger units of discourse than the figures of words (*PN* 1094–1587; *TS* 7.29–96). Because the *Poetria nova* is itself a poem, the illustrative examples that constitute most of the contents of these sections were composed by Geoffrey of Vinsauf, whereas those in the corresponding sections of *Tria sunt* were gathered from a wide range of sources, both ancient and medieval, both in prose and in verse. A second difference is that Geoffrey illustrated the "easy" figures of words and the figures of thought with two virtuoso poems in the *Poetria nova* (lines 1098–1217 and 1280–1527), in each of which he treats a unified topic while employing all of the respective figures in the strict sequence in which they are treated in the *Rhetorica ad Herennium* (also a popular text during the Middle Ages).[46] By contrast, the author of the *Tria sunt* alternated discussion and brief

45 Trans. Nims, p. 66, with one small change in wording and parenthetical additions to explain the grammatical variation.
46 As Ruth Taylor-Briggs notes, "The popularity of the *Ad Herennium* from the ninth century onwards is well attested by the survival of well over six hundred manuscripts" ("Reading Between the Lines: The Textual History and Manuscript Transmission of Cicero's Rhetorical Works," in Cox and Ward, p. 77).

illustrations of each figure in turn, in the same way that he and Geoffrey had treated the "difficult" figures. These materials were meant to help students identify the figures in any texts they might read, as well as to incorporate them in their own writing. Anyone who has read medieval texts in the original manuscripts will recognize the effects of such instruction in the marginal glosses that so frequently appear whenever an author employs a recognizable figure.

The "figures in their order" poems in the *Poetria nova* probably constitute an exercise that actually was used in the schools (see section 5, below), although this would have been a more advanced and perhaps for that reason less widely employed exercise than those that focused on producing individual figures through imitation of briefer models culled from authoritative sources. At some point students would have had to move from these smaller-scale exercises to compose larger-scale texts in which they would be expected to apply the techniques of figural ornamentation that they had mastered, but in less mechanical ways than in the sequential compositions of Geoffrey and others. In his *Metalogicon* (1159), John of Salisbury described a master teacher's use of what were probably small-scale, elementary exercises in imitating the figures similar to those facilitated by the *Poetria nova* and *Tria sunt*:

> [Bernard of Chartres] would also explain the poets and orators who were to serve as models for the boys in their introductory exercises in imitating prose and poetry. Pointing out how the diction of the authors was so skillfully connected, and what they had to say was so elegantly concluded, he would admonish his students to follow their example. And if, to embellish his work, someone had sewed on a patch of cloth filched from an external source, Bernard, on discovering this, would rebuke him for his plagiary, but would generally refrain from punishing him. After he had reproved the student, if an unsuitable theme had invited this, he would, with modest indulgence, bid the boy to rise to real imitation of the [classical authors], and would bring about that he who had imitated his predecessors would come to be deserving of imitation by his successors.[47]

As this account suggests, these pedagogical methods always carried the risk that students would struggle to make the transition from imitation to integration as they applied what they learned to their own compositions. With proper guidance and sufficient practice, however, such exercises empowered students not only to compose Latin verse and prose with ease but also to vary their discourse stylistically as the subject and the occasion demanded.

2. Transposition: Playing with What You've Got

In transposition exercises we are dealing with full-text variation. At the sentence level, this approach can overlap with the preceding variation exercises, in that

---

47 *Metalogicon*, ed. Hall, p. 53 (I.24.76–85); trans. McGarry, pp. 68–69. For a comparison of Bernard's exercises with those in the commentaries on the *Poetria nova* see Marjorie Curry Woods, "Some Techniques of Teaching Rhetorical Poetics in the Schools of Medieval Europe," in *Learning from the Histories of Rhetoric: Essays in Honor of Winifred Bryan Horner*, ed. Theresa Enos (Carbondale: Southern Illinois University Press, 1993), pp. 91–113.

changing the grammatical form of a key word can necessitate a full-scale change in the structure of the sentence (e.g., "The boy's face is white" becomes "Whiteness suffuses the boy's face"). Exercises in which material is reworked in another form could range from small-scale recastings such as translating individual sentences from the vernacular into Latin or vice versa (the texts to be translated were called *vulgaria* or *latinitates*)[48] to larger-scale exercises such as writing the same text as a letter in prose, a quantitative poem, and a rhythmical poem. Nicholas Orme cites the 1309 statutes of the grammar school at St. Albans, which specified that anyone wishing to rise to the status of senior scholar ("bachelor") "had to take a proverb from the master and compose verses, model letters, and a *rithmus* (species of verse) on the subject, as well as carrying on a disputation in the school."[49]

Once the means of transformation is chosen, it is applied to the entire source text uniformly. The proportions of the source text are retained more or less intact, but the format is altered throughout in any of a number of different ways. Recasting a narrative as a dialogue is illustrated by the Hunterian student poem based on Petrus Alphonsus, for example, which also involves prose into verse. In addition, medieval students might be assigned to rewrite the same text in different levels of style. Peter of Blois illustrates this exercise in his letter-writing treatise the *Libellus de arte dictandi rhetorice* (1181–1185). After he has discussed the five parts of a letter individually, he offers a brief letter, in which a student writes home from Paris asking his mother to send money, to illustrate how the parts work in conjunction. Peter calls this first model letter "naked and shapeless" (*nudam et informem*), by which he means that it is in the "low style" (*humilis stilus*). He then provides a second letter on the same subject, written "more carefully and and ornately" (*caucius et ornacius*), as befits the "middle style" (*stilus mediocris*). Although one could use the highest style, with its "more carefully chosen and less commonly employed vocabulary" (*magis exquisitis et minus vsitatis sermonibus*), Peter notes that it would be inappropriate in a letter of request from a student to his mother. Instead, he chooses to illustrate high style with a letter of request from the Bishop of Sens to the King of France.[50] As is often the case, here an exercise in *facilitas* also provides instruction in *proprietas*.

---

48 Martin Camargo, "If You Can't Join Them, Beat Them; or, When Grammar Met Business Writing (in Fifteenth-Century Oxford)," in *Letter-Writing Manuals and Instruction from Antiquity to the Present*, ed. Carol Poster and Linda C. Mitchell (Columbia: University of South Carolina Press, 2007), pp. 67–87, at p. 68.

49 Nicholas Orme, *Mediaeval Schools: From Roman Britain to Renaissance England* (New Haven and London: Yale University Press, 2006), p. 152. See also Martin Camargo, ed., *Medieval Rhetorics of Prose Composition: Five English* Artes Dictandi *and Their Tradition* (Binghamton NY: Medieval & Renaissance Texts & Studies, 1995), pp. 29–30.

50 Camargo, ed., *Medieval Rhetorics*, pp. 57–58. Cf. Chaucer's Host, who admonishes the Clerk of Oxford:

> Youre termes, youre colours, and youre figures,
> Keepe hem in stoor til so be ye endite
> Heigh style, as whan that men to kynges write.
> (*Canterbury Tales*, IV.16–18)

3. Expansion and Abbreviation: Picking a Path

This exercise requires a core text that is elaborated or compressed by means of specific applied techniques. The images that medieval teachers and rhetoricians used to describe this process are vivid and imply an almost physical wrestling with material that is at first obdurate but yields to training and craft. The epigraph at the beginning of this chapter comes from Geoffrey of Vinsauf's introduction to his discussion of amplification and abbreviation in the *Poetria nova*. The sentence that immediately follows sums up this attitude: "The hand of the mind controls [the material], either to amplify or curtail."

Amplification comes first, perhaps because it can be practiced on a unit as small as one word or as large as an already substantial text. The *Poetria nova* and *Tria sunt* recommend the same set of eight techniques for expanding an existing text (*PN* 219–689; *TS* 3.A.1–30). These include four that operate on a relatively small scale and belong to or resemble the figures of words—*interpretatio* (repeating the same thing several times in different words), *circumlocutio* (periphrasis: talking around a subject), *apostrophatio* (addressing an absent person or thing), and *locus oppositorum* (coupling a statement with the negation of its opposite: "I speak; I am not silent"). Another three are larger-scale strategies that are more like the figures of thought: comparison, *prosopopoeia* (speaking in character), and description. Indeed, any of these could form the basis of an independent text, as can be seen in several of the school poems from Hunterian MS. V.8.14. The remaining technique, digression, can take many forms (including comparison or description) but cannot exist independently of a larger narrative that it interrupts.

The *Tria sunt* also includes elaborate versions of amplification exercises that start with a single word rather than a full text. In the most radical version (*TS* 3.A.32–42), one begins by deriving a beginning, middle, and end from a verb, such as *lego* ("I read"), by making the "person" of the verb ("I") the beginning, the "matter" of the verb ("reading") the middle, and a time or place "external" to the verb the end. This produces an embryonic composition in the form of a bland core sentence: "I read in such a place," which can then be amplified by adding one of the eight artificial beginnings taught in the first chapter of *Tria sunt*: either by elaborating the middle or the end, or by employing a proverb or an exemplum related to the beginning, the middle, or the end. For example, an artificial beginning that elaborates the ending of the core sentence is "This place contains a double opportunity for study, being, on the one hand, pleasing in its beauty and, on the other hand, far removed from the noise of people." An artificial beginning with a proverb related to the beginning is "He whose spirit pants for the summit of supreme advancement longs with his whole being for the fruit and the abundance of readings." The artificial beginning provides a framework for the rest of the text, which the student begins to develop using the techniques of transition and continuation taught in the second chapter of *Tria sunt*.

A second exercise also begins with a subject matter that is encapsulated in a single verb, then opens the composition with a relevant proverb that has a specified grammatical form, and then derives the middle and end of the composition from two components of the initial proverb (*TS* 3.A.43–47). The example given is a composition on the subject matter "I teach" (*doceo*). The opening proverb should have two verbs, as in "Whoever *knows* ought to *teach*." The first of these verbs provides the nucleus of the middle or statement of facts (as in a letter), while the second provides the nucleus of the conclusion, producing a complete, if minimal "composition": "Whoever knows ought to teach. I know. Therefore I teach." Each element of this nuclear composition may then be elaborated as necessary. Thus, one can elaborate the statement of facts by adding "arguments" and evidence in support of them:

> I know because for some time now I have sought knowledge diligently among the experts. Truly among the experts because I have been among the Parisians, where knowledge of the trivium flourishes; among the Toledans, where knowledge of the quadrivium flourishes; among the Salernitans, where knowledge of medicine flourishes; and among the Bolognese, where knowledge of the laws and the decretals flourishes.

Finally, each part can be further elaborated stylistically, including the opening proverb:

> The one into whose mind the streams of knowledge have flowed should not refuse a drink to those who thirst but rather should disperse those streams broadly and distribute those waters even unto the highways and byways.

By such means, any student can develop a simple topic into as substantial a text as is desired.[51] With their well-articulated rules for generating a new text, these exercises could be included among the derivation exercises discussed in section 5, below (as we have done with one of them applied to letter writing), as easily as among the amplification exercises, where the author of *Tria sunt* put them.

Methods of amplification followed specific patterns and techniques, but we can think of them as opening up channels of invention so that the student was never at a loss for words. This kind of amplification exercise, like Geoffrey's example of conversion, above, works well as a group oral exercise in our own classes, in which every student, going in order around the room, contributes the next stage. Through such exercises one learns that one can always continue speaking or writing. Amplification is in all senses a primary skill.

Abbreviation, in contrast, appears to have been considered more difficult, perhaps because of necessity it involves working with longer and more complex texts. Geoffrey of Vinsauf employs the most violent of his images in his introduction to the techniques of abbreviation:

> Transfer the iron of the material, refined in the fire of the understanding, to the anvil of the study. Let the hammer of the intellect make it pliable; let repeated blows of that hammer fashion from the unformed mass the most suitable words.
>
> (*PN* 723–26)

---

51 It is not surprising that the word to be amplified in the exercises just described is a verb, for in Latin verbs also contain their subjects and hence comprise a complete statement. Verbs are thus, in general, a major focus of exercises in which a word is elaborated into a longer text. Verb morphology in Modern English carries less information, but one simply begins with a phrase rather than a single word.

The process of condensing is a powerful psychological experience. Rather than generating text, as with amplification exercises, abbreviations encapsulate texts, rendering them memorable and retrievable. Thus, assignments in abbreviation are particularly useful as a method of reviewing works read in the classroom, and one of the best ways for modern students to recall and retain the texts that they have read is to compose and share abbreviations of them as a review exercise.

Medieval exercises in abbreviation focused on the memorable, often horrible stories for which medieval pedagogy is becoming more widely known, as in Geoffrey of Vinsauf's version of the Snow Child, referred to in a commentary on the text as "that long story":[52]

> Her husband abroad improving his fortunes, an adulterous wife bears a child. On his return after a long delay, she pretends it begotten of snow. Deceit is mutual. Slyly he waits. He whisks off, sells, and—reporting to the mother a like ridiculous tale—pretends the child melted by sun.
>
> (PN 713–17)

Writers of modern synopses of operas, ballets, and dramas might benefit from deploying the crafted medieval approach (see Geoffrey's methods of abbreviation in Appendix A).[53]

What is counterintuitive about medieval instruction in abbreviation is the focus on nouns: "Do not be concerned about verbs; rather, write down with the pen of the mind only the nouns; the whole force of a theme resides in the nouns" (PN 719–22). A commentator on Geoffrey's story of the Snow Child describes it as "An example of a shorter composition exercise in which the five basic elements are touched on, namely man, woman, boy, snow, sun."[54]

Next we move into a different order of activity, since we are no longer building on a specific source text. The following techniques are used to produce a "new" text, albeit one that may contain quite a bit of preformed matter.

4. Initiation: Beginnings, Middles, and Ends

For medieval writers no less than for modern writers, getting started was the hardest part of the composing process. The difficulty was compounded by the heavy weight carried by the first few sentences of a composition, which not only announced a text's topic but also grounded its argument in authority (*auctoritas*) and established the hierarchical relationship between its author and the intended audience (*proprietas*). These multiple functions of beginnings are especially obvious in texts such as sermons, which begin with a "theme"—a short passage

---

52 "Istam longam fabulam" (Munich, Universitätsbibliothek, 4° 814, fol. 86v).

53 One of the most widely used medieval textbooks, the *Eclogue of Theodulus*, provided many examples of narrative abbreviation. It is comprised of matched pairs of quatrains narrating stories from the Hebrew Bible and the classical tradition that match up, often from an abstract or visual point of view. For a discussion of one matched set of abbreviations and their surprising content, see *SH2*, pp. 128–29.

54 "Exemplum breuioris tematis in quo tanguntur illa quinque principalia, scilicet vir, femina, puer, nix, sol" (Cambridge, Trinity College, R.14.22, fol. 17r); see also Woods, *Classroom Commentaries*, pp. 72–73.

from the Bible—that is subdivided and elaborated in the body of the sermon, and letters, which begin with strictly hierarchized formulas of greeting, usually followed by an authoritative statement, such as a proverb, an exemplum, or a quotation from scripture, that anticipates and underwrites the line of argument that will follow.

To prepare their students for the more stringent demands of letters and sermons, medieval teachers of general composition assigned exercises that focus on the beginnings of stories drawn from classroom texts. Robert Glendinning has suggested that specific composition assignments geared to the beginning of a story like that of Pyramus and Thisbe may have been classroom exercises in and of themselves; there is support for his argument in a gloss identifying the first two lines of one of Geoffrey of Vinsauf's examples of digression, which refer to lovers with one heart in two bodies, as a reference to that young couple, although the rest of Geoffrey's narrative does not follow their story.[55] Similarly, the surviving medieval student compositions on Niobe focus on her excessive pride in her fertility at the beginning of the story, rather than on her tears at the end that are the focus of the late antique exercise.[56] The student alters the proportions of his source by elaborating the emotional dimension of the opening topic while ignoring the ending. In the same way, one of the Dido lyrics in the *Carmina burana* stops when Dido and Aeneas get together in the cave, turning the tragedy of Virgil's Book 4 of the *Aeneid* into a happily-ever-after romance:

> And so in the union of them both
> the joyful heaven beamed:
> for on the joys of love
> they smile, and everything lay clarified.[57]

Other exercises emphasized a technical approach to devising a beginning to a story, such as Geoffrey of Vinsauf's eight varieties of **artificial order**, illustrated with the story of Minos, Nisus, and their children (*PN* 102–202). Here the variation involves a larger unit of text, usually at least a sentence. The first sentence of a work would be the logical place to start with this type of exercise, and that is indeed where the *Poetria nova* and the *Tria sunt* do begin (see Appendices A.A and B.A).

Exercises of this sort differ from those that generate a new text from a small kernel of text, whether a proverb or even a single word, which were discussed above. They are, in fact, exercises in textual interpretation as well as composition, and they demonstrate the ways in which the same text can express a range of different meanings. Geoffrey of Vinsauf's exercise, which is also found in *Tria*

55 Robert Glendinning, "Pyramus and Thisbe in the Medieval Classroom," *Speculum* 61 (1986): 60; see also Woods, *Classroom Commentaries*, p. 65.

56 Harbert summarizes her story as follows: "Niobe, wife of Tantalus, was proud that she had more children than Latona, mother of Apollo and Diana. Apollo and Diana punished her by killing all her children and turning her to stone" (p. 30).

57 "Troie post excidium," *The Love Songs of the Carmina Burana*, trans. E. D. Blodgett and Roy Arthur Swanson (New York: Garland Publishing, 1987), p. 114.

sunt, requires at least two levels of preliminary analysis of the base text before the act of (re)composition can begin. First, the narrative must be divided into three parts—the beginning, the middle, and the end—and then a meaning or what we might call a "moral" must be assigned to each part. These two acts of interpretation are, of course, reciprocal. In any chronologically structured narrative (what Geoffrey calls a narrative in "natural order") the boundaries between the parts could be drawn at different points, so the imposed meanings will dictate to a large extent the placement of the divisions. In the *Poetria nova* and *Tria sunt* the "beginning" is centered on King Minos of Crete, whose power and prosperity illustrate the gifts of Fortune; the "middle" is the murder of Minos's son Androgeus by his schoolmates at Athens, an example of envy; and the "end" is the abandonment of Scylla by Minos, which shows that those who betray others (as she had done to her father King Nisus of Athens) are themselves betrayed in turn.

Having thus analyzed the structural and thematic components of the text, the student is then asked to choose among nine options when rewriting it. One can retain the natural order, of course, and alter the text's meaning by strategic use of techniques such as amplification and abbreviation. More "fertile" (*PN* 102) options are the eight varieties of artificial order: beginning the story at the end, with the betrayal of Scylla; or at the middle, with the murder of Androgeus; or with a proverb on Fortune, envy, or the betrayer betrayed; or with an exemplum (here meaning an illustrative image or brief anecdote) pertaining to the meaning of the beginning, middle, or end of the narrative. Although the *Tria sunt* (and some copies of the *Poetria nova*) goes on to illustrate how one transitions from the various artificial beginnings to the body (or middle) of the new composition, neither the *Poetria nova* nor *Tria sunt* provides a complete example of such a composition. Presumably, the choice of beginning would have dictated the shape of that composition, which would amount to a reinterpretation rather than a simple retelling of the original story.

The treatises on letter writing often include collections of model letters which do illustrate how the kinds of beginnings practiced in the exercises just described are elaborated into full texts, albeit texts that are not adaptations of preexisting narratives. The parts of a letter and the sequence in which they occur are major concerns of such treatises, and it is common for them to devote special attention to alternatives for the opening two parts (*salutatio* and *exordium*). In that the *exordium* contains the authority or proof on which a letter's argument is based, such exercises could be aligned with the exercises on openings that are featured in the arts of poetry and prose.[58] In other words, both sets of exercises show how the choice of opening determines the meaning of the whole text. However, the teachers of letter writing (*dictatores*) appear to have used these sample beginnings differently, probably asking their students to choose a proverb or other authoritative text and use it to generate a letter on a specified topic, and so their exercises

---

58 In his *Formula moderni et usitati dictaminis* (Oxford, ca. 1390), Thomas Merke derives nine varieties of epistolary *exordium* from Geoffrey of Vinsauf's eight types of artificial order. Camargo, ed., *Medieval Rhetorics*, pp. 126–29.

on beginnings pertain more to text generation than to text variation and reinterpretation.[59]

The final part or conclusion of the composition gets similar treatment in several arts of poetry and prose (including the *Tria sunt* but not the *Poetria nova*) and to some extent in the *artes dictandi*. Thus, besides the focus on how to vary the all-important beginning of a composition, there is also a more general technique focused on the variation of one or more parts of a composition. Here again, the division of a text into three parts is fundamental. Even though the parts of a letter are most commonly identified as five—the greeting (*salutatio*), the introduction (*exordium*), the statement of facts (*narratio*), the request (*petitio*), and the closing (*conclusio*)—the first two and especially the last two have a tendency to aggregate, resulting in an underlying three-part structure that is often made explicit in the textbooks.[60] Since the structure of sermons also was built on triads, it may be that the more elementary instruction again reflected the demands of more advanced composition in its emphasis on beginnings, middles, and ends.

Such an approach could pay dividends in our own contemporary classrooms, and the specific techniques of varying the beginnings of compositions could be extended to reinterpretations of non-narrative texts. Exercises that require students to use "artificial order," however defined, to recast a given text compel them to reinterpret that text and in the process to experience the ways in which a variety of authoritative interpretations of the same text can be generated. Such exercises would have obvious value for teaching literary analysis and might be adaptable to teaching other varieties of textual analysis, as well. By changing the place from which a text starts and then rewriting it, in other words, a student can occupy simultaneously the positions of author and interpreter and thus engage actively and directly with the rhetorical production of meaning, evidence, and authority.[61]

5. Derivation: Filling in the Blanks

In these exercises, the student is given a structural framework within which to create his or her own text. These are important for the prose traditions of *ars dictaminis* (parts of a letter) and the *ars praedicandi* (parts of a sermon). One verse exercise produces connected discourse (rather than separate examples) using all the figures of words in the canonical order from the pseudo-Ciceronian *Rhetorica ad Herennium*, where they are presented individually and in prose. This exercise is extant in several versions, including a full virtuoso display using thirty-five figures of words, found in the *Poetria nova* (lines 1098–1217) and elsewhere,[62] and

---

59 For some examples, see Martin Camargo, "The Pedagogy of the *Dictatores*," in *Papers on Rhetoric V: Atti del Convegno Internazionale "Dictamen, Poetria and Cicero: Coherence and Diversification,"* Bologna, 10–11 May 2002, ed. Lucia Calboli Montefusco (Rome: Herder, 2003), pp. 65–94, at pp. 78–86.

60 In his *Summa dictaminis* (1228–1229), probably the single most influential textbook on letter writing in the Middle Ages, Guido Faba treats the *salutatio* as separate from the letter proper, whose three "integral" parts he identifies as the *exordium, narratio,* and *petitio.* "Guidonis Fabe *Summa dictaminis,*" ed. Augusto Gaudenzi, *Il Propugnatore,* n.s. 3 (1890), pt. 1: 287–338, pt. 2: 345–93, at p. 297.

61 Cf. Rita Copeland on translation as interpretation in *Rhetoric, Hermeneutics, and Translation in the Middle Ages: Academic Traditions and Vernacular Texts* (Cambridge: Cambridge University Press, 1991).

62 See Camargo, "Latin Composition Textbooks," in Cox and Ward, pp. 272–73.

the partial version in the longer Niobe poem, the first three figures of which are quoted above. There is also evidence that some teachers may have assigned just the first few figures, perhaps only six.[63]

Among the most common types of derivation exercises are those that combine a text form with techniques that overlap with the exercises mentioned above under amplification and/or initiation. A good example is an exercise used in letter-writing instruction, in which the student was asked to produce a complete, brief letter by starting from a proverb or some other "authority." Presumably, the teacher would have specified the topic of the letter, perhaps allowing the student to choose the initial proverb from one of those collections of proverbs that frequently accompany medieval treatises on letter writing. The teacher could complicate the exercise further by assigning two students to write a letter and its response, either assigning each the proverb to be used as the generative kernel for his respective text or giving them greater freedom to devise their argumentative strategies by making their own choice of proverb.

In one of its exercises for generating letters, the *Tria sunt* adapts the more general exercise discussed above in which a single verb is expanded into a complete composition. In this version a proverb or exemplum containing two verbs serves as the letter's *exordium*, the first verb of the *exordium* provides the nucleus for the *narratio*, and the second verb of the *exordium* provides the nucleus for the *petitio* and *conclusio*. All that remains to complete the letter is to supply the greeting (*salutatio*), which many teachers did not consider an integral part of the letter.[64]

6. Impersonation: Ethopoeia

Here is an obvious place where the *progymnasmata* overlap with medieval exercises, as students are invited to adopt another's voice and project themselves into alternative states. The goal of *proprietas*, here appropriateness of language and action to a specific character, is fostered by study of the "attributes" discussed in detail in the *Tria sunt*, but only mentioned in the *Poetria nova*. Carol Dana Lanham argues in the chapter preceding this one that in antiquity and the early Middle Ages, before the development of the *ars dictaminis*, exercises in *ethopoeia* were the basis of instruction in letter writing.[65] There are two classical versions of *ethopoeia*: the pathetic, in which the student writes a speech in the voice of a literary character in an emotional situation; and the ethical, which explores a character type rather than an individual.[66] We find both of these in medieval rhetorical treatises, although the second, rather than a first-person speech, is an address

---

63 For evidence of assigning a composition using the first six figures of words in the commentary on the *Poetria nova* by Reiner von Cappel, see Woods, *Classroom Commentaries*, pp. 76–79.

64 The *salutatio* was sometimes written on the outside of a letter, after it had been folded and sealed, as the author of the *Tria sunt* observes (*TS* 3.B.3).

65 See her chapter in this volume, (Chapter 3).

66 The *progymnasmata* are listed and summarized in James J. Murphy's chapter earlier in this volume (Chapter 2). For the complete texts in translation, see George A. Kennedy, *Progymnasmata: Greek Textbooks of Prose Composition and Rhetoric* (Atlanta: Society of Biblical Literature, 2003); also Malcolm Heath's translation of Aphthonius's *Progymnasmata* online at http://www.rhetcomp.gsu.edu/~gpullman/2150/Aphthonius%20Progymnasmata.htm (accessed November 14, 2011).

to—or sometimes a dialogue with—a particular kind of character. Geoffrey of Vinsauf, for example, has a series of apostrophes to specific character types, such as someone too presumptuous or too timid, in which he paints vivid pictures of the typical behavior of someone of that type and tells him how to shape up (*PN* 277–366). Laments, particularly of female characters, are a staple of late antique *ethopoeia* exercises (Niobe is the speaker in one of Aphthonius's examples[67]), and there is growing evidence of a continuation of this practice during the Middle Ages.[68] Geoffrey, however, provides laments spoken by inanimate objects such as the cross, a castle, and, perhaps most memorably, a worn-out tablecloth:

> I was once the pride of the table, while my youth was in its first flower and my face knew no blemish. But since I am old, and my visage is marred, I do not wish to appear. I withdraw from you, table; farewell!
>
> (*PN* 509–13)

We hope that it was performed in the classroom.

7. Contestation: War with Words

This is not really a separate category, but rather a way of showcasing other kinds of exercises in which paired and opposing approaches are presented. Its most sophisticated, extreme, and famous medieval form was the university *disputatio*, or debate.[69] But, just as the ancient *progymnasmata* provided practice in rhetorical techniques useful for more advanced oratorical compositions, a number of medieval exercises use "debate," broadly understood, as a structuring principle, as in collections of paired model letters, which suggests that this was an important category for the *dictatores*. In *Medieval Latin Poems of Male Love and Friendship*, Thomas Stehling translates a pair of letters from a *summa dictaminis* in which a man tries to seduce a boy using classical references, which the boy rebuffs with biblical references.[70] In another extant pair of epistolary declamations (letters meant to be performed) in the *Regina sedens Rhetorica*, two sisters debate what the modern editor calls "a young woman's right to choose a husband with sex appeal." The first sister notes that "the female kind . . . craves a respectable and attractive man just as matter craves form" and begs her sister "to secure me an absence from the paternal presence . . . as womankind is accustomed to remove a thorn from another's foot," while the other sister responds, "it is my special advice that, having wiped away all the inconstancies of lust whatsoever, you strive to obey in accordance with the deliberation and decision of our father and without stain of conscience take as your husband the one whom paternal

---

67 See Heath's translation of Aphthonius, "11. Characterisation."

68 See Marjorie Curry Woods, "Weeping for Dido: Epilogue on a Premodern Rhetorical Exercise in the Postmodern Classroom," in *Latin Grammar and Rhetoric: From Classical Theory to Medieval Practice*, ed. Carol Dana Lanham (London: Continuum, 2002): 284–94; and "Rhetoric, Gender, and the Literary Arts: Classical Speeches in the Schoolroom," *New Medieval Literatures* 11 (2009): 113–32.

69 Teeuwen discusses nine kinds of *disputatio* and a number of related concepts in *Vocabulary*, pp. 256–59.

70 Thomas Stehling, trans., *Medieval Latin Poems of Male Love and Friendship* (New York: Garland Publishing, 1984) nos. 88 and 89 and notes on pp. 156–57. Stehling comments, "Though they are in prose, the two letters are of sufficient interest to merit inclusion [in a collection of poems]" (p. 157).

kindness desires."[71] This basic oppositional technique is reflected in many kinds of exercises that produce pairs or even longer sequences of texts responding to other texts.[72] Thinking in opposites is a fundamental category for medieval teachers and manifests in all kinds of places. In Peter of Blois' *Libellus*, the author first describes seven methods for consoling a bereaved person—and then follows with seven methods for making such a person feel worse.[73] A more practical kind of opposition, that between praise and blame, is foregrounded in many paired medieval composition exercises.[74]

Conclusion

One of the most important aspects of medieval composition exercises is their flexibility. They can be adjusted and re-focused to reflect what the teacher wants to emphasize in the assigned readings and which skills the teacher wants the students to concentrate on during the composition process.[75] Thus, these exercises are well suited to the modern informal classroom with its emphasis on discussion and student input. The second edition of the *Short History* contained two lists of medieval exercises that had been tried successfully in two different kinds of classes: one on the history of rhetoric and one on medieval literature in translation; these are reproduced here in the first two parts of Appendix C.

Some modern teachers, however, might want to experiment with just one or two of the exercises at first to see how they work. For an exercise at the beginning of a course, we suggest a one-sentence imitation or amplification. If the experiment comes near the end of the term, a sequence of abbreviations (each

---

71 Martin Camargo, "Epistolary Declamation: Performing Model Letters in Medieval English Classrooms," in *Studies in the Cultural History of Letter Writing*, ed. Susan Green (San Marino: Huntington Library Press, 2011).

72 One of the methods of amplification discussed above, *locus oppositorum*, is a very small-scale version of this kind of exercise, in which something is said and then amplified by means of also negating its opposite in the same sentence (e.g., "The weather is hot and in no way is the temperature cold"). Although this example is not the kind of writing that we would necessarily want to find in student productions today, the exercise itself is a useful one in learning different ways to approach the same topic.

73 Camargo, ed., *Medieval Rhetorics*, pp. 69–71. For example, the third method of consolation, pointing out that the distress experienced is fleeting or of short duration, can be converted into a cause of despair thus: "This evil is lasting, nor can it be ended by any remedy." In fairness, Peter does point out that the arguments of consolation belong to the "useful and the good," while those of despair belong to their opposite.

74 Character sketches were an obvious occasion for praise and blame. Besides the examples from the Hunterian manuscript, see Matthew of Vendôme, *Ars versificatoria* I.50–59.

75 For example, the fourteenth-century statutes at Oxford for grammar-school masters gave the same requirements for instruction in both verse and letterwriting:

> Every two weeks, the grammar teachers "are required to assign (*dare*) **verses and letters** composed with proper words that are neither bombastic nor a yard long (*non ampullosis aut sexquipedalibus*), and with trim, graceful clauses, with metaphors that are clear and, as much as possible, full of wisdom; **which verses and which letters** the recipients [of the assignments from said teachers] should write down on parchment on the next feast day, or sooner, and then on the next day, when they come to school, they should recite them to their master from memory and submit them in written form.
>
> Strickland Gibson, ed., *Statuta antiqua universitatis oxoniensis*, qtd. in Camargo, "If You Can't Join Them," p. 68 (emphasis ours)

limited to a quatrain, a sentence, or even just a series of nouns) as a review of all of the works read in class. In the middle, when there is time to share the composition with peer reviewers and/or to rewrite it, then we suggest one of the longer sustained exercises, in which the students follow a specific structure, are given clear instructions or examples for each step, and draw on material read in the class. Each of these exercises, if the results can be shared even partially in class, has proven beneficial not just for the students' writing, but also for class discussion afterward.[76]

For all of these exercises, the more articulated the assignment the better. For many years Woods has assigned the exercise using all of the figures of words in the canonical order.[77] The rigid structure provides a framework for students to be creative in the individual steps, and the specific requirements force students to spend more time on details than traditional assignments allow. In each exercise the students have to study intensely and in detail the "base" or "shared" text (we avoid the term "original" here) upon which the exercise is based, but the students are also encouraged to make radical changes in that version.

The insights of medieval composition pedagogy are only beginning to be explored, and we encourage our readers to try the exercises here, to experiment with them, and to write about the results. One of the most successful ways we have found to teach initiation in its most absolute form, for example, is to read aloud, or better yet have read aloud by the student, the first sentence of every student's paper: a memorable sentence teaches itself. But it is the more extreme exercises—not just the figures in order but others like the amplification of one word into a whole paragraph—that have the strongest pedagogical effect. As teachers, our first reaction to reading about them may be, "But I don't want my students to write like that!" The results are so strange—dare we say it—so medieval. Here, as with almost every aspect of medieval pedagogy that we are familiar with, the performed experience is completely different from reading about it. The connections among play, performance, and verbal experimentation were well known to medieval teachers. A surprising result of a performance of the sisters' letters mentioned above turned out to be "how well the mannered language of the letters worked in oral performance . . . [T]he very artificiality of the language made it easier to adopt a persona and afforded many opportunities for dramatically heightened delivery."[78] One of the most difficult goals of modern teachers is to help students find a version of academic language that they can respond to and see as a form of personal articulation not possible in a more informal mode. This kind of exercise can be an important step in that direction. We might think of medieval exercises as functioning like modern invention and brainstorming exercises from the opposite point of view: as practice in hyper-articulation that gives students not just access to but control of a new form of expression. Try it.

---

76 The implications of these and similar exercises are discussed in two articles by Woods: "Weeping for Dido"; and "You May Have Changed My Life," Special Issue on Experimental Literary Education, ed. Jeffrey C. Robinson, *English Language Notes* 47.1 (2009): 159–65.

77 For the added advantages of asking students to write their own academic introductions to this exercise, see Woods, "Weeping for Dido," p. 290.

78 Camargo, "Epistolary Declamation."

Appendix A
Composition exercises and examples in Geoffrey of Vinsauf's *Poetria nova*, ca. 1200–1215.

A. Nine ways to begin a story based on the narrative of King Minos (see Initiation exercise above):

1. beginning according to natural order. 2. beginning at the end. 3. a beginning taken from the middle. 4. with a proverb from the beginning. 5. with a proverb from the middle. 6. with a proverb from the end. 7. with an exemplum from the beginning. 8. with an exemplum from the middle. 9. with an exemplum from the end.

B. Amplification: eight ways of expanding a subject (the first three are described in definitions that also exemplify them):

1. Repetition. 2. Circumlocution 3. Comparison 4. Apostrophe: lament for the death of King Richard Lionheart, expressed in a series of apostrophes to England, the day Richard died (Friday), the murderer (he was shot with an arrow that had been fired by one of Richard's own men and retrieved by the enemy from where it had stuck in the wall), Death, Nature, and God. 5. Personification, with examples of *ethopoeia* discussed above. 6. Digression: example of the story of separated lovers (identified as Pyramus and Thisbe in one manuscript) interrupted by digression on springtime as sexual union of masculine air with feminine earth. 7. Description (with examples of a naked woman; a dressed woman; a dressed table, and the feast for which it has been set). 8. A Double Statement: positive and negative versions of saying the same thing.

C. Abbreviation: very abbreviated summary of seven ways to condense a text, illustrated by successively shorter versions of the story of the Snow Child, the shortest ones using nouns almost exclusively:

1. Emphasis 2. Parataxis 3. Ablative absolute 4. Understanding one thing in another (implication) 5. Asyndeton 6. Avoidance of repetition 7. Meaning of many clauses contained in one.

D. Ornamentation in general: how a "rough" expression of a noble sentiment can be made elegant through the "clothing" of verbal ornament, described metaphorically.

E. Difficult Ornament: the Tropes:

1. Nine kinds of Transumption (kinds of metaphoric language), e.g., from the human to the non-human.

2. Six other tropes (957): metonymy (five kinds, e.g., the abstract for the concrete, cause for effect); hyperbole; periphrasis; synecdoche (two kinds: part for the whole and whole for the part); catachresis (deliberate misuse of a word for artistic effect); and hyperbaton (unusual word order).

F. Easy Ornament: patterns of words and thoughts, also called schemes:

1. The "figures in order" using, in a specific word order taken from the *Rhetorica ad Herennium*, <u>thirty-five</u> figures of words in connected discourse on a single subject or narrative (here based on the Bible).

2. The <u>nineteen</u> figures of thought (statements following set patterns of thought or approaches). These rhetorical colors are exemplified in a set piece on the responsibilities of the pope.

G. <u>Six kinds</u> of Emphasis (understatement, hyperbole, ambiguity, consequence, aposiopesis [implication], and analogy) with an example of an anecdote about Alexander the Great) [not in Appendix B].

H. The Theory of Conversion: <u>four</u> ways of altering a word for impact or to avoid repetition, such as using a noun in different cases. One example of converting uninflected words is a little dialogue between a teacher and student on needing more time to compose.

I. The Theory of Determination (qualifying one word by adding another), with examples of a badly set table; a description of Nero at table; a description of a dying body; and a comparison of the styles of Sidonius and Seneca.

[Items J. through P. in the outline of the *Tria sunt* below are not treated in the *Poetria nova*, except for a few lines on the circumstances and on the language suitable for the comic style (Appendix B, J.1. and O.1 below).]

Appendix B

A. <u>Nine ways</u> to begin a story, illustrated in prose and in verse:

1. beginning according to natural order. 2. beginning at the end. 3. a beginning taken from the middle. 4. with a proverb from the beginning. 5. with a proverb from the middle. 6. with a proverb from the end. 7. with an exemplum from the beginning. 8. with an exemplum from the middle. 9. with an exemplum from the end.

A., cont. How to manage a transition to the main narrative from each of the nine ways to begin, illustrated in prose and in verse.

B. Amplification (i): <u>eight ways</u> of expanding a subject matter, most of them copiously illustrated:

1. Interpretation (saying the same thing in different ways): examples from *Poetria nova*, *Complaint of Nature*, and other poems. 2. Circumlocution: examples from *Aeneid*, *Complaint of Nature*, and other poems and prose texts. 3. Comparison: examples from *Complaint of Nature*, *Architrenius*, poem praising the Bishop of Lincoln (also found in Hunterian MS. V.8.14), and the *Libellus de arte dictandi rhetorice* of Peter of Blois. 4. Apostrophe: examples from *Poetria nova*, *Aeneid*, Bernard Silvester's *Parricide*, *Metamorphoses*, and Lawrence of Durham's *Hypognosticon*. 5. Prosopopoeia: examples from *Poetria nova* and *Metamorphoses*.

6. Digression: examples from *Poetria nova*, poem praising Bishop of Lincoln, Horace's *Epistles*, *Thebaid*, Matthew of Vendôme's *Ars versificatoria*, *Complaint of Nature*, *Consolation of Philosophy*, and others. 7. Description: long example (coming of spring) from *Complaint of Nature*, shorter references to other examples. 8. Place of opposites: examples from "Sidonius," *Anticlaudianus*, and others.

B., cont. Amplification (ii): how to expand a very brief subject matter, such as a single word (using a variety of techniques, including the nine ways to begin): illustrated with the examples "I read" (*lego*) and "I teach" (*doceo*).

B., cont. Amplification (iii): letter writing as a special category of amplification that combines techniques like those described in (ii), above, with the *proprietates* or proper characteristics of persons and actions, derived from Horace's *Art of Poetry*: a letter mocking an ignoramus for his pretensions illustrates the artificial style and a letter from the imprisoned Duke Arthur of Brittany begging mercy of his uncle King John of England illustrates plain style.

C. Abbreviation (i): seven ways to condense a text, each method illustrated with short examples from medieval poets and Roman rhetoricians. The story of the Snow Child is then told in a version that illustrates all seven methods, followed by still shorter versions, as in the *PN*.

1. Emphasis. 2. Parataxis. 3. Ablative absolute. 4. Understanding one thing in another. 5. Asyndeton. 6. Avoidance of repetition. 7. Meaning of many clauses contained in one.

C., cont. Abbreviation (ii): condensing the text by focusing on its key nouns: illustrated with two extremely short versions of the Snow Child story.

D. Ornamentation in general: how a "rough" expression of a noble sentiment can be made elegant through the "clothing" of verbal ornament, with examples from *Poetria nova*, *Complaint of Nature*, *Cosmographia*, Matthew of Vendôme's *Ars versificatoria*, and others.

E. Difficult Ornament: produced by the ten types of transumption (*transumptio*) or transference (= the tropes), nine of meaning and one of order; those of meaning include four "weightier" and five "lighter" types; the first four types all involve shifts in animate/inanimate categories:

1. general techniques of transumption: exercises in how to shift a word from its "proper" meaning to a "transfered" meaning, including extensive directions on coining new words, with examples from Gervase of Melkley, Alan of Lille, and Horace.

2. weightier transumption: (a) Onomatopoeia, (b) Antonomasia, (c) Allegory, (d) Metaphor, with examples from *Poetria nova*, Gervase of Melkley, *Rhetorica ad Herennium*, and the *Libellus* of Peter of Blois, among others.

3. lighter transumption: (a) Periphrasis [said to be especially good for teaching boys], (b) Metonymy, (c) Hyperbole, (d) Synecdoche, (e) Catachresis, with many examples from a wide range of classical and medieval sources.

4. transumption of order: Hyperbaton, with subtypes Transposition and Anastrophe, citing *Rhetorica ad Herennium* and Matthew of Vendôme and illustrating with examples of medieval epistolary prose.

5. use of epithets, which can be transumptive or non-transumptive: examples from *Georgics, Alexandreis, Architrenius,* and *Poetria nova.*

E., cont. Adjectives and verbs that are especially useful for producing ornamented discourse, as illustrated in sample sentences: mainly derived from Matthew of Vendôme's *Ars versificatoria.*

F. Easy Ornament: produced by (1) Determination [I. in *PN*] and (2) Colors of words and thoughts:

1. Determination: how to embellish a word by modifying it with one or more additional words: (a) a proper noun with another noun, an adjective, or a verb; (b) an "appellative" noun, i.e., either a substantive or an adjective, with one or more verbs (including the special cases of zeugma and hypozeuxis), with one or more adjectives, with a noun in the genitive, dative, or ablative case, or with a prepositional phrase; (c) an adjective with a noun, an adjective, or a prepositional phrase; (d) a verb with an adverb, a noun or adjective functioning adverbially, or a prepositional phrase; and how to mix determinations of various sorts in elegant combinations; with examples from many sources, including Geoffrey of Vinsauf, with extensive description and illustration of the technique as an exercise.

2. Colors of words and thoughts: (a) thirty-six colors of words[79] defined and illustrated from many sources, including Geoffrey of Vinsauf's *Summa de coloribus rhetoricis,* but especially *Rhetorica ad Herennium;* (b) nineteen colors of thoughts defined and illustrated, also relying heavily on *Rhetorica ad Herennium* but supplemented by other sources, including *Poetria nova.*

[G. Kinds of Emphasis not in *TS*]

H. How to discover ornamented words through Conversion (rewriting sentences by changing a key word):

1. replacing an "indeclinable" word, such as an adverb, with a "declinable" one, either a noun or a verb.

2. converting a declinable word: (a) a substantive noun, into another noun in the same case or into a different case of the same noun; (b) a verb, into another verb or into a substantive noun; (c) an adjective, into a substantive noun; and

---

79 The *Rhetorica ad Herennium* (IV.xx.28) simply observes that the fifteenth figure of words (*similiter cadens*) regularly occurs together with the sixteenth (*similiter desinens*), but *Tria sunt* treats their mixture as a separate figure (*commixtum*). The *PN* appears to follow the *Rhetorica ad Herennium* more closely and therefore distinguishes 35 figures of words rather than the 36 listed in *TS.*

mixing and compounding these various types of conversion to create extended passages of elegant discourse.

[I. in Appendix A treated under F. above]

J. How to develop an original subject matter:

> 1. employ the seven "circumstances": (a) who? (b) what? (c) where? (d) with what means? (e) why? (f) how? (g) when?; citing *Topics* of Boethius, Horace's *Art of Poetry*, *Architrenius*, Gervase of Melkley.

> 2. imitate *auctoritates*, citing Horace's *Art of Poetry*, *Rhetorica ad Herennium*, *Poetria nova*.

K. How to develop a common subject matter using five methods adapted from Horace's *Art of Poetry*:

> 1. abbreviate where the source expands and vice versa

> 2. change the order of the parts

> 3. avoid a pompous, disproportionately long preface

> 4. avoid getting lost in excessive digressions

> 5. do not begin too far from the main point of a narrative (i.e., avoid excessive background detail).

A final counsel: observe the proper characteristics (*proprietates*) of the persons involved (also prescribed by Horace in the *Art of Poetry*).

L. Attributes of persons and actions: information directly relevant to the preceding exercise and to several of the earlier ones; draws on a wide range of sources, including Cicero's *De inventione* and several commentaries on it.

M. Levels and categories of "styles" (high, middle, low; "modern" styles: Tullian, Gregorian, Hilarian, Isidorian): information relevant to the transposing variety of exercise: e.g., rewrite a text in low style as one in high style, or one in Tullian style in Gregorian style.

N. Kinds of discourse and of narrative: also potentially relevant to exercises in transposition, such as one in which a narrative text is rewritten as a dialogue:

> 1. three kinds of discourse: (a) dramatic, in which only characters speak in their own voices; (b) hermeneutic or divided, in which the author speaks in his own voice throughout; and (c) didactic, in which the author engages in dialogue with a character.

> 2. three kinds of narrative (a category of hermeneutic discourse): (a) fable, which is neither factual nor plausible; (b) history, which is factual; and (c) argument, which is not factual but is plausible.

O. How to treat humorous subject matter:

1. use "light" and "common vocabulary"

2. employ the colors *praecisio* (cutting short) and *occupatio* (saying what you claim not to say).

P. Conclusions: created in three ways:

1. from the body of the subject matter, illustrated from Ovid's *Heroides* and a Troy poem

2. from a proverb, illustrated with a proverb that is applied to Troy

3. from an exemplum, illustrated from Horace's *Epistles*.

Also, a conclusion often is created by begging permission, as in the *Eclogues*, *Anticlaudianus, Architrenius,* and *Tristia*.

Finally, conclusions of letters are often indicated by certain transitional words; but a better method is to conclude with a proverb or exemplum, as illustrated in the model letters included in the discussion of letters (see the continuation of B., above).

Appendix C

A. A series of short written assignments for a <u>history of rhetoric class</u>, adapted from handbooks contemporary with the periods being studied. All of the student exercises should be read aloud (or better yet, performed) in class for comment and reaction.

1. Translate two paragraphs of academic prose taken from one of the class readings into dialogue form, either using characters and setting from an assigned Platonic dialogue or creating new ones.

2. Translate two pages of a Platonic dialogue into academic prose, taking as a model two paragraphs from the source used for the first "translation" assignment. Imitate as closely as possible the construction of the sentences, vocabulary, and diction of the academic piece.

3. Write your own defense of Helen of Troy.

4. Rewrite one of the reading assignments as a fable of no more than one page.

5. Summarize in one page or less one of the longer reading assignments. Summarize the same work in one sentence (see Appendices A.C and B.C).

6. Use all 35 figures of words in order from the *Poetria nova* in connected discourse based on a work read in class (see Appendices A.F.1 and B.F.2). A high-serious or comic approach works well, and this assignment also works

well as an exercise in character delineation, as with the first student exercise on Niobe in the Hunterian manuscript (no. 4).

7. Using Erasmus's exercise from *De copia* as a model, write one sentence 75–100 different ways. This works well as a group in-class oral exercise.[80]

8. Using as a model one of the Shakespearean passages brought in by each member of the class, imitate the form, structure, and diction as much as possible while creating an original context and characters.

B. For a class on <u>medieval literature</u> in translation, students write three papers, for each one of which the student has the choice of a modern analytical or a medieval rhetorical (creative) assignment. The three rhetorical assignments are typically the following:

1. Rewrite a passage of two or three pages of one of the assigned works in the style of one of the others (see student exercises nos. 1 and 2 from the Hunterian manuscript).

2. The figures in order exercise; see Appendix C.A.6 above.

3. Amplify in the style of Chrétien de Troyes an incident in one of the highly abbreviated texts of Marie de France; or abbreviate in the style of Marie de France one of the amplified romances by Chrétien de Troyes. This is a modern version of paired student exercises on Henry II [no. 2] and Niobe [no. 4] in the Hunterian manuscript). Or write a short abbreviation of every work read in class (see Appendix C.C.3 below).

C. Suggested assignments for <u>any class</u>; these can be assigned individually or as a sequence for the beginning, middle, and end of the semester:

1. Near the beginning of the course: a one-sentence imitation or amplification based on an assigned text. If possible, have the students read the results aloud in class.

2. Mid-course: a longer exercise in which the students follow the format of a very highly structured and detailed text or part of a text studied in class. We have used and recommend the "figures in order" (see Appendix C.A.6). Any composition with a specific sequence of steps or parts would also work well, such as a university sermon, an academic disputation, a letter of petition, a character delineation using the attributes of persons, etc. More than one of this kind of exercise can be assigned.

3. As a review exercise near the end of the course: an abbreviation, in only a few words, of <u>every</u> work read during the semester, including lyric poems (see

---

80 See the similar but more sophisticated exercise adopted by Lawrence Green from an earlier version of *De copia* (qtd. in Woods, "You May Have Changed My Life," pp. 162–63).

Appendices A.C and B.C). The use of alliteration, rhyme, or another kind of verbal patterning is highly recommended.

Acknowledgments

The authors are grateful to Rebecca Beal, Sandy Camargo, Ian Campbell, Vessela Valiavitcharska, and Jeffrey Walker for suggestions and corrections.

Chapter 5

Reading, Writing, and Rhetoric in the Renaissance

Don Paul Abbott

Key Concepts

Revival of classical rhetoric • English grammar schools • Continental Jesuit colleges • Humanism and rhetoric • Latin language • Erasmus's *De ratione studii* • Ascham's *The Scholemaster* • Vives's *On Education* • Imitation and invention • *Copia* and amplification • Commonplaces • Cicero as model for imitation • Citizen-orator • Union of wisdom and eloquence • Union of poetic and rhetoric • Double translation • Quintilian on pedagogy • Tyranny of the oration • Oratorical organization • "Elementarie" schools • *Progymnasmata* • Suárez's *De arte rhetorica* • *Ratio studiorum* and Jesuit education • *Eloquentia perfecta* • Female voice • Reintegration of rhetoric into contemporary curriculum.

If there is one school subject that seems to have pre-eminently influenced the writers, statesmen and gentlemen of the 16th and 17th century, in their intellectual outfit in afterlife, probably the claim for this leading position may justly be made for Rhetoric and the Oration.

Foster Watson[1]

Rhetoric dominated the education of the Renaissance and indeed of the wider culture beyond the classroom to an extraordinary degree. While rhetoric became a central subject of education almost from its origins in fifth-century Athens, probably at no time before or since was rhetoric as dominant in the curriculum as in the Renaissance. And although rhetoric originated as the art of public speaking, it soon came to exercise authority over the written as well as the spoken word. Thus in the Renaissance distinctions between oratory and poetry, speech and writing, talk and texts, persuasion and representation were rarely rigid. The oration maintained its place as the dominant template for expression; the written word emerged as an important artifact of that expression. The study of writing in the Renaissance is, therefore, inseparable from the study of rhetoric. Because rhetoric, oral and written, dominated the curriculum and pervaded

---

1 Foster Watson, *The English Grammar Schools to 1660: Their Curriculum and Practice.* (1908. reprinted, London: Frank Cass, 1968), 440.

the culture of the Renaissance, this period offers an especially bountiful field for investigating the teaching of writing.

However, because of this curricular and cultural bounty, Renaissance rhetoric is a vast subject that cannot readily be encapsulated in a single chapter. Fortunately, there are ample resources available for readers wishing to explore the intricacies of Renaissance rhetoric.[2] This subject becomes somewhat more manageable by keeping the focus on rhetoric, and writing, as it was taught. Therefore, I have chosen to look primarily at two institutions: the grammar schools of England and the Jesuit colleges of the Continent.

Scrutiny of these institutions offers a number of advantages for an investigation of the teaching of writing in the Renaissance. First, it was in these schools that rhetoric was most often taught. Although rhetoric was also a university subject, philosophy and theology, broadly defined, frequently overshadowed rhetoric in higher education. Second, an examination of the grammar school ensures an emphasis on the pedagogical rather than the theoretical issues. The schoolmasters were intensely interested in how their young students should be taught to write and, fortunately, left considerable testimony as to their methods. Third, a look at these schools maintains an emphasis on the development of the system of writing instruction ultimately inherited by the public and parochial schools of the United States. In particular, by contrasting grammar school and Jesuit college practices with current methods it may be possible to draw some conclusions that are relevant to current instructional needs. However, a focus on institutions alone cannot fully describe cultural practices. This is certainly true of the Renaissance, in which so many were excluded from formal schooling. The exclusion of females from educational institutions was especially egregious and so I will briefly discuss women and the teaching of writing. But first I begin by outlining the nature of the English grammar school.

The English Grammar School

Rhetoric and writing were taught most extensively in the English grammar school. Indeed, this institution was invented in the sixteenth century for that purpose. Although the term "grammar school" was mentioned in England as early as 1387, Dean Colet's founding of St. Paul's School in 1510 marks the real beginning of a new educational movement. The grammar schools were inspired by the ideals of the European humanists and, in the case of St. Paul's, directly

---

2 For a brief overview see my "Renaissance Rhetoric," *Encyclopedia of Rhetoric*, ed. Theresa Enos (New York: Garland, 1996), 594–600. For England see Peter Mack, *Elizabethan Rhetoric: Theory and Practice* (Cambridge: Cambridge University Press, 2002). The scholarship on Renaissance rhetoric is extensive. For a survey of recent research see my chapter "The Renaissance" in *The Present State of Scholarship in the History of Rhetoric: A Twenty-First Century Guide*, ed. Lynée Gaillet (Columbia: University of Missouri Press, 2010), 82–113. The most comprehensive bibliography of rhetorical treatises is Lawrence D. Green and James J. Murphy, *Renaissance Rhetoric Short-Title Catalogue 1460–1700* (Aldershot, UK: Ashgate, 2006). This bibliography "presents 1,717 authors and 3, 842 rhetorical titles in 12,325 printings, published in 310 towns and cities by 3,340 printers and publishers from Finland to Mexico" (xi). A convenient collection of key works is assembled in Brian Vickers, ed., *English Literary Criticism in the Renaissance* (Oxford: Oxford University Press, 1999).

encouraged and assisted by Desiderius Erasmus. These schools were, in a very real sense, an effort to put the educational theories of the Humanists into pedagogical practice. Thus the main aim of the schools was also a major goal of Renaissance humanism: the creation of elegant and eloquent expression. The grammar schools sought to teach the kind of expression known to Cicero, but lost in the Middle Ages. Thus the art of expression was necessarily conceived in the language of classical rhetoric. In the minds of the humanists and in the grammar school classrooms rhetoric and humanism were intertwined.[3]

The term "grammar," therefore, had a more expansive meaning in the sixteenth century than it does for modern readers. In its narrowest sense, grammar meant simply Latin grammar. Knowledge of Latin gave students access both to the classical masters of expression and to the current scholarly and political communication in the international language. The educational goal, therefore, was to provide something far more than a rudimentary acquaintance with a foreign tongue. What grammar really meant to the masters of the grammar schools was what it meant to Quintilian. After a boy has learned to read and write, says Quintilian, he is then turned over to a *grammaticus*, a teacher of literature and language. The concern of this profession, says Quintilian, "may be most briefly considered under two heads, the art of speaking correctly and the interpretation of the poets; but there is more beneath the surface than meets the eye. For the art of writing is combined with that of speaking, and correct reading precedes interpretation, while in each of these cases criticism has its work to perform."[4] Grammar, then, may be best understood as signifying an integrated curriculum of oral and written composition combined with literary criticism.

This literary and Latinate curriculum was advocated by a wide variety of humanists, but it was Erasmus who most directly inspired the English Grammar Schools. In T. W. Baldwin's phrase, Erasmus "laid the egg" of the grammar schools. Baldwin asserts that "anyone who wishes to understand the principles upon which the sixteenth-century grammar school was founded in England would be very unwise to begin anywhere else than with Erasmus."[5] In his small book *De ratione studii* Erasmus proposes a course of study which would become the basis of the grammar schools. Although not published until 1512, earlier versions of *De ratione studii* were circulated, including one which Erasmus sent to Colet for the latter's reaction. Colet responded that he read the "epistle about studies" and told Erasmus that "I not only approve it all, but I truly admire your genius, and art, and learning, and copiousness and eloquence. I have often

---

3 For an excellent survey of the relationship between rhetoric and humanism see John Monfassani, "Humanism and Rhetoric," in *Renaissance Humanism: Foundations, Forms, and Legacy*, ed. Albert Rabil, Jr., Vol. 3, *Humanism and the Disciplines* (Philadelphia: University of Pennsylvania Press, 1988), 171–235. For a discussion of the educational practices of the humanists see Anthony Grafton and Lisa Jardine, *From Humanism to the Humanities* (Cambridge MA: Harvard University Press, 1986). For an excellent overview see Peter Mack, "Humanistic Rhetoric and Dialectic," in *The Cambridge Companion to Renaissance Humanism*, ed. Jill Kraye (Cambridge: Cambridge University Press, 1996), 82–99.

4 Chapter 38, Quintilian, *Institutio oratoria*, trans. H. E. Butler (Cambridge MA: Harvard University Press, 1980), I.IV.2–4.

5 T. W. Baldwin, *William Shakspere's Small Latine and Less Greeke* (Urbana: University of Illinois Press, 1944), I:77.

wished too, that the boys at our school could be taught in the way you explain."[6] In due time the boys at St. Paul's and the other grammar schools would indeed come to be taught in the way Erasmus had explained. The method of study which Erasmus advances is very much dependent on Quintilian, "who has left a very thorough treatment of these matters, so that it would seem the height of impertinence to write about a subject he has already dealt with."[7] So agreeable is Quintilian to humanists like Erasmus that it is reasonably accurate to say that the grammar school curriculum is a combination of Quintilian and Christianity. Quintilian's influence is so strong that the methods outlined by Professor Murphy in Chapter 2, could, with slight revision, serve to describe the education of sixteenth-century England.

Erasmus begins *De ratione studii* by concurring with the ancient position that knowledge is "of two kinds: of things and of words," that is, of ideas, truths, and of language.[8] The knowledge of words comes first, but knowledge of things is ultimately more important. Although Erasmus distinguishes two types of knowledge, the two are interdependent, and "a person who is not skilled in the force of language is, of necessity, short-sighted, deluded, and unbalanced in his judgment of things as well."[9] Knowledge of Latin and Greek is essential in the acquisition of knowledge because humankind's greatest ideas are to be found in these two languages. Thus grammar comes first, but only as a means to an end. Erasmus recommends only enough grammar as is necessary to allow the students to get on with the important tasks of reading, writing, and speaking. As students become increasingly familiar with the classical languages, more complex grammatical matters can be introduced. Erasmus is generally impatient with excessive attention to rules. He wishes Latin to be a truly living language to be used, rather than to be analyzed and systematized. As soon as the basics have been mastered, then, students should begin to read increasingly complex classical and Christian sources. These texts become the objects of imitation; students are expected to imitate both the eloquence of the "words" and the morality of the "things." Thus the educational program of Erasmus is at once both literary and moral. So confident is Erasmus of his approach that he makes this promise: "given youth who are not totally incompetent intellectually, I would with less trouble, and within fewer years, bring them to a credible degree of eloquence in each language than those notorious instructors who force their charges into their own stammering form, or rather lack, of expression."[10]

Precisely how the followers of Erasmus would bring students to "a credible degree of eloquence" can be seen from the records of what was taught in the grammar schools. That curriculum is particularly remarkable because the grammar school was intended to educate boys from about the ages of seven to fifteen. Before attending a grammar school, students would likely have gone to a "petty" or "elementarie" school. Richard Mulcaster, in *The Elementarie* (1582)

6 Cited in Baldwin, I:78.
7 Erasmus, *Collected Works of Erasmus*, ed. Craig R. Thompson, Vol. 24, *Literary and Educational Writings: De copia / De ratione studii*, trans. Betty I. Knott (Toronto: University of Toronto Press, 1978), 672.
8 Ibid., 666.
9 Ibid.
10 Ibid., 691.

says that such a school should consist of five activities: "reading, writing, drawing, singing, & plaing."[11] The first two of these activities were typically the most important. The primary accomplishment of most petty schools was probably the teaching of the alphabet and basic vernacular literacy. The grammar school thus served a kind of middle school between the "elementarie" and the university. Yet the grammar school was, in many ways, the heart and soul of English education: students attended it longer than any other stage of education and in the sixteenth century, at least, the grammar school was at the forefront of educational innovation.

The humanistic curriculum of the grammar schools was predicated upon the recommendation of Erasmus that students be given a grammatical introduction followed by increasingly complex reading and writing accompanied by additional grammar when necessary. The schools were divided into five to eight classes or "**forms**." These forms were in turn divided into two broad groupings according to the instructor. The lower forms usually presented the rudiments of Latin grammar and were taught by an "usher." Beginning typically with the third form a more accomplished teacher, the "master," took over to teach advanced Latin grammar, Greek grammar, and, especially, rhetoric. The following specimen of a late sixteenth-century grammar school timetable illustrates the thoroughness and complexity of the teaching methods in the advanced forms. The numbers in parentheses indicate the days of the week each subject was taught (2=Monday and so on).

MASTER'S FORMS
Third Form
7–11 A.M.
Lecture on the Letters of Ascham, or Sturm's Cicero's Letters, or Terence. Paraphrase of a sentence (2).
Lecture on Ascham, etc., as on Monday. Vulgaria in prose (3).
Lecture on Palingenius, or the Psalms of Hess. Paraphrase of a sentence (4).
Lecture on Palingenius, or the Psalms of Hess (5).
Vulgaria in prose, and repetition of the week's lectures (6).
Examination in lecture of the previous afternoon (7).

1–5 P.M.
Latin syntax, or Greek grammar, or the figures of Sysenbrote [Susenbrotus].
Home lessons given out and prepared (2; 3; 4).
Half Holiday (5).
Repetition of the week's work continued. Lectures on Erasmus's Apothegms (6).
Catechism and New Testament (7).

Fourth Form
7–11 A.M.
Lecture on Cicero de Senectute, or de Amicitia, or on Justin (2; 3).

11 Mulcaster's *Elementarie*, ed. E. T. Campagnac (Oxford: Clarendon Press, 1925), 59.

Lecture on Ovid's Tristia, or de Ponto, or Seneca's Tragedies (4; 5).
Verse Theme, and repetition of the week's lectures (6).
Examination on the lecture of the previous afternoon (7).

1–5 P.M.
Prose Theme (2; 4).
Latin Syntax, or Greek Grammar, or Figures of Susenbrotus. Home lessons and exercises given out and prepared (2; 3; 4).
Half Holiday (5).
Repetition of the week's lectures continued, and lecture on Ovid's Fausti (7).
Catechism and New Testament (7).

Fifth Form
7–11 A.M.
Prose Theme (2; 4).
Lecture in Cicero or Sallust or Caesar's Commentaries (2; 3).
Verse Theme (3; 6).
Lecture in Virgil or Ovid's Metamorphosis, or Lucan (4; 5).
Repetition of the week's lectures (6).
Examination of the lecture of the previous afternoon (7).

1–5 P.M.
Latin Syntax, or Greek Grammar, or Figures of Susenbrotus. Home lessons and exercises given out and prepared (2; 3; 4).
Half Holiday (5).
Repetition of the week's lectures continued, and lecture on Horace, or Lucan, or Seneca's Tragedies (6).
Declamation on a given subject by several senior scholars. Catechism and New Testament (7).[12]

This timetable presents a reasonably complete view of what an English grammar school student would have been expected to endure. While there was some variation in texts and assignments, the pattern of teaching was remarkably constant throughout England. Students at St. Paul's, Eton, Winchester, Rotherham, and the other grammar schools could expect to engage in much the same grammar, reading, lectures, examinations, themes, and declamations. What the timetable does not fully reveal are the exact methods used to teach the attainment of elegant expression in Latin. Teaching methods, however, were remarkably consistent from school to school.

With this brief sketch of the English grammar school curriculum we are now in a position to look more closely at the nature of writing instruction in sixteenth-century England. A closer look at the master's forms will make clear certain critical features of the grammar school approach to writing. Perhaps the most fundamental aspect of the grammar school curriculum was that it was in its

12 Appendix P, A. Monroe Stowe, *English Grammar Schools in the Reign of Queen Elizabeth* (New York: Teachers College, Columbia University, 1908), 185–188.

entirety a linguistic and literary curriculum. The original and fundamental purpose of the institution was to make the students eloquent in Latin. This intent is clearly revealed in the complete title of Roger Ascham's educational treatise of 1570: *The Scholemaster, Or plaine and perfit way of teachyng children, to understand, write, and speake, the Latin tong, but specially purposed for the private brynging up of youth in Jentlemen and Noble mens houses, and commodious also for all such, as have forgot the Latin tonge, and would, by themselves, without a scholemaster, in short tyme, and with small paines, recover a sufficient habilitie, to understand, write, and speake Latin.*[13]

In order to ensure that children would indeed understand, write, and speak the Latin tongue, grammar school statutes commonly required both masters and scholars to speak Latin at all times while on school premises. The instruction in Latin was to be so complete and unremitting that the ancient language could not help but become as familiar as the vernacular. Thus Charles Hoole, in *A New Discovery of the Old Art of Teaching Schoole* (1660), would have his scholars in the fifth form translate an oration or a passage from Sallust, Livy, or Tacitus every day and then recite these efforts in Latin and English each week. In the sixth form Hoole requires that the students "continue to make *themes* and *verses*, one week in Greek and another in Latine; and ever and anon they may contend in making Orations & Declamations."[14]

This intensive instruction in Latin was not designed to teach the vernacular, but of course a second language can only be taught by employing the native tongue of the students. Consequently, the grammar schools also taught composition in English. The process of translating from English to Latin and back into English began early and continued throughout the forms. Juan Luis Vives, who, like his mentor Erasmus, exercised considerable influence on English education, recommends that "as soon as they have learned syntax, let the pupils translate from the mother-tongue into Latin, and then back again into the mother-tongue."[15] Ascham enthusiastically endorses this "double translation" as far superior to a single translation from one language to another. Invoking the authority of Pliny the Younger, Ascham claims that "this exercise of double translating is learned easily, sensiblie, by litle and litle, not onlie all the hard congruities of Grammar, the choice of aptest wordes, the right framing of wordes and sentences, cumlines of figures and formes, fite for everie matter and proper for everie tong." The result of these exercises is that "your scholar shall be brought not only to like eloquence, but also to all trewe understanding and right judgement, both for writing and speaking.[16]

13 Roger Ascham, *The Scholemaster*, ed. John E. B. Mayor (London: Bell and Daldy, 1863; reprinted, New York: AMS Press, 1967).

14 Charles Hoole, *A New Discovery of the Old Art of Teaching Schoole, English Linguistics 1500–1800*, ed. R. C. Alston, no. 133 (Menston, UK: Scolar Press, 1969), 173, 200.

15 Juan Luis Vives, *On Education [De tradendis disciplinis]*, ed. and trans. Foster Watson (1913; reprinted, Totowa NJ: Rowman and Littlefield, 1971), 114. Although born in Spain in 1493, Vives spent most of his adult life in the Low Countries and England where, for a time, he lectured in Greek, Latin, and rhetoric at Cardinal College, Oxford. Vives died in Bruges in 1540. For an account of Vives's consti- tutions to Renaissance rhetoric see my "Juan Luis Vives: Tradition and Innovation in Renaissance Rhetoric," *Central States Speech Journal*, 37 (1986), 193–203.

16 Ascham, *The Scholemaster*, 103–104.

For these reasons, says Ascham, "I am moved to think this way of double translating, either onlie or chiefly, to be the fittest for the spedy and perfit atteyning of any tong."[17] The act of translating from English to Latin and back again, all the while attending to the principles of rhetoric, could not help but perfect the student's ability to compose in English. Moreover, the vernacular made steady inroads into the province of rhetoric in the late sixteenth and seventeenth centuries. Many vernacular textbooks' authors simply adapted, with little alteration, the methods of teaching Latin composition and applied them to English.[18] The program of the grammar school might best be thought of, then, as a kind of bilingual education. Latin was the primary language, but English was never far behind.

So complete was the domination of rhetoric and Latin in this curriculum that there was simply very little room for anything else. For example, what science was taught was often subservient to literary demands. In *De ratione studii* Erasmus recommends wide knowledge in order to facilitate the literary explication of ancient poets and other writers. Astronomy, says Erasmus, is useful because "the poets liberally sprinkle their creations with it." In short, he concludes, "there is no branch of knowledge, whether military, agricultural, musical, or architectural which is not useful for those who have undertaken an exposition of the ancient poets or orators."[19] For Erasmus and his followers in the grammar schools, non-literary knowledge was useful primarily for its ability to assist in the development of eloquence.

Language occupied this preferred position in the grammar school curriculum because it is a defining characteristic of the human being. Vives says: "The first thing man has to learn is speech. It flows at once from the rational soul as water from a fountain. As all beasts are bereft of intellect, so are they also lacking in speech. Discourse is also the instrument of human society, for not otherwise could the mind be revealed, so shut in is it by the grossness and density of the human body. Like as we have the mind by the gift of God, so we have this or that language, by the gift of art."[20] Vives continues by noting that "language is the shrine of erudition, and as it were a storeroom for what should be concealed, and what should be made public. Since it is the treasury of culture and the instrument of human society, it would therefore be to the benefit of the human race that there should be a single language, which all nations should use in common."[21] Latin was, of course, just such a "single language" and as such well deserved its singular place in the schools. Latin made possible, for the Europeans and the English, at least, an international exchange of ideas, commerce, and diplomacy. While suited to the needs of the present, Latin, without any native speakers, inevitably also kept its users cognizant of the past. Its users were especially cognizant of the literature of the Romans and were well aware that the oration was the literary form that dominated Rome. So it was in the grammar school classroom.

---

17 Ibid., 104.
18 David Thomson demonstrates that late medieval grammar masters in England simply translated the Latin grammars of Priscian and Donatus into English. See *A Descriptive Catalogue of Middle English Grammatical Texts* (New York: Garland, 1979), esp. 1–49.
19 Ibid., 674–675.
20 Vives, *On Education*, 90.
21 Ibid., 91.

Oratorical Form and the Written Text

The technological advances of the Renaissance made the teaching of writing more possible and practical than ever before. The printing press arrived in England in 1477 and paper production began in the first years of the sixteenth century. The use of books—textbooks for students to read and **copy books** in which to write—made the act of writing far more central to the educational endeavor. Thus John Brinsley in *Ludus Literarius: or, The Grammar Schoole* (1612) devotes an early chapter to a discussion of how the act of writing might be accomplished. Students should write at least an hour every day and to do that they must have "all the necessaries belonging thereunto; as penne, inke, paper, rular, plummet, ruling-pen, pen-knife, &c"[22] Students must know how to make their own pens because "when they are away from their Masters (if they have not a good pen made before) they wil write naught; because they know not how to make their pens themselves.[23] Brinsley then presents an equally detailed account of how a pen is to be made, from the selection of the quill to the cutting of the nib. The remainder of the chapter involves instructions for holding the pen and for perfecting the techniques of writing. All of this detail is, in part, necessary because of the relative newness of writing with pen and ink in the classroom. Yet despite the obvious importance and practicality of writing in the grammar school, treatises present writing primarily as a physical activity (orthographia), while the mental activities continue to be expressed in oral terms. That is, the conceptual and expressive functions of composition continue to be expressed in the terminology of classical oratory. Despite the rapid advances in printing, the oration remained fixed as the supreme form of discourse, just as it had been for the Romans. In the opinion of Walter Ong, the oration "tyrannized over ideas of what expression as such—literary or other—was."[24]

This oratorical "tyranny" is certainly apparent in the four principal composition exercises of the grammar school: letter-writing, verse-making, the **theme**, and the oration. The oration is invariably the final, and hence presumably the most difficult to accomplish, of these various assignments. Practically speaking, however, the three exercises which preceded the oration followed much the same rules of composition. This is especially true of the disposition or organization of discourse. In *The Arte of Rhetorique* Thomas Wilson recommends one pattern for virtually all composition:

> *There Are Seven Parts in Every Oration*
> 1. The entrance or beginning
> 2. The narration
> 3. The proposition
> 4. The division or several parting of things
> 5. The confirmation

22 John Brinsley, *Ludus Literarius, English Linguistics 1500–1800*, no. 62 (Menston, UK: Scolar Press, 1968), 29.
23 Ibid.
24 Walter Ong, "Tudor Writings on Rhetoric, Poetic, and Literary Theory," in *Rhetoric, Romance, and Technology: Studies in the Interaction of Expression and Culture* (Ithaca: Cornell University Press, 1971), 53.

6. The confutation
7. The conclusion[25]

Wilson, of course, had adapted this structure from his classical predecessors although they typically had recommended six parts (Wilson adds the proposition as a separate section). While the exact number of parts varies slightly, this pattern is recommended by most authorities as the template for all forms of written composition. Thus in *The English Secretorie. Wherein is Contayned, a Perfect Method, for the inditing of all manner of Epistles and familiar letters* . . . (1586) Angel Day indicates that letter-writing may be divided into three parts: invention, disposition, and elocution. Of the five parts of classical rhetoric, Day omits only memory and delivery, the two most fully oral parts of the ancient division.[26] Likewise, Day also directs that the letter be organized precisely as a classical oration: *exordium, narratio, propositio, confirmatio, confutatio,* and *peroratio.*[27] Indeed, any kind of discourse could be, and should be, organized in just this way. Citing Aphthonius, Brinsley says that he gives his students "a Theame to make, following the example in their booke, to prosecute the same parts of the Theame; as Exordium, narratio, confirmatio, confutatio, conclusio."[28] It is no exaggeration to say that the rules of the classical oration were applied to every kind of discourse.

The oratorical domination of poetry is perhaps most surprising today, but it is simply another example of how completely ancient rhetoric governed all expression. There is no very clear demarcation between rhetoric and poetry in the Renaissance and the language of rhetoric is always deemed the appropriate idiom for the analysis of the poetry.[29] Thus Abraham Fraunce's *Arcadian Rhetorike* (1588), is, as the title suggests, a rhetoric which uses Sir Philip Sidney's pastoral romance, as well as the poetry of Boscán, Garcilaso, Tasso, and other vernacular poets as a source of rhetorical precepts. Similarly, John Hoskyns' *Directions for Speech and Style* (ca .1599) employs the *Arcadia* as his principal source for illustrating the figures of speech. Sidney himself, in his *Defence of Poesie*, defines poetry as "an art of imitation . . . a representing, counterfitting, or figuring forth—to speak metaphorically, a speaking picture—with this end, to teach and delight."[30] A few pages later Sidney says that poets "imitate, both to delight and teach; and delight, to move men . . ."[31] Thus Sidney justifies poetry because it seeks the same ends as rhetoric: it is both an art of imitation and an art of persuasion. It is not surprising, then, that Sidney composed his *Defence of Poesie* (1595) in the form of a persuasive oration.[32]

---

25 Thomas Wilson, in Vickers, ed., *English Renaissance Literary Criticism*, 81.
26 Angel Day, *English Secretorie, English Linguistics 1500–1800*, no. 29 (Menston, UK: Scolar Press, 1967), 19–20.
27 Ibid., 22.
28 Brinsley, *Ludus Literarius*, 172–173.
29 For a complete treatment of this relationship see Bryan Vickers, *Classical Rhetoric in English Poetry* (London: Macmillan, 1970; reprinted, Carbondale: Southern Illinois University Press, 1989).
30 In Vickers, ed., *English Renaissance Literary Criticism*, 345.
31 Ibid., 346.
32 See K. O. Myrick, *Sir Philip Sidney as a Literary Craftsman* (Cambridge MA: Harvard University Press, 1935), especially 46–83. In the text of the *Defence* in *English Renaissance Literary Criticism* Vickers has marked the oratorical divisions (336–391).

This union of rhetoric and poetic and all other genres was possible, indeed even essential, because all discourse shared the same end: to speak eloquently and to speak persuasively. The civic and forensic origins of rhetoric are almost always present in Renaissance literature. That is, literature, like rhetoric itself, is always argumentative and persuasive, never neutral.[33] There is no conception of a use for language that is merely expository, or merely descriptive, or merely narrative. Such functions existed only insofar as each promoted the ultimate end of persuasion. Nowhere is this more apparent than in the work of John Milton. D. L. Clark has demonstrated that Milton, while a student at St. Paul's School in London, had learned his lessons well. Milton's famous essay on freedom of the press was modeled after an Isocratean oration and is entitled "Areopagitica; A Speech of Mr. John Milton For The Liberty Of Unlicensed Printing. To The Parliament Of England."[34] Similarly, "Paradise Lost" is "An Oration to Justify The Ways of God to Men."

Imitation and Invention

The Areopagitica demonstrates the appeal of classical models to even a creative genius like Milton. "That Milton should aspire to such literary and oratorical ideals as moved the orators and poets of antiquity is natural enough," says Clark, "for he had an early education very like their own."[35] In basing his essay on a classical pattern Milton was simply doing what he had been taught to do. If there is one constant in Renaissance education it is a belief in the necessity, indeed, the inevitability of imitatio as the principal method of learning. Imitation is made necessary by the human condition. Says Vives: "Although it is natural to talk, yet all discourse whatsoever belongs to an 'art' which was not bestowed upon us at birth, since nature has fashioned man, for the most part, strangely hostile to 'art.' Since she lets us be born ignorant and absolutely skilless of all arts, we require imitation. Imitation, furthermore, is the fashioning of a certain thing in accordance with a proposed model."[36] Human expression, in particular, requires imitation to perfect. According to Ascham, "all languages, both learned and mother tonges, be gotten onlie by Imitation. For as ye used to heare, so ye learne to speake . . . And therefore, if ye would speake as the best and the wisest do, ye must be conversant, where the best and the wisest are."[37] The best and the wisest are to be found, more often than not, in classical literature: "in the Greek and Latin tong, the two onlie learned tonges, which be not kept in common taulke, but in private bookes, we finde alwayes wisdom and eloquence, good matter and good utterance, never or seldom a sonder."[38]

The belief in a literary education which favors imitation over rules naturally requires great authors to imitate. But which great authors? The answer,

---

33 See Ong, "Tudor Writings," 65.
34 Donald Lemen Clark, John Milton at St. Paul's School: A Study of Ancient Rhetoric in English Renaissance Education (New York: Columbia University Press, 1948). See also Wilbur E. Gilman, Milton's Rhetoric: Studies in His Defense of Liberty, University of Missouri Studies 14 (1939), 12–13.
35 Clark, John Milton at St. Paul's School, 3.
36 Vives, On Education, 189.
37 Ascham, Scholemaster, 134.
38 Ibid., 136.

invariably, was the best writers from the best periods. That, in turn, almost always meant Cicero. There was considerable debate about whether or not Cicero was the only model for imitation, but there was little disagreement that he should be, at the very least, one of the models.[39] Says Vives: "There are those who, out of all authors, select only Cicero, whom alone they imitate. Cicero is indeed the best, though he does not contain every merit. Nor is he the only author with good style. When he delights and teaches us he is admirable beyond the rest." The conclusion, says Vives, is that "if Cicero is the best and most eminent stylist, others are not, on that account, bad or contemptible."[40] In other words, Cicero is first among the ancients, but only one of a number of worthy models. Among many others, Vives himself suggests, "for an intellectual and learned circle, the speeches of Demosthenes are suited. So, too, are those to be found in Livy, in whose histories orations are interwoven. For sweetness and rhythm we have Isocrates. Plato has a still higher flight."[41] Each Renaissance educator has a favorite list of authors, but all agree on the need to imitate the greats of antiquity.

Vives suggests how this process of imitation should proceed: "the zealous imitator will study, with the greatest attention, the model he has set up for himself, and will consider by what art, by what method, such and such was achieved by the author, in order that he himself with a similar artifice may accomplish his own intention in his own work."[42] With the assistance of the master, then, the student should first analyze the appropriate model to determine the method of composition and then gradually attempt to apply these methods in their own writing. Naturally, a child needs considerable assistance in analyzing models and generating sophisticated prose and verse. The grammar school sought to facilitate this process by engaging the students in a series of increasingly complicated imitative exercises. Ascham discusses five such exercises. Although the fifth is explicitly called "imitation," all five are predicated on the emulation of models. The five are: 1) translation, especially double translation; 2) paraphrase, "not onlie to expresse at large with more wordes, but to strive and contend (as Quintilian saith) to translate the best latin authors into other latin wordes";[43] 3) metaphrase, the translation of prose into verse and verse into prose; 4) epitome, the distillation of classical works into their essences. This is an exercise Ascham much "mislikes" for it emphasizes only matter and disregards expression and it can cause students to lose sight of the original model. Finally, after much translation, paraphrase, metaphrase, and perhaps epitome, the student is ready for 5) imitation proper: the careful scrutiny and creative emulation of an approved model.

---

39 In the *Ciceronianus* Erasmus rejects the imitation of Cicero to the exclusion of all other models. See *The Ciceronian: A Dialogue on the Ideal Latin Style*, trans. Betty Knott, Vol. 28, *Collected Works of Erasmus*. For an account of the debates about Ciceronianism, see Izora Scott, *Controversies over the Imitation of Cicero as a Model for Style and Some Phases of their Influence on the Schools of the Renaissance* (New York: Teachers College, 1910). For a thorough discussion of Cicero's place in the schools of the Renaissance see Joseph S. Freedman, "Cicero in Sixteenth- and Seventeenth-Century Rhetoric Instruction," *Rhetorica*, 4 (1986), 227–254.

40 Vives, *On Education*, 191–192.

41 Ibid., 194.

42 Ibid., 195.

43 Ascham, *Scholemaster*, 106.

This emphasis on imitation inevitably required sufficient material to imitate. And that material could only come from the student's careful reading of approved texts. Erasmus recommends that students follow this procedure as they read:

> Review immediately a reading you have heard in such a way that you fix the general meaning a little more deeply in your mind. Then, go back over it, starting at the end and working back to the beginning, examining individual words and observing only points of grammar in the process . . . After doing this, run through the passage completely again with particular attention to points of rhetorical technique. If any phrasing seems to have special charm, elegance, or neatness, mark it with a sign or asterisk . . . if there is some saying, maxim, old proverb, anecdote, story, apt comparison, or anything that strikes you as being phrased with brevity, point, or in some other clever way, consider it a treasure to be stored carefully in the mind for use in imitation. When you have attended to those things carefully, do not be reluctant to go over the passage a fourth time . . . . Seeking out what seems to relate to philosophy, especially ethics, to discover any example that might be applicable to morals . . . .[44]

This four-part procedure of reading generally, grammatically, rhetorically, and morally foreshadows the "close reading" of the New Critics. But whereas close reading enables textual explication, Erasmian reading facilitates the students' invention and composition.

Students were expected not only to absorb the content of their reading, but to extract exceptional elements and then record these in their own collections of commonplaces. After recommending a number of authors which students might profitably read, Hoole next advises: "let every one take one of those books forementioned, and see what he can finde in it for his purpose, and write it down under one of those heads in his Commonplace book."[45] The students should then "all read what they have written, before the Master, and every one transcribe what others have collected, into his own book; and thus they may alwayes have store of matter for invention ready at hand, which is far beyond what their own wit is able to conceive."[46] These student **commonplace books** functioned in concert with the various published collections to insure that the students would have a sufficient storehouse of material for the process of writing. Thus, says Ann Moss, these commonplace books were "the principle support system of humanist pedagogy. Pupils were required to make themselves commonplace-books, and to collect excerpts from their reading under appropriate heads. When they came to construct compositions of their own, they were encouraged to use their commonplace-books as a resource, culling from them quotations, examples, and other illustrative material."[47]

---

44 *De Conscribendi Epistolis*, trans. and annotated by Charles Fantazzi, Vol. 25, *Collected Works of Erasmus* (1985), 194–195.
45 Hoole, *New Discovery*, 183.
46 Ibid.
47 Ann Moss, *Printed Commonplace-Books and the Structuring of Renaissance Thought* (Oxford: Clarendon Press, 1996), v.

While students were expected to compile their own commonplace books, there were also innumerable printed books which serve as guides for composition. These collections, compendia, and anthologies of adages, apothegms, commonplaces, and figures all provide handy sources of the wisdom of the ancients. For example, Erasmus's *Adagia* began as a collection of 818 proverbs and ultimately grew to include 4,151 adages. These proverbs, which Erasmus culled from classical sources, contributed, he says, four things to discourse: "philosophy, grace and charm in speaking, and the understanding of the best authors."[48] Thus the proverbs contained in this collection should be studied for their merits and then applied where appropriate in a composition. A similar work is Robert Cawdrey, *A Treasvrie or Storehouse of Similes: Both pleasaunt, delightfull, and profitable, for all estates of men in general. Newly collected into Heades and Common places* (1600). Cawdrey's 858-page book contains similes arranged alphabetically from "Accusation" to "Zeale." Much like the apothegms of Erasmus, these similes serve as a ready source of philosophically sound illustrative material for composition. The term "commonplace" in the title is indicative of Cawdrey's purpose. As Joan Lechner explains, the commonplace, in this sense, may be thought of as "as a little oration or as a 'speech within a speech.'"[49] These "little speeches which were regularly inserted in longer orations for purposes of amplification, exposition, persuasion, and description were thought of as 'commonplaces' because they provided ready-made 'arguments' which in some way magnified (or minimized) a subject."[50] These collections of commonplaces, figures, proverbs and all the rest served as a source of approved material which could be inserted directly or altered to fit individual needs.

In addition to these collections of "little speeches" and other relatively short devices, students could also make use of collections of more complete discourses. Angel Day's *English Secretorie*, for example, is comprised of "sundry examples of euery Epistle." Day includes at least one example of deliberative, confirmatory, laudatory, hortatory, dehortatory, suasory, disuasory, and all the other genres of letters that he identifies. Another work which provides complete examples of discourse is Richard Rainolde's *A Booke called the Foundacion of Rhetorike* (1563). *The Foundacion of Rhetorike* is an English adaptation of Reinhard Lorich's Latin version of Aphthonius's *Progymnasmata*.[51] The *Progymnasmata*, or a set of introductory exercises, is comprised of fourteen progressively more difficult compositional models from simple fables to complex questions of law. Rainolde readily acknowledges his debt to his ancient source:

> Aphthonivs a famous man, wrote in greke of soche declamacions, to enstructe the studentes thereof, with all facilitie to grounde in them, a most plentious and rich vein of eloquence. No man is able to inuente a more

48 Erasmus, *Adages*, trans. Margaret Mann Phillips, Vol. 31, *Collected Works of Erasmus*, 14.
49 Sister Joan Marie Lechner, O.S.U., *Renaissance Concepts of the Commonplaces* (New York: Pageant Press, 1962, reprinted, Westport CT: Greenwood Press, 1974), 3.
50 Ibid.
51 Richard Rainolde, *The Foundation of Rhetoric, English Linguistics*, no. 347 (Menston, UK: Scolar Press, 1972). Aphthonius's *Progymnasmata* was widely printed in the Renaissance and Lorich's version, with twenty-eight editions in the sixteenth and seventeenth centuries, was especially popular. See James J. Murphy, *Renaissance Rhetoric: A Short Title Catalogue* (New York: Garland Publishing, 1981), 22.

profitable waie and order, to instructe any one in the exquisite and absolute perfection, of wisedome and eloquence, then Aphthonius Quintilianus and Hermogenes.[52]

Thus Rainolde expresses both his conviction in the efficacy of imitation and his faith in the ancients whom he is himself imitating. In his enthusiasm for Aphthonius Rainolde is by no means alone; Aphthonius is one of the most widely accepted authorities for writing instruction. Brinsley, for example, bases his instructions for the teaching of themes on Aphthonius.[53]

Works like those of Rainolde and Day, together with the various printed "storehouses" of epitomes, adages, and figures, and the students' own personal commonplace books presumably provided the boys with all the resources necessary for composition. Thus when grammar school students were finally faced with actually writing a theme they were at least theoretically well stocked with material which would make the process relatively easy. In actual fact, of course, the process could be painful. In his dialogue *Ludus Literarius* one of Brinsley's characters admits that the themes which "my children have done hereby for a long time, they have done it with exceeding paines and feare, in harsh phrase, without any inuention, or iudgement; and ordinarily so rudely, as I have been ashamed that anyone should see their exercises. So as it hath driuen mee into exceeding passions, causing me to deale ouer rigorously with the poore boies."[54] Indeed, the grammar school curriculum appears extremely rigorous by any standard, and it is easy to imagine that many of those who experienced it were less than enthusiastic in their studies. Despite the frustrations of the Masters and the recalcitrance of the boys, the grammar schools certainly provided their charges with the opportunity to develop the ability to write comprehensively on virtually any subject.

Grammar school students were rather young, and they were never really expected to write discourses which would exceed the models they were constantly reading. Nevertheless, students in the later forms were expected ultimately to write themes that, while in the spirit of their models, were not simply slavish reproductions of them. Thus Hoole recommends that the master should not tie the students "to the words of any Authour, but giving them liberty to contract, or enlarge, or alter them as they please; so that they still contend to go beyond them in purity of expression."[55] Ultimately, says Hoole, once the master determines that "they have gained a perfect way of making Themes of themselves, you may let them go on to attain the habit by their own constant practice."[56]

The "perfect way of making themes" was naturally dependent on the accumulation of material for imitation. The actual assembly of this previously gathered material was governed by the process of *amplificatio*—the achievement of copiousness or "copie." Amplification was, in effect, the active implementation of

---

52 Rainolde, "To the Reader", *The Foundation of Rhetoric.*
53 See *Ludus Literarius*, 172–190.
54 Brinsley, *Ludus Literarius*, 173.
55 Hoole, *New Discovery*, 185.
56 Ibid., 186.

imitation. As such, the process combined the classical divisions of invention, style, and arrangement. Although the sixteenth-century educational reformer Peter Ramus had attempted to make invention the sole property of logic, this re-arrangement did little to banish invention from the grammar school where invention and style combined in the process of amplification.[57] Brinsley and Hoole could, therefore, recommend Ramistic texts and still discuss invention without any sense of anomaly. Brinsley advises that students should "trie what reasons they can inuent of themselves according to the chiefe heads of Inuention" such as causes, effects, subjects, and adjuncts.[58] Later he admits that this approach may be too hard for children "who haue read on Logicke," but he nevertheless continues to advocate the use of these topics.

It is in the work of Erasmus, however, that the union of invention and elocution within the rubric of amplification is most apparent. Ascham calls Erasmus "the ornament of learning in our tyme"[59] and this veneration in large part is due to Erasmus's *De duplici copia verborum et rerum*. *De copia* may be thought of as the first grammar school textbook; in fact Erasmus wrote it for that purpose. In a letter to Dean Colet, the founder of St. Paul's School, he says:

> I thought it would be appropriate for me to make a small literary contribution to the equipment of your school. So I have chosen to dedicate to the new school these two new commentaries *De copia*, inasmuch as the work in question is suitable for boys to read and also, unless I am mistaken, not unlikely to prove helpful to them, though I leave it to others to judge how well-informed this work of mine is, or how serviceable it will be.[60]

De copia was judged very serviceable as a textbook upon its first publication in 1511. Indeed, "so widespread did its use become that it was worth pirating, summarizing, excerpting, turning into a question-and-answer manual, and making the subject of commentaries."[61] The frequency with which *De copia* was reprinted "testifies to the significance of the work and to its influence during the first three-quarters of the sixteenth century in both arousing and ministering to a particular stylistic ideal."[62]

That stylistic ideal is captured in the Latin word *copia*, which is rendered as "abundance" in the standard English translation of the work.[63] But as Donald B. King explains, there is no entirely suitable English word: "as used by Erasmus, *copia* encompasses within its meaning the meaning of four English words: variation, abundance or richness, eloquence, and the ability to vary and enrich

---

57 The standard account of "Ramism" is Walter Ong, S.J,. *Ramus, Method, and the Decay of Dialogue* (Cambridge MA: Harvard University Press, 1958). For the first modern English translation of a work by Ramus see *Arguments in Rhetoric Against Quintilian: Translation and Text of Peter Ramus's Rhetoricae Distinctiones in Quintilianum (1549)*, trans. Carole Newlands, with an introduction by James J. Murphy (DeKalb: Northern Illinois University Press, 1986).

58 Brinsley, *Ludus Literarius*, 180.

59 Ascham, *Scholemaster*, 140.

60 *Collected Works of Erasmus*, 24:285.

61 Translator's Introduction, ibid., 283.

62 Ibid.

63 *Copia: Foundations of Abundant Style, Collected Works of Erasmus*, Vol. 24.

language and thought."[64] Erasmus believes that the development of *copia* is necessary because "exercise in expressing oneself in different ways will be of considerable importance in general for the acquisition of style."[65] More particularly, "variety is so powerful in every sphere that there is absolutely nothing, however brilliant, which is not dimmed if not commended by variety. Nature above all delights in variety; in all this huge concourse of things, she has left nothing anywhere unpainted by her wonderful technique of variety."[66] Practically speaking, "this form of exercise will make no insignificant contribution to the ability to speak or write extempore, and will prevent us from standing there stammering and dumbfounded."[67] Ultimately, says Erasmus, "if we are not instructed in these techniques, we shall often be found unintelligible, harsh, or even totally unable to express ourselves."[68] *Copia*, then, is the very foundation of style.

After these introductory remarks Erasmus says that he will now "give some brief advice on the exercises by which this faculty may be developed."[69] The next three hundred or so pages are devoted to this "brief advice" on achieving copiousness in both words and ideas. For the most part, variety in words is achieved by the use of figures and tropes, variety in ideas by the rhetorical topics. There is, however, very little discussion of the theory of figurative or topical language in *De copia*. Rather, the emphasis in Erasmus's book, as in the grammar school classroom, is on practical application in discourse. This approach culminates in a "practical demonstration" of abundance in Chapter 33 of *De copia*. Erasmus promises to "take one or two sentences and see how far we can go in transforming the basic expression into a Protean variety of shapes."[70] As it turns out, Erasmus can go so far as to produce 195 variations on the sentence "your letter pleased me mightily."[71] This demonstration is followed by 200 variations on "always, as long as I live, I shall remember you."[72] In this virtuoso performance Erasmus is being intentionally extreme. He deliberately takes a "not particularly fertile" sentence and creates some 200 variants to show his readers the infinite fecundity of human language. Erasmus does not recommend going quite this far in the classroom; it is rather a dramatic testimony to the plasticity of language to those who might not believe it.

There is nothing terribly original about Erasmus's *De copia*. The work is based on broad reading in the classics, knowledge of rhetorical theory, and great practice in composition. In short, Erasmus's work is the result of an education much like that he had in mind for young boys. *De copia*, and the grammar school curriculum, were together a celebration of the centrality of language in human affairs. When a student left the grammar school, he might not be able to generate

---

64 Erasmus, *On Copia of Words and Ideas,* trans. Donald B. King and H. David Rix (Milwaukee: Marquette University Press, 1963), "Note to the Reader," 9.
65 *Collected Works of Erasmus*, 24:302.
66 Ibid.
67 Ibid.
68 Ibid.
69 Ibid., 303.
70 Ibid., 348.
71 Ibid., 348–354.
72 Ibid., 354–364.

two hundred versions of the same sentence, but he would certainly be prepared to write on any subject with skill, dispatch, and perhaps even eloquence.

Eloquentia Perfecta: The Jesuit Plan of Studies

An examination of the grammar school demonstrates just how thoroughly rhetoric dominated the curriculum and directed the teaching of writing in England. This rhetorical domination was not limited to England but was typical of European education as well. The Jesuit educational system, "undoubtedly the most successful and influential to come out of the Renaissance," is proof of this rhetorical emphasis.[73]

Not long after its founding (the Jesuit order was sanctioned by Pope Paul III in 1540) the order became deeply involved in education, an association which has, of course, persisted to the present. The founder of the order, Ignatius of Loyola, had himself established both a primary school and a college. By the early seventeenth century there were nearly 300 Jesuit colleges in existence. These colleges were the backbone of the Jesuit educational mission. They were secondary schools, offering an education between the elementary and university levels. As such, they roughly parallel the English grammar schools. Students in the humanities courses were typically between ten and sixteen years of age.

Beginning in the middle of the sixteenth century and lasting well beyond the Renaissance the order's schools were guided by the *Ratio studiorum*, the Jesuit plan of studies. The educational objectives of the *Ratio studiorum* were being developed as early as 1540, preliminary versions were issued in 1586 and 1589, and the definitive version was promulgated in 1599. The *Ratio studiorum* was itself derived from the pedagogical precepts of antiquity and like classical education was intended to produce students who were masters of eloquence.[74]

To achieve this goal the *Ratio studiorum* stipulated that five courses were to be taken over a period of five years: three courses in progressively advanced Latin and Greek grammar, followed by a course in humanities, and culminating in the study of rhetoric. The humanities class acted as a kind of transition between the grammatical studies and rhetorical studies. Edward Lynch summarizes the content of this course:

> The aim of this class is to lay the foundation for eloquence, after the pupils have finished the grammar classes. This is done in three ways: by a knowledge of the language, some erudition, and a sketch of the precepts pertaining to rhetoric. For a command of the language, which consists chiefly in acquiring propriety of expression and fluency, the one orator used in daily prelections is Cicero; among historians, Caesar, Sallust, Livy, Curtius, and

---

73 Aldo Scaglione, *The Liberal Arts and the Jesuit College System* (Amsterdam: Benjamins, 1986), 51.

74 The literature about Jesuit education is vast. For discussions of rhetoric's place in it see, in addition to Scaglione, Edward Lynch, S.J., "The Origin and Development of Rhetoric in the Plan of Studies of 1599 of the Society of Jesus " (Ph.D. diss., Northwestern University, 1968), Jean Deitz Moss, "The Rhetoric Course at the Collegio Romano in the Latter Half of the Sixteenth Century," *Rhetorica*, 4 (1986): 137–152, and Marc Fumaroli, "The Fertility and Shortcomings of Renaissance Rhetoric: The Jesuit Case," *The Jesuits: Cultures, Sciences, and the Arts, 1540–1773*, ed. John W. O'Malley et al. (Toronto: University of Toronto Press, 1999), 90–106.

others like them; among the poets, Virgil, excepting some of the eclogues and the fourth book of the *Aeneid*, as well as Horace's *Odes*, and elegies, epigrams, and other works of classic poets.[75]

After completing the class in humanities the student was ready for the study of rhetoric, the goal of which was to attain

> perfect eloquence, which comprises two great faculties, the oratorical and the poetical. It regards not only the practical but also the cultural. For the precepts of oratory, Cicero may be supplemented by Aristotle and Quintilian. Style is to be formed on Cicero, though help may be drawn from approved historians and poets. Erudition will be derived from the history and manners of nations, and from the authorities of writers and every sort of learning.[76]

The rhetoric text specified in the 1599 *Ratio studiorum* was *De arte rhetorica libri tres, ex Aristotele, Cicerone, et Quinctiliano praecipue deprompti* (1557?) of Cypriano Suárez, S.J. (1524–93). Although Suárez's *De arte rhetorica* was not required until 1599 it was in use in Jesuit colleges well before that date. Because of its association with the *Ratio studiorum*, *De arte rhetorica* became one of the most widely used of all Renaissance rhetoric textbooks in Europe and, of course, in the New World as well. The *Ratio studiorum* of 1599 was made mandatory in some 245 Jesuit schools in Europe and in Europe's overseas empires.[77] And while Suárez's book was not used at all Jesuit institutions, it was the required text in a great many of these schools.[78]

Suárez's book is well suited to the Jesuit goal of *eloquentia perfecta*—it is a distillation of the precepts from the great rhetorical triumvirate of antiquity: Cicero, Aristotle, and Quintilian. As much as he admires these three authorities, Suárez believes that no single ancient text dealt adequately with the entire art of rhetoric. Suárez proceeds to enumerate the faults of each of the basic treatises written by his three sources.[79]

Because of these inadequacies, Suárez says, "our [Jesuit] teachers desired: to collect all the elements of eloquence in some book, method, and plan; to explain these with definitions and to illustrate them with examples from the teaching of Aristotle; in the case of Cicero and Quintilian to include not only their teaching but usually their very words."[80] This is precisely what Suárez does, with the intention of assisting "young men to read the learned books of Aristotle, Cicero, and Quintilian wherein lie the well-springs of eloquence."[81]

---

75 Lynch, 261.
76 Ibid., 262.
77 Ibid., 258.
78 For a discussion of the Jesuit teaching of rhetoric in Spain's American colonies see my *Rhetoric in the New World* (Columbia: University of South Carolina Press, 1996), 102–120.
79 "The *De Arte Rhetorica* (1568) by Cyprian Soarez, S. J.: A Translation with Introduction and Notes," Lawrence J. Flynn, S. J. (Ph.D. diss., University of Florida, 1955), 105–107.
80 Ibid., 108.
81 Ibid., 108.

Suárez is committed to the utility of ancient precepts, and sees no reason to tinker with them in the sixteenth century. He is aware, he says,

> that many of the teachings handed down by the ancients are attacked even in published books by people who should more reasonably have defended them. However, since many persons of exceptional learning have defended these teachings, I have decided not to change, without a good reason, what the judgment of so many centuries of learning has approved. In fact, I strongly urge you, Christian reader, to uproot completely from your mind this inordinate desire to contradict ancient writers rashly, so that it does not then proceed further towards the undoing of your intellect.[82]

Having thus affirmed the superiority of ancient precepts, Suárez proceeds to present a compendium of classical rhetoric. In his introduction Suárez summarizes *De arte rhetorica* in this way:

> In the first book, which concerns invention, sixteen topics for arguments are explained, and at the same time the matter suitable for arousing hearers is extracted from them. Certain rules are also set forth adapted to embellishment and deliberation [demonstrative and deliberative speaking].
>
> The second book which contains rules for arrangement treats the divisions of a speech, the status, judgment, and the kind of dispute which arises over the meaning of a writing. Also, syllogistic reasoning, enthymeme, induction, and example are treated. Besides, since ancient writers frequently refer to the epichereme, sorites, and dilemma, the effectiveness of these is explained.
>
> Finally, the third book teaches the embellishment of speech contained in words, either simple or compound. It also discusses rare and new words, tropes, ornaments of words and of thoughts; the origin, cause, nature, and use of well knit metrical prose; and finally, it treats memory and delivery.[83]

Thus students in Jesuit colleges could expect to be inundated with unadulterated classical rhetoric, whether in Europe, or Mexico, or Peru. The similarities between the curricula of the Jesuit colleges and the English grammar schools are striking. These commonalties derive, in large measure, from the common humanistic origins of both Catholic and Protestant educational objectives. Gabriel Codina's observation about the *Ratio studiorum* might be applied with equal accuracy to the grammar school: "Rhetoric became the art of arts, the science of sciences, the culmination of all literary studies. For Erasmus, as for all the humanists, the study of grammar, Latin, Greek was all oriented toward the attainment of eloquence. It is not strange that the Jesuits proposed eloquence as the ideal of their formation—*eloquentia perfecta*."[84]

---

82 Ibid., 108–109.
83 Ibid., "Introduction II," 112–113.
84 Gabriel Codina, "The 'Modus Parisiensis,'" *The Jesuit* Ratio Studiorum: *400th Anniversary Perspectives*, ed. Vincent J. Duminuco, S.J. (New York: Fordham University Press, 2000), 40.

The Female Voice in Renaissance Education

An examination of the curricula of the grammar schools and the Jesuit colleges furnishes a great deal of information about the practice of literary pedagogy in the Renaissance. Such an institutional approach does not, of course, tell us very much about those excluded from these institutions. The grammar schools and the Jesuit colleges were concerned almost exclusively with the education of young boys of the upper class and nobility. English boys of the lower classes had much less opportunity to participate and girls, of whatever class, had even less opportunity for an institutional education. The Jesuits taught only boys. The exclusion of women from these schools is especially striking in light of the humanists' acknowledgment of the need, indeed the duty, to educate women as well as men. The educational reformers recommended a classical and humanistic education for girls which was similar in methods and materials to those recommended for boys. Despite the similarity of male and female education the humanists believed that there must be fundamental differences between the teaching of girls and boys. One of the most striking distinctions between the two programs is seen in the humanists' conviction that, unlike men, women should not be taught rhetoric. Leonardo Bruni, in a letter to Baptista Malatesta written in 1405 or 1406, proposes what an educated lady should study and should not study. Bruni says that the "subtleties of Arithmetic and Geometry are not worthy to absorb a cultivated mind, and the same must be said of Astrology." He then adds that "the great and complex art of rhetoric should be placed in the same category. My chief reason is the obvious one, that I have in view the cultivation most fitting a woman. To her neither the intricacies of debate nor the oratorical artifices of action and delivery are of the least practical use, if indeed they are not positively unbecoming. Rhetoric in all its forms—public discussion, forensic argument, logical fence, and the like—lies absolutely outside the province of woman."[85] Vives makes much the same point in *The Instruction of a Christian Woman*: "The study of wisdome, the which doth enstruct their maners, and enfourme their lyving, and teacheth them the waye good and holy lyfe. As for eloquence, I have no great care, nor a woman nedeth it not, but she nedeth goodnes and wysedome."[86] Both Bruni and Vives make clear that instructing a woman in rhetoric, the most public of arts, is unproductive because women were, for the most part, excluded from public life. As Margaret King says of the educated women of the Renaissance: "Such women had been educated to do nothing and go nowhere."[87] Girls were educated to participate in the private life of the home, whereas boys were educated to participate in the public life of the Church and the state.

The exclusion of women from public life, and hence from instruction in rhetoric, would have obvious implications for the teaching of writing to women. It is not necessarily the case, however, that excluding women from instruction in rhetoric resulted in a female education entirely separated from the rhetorical tradition. Most humanists agreed that women needed many, but of course not

---

85 "Leonardo D'Arezzo Concerning the Study of Literature," *Classics in the Education of Girls and Women*, ed. Shirley Nelson Kersey (Metuchen, NJ: Scarecrow Press, 1981), 23.

86 Ibid., 40.

87 Margaret King, *Women of the Renaissance* (Chicago: University of Chicago Press, 1991), 213.

all, of the skills required by men. Thus Richard Mulcaster identifies four subjects which the "young maiden" must master: "*reading* well, *writing* faire, *singing* sweet, *playing* fine."[88] Mulcaster even adds that the "young gentlewoman" should also "speake the learned languages . . . with some *Logicall* helpe to chop, and some *Rhetoricke* to brave."[89] A significant portion of a girl's, as well as a boy's education, must be devoted to reading and writing. Rarely do the humanists make distinctions about the methods used to impart basic literacy to either boys or girls, but beyond the elementary level the approaches begin to diverge. This is particularly true when it comes to reading material. Bruni says that the gentlewoman has before her "as a subject peculiarly her own, the whole field of religion and morals."[90] The goal of Bruni, and other humanists, is to instill in the young gentlewoman a sense of prudent and chaste behavior appropriate to the good wife and caring mother. This can be accomplished, says Bruni, not only by the careful reading of Christian texts, but by the "noblest intellects of Greece and Rome."[91] Bruni recommends the ancient historians as especially instructive, but also emphasizes that "the great Orators of antiquity must by all means be included. Nowhere do we find the virtues more warmly extolled, the vices so fiercely decried."[92] While there was little need for women to practice oratory, there was every reason for women to read the speeches of orators past. At least since Isocrates, a rationale for rhetoric was that it offered moral inculcation, and that rationale obtained in the Renaissance. Indeed, Bruni claims that questions of morality and virtue be pursued by "men and women alike," but religion and morals "hold the first place in the education of a Christian lady."[93] Thus, while there was, therefore, no need to train women to be orators, there was every reason, literary and moral, that they should be acquainted with the rhetorical tradition.

Thus while many European educators would restrict women's education, others would not. Catherine R. Eskin observes that there was a "range of attitudes toward female education and speech" which makes it clear that "the Renaissance did accept this idea of the female voice and, by extension, of female agency."[94]

Moreover, there were those who ignored the injunction against teaching women rhetoric. Perhaps the most notable exception was the education of Mary and Elizabeth Tudor. Vives supervised the education of Mary and Roger Ascham taught Elizabeth. Ascham appears to have used his tutelage of Elizabeth as an opportunity to test the methods recommended in the *Scholemaster*. Mary and Elizabeth are, however, special cases because, as potential rulers, they were given what was essentially a man's education. Other women also received classical and humanistic training. Thomas More ensured that his three daughters, Margaret,

88 Richard Mulcaster, "Education of Girls," in *Classics in the Education of Girls and Women*, 64.
89 Ibid., 65.
90 "Leonardo D'Arezzo Concerning the Study of Literature," ibid., 23.
91 Ibid.
92 Ibid., 24.
93 Ibid.
94 Catherine R. Eskin, "The Rei(g)ning of Women's Tongues in English Books of Instruction and Rhetoric," *Women's Education in Early Modern Europe: A History, 1500–1800*, ed. Barbara Whitehead (New York: Garland, 1999), 124.

Cecilia, and Elizabeth, together with Margaret Giggs, a relative, were taught the complete humanistic curriculum.

Although few households were as enlightened as More's, women were typically educated at home by a tutor or family member. Frequently, initial literacy in the vernacular was the responsibility of the women of the household. Thus, when there emerged in the Renaissance a female voice that voice was typically expressed in the vernacular.

Relatively few girls attended a school beyond the most elementary. This, of course, was true of boys as well. Few children, male or female, were sufficiently privileged to enjoy the benefits of an institutional education. Boys were excluded from education by class and economics; girls were excluded for these reasons as well as gender. Thus the education of women occurred outside educational institutions, learning to speak and write in a manner influenced by the rhetorical tradition, but not truly a part of it.[95]

Renaissance Rhetoric in the Twenty-First Century

The study of language is certainly a major preoccupation of the twenty-first century. Yet such study is dispersed over a wide variety of fields, some of which are oblivious to the practical pursuit of any kind of eloquence. In the Renaissance the interest in language was concentrated in the study of "grammar," broadly defined, and of rhetoric. Brian Vickers argues that the Renaissance "reintegrated" the study of rhetoric after the "fragmentation" of the art following the fall of Rome.[96] It is this concentration that gives Renaissance rhetoric much of its effectiveness. But what Renaissance educators reintegrated, later generations have fragmented and departmentalized. This fragmentation has resulted in subjects once conceived of as unitary and complementary coming to be regarded as binary and competitive. Thus the integrated rhetoric so valued by Renaissance humanists gradually disintegrated into dualities of literature and composition, writing and speaking. The incentives for this disintegration are both institutional and intellectual and these centrifugal forces remain powerful. By the mid-nineteenth century the study of literature and the teaching of writing came to be increasingly regarded as distinct, and perhaps even incompatible, subjects.[97] Indeed, these formerly united subjects had become so disparate that some would argue that the contemporary composition classroom was "no place for literature."[98] At about the same time that literature and composition were divorcing, teachers of writing and speaking were also separating. Thus in the early twentieth century teachers of public speaking would declare their independence from

95 For an excellent treatment of women's education in the Italian Renaissance see Anthony Grafton and Lisa Jardine, *From Humanism to the Humanities* (London: Duckworth, 1986), 29–57. Their account asks the crucial question: "Women Humanists: Education for What?"

96 Brian Vickers, *In Defence of Rhetoric* (Oxford: Clarendon Press, 1988), Chapter 5, "Renaissance Reintegration," 254–293.

97 The literature on the evolution of separation of literature and composition is extensive. For a useful survey of available resources see Lynée Gaillet, "The Nineteenth Century," in *The Present State of Scholarship*, 152–184. See especially 156–158.

98 Erika Lindemann, "Freshman Composition: No Place for Literature," *College English* 55 (1993), 311–316.

the discipline of English. These relatively recent divisions between literature and composition and between writing and speaking into separate departments would confound any grammar school master or, for that matter, virtually any rhetorician before, say, 1800.[99]

The revival of rhetoric in the late twentieth century has perhaps partially subverted this division, but the centrifugal forces of departmentalization and disciplinarity remain potent. There are, however, signs that writing should again be central to education. "Writing across the curriculum" is the most obvious manifestation of this attitude. Yet the efforts to disperse writing across fields and departments are frequently accompanied by the creation of writing programs and writing centers often entirely independent of English departments. And so the segregation of composition and literature continues.

It is probably this dispersal of reading, writing, and speaking across both departments and disciplines that most differentiates Renaissance instruction from our own. Writing was not dispersed across the curriculum; it *was* the curriculum. The curricula of the grammar schools and Jesuit colleges were almost entirely literary; the teaching of reading, writing, and speaking was the sole effort of the master, every day and every form. The goal was not mere competence but eloquence. Furthermore, this eloquence was to be of a special kind: the classical eloquence of Cicero's citizen-orator. The theory and practice of Cicero and the pedagogy of Quintilian shaped a curriculum reverential toward the past and yet attentive to the present.

While the rhetorical curriculum of the Renaissance has an obvious appeal for writing instructors, it is improbable that the concentrated and unified curriculum could replace the infinitely more diverse curriculum of our own time. Nor could a technological society ever accept an exclusively literary education. So while the preeminence of rhetoric within the entire curriculum is unlikely to return, the reintegration of literature and writing on a less grand scale is certainly possible. Indeed, individual teachers can find ways, and in fact are doing so, to reunite literature and composition in the classroom.[100]

While we cannot return to the Renaissance we can remember the best of its cultural aspirations and find in the work of great educational theorists and practitioners inspiration for present efforts. Perhaps it is not too much to hope that histories such as this one might further the reintegration of rhetoric into the twenty-first-century curriculum, helping to restore rhetoric to its historical mission of teaching literature and composition, writing and speaking and, ultimately, eloquence.

---

99 For discussions of the separation of the written and spoken word in American education see James A. Berlin, *Rhetoric and Reality: Writing Instruction in American Colleges, 1900–1985* (Carbondale: Southern Illinois University Press, 1987); James J. Murphy, *The Rhetorical Tradition and Modern Writing* (New York: Modern Language Association, 1982); and Steven Mailloux, "Disciplinary Identities: On the Rhetorical Paths between English and Communication Studies," *Rhetoric Society Quarterly* 30 (2000), 5–30. See also responses to Mailloux by Michael Leff and William Keith, *Rhetoric Society Quarterly* 30 (2000), 83–106.

100 For a discussion of this issue and many case studies see *Integrating Literature and Writing Instruction: First-Year English, Humanities Core Courses, Seminars*, ed. Judith H. Anderson and Christine R. Farris (New York: Modern Language Association, 2007).

Chapter 6

Writing Instruction in Eighteenth- and Nineteenth-Century Great Britain
Continuity and Change, Transitions and Shifts

Linda Ferreira-Buckley

Key Concepts

Social, economic, and political changes affected and were effected by changes in education • Religions control much education • English vernacular versus Latin • Writing versus oratory • Methods of writing instruction • Early continuity of medieval pedagogy • Imitation and memorization • Study of 'belles lettres' as models • Hugh Blair's *Lectures on Rhetoric and Belles Lettres* • Richard Whately's "Argumentative Composition" • George Jardine's objection to dictation • Dissenting academies • Examinations and themes • 1831 Report of the Royal Commission • "Redbrick" universities • Writing instruction for working people • Writing instruction in Scotland, Wales, and Ireland • Scottish universities on continental plan • Three Scottish educators: Aytoun, Bain, and Jardine • Gaelic and Welsh vernaculars discouraged • Improvement of female education • University Extension Lecture movement • Salons • Entrance of women into universities • Foundation of women's colleges • British education exported to colonies across the globe.

> *The word eloquence in its greatest latitude denotes, "That art or talent by which the discourse is adapted to its end." All the ends of speaking are reducible to four; every speech being intended to enlighten the understanding, to please the imagination, to move the passions, or to influence the will.*
>
> George Campbell, "The Nature and Foundations of Eloquence"

The epigraph to this chapter, taken from the opening of George Campbell's popular *Philosophy of Rhetoric* (1776), conveys the widening of rhetoric's aims that will distinguish the eighteenth and nineteenth centuries in Great Britain. While Campbell affirms the importance of persuasion, or "influencing the will," he includes three other aims—enlightening the understanding, pleasing the imagination, moving the passions—and all four figure prominently in his treatise. Increasingly, the discipline of rhetoric or "eloquence" was understood to have this broader scope. Although Campbell here focuses on oral communication, those who studied his work in the eighteenth and nineteenth centuries recognized that his theory applied to all communication. Over the course of our period, adult Britons were increasingly less likely to need to compose and deliver speeches and increasingly more likely to need to produce written communication, leading to an increased demand for writing instruction. Unsurprisingly, Campbell's *Philosophy of Rhetoric*, like those of Hugh Blair and other theorists of our period, would be interpreted, misinterpreted, applied, rejected, and ignored, giving rise to significantly different theories about discourse and pedagogy. Girls and boys and women and men from every social class received increased instruction in writing, albeit to varying degrees, from the rudimentary practices taught to the poor to the range of genres favored for gentlemen or gentlewomen of means. This chapter will map out the range of principles and practices that characterize approaches to writing instruction across the British Isles of England, Ireland, Scotland, and Wales over two centuries of complex change.

Eighteenth- and nineteenth-century British society, the focus of this chapter, is more complex than the comparatively uniform culture of the previous chapter. As the preceding chapters have made clear, the reign of classical languages as the medium of scholarship, learning, and culture had meant the study of Latin and Greek long dominated the curricula of schools and universities in Great Britain. Over the course of the eighteenth and nineteenth centuries, however, the sovereignty of the classical languages was increasingly challenged, and instruction in English, including English composition, became more common in response to evolving social, political, religious, and economic developments. Two related linguistic factors also influenced the way writing was perceived and taught: the shift from an oral culture to a basically literate one—that is, from an emphasis on speaking to an emphasis on writing—and the proliferation of books and periodicals at more affordable cost. This chapter looks at how these and other developments affected the teaching of rhetoric and writing in schools and universities in eighteenth- and nineteenth-century Great Britain, that territory encompassing England, Scotland, Wales, and Ireland. While the generalizations offered here suggest the diversity of language instruction of the period, readers should nonetheless bear in mind that they do not capture the range of practices, nor do they fully capture how competing beliefs about class, gender, region, language, and pedagogy ensured heterogeneity of practice.

Transformative change characterizes our period. The eighteenth and nineteenth centuries saw rapid industrialization, and across Britain, the rural agricultural population migrated to cities in large numbers. Between 1700 and 1800, for example, Manchester and Liverpool mushroomed into industrial centers. Between 1800 and 1900, Ireland lost half of its population to famine and emigration, but Scotland changed from a poor agricultural society to a relatively industrialized one, with its population increasing from 84,000 to 500,000, and Wales became a leading exporter of coal and iron, with its population quadrupling.

Along with such shifts came economic growth and political unrest, activism, and reforms that dispersed power beyond the traditional power bases, and the demand for education escalated. Eighteenth-century grammar schools, which developed out of a variety of cathedral, abbey, collegiate, parish, and song schools from the fifteenth and sixteenth centuries, aimed to turn out students who could read and write Latin. As the name "grammar school" suggests, students embarked on an intensive course of Latin grammar. They went on to study Greek and rhetoric while continuing to improve their proficiency in Latin by writing verse.

After attending the equivalent of high school, a privileged few entered university. Existing preparatory schools and universities were not sufficient; since they could neither enroll more than a tiny percent of the nation's children, nor were their curriculums suitable to new realities. At the beginning of the eighteenth century, England had only two universities (Oxford and Cambridge), Ireland one (Trinity), Scotland four (Edinburgh, Glasgow, St. Andrews, and Aberdeen), Wales none. By the end of the nineteenth, dozens had been established. Primary and secondary schools also proliferated. More economically secure, the middle classes, especially the large and powerful merchant class, sought access to quality education, including training in reading, writing, and speaking the vernacular. A sign of good breeding, "proper English" was perceived as a rung on the ladder of upward mobility for the native English and the provincial alike. Poor children had little hope of crossing class lines and they received what little education they could from church-sponsored schools or foundations.

The interplay between religion and politics, never separate after the Jacobite defeat in 1746, contributed to the drama of education and writing instruction in the eighteenth and nineteenth centuries. Indeed, through much of the period, religion and education seemed to be inextricably bound, and secular educational institutions were rare. Religion provided a rationale for education: proponents maintained that when designed appropriately for gender and class, it fostered virtue by teaching the skills required to read holy texts and instilling personal discipline. Those who were not members of the Anglican Church faced serious educational obstacles; allegiance to the Established Church of England was required at the great public schools and Oxford and Cambridge. In fact, in order to obtain a degree from those universities, students had to affirm its doctrine. Other restrictions applied. The 1800 Act of Union dissolved the Dublin Parliament, and Ireland came fully under British control. While uniting the parliaments of England and Scotland, however, the 1707 Act of Union allowed Scotland to retain independence in education and religion. Its well-established universities—highly respected academically in England and on the continent, and with no religious constraints—attracted numerous students. At the beginning of the period, non-Anglicans who wished to remain in England turned to the many **dissenting academies** run by religious nonconformists, which provided a university-equivalent education; later, they might attend one of the "**redbrick**" universities founded to provide the middle classes with a practical education. Anglicans serious about education often chose one of these options since Oxford and Cambridge were reputed to have become morally and educationally decadent. It is in these academies and in the Scottish and English redbrick universities that disciplinary innovations took place, where English as an academic subject flourished and where instruction in writing came to mean writing in English rather than writing in Latin, topics discussed next.

Since most eighteenth-century teachers were clergymen and many university students were training for the ministry, education was often allied with religious authorities. Females were rarely the recipients of this instruction; notable exceptions were those in John Wesley's community, who, Vicki Tolar Burton maintains, benefited greatly from Wesley's cultivation of "spiritual literacy" and were in effect schooled, as were males of all classes in his community, in the practices of reading, writing, and speaking.[1] Not surprisingly, much secondary and post-secondary writing instruction centered on sermon writing, as young men were trained to decipher the lessons of the scriptures to instruct lay people. Of course, instruction for sermon writing sometimes varied according to the propensities of Anglicans, Dissenters, and Catholics. Some manuals focused exclusively on sermon writing; in dozens more, sermons were one of many genres for which guidance was proffered. Not only do many of the distinguished rhetoricians of the time include advice for writing sermons in their rhetoric manuals, many rhetoric teachers regularly composed sermons they delivered as part of their clerical duties. Many of these sermons were later published for wider distribution. Sometimes, however, sermons were composed exclusively for readers. In any case, collections of sermons enjoyed brisk sales, and students of all ages, whether bound for the ministry or not, developed their prose style by studying sermons according to the dictates of imitation exercises.

The literary scenes of London, Edinburgh, and Dublin were intellectually lively, giving rise to such journals as the *Spectator, Rambler,* and *Edinburgh Review,* all of which helped to standardize, even valorize, English. They published good prose and celebrated it. Hundreds of other less famous newspapers and periodicals surfaced locally or nationally and further encouraged interest in the vernacular.[2] **Lectures**, coffee houses, clubs, and societies proliferated, providing active forums for such interests.[3] In the middle of the eighteenth century in Edinburgh, for example, Adam Smith, Robert Watson, Hugh Blair, and Thomas Sheridan delivered rhetoric lectures at the urging of Henry Homes, later Lord Kames, who believed that such refinements were necessary if Edinburgh professionals were to advance. The lectures were well attended and eventually became part of the regular university curriculum. Just so, in towns and cities across the British Isles, in single and serial lectures, specialists (and a few charlatans) lectured either or both men and women, young and old, on the proper uses of spoken and written English.[4]

Local Vernaculars, "Proper" English, and the Ancient Languages

A rise in nationalism contributed to the growing valorization of English language and literature. Although men and women of culture had long read English literature at home, for much of the period it was still considered popular literature unworthy of formal instruction. But as the demographics of schooling changed, not all students would enter with a command of "proper" English, and thus

---

1 Vicki Tolar Burton, *Spiritual Literacy in John Wesley's Methodism: Reading, Writing, and Speaking to Believe.* Waco, TX: Baylor University Press, 2008.

2 Stephen M. North, *The Making of Knowledge in Composition: Portrait of an Emerging Discipline* (Upper Montclair NJ: Boynton/Cook, 1987), especially 3–20; Lionel Madden and Diana Dixon, "Histories and Studies of Individual Periodicals," in J. Don Vann and Rosemary T. VanArsdel, *Victorian Periodicals: A Guide to Research,* Vol. 2 (New York: MLA, 1989), 98–122; Joanne Shattock, *Politics and Reviewers: The Edinburgh and the Quarterly* Leicester, UK: Leicester University Press, 1989), see especially 82–97.

3 Peter Clark, *British Clubs and Societies 1580–1800,* New York: Oxford University Press, 2000.

4 D. D. McElroy's *Scotland's Age of Improvement: A Survey of Eighteenth-Century Clubs and Societies* (Pullman: Washington State University Press, 1969) remains the best first source.

English became a regular part of the curriculum, English literature serving as, in J. D. Palmer's words, "the poor man's classics," and we might add the British provincial's classics, gaining full respectability only in the twentieth century.[5] Nationalism also gave rise to a reverence for the past, hence the nostalgia for local vernaculars such as Scots and Gaelic, manifesting itself in the recovery, study, and promotion of folk literatures. The Edinburgh literati, for example, sponsored James McPherson's "recovery" of the Ossian poems. They longed for a record of a Scots literary tradition, even as they repudiated "Scotticisms" in their own written prose. Many Irish and Welsh citizens also cherished their indigenous literature, even as their own use of the vernacular was deemed unlearned, vulgar, and an impediment to British nationalism.[6] Local vernaculars were banished from provincial classrooms. Such prejudice helped to legitimate the study of English. Teachers, elocutionists, grammarians, and lexicographers—with Enlightenment faith in rationality and rules—set out to understand and standardize English, firm in the belief that change indicated deterioration and that Latin grammar was the standard by which all languages should be measured. Such beliefs would eventually be challenged. The eighteenth century saw the publication of Nathaniel Bailey's *Universal Etymological Dictionary* (1721) and Samuel Johnson's *Dictionary of the English Language* (1755); the late nineteenth, of the *Oxford (or New) English Dictionary*. These and other English language resources indicate the growing respectability of English in learned circles.

This interest in national language encouraged reexamination of older English texts stored in libraries such as the British Museum, the Bodleian at Oxford, and the University Library at Cambridge. As Jo McMurtry explains, by the end of the nineteenth century, Victorians "had found, edited, and published virtually the entire canon of English literature" and compiled concordances and other scholarly tools.[7] All of these activities influenced instruction. Some left a major imprint: for example, early in the eighteenth century, university students would hear about word histories as they were schooled in proper usage; by the end of the nineteenth, they would be examined extensively in **philology**, that is, historical and comparative linguistics. Accordingly, new guidelines for academic writing were developed and passed on.

During the eighteenth and nineteenth centuries, most schools, dissenting academies, and universities shifted to English, but the shift was gradual and contested, and the ancient educational establishments that had long served the sons of elite families and formed the generations of scholars continued to insist that students read and write in Latin and other classical languages. Oxford,

---

5 J. D. Palmer, *The Rise of English Studies* (London: Oxford University Press, 1965) 78.

6 The diminishment of Scots, Gaelic, and Welsh has been well documented, including the role played by British educational policies. For example, Parliament's mid-nineteenth-century educational reforms cautioned against allowing Welsh to be used in school; by century's end, only half of the population spoke Welsh, and very few could write it. Gaelic also suffered. In 1800, half of the Irish population spoke only Gaelic; by mid-century, only a quarter of the population could even speak Gaelic (of these, only 5 percent were monolingual). Many families, eager for their children to prosper, supported these early English-only policies. For additional information, see, for example, David Williams's *A Short History of Modern Wales* (London: J. Murray, 1962) and Sean O'Tuama's edited collection, *The Gaelic League Idea* (Cork: Mercier, 1972).

7 Jo McMurtry, *English Language, English Literature: The Creation of an Academic Discipline* (Hamden: Archon, 1985).

Cambridge, and Trinity Universities clung to traditional approaches. In English, Scottish, Welsh, and Irish grammar and public schools, students learned Latin grammar and wrote extensively—in Latin. Their religious exercises, too, were in Latin, and they sang psalms in the classical languages. At many of these schools, regulations mandated that all discussions, save those in family groups, were to be in Latin, although it is difficult to determine how steadfastly such rules were observed. What's more, in such circles literacy itself *was defined as* the ability to read and write Latin. Objections to the **dominance** of the classical languages were increasingly raised by individuals within many of these institutions, however, as education elsewhere began to address more utilitarian ends for merchants and other men of business.

Another consequential linguistic shift, mentioned above, is that from the spoken to the written form of language. Writing pedagogies drew upon rhetorical theory. Even though rhetoric had long privileged the study of oratory, students had always been immersed in various written exercises to develop their stylistic virtuosity and had composed themes to master organization and form, although these had been considered scripts for oral delivery or preparatory training for writing speeches.[8] For most of our period, writing instruction built explicitly on this rhetorical tradition. Although "rhetoric" long referred to "public *Speaking* alone," Richard Whately explains in *Elements of Rhetoric* (1828), "as most of the rules for Speaking are of course applicable equally to Writing, an extension of the term naturally took place; and we find even Aristotle, the earliest systematic writer on the subject whose works have come down to us, including in his Treatise rules for such compositions as were not intended to be publicly recited."[9] Whately goes on to observe that

> [t]he invention of Printing by extending the sphere of operation of the Writer, has of course contributed to the extension of those terms which, in their primary signification, had reference to Speaking alone. Many objects are now accomplished through the medium of the Press, which formerly came under the exclusive province of the Orator; and the qualifications requisite for success are so much the same in both cases, that we apply the term "Eloquent" as readily to a Writer as to a Speaker [. . .] because *some part* of the rules to be observed in Oratory, or rules analogous to these, are applicable to such compositions. Conformably to this view, therefore, some writers have spoken of Rhetoric as the Art of Composition, universally; or, with the exclusion of Poetry alone, as embracing all Prose-composition.
>
> (2–3)

Other theorists, he notes, confine the term to "Persuasive Speaking" (4) or extend the discipline more widely to include discourses in art, law, logic, ethics, and politics. Indeed, in the eighteenth and nineteenth centuries, theorists and

---

8 See David Vincent, *The Rise of Mass Literacy: Reading and Writing in Modern Europe* (Malden MA: Blackwell Publishers, 2000).

9 Richard Whately, *Elements of Rhetoric*, ed. D. Ehninger (Carbondale: Southern Illinois University Press, 1963) 2.

teachers variously defined rhetoric and writing instruction narrowly or broadly, and ought to caution us against overgeneralization.

As before, then, much instruction included writing scripts for oral delivery. Prior to the eighteenth century, writing in schools had emphasized oratory, sermons, and letters. During the eighteenth century, as people's interests were increasingly served by government representatives and the legal profession and as writing became the medium of communication and record, the **dominance of oratory** decreased. Although oratorical exercises lost favor in some schools, "elocution"—a truncated rhetoric of delivery (rhetoric's fifth canon or office)—enjoyed great popularity throughout the period, even as critics decried its limitations and excesses.[10]

However, other uses of oral language drew the attention of school and university students, as they did that of George Drummond, a student in John Stevenson's logic course at Edinburgh, whose theme "Rules of Conversation," dated April 25, 1740, is one of many compositions on such topics housed in university archives across Great Britain. Essays in periodicals and even whole books also celebrated the virtues of conversation, setting down its rules in print and encouraging adults to write about it. Thomas De Quincey's "Conversation," which appeared in 1847 in *Tait's Magazine*, maintained that "[w]ithout an art, without some simple system of rules, gathered from experience of such contingencies as are most likely to mislead the practice when left to its own guidance, no act of man nor effort accomplishes its purposes in perfection."[11] It was assumed that facility in conversation, disciplined by careful study, would also foster facility in writing. In this and other ways, the study of the oral uses of language changed, but it continued to play a part in writing instruction.

Over the course of two centuries, with cheaper materials and production costs, books became affordable to more families than ever before, though by no means most. In addition, public and private libraries increased in number and size. The rapid increase in the reading populace in turn helped to produce an expanded class of writers who looked to be remunerated for their work. Spirited exchanges on a broad array of topics ensued in books, pamphlets, and periodicals. Accordingly, more readers wished to write proficiently, if not expertly. Writing manuals and textbooks multiplied to serve this reading and writing public, helped by new printing technologies that cheapened production costs.[12]

---

10 Wilbur Samuel Howell emphasizes the reductive nature of elocution by quoting the opening line of an elocutionary manual—"Always breathe through the nostrils"—alongside that of Aristotle's *Rhetoric*—"Rhetoric is the counterpart of dialectic." See Wilbur Samuel Howell, *Eighteenth-Century British Logic and Rhetoric* (Princeton: Princeton University Press, 1971) 145–256. Howell's criticisms notwithstanding, elocution sometimes constituted a rich component of rhetorical education.

11 Thomas De Quincey, *Selected Essays on Rhetoric by Thomas De Quincey* (Carbondale: Southern Illinois University Press, 1967) 264.

12 Ian Michael's *The Teaching of English: From the Sixteenth Century to 1870* (London: Cambridge University Press, 1987) documents three centuries of British textbooks dedicated to the study of English and thus serves as an invaluable reference. Although Michael devotes only a dozen pages (303–316) to those texts explicitly teaching "written expression," other sections also pertain to composition instruction. Also see Louis G. Kelly's *Twenty-Five Centuries of Language Teaching: An Inquiry into the Science, Art, and Development of Language Teaching Methodology, 500 BCE–1969* (Rowley: Newbury, 1969).

Methods of Writing Instruction

Although a full understanding of the ways writing was taught in the eighteenth and nineteenth centuries is beyond reach since much instruction was strictly oral, extant materials—textbooks, instructor lectures, student notes, books on education, university calendars, etc.—provide a reasonable basis for characterizing many practices. Of course, it's wise to keep a few cautions in mind: such sources are hardly infallible, for, at least in some cases, they indicate what individuals felt ought to be done, not what was actually done; in some cases, writing instruction drew on a hodgepodge of the methods discussed below. For such reasons, understanding any specific site of instruction requires local evidence.

During the second half of the eighteenth century, Scottish rhetorics, informed by disciplines such as classical rhetoric, French **belletristic** theory, Common Sense Philosophy, and Faculty Psychology, proved especially popular.[13]

Language Exercises and Grammatical Study

Medieval pedagogy prevailed well into the period. The trivium of grammar, logic, and rhetoric provided solid, if somewhat tired, training in communication skills. Texts such as John Holmes's *The Art of Rhetoric Made Easy* (London, 1739), John Lawson's *Lectures Concerning Oratory* (Dublin, 1758), and John Ward's *System of Oratory* (London, 1759) reveal typical pedagogical approaches. Instructors believed that in order to learn to read, one first had to learn to spell and that, in like fashion, in order to learn to write, one first had to learn grammar. Students thus progressed from words to sentences to paragraphs to themes and finally to lengthier compositions or orations. Memorizing and modeling were common methods of improving student writing. Well into the twentieth century, grammar instruction remained inextricably bound to writing instruction.

As earlier noted, at the start of our period, grammar was the grammar of Latin since writing instruction focused on writing Latin; as part of this instruction, however, students were required to translate "into a good English stile,"[14] and as late as the end of the nineteenth century, proficiency in English was often tested by translation from Latin. Writing and speaking, English and Latin were likely to be taught side by side, instruction in one reinforcing instruction in the other, making the commonplace that classical languages prevailed somewhat misleading. For example, a master might dictate a letter for the student to write out in Latin, then transpose into English.[15] Whether in Latin, in English, or in Latin and English, medieval exercises comprised an integral part of writing instruction. Eventually, as modern foreign languages came into the curriculum, studying them was also considered a viable means of improving English. In 1867, for instance, a master at Eton urged that French or another modern language be

---

13 Linda Ferreira-Buckley, "The Eighteenth Century," *The Present State of Scholarship in the History of Rhetoric* (Columbia: University of Missouri Press, 2010) 114–150; Linda Ferreira-Buckley and S. Michael Halloran, "Introduction," *Hugh Blair's Lectures on Rhetoric and Belles Lettres* (Carbondale: Southern Illinois University Press, 2001).

14 Michael 274.

15 Michael 308.

substituted for Latin as a means of improving English.[16] The redbrick universities and academies often taught such languages as German, French, Arabic, and Punjab alongside the classical ones, which contributed somewhat to the students' abilities in English. Not everyone approved since Latin structure had long been considered paradigmatic, and so arguments about what language ought to be primary in school continued throughout our period.

What we today call "basic English" was sometimes part of writing instruction. Because, unlike elitist Oxford and Cambridge, the more democratic Scottish universities and redbrick universities served many students who were not proficient speakers and writers in the standard received British dialect, language instruction covered fundamentals.[17] Eradicating provincialisms became part of the educational mission of individuals and institutions.

Considered fundamental to all composition instruction of the period, grammar was stressed at all levels.[18] Based on the assumption of a **universal grammar** common to all languages, the Latin system was at first adapted without change to English. Grammar exercises associated with the ancient rhetoric were widely used by students at all levels: imitation; varying (which involved changing a sentence into all of its possible forms); paraphrasing; and prosing (turning verse into prose). Transposition, a common exercise, entailed "the placing of Words out of their natural Order, to render the Sound of them more agreeable to the Ear."[19] **Elliptical exercises** were sentences with some omitted words that the student was expected to supply. In the grammar schools, the students were expected to know their grammar books by heart; instruction might then proceed in **catechetical** fashion. These exercises were used in the nineteenth century, though perhaps less frequently; translation from Latin into "correct English" and later from a modern foreign language continued to be used well into the twentieth century.

The practical benefits of ridding students of "rusticisms" and of training them in mechanics of a written standard were rarely questioned, even as we lament cultural biases. Usage lessons, designed especially for students trying to eradicate traces of a provincial dialect, supplemented textbooks and became part of instruction in writing. Parsing sentences and correcting "false English" were also widely practiced. Students were expected to correct sentences that had errors of spelling, syntax, or punctuation and to cite the rule that had been violated. Or the master might correct the exercises, usually orally, and return them to the students, who, sometimes with the help of classmates, made their own corrections in writing. Since paper was expensive, students often wrote their first versions on slates and then copied the corrected versions into their notebooks. University students often continued these preparatory school exercises, inherited from the classical tradition.

---

16   Michael 311.
17   Franklin Court, *Institutionalizing English Literature: The Culture and Politics of Literary Study, 1750–1900* (Palo Alto: Stanford University Press, 1992); Thomas P. Miller, *The Formation of College English: Rhetoric and Belles Lettres in the British Cultural Provinces* (Pittsburgh: University of Pittsburgh Press, 1997).
18   Linda C. Mitchell, *Grammar Wars* (Aldershot, UK: Ashgate Publishing, 2001).
19   Cited in Michael 283.

The Belletristic Approach

Throughout the period, reading and writing remained closely associated with literature, defined broadly as polite or humane learning. Literary texts, including classical texts in translation and texts originally written in English, served the rhetoric course as models for good oratory and writing, what McMurtry describes as a sort of "window display, to be taken in snippets [. . .] as illustrations for rhetorical techniques."[20] Although there was little attempt to explore the meaning, literature served rhetoric in a very real way since students were often required to imitate models. Memorizing books and literary passages remained a common practice even at the university level, for students were expected to have patterns of good writing in their heads.

The nineteenth century saw a significant change, for pedagogical material began to be drawn more from vernacular literature and less from the classical to illustrate grammatical patterns and rhetorical effects. Nevertheless, the early teachers of literature considered instruction in writing part of their mission until newer, more "efficient" methods of inculcating rules and evaluating proficiency in English came to eclipse essay and oratorical forms, even though testing a student's knowledge of philological and historical facts offered no indication of writing ability. English literature came to dominate newly formed English departments, but writing instruction remained a part of courses. Communication skills, written and spoken, were recognized as central to the entire educational endeavor.

Although classical rhetorical approaches had always relied upon literary examples, the new Scottish rhetoric foregrounded the study of the *belles lettres*, or literature. Drawing upon continental (especially French) theorists and upon his own training in classical rhetoric at the University of Edinburgh, Hugh Blair compiled a broad and accessible guide to reading and writing, *Lectures on Rhetoric and Belles Lettres* (1783). He wished to revise classical rhetoric—for which he professed great respect—in view of Enlightenment thinking. Characterizations of Blair seem at odds: is he the British Quintilian or the bridge between Enlightenment and Romantic theories of writing?[21] The teaching of oral and written skills were closely linked; such study profited equally the writer or speaker, and the reader or hearer. (Not until late in the nineteenth century did oral and written skills begin to be separated into different courses and different departments.)

Blair's text, in full and abridged form, sold well throughout Great Britain in the late eighteenth and nineteenth centuries. It also inspired such other books as William Barron's *Lectures on Belles Lettres and Logic* (London, 1806) and Alexander Jamieson's *A Grammar of Rhetoric and Polite Literature* (London, 1818). Although the full extent of belletristic rhetoric's reach has not yet been determined, Blair, along with fellow Scots like George Campbell and Henry Homes, Lord Kames, helped to shape the course of writing instruction in nineteenth-century Britain and elsewhere, broadening the range of texts studied and linking it with literary appreciation. (The work of these Scots was also strongly felt in North America,

20 McMurtry 122.
21 See, for example, George A. Kennedy, *Classical Rhetoric and Its Christian and Secular Tradition from Ancient to Modern Times* (Chapel Hill: University of North Carolina Press, 1980) 235.

as Suzanne Bordelon, Elizabethada Wright and Michael Halloran make clear in Chapter 7 of this volume.)[22]

Argumentation

In his "Preface," Richard Whately recalls that *Elements of Rhetoric* (1828) was used in colleges, schools and homes, its practical orientation a welcome relief from more theoretical treatments. Some females studied it surreptitiously. Whately had been especially interested in composition instruction as a tutor at Oriel College, Oxford, as principal of St. Alban's Hall, and when, as Archbishop of Dublin, he worried about cultivating new generations of ministers. He revised and expanded *Elements*, each edition attending more to pedagogical concerns, culminating in the seventh edition of 1846. Whately restricted writing instruction exclusively to "Argumentative Composition," "considering Rhetoric (in conformity with the very just and philosophical view of Aristotle) as an off-shoot from Logic."[23] Whately's popular treatise lays out rules necessary to "*establish*" or "prove" notions "to the satisfaction of *another*."[24] Although he assumes that written rhetoric is often a script for spoken rhetoric, his work and those it inspired formed the bases of much nineteenth-century writing instruction. Along with its companion volume, *Elements of Logic* (1826), it guided teaching practices into the twentieth century.

By the time *Elements of Rhetoric* was published, many writers and teachers were loath to admit studying "rhetorical" precepts, so excessive had been earlier dependence on detailed artificial systems of rhetoric. While deploring such excess, Whately observes: "The simple truth is, TECHNICAL TERMS ARE PART OF LANGUAGE."[25] He presents philosophical and practical principles to guide understanding. Despite the treatise's limitations—it rejects the full rhetorical art of invention, it rejects probable truths, it prefers inference and neglects empirical knowledge, it neglects forensic and deliberative topics and it embraces faculty psychology—the textbook and its author taught generations of students to argue convincingly, if not persuasively. His student John Henry Newman recalled how the prose and reasoning abilities of his Oxford classmates benefited from Whately's unstinting attention. Indeed, Newman emulated many of his mentor's methods when teaching at schools and universities in England and Ireland. His influence is evident in Newman's own rhetorical treatise, *The Grammar of Assent*.

The Lecture System as Writing Instruction

While the tutorial system, discussed in the previous chapter, continued at Trinity, Oxford, and Cambridge, the lecture system was favored by the Scottish and English redbrick universities and by the dissenting academies. In the latter,

---

22   The essays collected in Lynee Lewis Gaillet, ed., *Scottish Rhetoric and Its Influences* (Mahwah: Erlbaum, 1998), examine the far-reaching dominance of the Scots in America.

23   Whately, *Elements* 4.

24   Whately, *Elements* 5.

25   Whately, *Elements* 19, emphasis in original.

lectures were augmented by the catechetical system whereby the professor lectured for an hour a day and spent an additional hour or two questioning students about the material covered in the lecture. The custom of "dictates," where the professor spoke slowly enough so that the student could take down the lecture word for word, provided accurate textbooks for the student and required him to practice composition. But there were abuses. In a moral philosophy course, one student complained that the professor was dictating "fast enough in all conscience to keep 20 persons writing" and that he "does not feel very morally philosophical."[26] Some faculty seemed unable or unwilling to update their lessons: student notes from David Masson's course, for example, vary little over thirty years. Robert Schmitz tells the story of students who were following Masson's lecture from an earlier set of student notes. Objecting to changes when Masson deviated from their copies, they would shuffle their feet in protest, whereupon Masson, rising, would remark, "Gentlemen . . . as I have been in the habit of saying" and would return to his previous years' notes.[27] Nonetheless, **dictation** was a component of writing instruction: it familiarized students with the physical practice of writing and instilled codes of formal English. The methods employed at the dissenting academies are characteristic. Some of the later tutors dictated word by word. Others such as Doddridge and Priestley read their lectures and then handed over the MSS. to be copied by their pupils at leisure. Belsham spoke from brief hints and imperfect notes. Pye Smith provided pupils with an outline of his principal course.[28] Working from the broad outline, students then wrote out the details. Sometimes students were given printed lectures, as by Priestley at Hackney College and Warrington. Aided by their small size, the dissenting academies favored free discussion. They departed from the traditional lecture course; after a brief lecture commenting on a text, the sessions were fashioned to suit their students' and their own needs.[29] Students often used their course notes as their text after the medieval fashion. Some embellished their notes with drawings and bits of humor; one set contains scenes from Glasgow in the margins and a reference to Aristotle as the "Rev. J. G. Aristotle."[30] Some bound the notes into book form.

In the nineteenth century, students were often assigned textbooks in addition to the theoretical rhetorical text. Textbooks were expensive, students often poor. Students who could not afford textbooks used their professors' personal libraries, although poorly paid academy professors had few to lend. Few dissenting academies had substantive libraries, although university libraries fared better. The redbricks and provincial libraries housed both classical and contemporary guides to writing, as did the better high school libraries. (The work of Hugh Blair, George Campbell, Lord Kames, Lindley Murray, and Richard Whately served as

---

26 EUL Ms. Gen. 850. We include manuscript references within the text, employing the following abbreviations: University of Edinburgh Library, EUL; Glasgow University Library, GUL; and National Library of Scotland, NLS. We also include each library's catalogue numbers.

27 Cited in Robert Morrell Schmitz, *Hugh Blair* (Morningside Heights: King's Crown) 67.

28 Herbert McLachlin, *English Education under the Test Acts: Being the History of Non-Conformist Academies 1662–1820* (Manchester: Manchester University Press, 1931) 23.

29 J. W. Ashley Smith, *The Birth of Modern Education: The Contribution of the Dissenting Academies 1660–1800* (London: Independent Press, 1954) 263.

30 GUL BCE 28–H.3.

textbooks for almost a hundred years in Britain and elsewhere and were usually available in multiple copies in libraries.)

Some students developed a shorthand in which they took notes,[31] while others used phonetic spellings, a popular movement in the nineteenth century.[32] The professorial practice of dictating notes was indeed common and might well be considered part of writing instruction, drawing on one facet of classical imitation exercises. The extent to which dictates contributed to students' skill in composition undoubtedly varied radically from classroom to classroom, however. The one extant set of notes of Adam Smith's rhetoric lectures appear to be by two students collaborating.[33] At Glasgow, Jardine objected to this procedure since the student "is constantly occupied with the mechanical operation of transferring the words of the lecture to his note-book." Consequently, because his mind is unengaged, "when he leaves college, accordingly, his port-folio, and not his memory, contains the chief part of the instruction he carries away." Jardine maintained that, after leaving the classroom, students should immediately review the lecture in their minds and "commit to writing in their own composition, whatever they judge to be of leading importance."[34] In so doing, "the students have to remember,—to select and arrange the materials furnished to them, and to express, on the spur of the occasion, their ideas in plain and perspicuous language."[35] Jardine's suggestion of summarizing the lectures in a written composition proved invaluable as a productive exercise in selecting and organizing a body of information, and his observations shaped teaching practices elsewhere in the British Isles.

The Role of Examinations and Themes in Writing Instruction

The catechetical system, whereby students were quizzed on lecture materials, was initially oral, but toward the middle of the nineteenth century the written examination began to replace the oral question-and-answer format. In the description of his course on moral philosophy, Professor Henry Calderwood, who had also served as Examiner of Mental Philosophy, and chaired the first School Board for the City of Edinburgh, reported that written and oral examinations were part of instruction and that "subjects are also prescribed for elaborate Essays, as well as for briefer occasional exercises."[36] In the same calendar, Alexander Campbell Fraser, professor of logic and metaphysics, wrote that class hours were devoted to lectures and "also to discipline, by means of Conversations,

---

31 E.g., EUL Ms. Gen 49D.
32 E.g., EUL Ms. Gen. 700.
33 J. C. Bryce, "Introduction" to *Adam Smith Lectures on Rhetoric and Belles Lettres*, gen. ed. A. S. Skinner (Indianapolis: Liberty Classics, 1985) 4.
34 George Jardine, *Outlines of Philosophical Education Illustrated by the Method of Teaching Logic, or First Class of Philosophy in the University of Glasgow* (Glasgow: Printed by Andrew & James Duncan, Printers to the University, 1818) 278. For a fuller discussion of Jardine's instructional practices see Lynée Lewis Gaillet, "George Jardine's Outlines of Philosophical Education: Prefiguring 20th-Century Composition Theory and Practice," in *Scottish Rhetoric and Its Influences* (Mahwah: Hermagoras Press, 1998) 193–208. Also see Gaillet, "George Jardine: Champion of the Scottish Philosophy of Democratic Intellect," *Rhetoric Society Quarterly* 28 (1998): 37–51.
35 Jardine 289.
36 EUL Calendar 1859–60.

short Exercises, and Essays, meant to train the members to logical habits and a reflective life. General Examinations, at which answers are returned in writing to questions proposed by the Professor, are held at intervals the course of the Session."[37] In many universities, especially those in Scotland, writing instruction took place across the curriculum in accord with the *1831 Report of the Royal Commission:* "In addition to Examinations, Exercises and Essays should be required from all the regular Students in each class, and ought to be criticized by the professor."[38] Consequently, instruction in writing was never confined to any single course, though, to be sure, language arts instructors sought to develop students' prose style in particular ways.

Giving evidence before the Commission in 1827, Professor Robert Scott had described his class in moral philosophy, which met for two-and-a-half hours during the day. The first half-hour was spent in oral examination of the preceding day's lecture "with the students reading aloud their written answers to questions assigned the day before." A considerable part of the afternoon hour was spent "in the practice of composition"; subjects were prescribed "and a time fixed, before which the essays must be left by the authors at the Professor's house."[39] Jardine's approach at Glasgow is described in his 1825 *Outlines of a Philosophical Education.*[40] Themes should be "prescribed frequently and regularly," and the subjects should be "numerous and various." In a four-ordered sequence, Jardine described his assignments. In the first order, during the first two months, there was a theme almost every day, "the subject proposed in the form of a question." Following that, students were required to use analysis and classification: "How may books in a library be arranged?" Students were then asked to prove a proposition: "The hand of the diligent maketh rich," "Do holidays promote study?" or "Personal talents and virtues are the noblest acquisition." The fourth and final order engaged the student "in the higher processes of investigation," which "may be said to constitute the envied endowment of genius."[41]

Student-Centered, Authentic Writing

Some educators advocated a more authentic curriculum. Whately's pedagogy, for instance, was student centered, as he reminded teachers to assign relevant writing topics that engage the learner. The young writer "must be encouraged to express himself (in correct language indeed, but) in a free, natural, and simple style; which of course implies (considering who and what the writer is supposed to be) such a style as, in itself, would be open to severe criticism, and certainly very unfit to appear in a book."[42] He goes on: "the compositions of boys *must* be puerile," but "to a person of unsophisticated and sound taste, the truly

37 J. C. Bryce, "Introduction" to *Adam Smith Lectures on Rhetoric and Belles Letters*, gen. ed. A. S. Skinner (Indianapolis: Liberty Classics, 1985) 4.

38 *Public Records: A Description of the Contents, Objects, and Uses of the Various Works Printed by Authority of the Record Commission, etc. Great Britain Record Commission* (London: Baldwin and Cradock, 1831) (hereafter *Royal Commission*) 34.

39 *Royal Commission* 40.

40 Gaillet, "George Jardine's Outlines."

41 Jardine 291–360.

42 Whately, *Elements* 23.

contemptible kind of puerility would be found in the other kind of exercises": those "*dried specimens*" "on any subject on which one has hardly any information, and no interest; about which he knows little, and cares still less."[43] Thus dismissing the traditional subjects of declamations and other composition exercises, Whately urged the teacher instead to

> Look at the letter of an intelligent youth to one of his companions, communi-
> cating intelligence of such petty matters as are interesting to both—describing
> the scenes he has visited, and the recreations he has enjoyed during a vacation;
> and you will see a picture of youth himself—boyish indeed in looks and in
> stature—in dress and in demeanour; but lively, unfettered, natural, giving a
> fair promise for manhood, and, in short, what a boy should be. Look at a
> theme composed by the same youth, on "Virtus est medium vitiorum," or
> "Natura beads omnibus esse dedit," and you will see a picture of the same boy,
> dressed up in the garb, and absurdly aping the demeanour of an elderly man.[44]

Although his ultimate goal was argumentative writing, Whately and those who follow him ushered in a new kind of writing in Britain: the personal essay. Specifically, he recommended drawing up an outline, or "skeleton [. . .] of the substance of what is to be said," one from which the writer could freely deviate, "a *track* to mark out a path for him, not as a *groove* to confine him."[45] He also offered detailed guidance for discovering and arranging propositions and argu-ments[46] and for forming a natural prose style and delivery.

Responses to Writing

How teachers responded to student writing is difficult to discern since such evidence tends to be ephemeral. Extant evidence suggests that teachers at both the secondary and university levels paid close attention to student work but that prac-tices varied. Teachers checked traditional writing assignments, like those requiring students to translate from Latin into English, for correctness. Such exercises were intended to inculcate correctness, form a writer's style, and extend his (or, more rarely, "her") stylistic range. The instructor's markings were suited to those ends: sometimes the instructor corrected the work; other times they marked errors that students were then expected to correct; still other times, the students themselves were expected to self-correct it. Exercises and themes were frequent.

Edinburgh University Library has in its manuscript archive a collection of twelve essays written by John Dick Peddies for William Spalding's course in Rhetoric and Belles Lettres in 1844–45.[47] Written during Peddies' last year in the university, the themes vary from twelve to forty-two pages and cover such topics as "Remarks on Harris' Treatise on Music, Painting, and Poetry" and "Remarks on different points in the Association Theory of Beauty." Professor Spalding's comments, brief and complimentary, were likely augmented by oral

43   Ibid.
44   Whately, *Elements* 23–24.
45   Whateley, *Elements* 25.
46   It dealt with methods of proof, not methods of inquiry. The philosopher seeks, the rhetor communicates.
47   EUL Ms. Gen. 769D.

comments. It was common for teachers to read the themes, either in class or after, and to discuss the student's work with him. Spalding, for example, corrected errors in agreement and the use of "will" for "shall." Other papers displayed common confusions like "principle" for "principal" and "their" for "there." (Popular textbooks of the period reviewed such matters.)

Throughout the eighteenth and nineteenth centuries, then, with few exceptions, responding to student writing was a matter of correction rather than appraisal, and more often than not it was oral. In the lower schools, it was largely correction of mechanical errors, as described in John Walker's "Hints for correcting and improving juvenile composition":

> The pupil writes a draft on loose paper. Next day he copies it, with amendments, on the lefthand side of the paper of an exercise book. He reads the theme, without interruption, to the teacher, who then takes it sentence by sentence and shows the pupil where he has erred, either in the thought, the structure of the sentence, the grammar of it, or the choice of words.[48]

The pupil then made a fair copy on the right-hand page of his **exercise book**. Walker urged that course enrollment be kept as low as possible to ensure that students receive the necessary attention.[49] Instruction sometimes seemed concerned with presentation—not with a critically engaged mind.

Often students read their work aloud so that it might be criticized publicly either by the professor or classmates or both. In describing his course, Professor Robert Scott reported: "After being examined in private by the Professor, and the inaccuracies, whether of thought or composition, carefully marked, they are returned to the authors, by whom they are read publicly in the class; their inaccuracies are pointed out, and commented on, and an opinion as to their merits or defects publicly expressed."[50] The first set of essays "is generally read by the Professor, without mentioning the names of the authors [. . .] to save the feelings of individuals," Scott added.[51]

Jardine's method of responding to themes, outlined in a chapter titled "On the Method of Determining the Merits of the Themes," sounds remarkably modern and influenced many British teachers during the nineteenth century. Faced with a class of nearly two hundred students, he contended that "experience and habit enable the teacher to execute his work more expeditiously than might at first be believed."[52] He further suggests for large classes the use of "**examinators**," ten or twelve students from the class who read other students' work, with the professor selecting works that "abound with defects" for his own inspection, which he returned with remarks "most likely to encourage, and to direct future efforts."[53] (Indeed, he urged that "the professor must touch their failings with a gentle

---

48 Cited in Michael 222.
49 Ibid.
50 *Royal Commission* 40.
51 Ibid.
52 George Jardine, *Outlines of Philosophical Education Illustrated by the Method of Teaching Logic, or First Class of Philosophy in the University of Glasgow* (Glasgow: Printed by Andrew & James Duncan, Printers to the University, 1818) 364.
53 Jardine 371.

hand."[54]) In notes from David Masson's class in 1881, the student jots down the assignment and instructions on the last page of volume four: "Attend to neatness of form, expression, and pointing, as well as the matter."[55] Masson, who taught first at University College London, and subsequently at Edinburgh, commented on both form and content. Somewhat unusually, John Hoppus, a professor at University College London, for nearly forty years, determined prize essays by student vote.

Education in the British Isles

British students in the eighteenth century who sought out higher education might attend one of the universities—Oxford, Cambridge, Trinity, St. Andrews, Aberdeen, Glasgow, or Edinburgh—or one of the dissenting academies. In the nineteenth century, they might also attend Catholic University, Dublin, the University of Wales, or any of the new English redbrick universities.[56] Students' choices depended largely on religious affiliation, economic status, and the region in which they lived.

England

By the eighteenth century Oxford and Cambridge had degenerated into a "preserve for the idle and the rich."[57] Their cost—between 200 and 300 pounds per annum in the 1830s—was prohibitive to most citizens. They were also elitist institutions: undergraduates of noble birth wore embroidered gowns of purple silk and a college cap with a gold tassel, which distinguished them from poor students, who donned simple attire. What's more, such students were excused from all examinations leading to a degree (even though test standards were dismally low) and were required to be in residence only thirteen weeks out of the year. "[A]ll the leading men of the eighteenth century—Bentham, Butler, Gibbon, Adam Smith, Vicesimus Knox and many lesser lights," Nicholas Hans points out, "condemned the two Universities from their personal experiences as students."[58] Knox, headmaster of Tonbridge School from 1778 to 1812, called the requirements for the Oxford degree a "set of childish and useless exercises" which "raise no emulation, confer no honour and promote no improvement." Fellows "neither study themselves nor concern themselves in superintending the studies of others."[59] Scholar R. L. Archer describes Oxford of the time as "a university in which professors ceased to lecture, and where work was the last thing expected." Students "entered the University not to feed on solid intellectual food, but to

---

54 Jardine 365.
55 EUL Ms DK. 4.28–30.
56 Because females of means were eligible for few of the educational opportunities enjoyed by boys and men of means in the eighteenth and nineteenth centuries, our discussion here refers to male students only, unless we indicate otherwise. We devote a later section to female education.
57 H. C. Barnard, *A History of English Education from 1760*, 2nd ed. (London: University of London Press, 1961) 24.
58 Nicholas Hans, *New Trends in Education in the Eighteenth Century* (London: Routledge & Kegan Paul, 1955) 42. Hans attempts to refute charges commonly made against eighteenth-century Oxford and Cambridge, especially that poor students had deserted them. His arguments are not convincing against substantial evidence to the contrary.
59 Cited in Barnard 25–26.

enjoy a costly luxury." Indeed, Oxford was marked by "extravagance, debt, drunkenness, gambling, and an absurd attention to dress."[60] While Cambridge fared better, both southern universities were preserves of the cultural elite.

In the late eighteenth century, class attendance was low. At Oxford in 1850, "out of 1500 or 1600 undergraduates, the average annual attendance at the modern history course was 8; at botany 6 and at Arabic, Anglo-Saxon, Sanskrit and medicine, none."[61] Lectures were dubbed "wall lectures" because the lecturers had no audience but the walls. Oxford and Cambridge offered little for students who came well prepared, and preparatory school students beat university students to capture many of the universities' classical prizes. Reform came slowly in the middle of the nineteenth century under the Oxford University Act and the Cambridge Reforms of 1854–56. Founder's Kin scholarships were opened to competition, and for the first time University business could be carried out in English instead of Latin.[62] Life fellowships were abolished, and celibacy was no longer required for college fellows. In 1871, religious tests for the degree were finally abolished. New professorships were established, the curriculum was broadened, and examinations were made more stringent.

In spite of these nineteenth-century reforms, however, Oxford and Cambridge continued to be aristocratic and conservative. Under the direction of their college tutor, Oxford and Cambridge students were instructed first in Latin and then in Greek composition. Tutors varied greatly in expertise and commitment, and some colleges offered quite a strong classical education. Both Matthew Arnold (at Balliol) and John Henry Newman (at Trinity) were schooled in classical language studies, going through language exercises like those described by Don Paul Abbott in Chapter 5 of this volume. Translation exercises not only developed students' command of Latin and Greek but of English as well. When the tutor was qualified (as the tutors of Arnold and Newman apparently were) and his charges studious, writing instruction was well served. More often, it seems, studies were unfocused, with the student dabbling in Latin and Greek, never understanding the relevance of the classics, never understanding how rhetoric might draw connections between education and life.

It was left first to the Scottish universities and English dissenting academies, then to the English redbricks and new provincial universities, to inspire educational innovations, including the establishment of English vernacular as an academic study. Under pressure and with reluctance, Oxford and Cambridge institutionalized English studies only at the end of the nineteenth century, long after the dissenting academies, the provincial universities, and redbrick universities had done so.

Dissenting Academies

Dissenting academies, sponsored by Protestants who opposed the prevailing Anglican-controlled education, were innovative and strong in the eighteenth century. As Thomas P. Miller has established, as early as the last quarter of the

60 R. L. Archer, *Secondary Education in the Nineteenth Century* (Cambridge: Cambridge University Press, 1921) 7.
61 Barnard 82.
62 Barnard 123.

seventeenth century, English composition and literature were taught to college-age students in purposeful, systematic ways.[63] The academies had begun as a response to the 1662 renewal of the Act of Uniformity, originally passed in 1559, by which all schoolmasters and students were required to take the oath of conformity and to renounce the Scottish covenant. On August 24 of that year, nearly 2,000 rectors and vicars resigned.[64] The early academies were illegal, but after the Act of Toleration in 1689, the English grammar schools and high schools were opened to all comers, though the universities maintained religious restrictions. The academies filled the gap by offering education equivalent to that of the universities, but distinguished themselves by being the first to offer modern subjects, including English composition and literature. Founded by fine scholars, many of whom were themselves educated in Scotland or on the continent, the academies were marked by a seriousness and a political activism lacking at the two ancient universities. Originally designed to educate ministers, in the eighteenth century the academies broadened their scope and took on utilitarian purposes. English studies served the dissenters' economic and political reform agendas.[65]

In general, the academies were superior to the colleges of Oxford and Cambridge, for they boasted much stricter curriculums. Terms were longer, vacations shorter. Students were as young as fourteen since preparatory opportunities were limited: freed from religious restrictions, these institutions served the brightest eighteenth-century British youth, turning out a generation of brilliant men of letters as well as an avid reading public. Students often began to study in the early morning, hearing lectures at six and seven, and they continued through the evening.[66] Non-conforming academies, which proliferated during the eighteenth century, tended to be small in faculty and students. Students moved from one school to another, taking advantage of each institution's academic strengths.[67]

According to Miller, dissenters embraced a comparative method of instruction, in which "conflicting views of controversial issues were presented, and then students researched and composed essays arguing their positions," a method "consistent with the dissenters' belief that free inquiry would advance political reform and economic and moral improvement."[68] In so doing, they rejected the conservative approaches to classical language instruction then dominant. At John Jennings's early eighteenth-century academy, for example, students were ordered not to draw upon the received truths of tradition but rather, as Philip Doddridge remembered, to focus on "such subjects as are discoverable by the light of nature."[69] Liberal reformers, they marshaled the power of language instruction in "the progress of reason toward a utopia of free trade, scientific innovation, and rational religion."[70] Writing

---

63 See Chapter 3 ("Liberal Education in the Dissenting Academies") of Thomas Miller's *The Formation of College English* (Pittsburgh: University of Pittsburgh Press, 1997) for a discussion of how dissenters taught English. Our account draws upon Miller's work.
64 McLachlin 1.
65 See Miller; also see McMurtry.
66 McLachlin 25.
67 McLachlin 23–25.
68 Miller 86.
69 Quoted in Miller 89.
70 Miller 88.

instruction helped to fulfill the pedagogical goals of such teachers as Isaac Watts, Philip Doddridge, and Joseph Priestley.

In *The Compleat English Gentleman*, written in 1728, Daniel Defoe recommends studying English along the lines his teacher Charles Morton promoted: each week students, under the guise of public figures, wrote an oration and two compositions. "Thus he taught us to write a masculine and manly stile, to write the most polite English, and at the same time to kno' how to suit their manner as well to the subject they were to write upon as persons or degrees of persons they were to write to; and all equally free and plain, without foolish flourishes and ridiculous flights of jingling bombast in stile, or dull meanness or expression below the dignity of the subject or the character of the writer."[71] Differences with classical traditions notwithstanding, these new approaches to writing instruction remained strongly rhetorical. Though writing instruction varied by individual teacher, some practices were common. Students often debated orally as preparation for writing, critiqued discourse (including sermons), rejected dependence upon traditional invention and syllogistic reasoning, favored empiricism, promoted enlightenment values like individualism, encouraged student discussion, respected the vernacular, and favored plain styles and practical forms and genres likely to be useful in public life and future employment.

Part of the curriculum at all levels, writing instruction took its place variously alongside the study of elocution and *belles lettres*, as well as alongside mathematics, geography, classical and modern languages, history, political economy, and science. The practical was valued over the aesthetic, composition over literature. In fact, Joseph Priestley, who taught at Warrington Academy, pioneered forms of scientific and political writing.[72] Miller credits thinkers like Smith and Priestley with developing "a modern philosophy of public education."[73] During the first quarter of the nineteenth century, however, the academies lost much of their vitality as they became more narrowly practical and abandoned the working classes and the poor.

The New Universities

Another development in the nineteenth century was the founding of the English "redbrick" universities, whose facades contrasted markedly with the stone that was characteristic of the ancient universities. The first of these, London University (later University College London), was founded in 1828. Not only was there no religious test for admission and degree, theology was pointedly excluded from the curriculum. Although classical studies found an honored place, science, medicine, and other modern, practical studies, including the vernacular, were favored. Indeed, it was here that the first formal professorship explicitly devoted to English was established. In the earliest years, writing instruction in the English courses was modeled after Scottish belletristic pedagogy.[74] Under the Rev.

---

71 Cited in Miller 90.
72 See Charles Bazerman, *Handbook of Research on Writing: History, Society, School, Individual, Text* (New York: Lawrence Erlbaum, 2008).
73 Miller 105.
74 See Linda Ferreira-Buckley, "Scotch Knowledge and the Formation of Rhetorical Studies in 19th-Century England," *Scottish Rhetoric and Its Influences*, ed. Lynée Gaillet (Mahwah: Hermagoras, 1998) 163–75.

Thomas Dale, students at University College took "Principles and Practice of English Composition," in which they studied the philosophy of language and the fundamentals of speaking and writing. Earlier as tutor to John Ruskin and other children, and later as professor of English at University College London, and at King's College London, Dale drew upon Blair's *Lectures on Rhetoric and Belles Lettres*, an edition of which he later produced. In Dale's literature course, students also applied these principles to works of English letters and to their own compositions on polite subjects. Decades later, when David Masson assumed the English professorship at University College London, he paid more attention to great literary traditions, to philology, and to classical rhetoric, confirming that classical rhetoric was esteemed by some new literature professors. Successors taught much the same way, although, as the century wore on, philology and English literature came to occupy more course time, composition less.

Until the later third of the nineteenth century, professors of English worked from different philosophies of composition, but they all required that students compose frequently. What's more, students wrote in most courses since professors of other disciplines recognized the role of writing in learning and professional life. Moreover, students wrote constantly in their foreign language courses (ancient and modern), where translation and style exercises sharpened their command of both languages; they also wrote in courses like moral philosophy, where, for example, for nearly forty years John Hoppus, a dissenting minister, drew explicitly upon the writing-to-learn theories promoted by his mentor George Jardine. Indeed, courses taught by Hoppus and others employed the range of exercises practiced today under the rubric of writing across the curriculum and collaborative pedagogy.

Upset that London was served only by this secular institution, Anglicans founded King's College London, in 1831. Due largely to opposition from Oxford and Cambridge, neither college was at first allowed to grant degrees, but beginning in 1836, the University of London was chartered to grant degrees, with students from University and King's among those sitting for examinations. From this beginning, other nonsectarian and nonresidential institutions were founded during the second half of the nineteenth century as instructional rather than degree-granting colleges, among them the universities of Manchester (1871), Liverpool (1881), Leeds (1877), and Newcastle (1871). Many institutions evolved from colleges of various types, originally supported by funds from private individuals and business and civic institutions. Not until 1898 were these institutions permitted to grant degrees, all such credentialing until that time being through the University of London. All of these institutions departed from purely classical education since proficiency in writing English was now considered an indispensable component of education.

Writing Instruction for Working Men and Women

Writing instruction also figured in diverse adult working-class educational enterprises in the nineteenth century: public lectures, scientific, philosophical, and literary societies, mechanics' institutes, book clubs, reading rooms and libraries, and the like. All sought the mutual improvement of members, most usually middle-class or skilled working men, though some women and unskilled laborers benefited as well.[75] Most often such efforts were led by volunteers (often middle-class men and woman or clergy). Sometimes funded by wealthy donors, the organizations and institutions charged small fees (not insignificant to working people, who suffered poor salaries) to cover expenses. Procedures varied: Volunteers taught groups; members formed study groups; individuals engaged in self-study, sometimes guided by another.

Though the diversity of adult education needs to be stressed, some generalizations hold. Liverpool and Manchester boasted large mechanics' institutes that drew many of their members from the middle classes. Subjects such as English language and literature, botany, history, music, and art were included in the afternoon offerings at Manchester, which attracted older middle-class "ladies" with the opportunity to acquire the "intellectual culture" befitting their station in life, while day offerings attracted daughters of the lower-middle class with the "knowledge and skills" suitable for a "young lady."[76] In the latter especially, English skills were stressed: "considerable attention was given to the spoken word and art of conversation and writing, which included not only letter writing but also writing bills, keeping cash accounts, sealing letters and penmaking," for "[s]uch skills," June Purvis observes, "might help young women become competent in middle-class rituals of 'calling' as well as in managerial skills as a future mistress of a household."[77] At Manchester, the superintendent, a Miss Wood, took responsibility for the English Department and taught English reading, grammar, and writing, a sign of the respect accorded the vernacular. Miss Askew assisted. These studies occupied three hours each day. Mr. Daniel Stone taught Biography and Criticism of English Literature on Thursdays from 4 p.m. to 5 p.m.[78] Despite gains in adult education, literacy remained under guard: "controversial" literature was banned in the reading rooms and from the curriculum for both men and women. Class anxiety could not be dispelled—those running the institutes did not want to incite working class men and women.[79] Studies for men focused on rudimentary language skills that might foster the technological expertise useful for their livelihood. Defying the many who believed that the poor should remain illiterate, the evangelical Hannah More pioneered efforts to teach reading to the poor (typically, the aim was to make the Bible accessible), but she too refused to teach writing on the grounds that such skill might make them ungovernable.[80]

75 Historical inquiries have not yet yielded detailed accounts of writing instruction at such locations. Local histories provide a useful beginning point for primary work: see, for example, W. S. Porter, *Sheffield Literary and Philosophical Society* (Sheffield, 1922), and E. K. Clarke, *History of the Leeds Philosophical and Literary Society* (Leeds, 1924).

76 June Purvis, *Hard Lessons: The Lives and Education of Working-Class Women in Nineteenth-Century England* (Cambridge: Polity Press, 1989) 134.

77 Purvis 135.

78 *Twenty-Second Annual Report of the Directors of the Manchester Mechanics' Institution* (Manchester: Johnson, 1846) cited in Purvis 135.

79 Purvis 160.

80 On the positive side, her *Cheap Repository Tracts*, published between 1795 and 1798, sold millions of copies, and in so doing, "pioneered female writing for the mass market of the lower classes." Bonnie S. Anderson and Judith P. Zinsser, *A History of Their Own: Women in Europe from Prehistory to the Present*, vol. 2 (New York: Harper & Row, 1988).

Working men's colleges were another influential component of adult education. The People's College in Sheffield (1842) and the London Working Men's College (1854) were the first of dozens that would spread throughout Britain. Unlike the institutes, whose focus was practical, the colleges valued "humane culture," "democratic comradeship," and "enrichment of personality."[81] Admission was open to any working man who could read and write, the skills upon which their studies were to build. The study of English (including essay writing) flourished— Thomas Kelly compares their curriculums to those offered earlier at dissenting academies.[82] When women were finally admitted, they were refused the composition and elocutionary instruction offered to men on the assumption that such skills were appropriate to the public sphere, not the domestic sphere.

Scotland

More democratic and with fewer religious restrictions for admission or degrees, the Scottish philosophy of education was distinctive. While the ancient English and Irish universities restricted higher education to a tiny percentage of the population, Scottish universities admitted all talented students who sought an education and thus attracted students from the families of merchants, farmers, and factory and land workers, for in the north education was considered a public and state responsibility in addition to an individual and voluntary one. Thus throughout our period, all Scottish children received a primary education that stressed basic literacy skills in English (or occasionally the local vernacular).[83] Some Scottish students proceeded to university with no Latin, though with some proficiency in English composition. Those fortunate enough to attend traditional schools like Edinburgh High School came steeped in classical rhetoric, much like their counterparts in England, having gone through style exercises as preparation for writing orations, the pinnacle of their high school experience.[84] So firm was the faith in the universal applicability of classical study that English was not officially made part of the curriculum at Edinburgh High School until 1827, when it was made one of four optional "General Knowledge" classes available to students who paid additional fees, and then largely because the institution feared losing students to other more "modern" programs. Not until midcentury was a regular English master employed. Because preparatory schools were scarce, allowance was always made for the "lad o'parts"—usually a gifted young man tutored by the local parson in a parish school who then went early to university, sometimes as young as fourteen.[85] Thomas Carlyle, the eldest of five children, walked eighty miles from his home in Ecclefechan to the University of Edinburgh at that young age.[86] University courses were designed to fill in predictable deficiencies in preparation.

---

81 Purvis 164.
82 Thomas Kelly, *History of Adult Education in Great Britain*, 3rd ed. (Liverpool: Liverpool University Press, 1992) 182.
83 Hans 31. For a different perspective, see McElroy, who has challenged claims of Scottish superiority in education.
84 See Ferreira-Buckley and Halloran.
85 Ian R. Findlay, *Education in Scotland* (Hamden CT: Archon Books, 1973) 9–10.
86 See Ian Campbell, *Thomas Carlyle* (New York: Charles Scribner's Sons, 1974), for details of Carlyle's education.

The Scottish universities of Glasgow, St. Andrews, and Aberdeen, all founded in the fifteenth century, were modeled on the continental rather than the English pattern, a fundamental difference that became particularly significant during the eighteenth century. That century, their universities attracted students not only from the surrounding regions but also from England and the continent.[87] The Scottish universities had offered a more philosophically based general education with a more broadly democratic purpose, ordered by the **regent system** in which a single professor stayed with one group of students during their entire program. He was expected to teach all the subjects in the arts curriculum: Latin, Greek, mathematics, chemistry, natural philosophy, and, in the final year, logic, moral philosophy, and rhetoric. Practice in composition—Latin composition—came under the regent's purview and thus did not differ fundamentally from other universities following the dictates of ancient rhetoric. Regenting was abolished at Edinburgh in 1708, at Glasgow in 1727, and at St. Andrews in 1747 but persisted in King's College in Aberdeen until 1798 because of the influence of Thomas Reid. The students seemed not to suffer since professors often had quite able assistant lecturers, who conducted classes, lectured, and commonly assumed their positions upon the chairholder's death.

To be sure, during both the eighteenth and nineteenth centuries, Scottish universities and dissenting academies were distinguished by able professors who wrote widely in the journals of the day and were innovators in philosophy and rhetoric, among other fields. Although Adam Smith is better known today for *Wealth of Nations* (1776) than for his course in rhetoric, for example, his influence in language education was consequential. The broad influence of Hugh Blair and George Campbell, whose books were used on both sides of the Atlantic in the eighteenth and nineteenth centuries, has also been well documented.[88]

In the nineteenth century, Scotland had less well-known but nonetheless influential educators who had a profound effect on the future of English studies and writing instruction at both British and American universities. Three deserve special note to show the range and variety of writing instruction there: Edward Edmondstoune Aytoun, Alexander Bain, and George Jardine.[89] Edward Edmondstoune Aytoun, who held the Chair of Rhetoric and Belles Lettres at Edinburgh from 1845 to 1865, did not believe in instruction in classical rhetoric: "I believe the ancient systems to be unsuited to the circumstances of our

87 George Elder Davie, *The Democratic Intellect: Scotland and Her Universities in the Nineteenth Century* (Edinburgh: Edinburgh University Press, 1961).

88 See the critical introductions to British rhetoricians provided in Michael Moran, ed., *Eighteenth-Century British and American Rhetorics and Rhetoricians* (Westport: Greenwood, 1994) and the description of nineteenth-century Scottish educators and curriculum in Winifred Bryan Horner's *Nineteenth-Century Scottish Rhetoric* (Carbondale: Southern Illinois University Press, 1993). Also see the essays collected in Gaillet, *Scottish Rhetoric*.

89 Our characterizations of Scottish universities are based on lecture notes taken by students, which are housed in the manuscript sections of Scottish libraries. These notes are "dictates" and represent, in many cases, word-for-word representations of a professor's lectures. For a more detailed account see Winifred Bryan Horner, "Rhetoric in the Liberal Arts: Nineteenth-Century Universities," *The Rhetorical Tradition and Modern Writing*, ed. James J. Murphy (New York: MLA, 1982); and, especially, Horner, *Nineteenth-Century Scottish Rhetoric*, which documents the archives in the Scottish universities.

time."[90] Aytoun covered the principles of vernacular composition with an examination of style as exhibited by eminent English authors, along with the rules of spoken discourse. He also offered a critical review of British literature and occasional lectures on ancient and medieval literature. His course came to include more and more English literature, however, a trend popular with students, who paid course fees directly to Aytoun. At his request, the title of his chair was altered to Professor of English and Literature. When in 1861 a Royal Commission recommended that English be offered by all four Scottish universities—none but Edinburgh had a course at the time—writing instruction was assigned to professors of logic. At the outset, the "English" course might well include English history and geography, itself reminiscent of the way such disciplines comprised classical studies. At the time, the concept of literature was broad enough to include historical and scientific essays as well as "works of the imagination," and students usually wrote themes, with varying degrees of instruction. In writing to a friend about his teaching, Aytoun complained that he had enough themes to read to "roast an ox," wry testimony that his students wrote frequently.

Professor of Logic and Rhetoric from 1860 to 1880 at Aberdeen, Alexander Bain moved writing instruction in a markedly different direction. His 1864 course description indicates his emphasis. The Professor of Logic, the Calendar reads, "has two classes, one in English Language and Literature, and the other in Logic." The English class would include "the higher Elements of English Grammar; the Principles of Rhetoric, applied to English Composition, and some portion of the history of English literature."[91] Drawing students from northern districts, Bain faced problems different from those of his Edinburgh colleagues. The students who went to Aberdeen were in general younger, less well prepared, with dialects marked by rusticisms. The perceived duty of the universities became to teach such students to speak, read, and write "cultivated" English (at the time the London received standard). Coming from just such a background, Bain took as his own the responsibility of educating these students. An immensely popular psychology teacher now recognized as a leader in the discipline, he was an immensely *unpopular* rhetoric teacher, for he conceived of the rhetoric course largely in terms of grammar and basic writing, a remedial course in English. Many characteristics of early twentieth-century composition classes can be traced directly to his influence: the **modes of discourse**, which he delineated as narration, description, exposition, argument, and poetry; the topic sentence; and the organic paragraph. His textbook, *English Composition and Rhetoric* (1866), went through six editions in ten years; his several grammar books also sold well. Bain felt strongly that the way to good English, written and spoken, was primarily through a knowledge of grammar, which he conscientiously drilled into his students. His pedagogy reduced composition to the teachable forms that are his legacy.

90   NLS MS 4913, fol. 29v. According to the *Dictionary of National Biography,* thirty students were enrolled in his classes in 1846; an astonishing 1,850 by 1864. Aytoun's lectures in his own hand are contained in manuscripts 4897–4911 in the collection of the National Library of Scotland. These manuscripts attest that Aytoun was constantly changing and updating his lectures and was a lively and informative lecturer. Excerpts from his lectures are published in Erik Frykman, *W. E. Aytoun, Pioneer Professor of English at Edinburgh,* Gothenburg Studies in English 17 (Gothenburg, 1963). Also see Horner, *Nineteenth-Century Scottish Rhetoric.*

91   Alexander Bain, *English Composition and Rhetoric: A Manual* (London: Longmans, 1866) n.p.

Like Bain, George Jardine recognized Scottish students as ones "who are not qualified, either in respect to age or previous acquirements," but he approached this challenge in a very different way, his enlightened teaching methods prefiguring those of modern composition.[92] During his long tenure as Professor of Logic and Rhetoric at the University of Glasgow from 1774 to 1824, Jardine was deeply involved in the educational issues of the day, a strong champion of the Scottish system. While formerly education was preparation for church and state, he recognized that modern Scottish universities were designed for young men "destined to fill various and very different situations in life."[93] He understood that knowledge was not enough and admonished his students that "a man may be capable of great reflections but if he cannot communicate it to others, it can be little use."[94] His remarkably enlightened teaching methods, described in his book *Outlines of Philosophical Education Illustrated by the Method of Teaching Logic, or First Class of Philosophy in the University of Glasgow*, urged peer review, promoted writing as a way of learning, and made frequent sequenced writing assignments. Writing instruction was necessarily dispersed throughout the curriculum. The extent of his influence is only beginning to be understood.

Wales

Welsh students had few school options. Due largely to the system of circulating schools launched in the 1830s by the Rev. Griffith Jones, many of the poorer classes were taught the rudimentary reading skills so that they were able to read the Welsh translation of the Bible. Apparently, instruction in writing rarely moved much beyond teaching students to spell and write their names. Wales had a few grammar schools but no universities until the founding of University College Wales in 1872, of the University College of South Wales and Monmouthshire in 1883, of University College of North Wales in 1884, and of Wrexham School of Science and Art in 1887.

Functional illiteracy was pervasive. The Registrar-General reported in 1864: "In south Wales, an average of 64 per cent of men and 48 per cent of women were able to write their names."[95]

As in Scotland, much Welsh education stemmed from provincial linguistic anxiety. Middle-class parents often wished their sons and daughters to lose tell-tale signs of Welsh in written and spoken language, the well-off sometimes sending their children to England to "finish" their schooling. As W. Gareth Evans remarks, "the ethos of the middle-class girls' schools was English rather than Welsh."[96] In fact, Welsh was strictly forbidden. By the middle of the nineteenth century, at the most prestigious schools, girls would also study French, the

---

92 George Jardine, *Outlines of Philosophical Education Illustrated by the Method of Teaching Logic, or First Class of Philosophy in the University of Glasgow* (Glasgow: Printed by Andrew NS James Duncan, Printers to the University, 1818) 427. See Gaillet, "George Jardine's Outlines," for a fuller discussion of Jardine's instructional practices.

93 Jardine 31.

94 GUL Ms. Gen. 737, vol. 2, 157.

95 W. Gareth Evans, *Education and Female Emancipation: The Welsh Experience, 1847–1914* (Cardiff: University of Wales Press, 1960) 53.

96 Evans 60.

only foreign language permitted. H. M. Bompas, who authored the eighth volume of the *Taunton Report*, expressed the common view that the native language "interferes with education" and reported that "in some parts" knowing Welsh was "considered unfashionable for girls," observing that "this feeling is likely to make the language die out rapidly, at least among the middle classes."[97] Since boys of some means were expected to acquire the classical languages as well, they were even less likely to study Welsh in school.

At the end of the nineteenth century some citizens reclaimed the right to study their home language. In her prize-winning essay on the set topic, "The Higher Education of Girls in Wales with practical suggestions as to the best means of promoting it," for example, student Elizabeth Hughes argued for the study of Welsh in schools and colleges:

> Let us have a national education to preserve and develop our national type [. . .]. An ideal Welsh education must be national. It must differ from an ideal English education primarily because of the difference of race [. . .]. Difference of race, far from being a subject for regret, as far as possible should be deepened and perpetuated. The differences of race found within the bounds of the British Empire can become a source of strength and completeness.[98]

The language spoken by a million people was not accorded this sign of respect until the following century, however.

Some of the most powerful literacy movements took hold beyond school walls and without educational texts per se. For example, Sarah Yoder Skripsky revealed the rhetorical efficacy of the Young Wales nationalist movement of the late nineteenth and early twentieth centuries in its literary magazines, especially in light of long-running debates about the Welsh versus the English language.[99] These magazines championed Welsh communal agency to combat cultural disempowerment.

Educational Reform in the Closing Decades of Nineteenth-Century Britain

The impoverished literacy skills of most Britons were troubling: too few members of the working classes could read; fewer still could write. In England and Wales, the 1860s educational reforms tended to reify class divisions, with the *Newcastle Report* (1861) examining education for the masses, the *Clarendon Report* (1864) studying education for the elite in the nine most eminent "public" (i.e., private) schools, and the *Taunton Report* (1868) weighing in on that for the middle classes. The six-volume *Newcastle Report* underscored the deficiencies in mass education: random lessons were too often taught by incompetent teachers in a hodgepodge of situations. The costs of improvement to the state would be great (it would be three decades before the government required that education be free of cost to

---

97 *Report of the Taunton Commission*, vol. 8, cited in Evans 61.
98 *Transactions of the Liverpool National Eisteddfod*, 1884, 40–62, 49–50; cited in Evans 137.
99 Sarah Yoder [Skripsky], "Miscellany Rhetoric(s) of Nationalism: Postcolonial Epideictic and the Anglophone Welsh Press, 1882–1904" (PhD thesis, Texas Christian University, 2008).

students), and leaders demanded measurable outcomes on set subjects. The Revised Code of 1861 set six standards—writing among them—on which students' progress was to be measured. Soon after, in 1862, the "Payment by Results" system required elementary students to take Her Majesty's Inspectors' end-of-year examinations, and teachers' pay was in part funded by student pass rates. Evidence suggests that, soon after, writing instruction was quickly "taught" in overly formulaic ways by teachers determined to teach their students a formula for passing the test. Rates of basic literacy began to rise more substantially after the 1870 Education (or Forster) Act, which guaranteed nondenominational public education for all children aged 5 to 13, and again after the 1891 Education Act, which for the first time mandated that instruction be free.[100]

Ireland

Ireland, with its largely Catholic population, did not fare well. Irish education also suffered under colonial control. Irish or Gaelic, the indigenous language, was not a school or official language and languished correspondingly. Well-off Protestants founded so-called "English schools" to promote British education, not least of which was a command of the King's English. As Miller points out, such efforts affected not only schools but university study as well. John Lawson, professor in oratory and history, whose *Lectures Concerning Oratory* (1758) draws upon classical precepts in discussing rhetoric and poetry, was the first university professor in Ireland to publish language lectures in English, Miller notes.[101] In this regard, Lawson typified Protestant educators in Ireland of our period who felt the pressures of residing in a cultural province and thus sought to "meet the Irish gentlemen's need to know the language and literature of England."[102] Anglicans in Ireland continued to attend Trinity College, Dublin, whose classical curriculum and academic seriousness offered a solid if somewhat old-fashioned education in writing. A full archival record documents instruction in rhetoric and writing there, including curriculum records and prize essays.[103] Founded in 1592, Trinity College introduced students to rhetoric in a variety of contexts, including in the lectures of the "Professor of Theological Controversies," and, beginning in 1724, in the lectures given by the holder of the Erasmus Smith Chair of Oratory and History. In formulating instruction in rhetoric, holders of the chair, John Lawson beginning in 1750, but especially Thomas Leland beginning in 1761, drew upon classical rhetoric but sought to correct and enrich it in light of the new rhetoric. Both Lawson's *Lectures Concerning Oratory* (1758) and Leland's *Dissertation on the Principles of Human Eloquence* (1765) suggest the coming together of the old and new rhetorical principles and eloquence's broadening to include both oratory and poetry.

100 See David Vincent, "The Progress of Literacy," *Victorian Studies* 45.3 (Spring 2003): 405–431.
101 Our discussion of Irish education draws upon the helpful accounts offered by Thomas Miller in *The Formation of College English* (1997) and by Jean Dietz Moss in "Discordant Concensus': Old and New Rhetoric at Trinity College, Dublin," *Rhetorica* 13.4 (1996): 383–411.
102 Miller 118.
103 See Moss's rich account.

Students practiced classical language exercises, written and oral, as part of their formal study, but, just as important, they fostered those language skills in extracurricular societies. In 1747, for example, Edmund Burke founded the "Academy of Belles Lettres" at Trinity, a forum for lively debate (it would lead to the Historical Society and the College Historical Society, the latter for the expressed purpose of the "Cultivation of History, Oratory, and Composition".[104] Students longed for "practical experience." Jean Dietz Moss, quoting from the club's early minutes, makes clear that its "business" was "speeching, reading, writing and arguing, in Morality, History, Criticism, Politicks, and the useful branches of philosophy."[105] In *Chironomia* (1806) Gilbert Austin writes that "The speaking societies set up at various times in London and in Dublin, and perhaps in other cities, have had the practice of declamation for their object. Imaginary subjects have been discussed and debated with all the interest of real occasion, and with all the efforts of declamation; and not infrequently with considerable powers of eloquence. These societies operated as incentive to oratory, and awakened love of eloquence, if they did not teach it."[106] At various times and places, however, anxious administrators banned student debate about controversial contemporary issues. About such efforts at the University of Dublin, Austin writes that they are "flourishing in all the acquirements of classical knowledge, classical eloquence, morality, loyalty, and religion; a nursery of oratory, learning, and taste."[107]

The Irish Catholic population did not fare as well. Some risked punishment by relying on illegal "hedge" schools, which educated students in Gaelic culture and the classics.[108] Catholic aristocracy in Ireland employed private tutors and sent their children to continental universities. As government restrictions eased in the nineteenth century, Catholics were permitted to attend state schools (Trinity had begun admitting Catholics in the 1790s), but as John Henry Newman argued, British Catholics needed an institution of their own. "Robbed, oppressed, and thrust aside, Catholics in these islands have not been in a condition for centuries to attempt the sort of education which is necessary for the man of the world, the statesman, the landholder," he observed. "Only advanced and rigorous study"—liberal education that aimed at "cultivation of the mind" and thus fostered thinking, speaking, and writing—would politically empower Catholics.[109] When, in the 1850s, Newman helped to found the Catholic University in Dublin, he insisted that students be immersed in classical language study, much like that which he had enjoyed at Trinity College, Oxford. Grammar and rhetoric were central in writing instruction in Latin and Greek. They studied English language and literature as well, a sign of the vernacular's growing acceptance in higher education.

---

104   Quoted in Moss 407.
105   Moss 403.
106   Gilbert Austin, *Chironomia, or a Treatise on Rhetorical Delivery* (1806), ed. Mary Margaret Robb and Lester Thonssen (Carbondale: Southern Illinois University Press, 1966) 212.
107   Ibid.
108   Moss 385.
109   John Henry, Cardinal Newman, *The Idea of a University* (Garden City: Image Books, 1959) 12.

Female Education

No matter what their class or regional affiliation, British girls were not permitted the level of education afforded boys.[110] A few eighteenth-century girls attended grammar schools, but most of those fortunate enough to receive an education received it at home, often under the tutelage of their mother or governess. Boys could go away to school—a move toward intellectual and social independence; girls rarely did. "School parted us," lamented George Eliot, looking back on her own brother's departure.[111] The distance was both physical and psychological, of course, for the boy would be immersed in Latin and eventually Greek languages and literatures, in reading, speaking, and writing—intellectual activities made to foster in him a public sense of self. Traditionally the purpose of secondary and higher education was to train young men for service to church and state, roles then unthinkable for women. Some girls might study from a brother's books, but most parents discouraged the practice. Some might go to an academically weak finishing school, where writing instruction would be limited to learning/ practicing discursive forms suitable for social occasions or to composing light verse. Very early on, Quakers and a few nonconformist schools defied cultural mores to offer girls serious academic educations and deemphasize "accomplish-ments."[112] Although some men became advocates of women's education—Daniel Defoe, for example, decried the "barbarous custom of denying the advantages of Learning to Women" as early as the seventeenth century, observing, "We reproach the Sex everyday with Folly and Impertinence, while I am confident, had they the advantages of Education equal to us, they wou'd be guilty of less than ourselves"[113]—the Defoes were few, and their arguments went largely unheeded until the end of the nineteenth century.

Prohibitions against female education were made on both biological and cultural grounds. One commonly held fear was that rigorous study led to infer-tility and insanity—a woman thus defying her God-given limitations would be unsexed, dehumanized.[114] Medical officials warned that females were ill-equipped to handle the rigors of study: overtaxed by the demands of learning the classical languages, for instance, a female might be driven insane. Even Charles Darwin and Herbert Spencer believed that scientific evidence confirmed such lore.[115] Society feared that educated women would be "argumentative wives"

110 Although literacy statistics are not wholly reliable (not least because definitions of what constitutes "literacy" differ radically) historians have arrived at rough estimates: "While women's ability to read and write trailed behind men's (by twenty to twenty-five percentage points in this era), literacy became standard for girls above the working class. By 1750, 40 percent of English women and 27 percent of French women could sign their names—not an adequate test of literacy, but one of the few ways of assessing it before the nineteenth century" (Anderson and Zinsser 139).

111 Ruby V. Redinger, *George Eliot: The Emergent Self* (New York: Knopf, 1975) 610.

112 Gillian Avery, *The Best Type of Girl: A History of Girls' Independent Schools* (London: André Deutsch, 1991).

113 Quoted in D. P. Leinster-Mackay, *The Educational World of Daniel Defoe* (University of Virginia, 1981) 37.

114 Carol Dyhouse, *Girls Growing up in Late Victorian and Edwardian England* (London: Routledge & Kegan Paul, 1981), and "Good Wives and Little Mothers: Social Anxieties and the School Girls' Curriculum 1890–1920," *Oxford Review of Education* 3.1: 21–35. Showalter, Elaine, "Victorian Women and Menstruation," in *Suffer and Be Still: Women and the Victorian Age*, ed. Martha Vicinus (Bloomington, IN: Indiana University Press, 1972) 38–44.

115 Anderson and Zinsser 151–152.

who would undermine the institution of marriage. They "would join in discussions of public affairs and disturb the household by challenging the opinions of their husbands and sons." Accordingly, learned women were undesirable, destined most likely to become "old maids."[116] Would a man be happier "if he were mated with a 'being' who, instead of mending his clothes and getting his dinner cooked, had a taste for a literary career upon the subject of political economy?" asked a *Saturday Review* writer in 1864. Decidedly not. "There is a strong, an ineradicable male instinct, that a learned, or even an over-accomplished young woman is one of the most intolerable monsters in creation."[117] High-level literacy—especially the skills of rhetorical education—endangered the domestic ideal.

Even advocates of female education disagreed on its end: some, like Emily Davies, argued that females must have a liberal education identical to that enjoyed by males in order to avail themselves of professional opportunities. Others, like Hannah More and Dorothea Beale, argued for a distinctly female education that prepared them to fulfill the special role God ordained for "the fairer sex." Still others, like Frances Mary Buss, under whose leadership the North London Collegiate School and Camden Girls' School flourished, emphasized modern subjects likely to help women find full employment.[118] All of these orientations specified a type of writing instruction.

Given the state of female education, it is remarkable that the eighteenth and nineteenth centuries produced so many strong female writers. Many were self-taught, using manuals such as those by Hugh Blair, Alexander Jamieson, and Lindley Murray. Many wrote prolifically in diaries and letters, two discursive forms readily available to them. Letter-writing manuals, some newly published and some centuries old, offered pointed rhetorical advice on topics, genre, and style and schooled readers in grammatical matters. Harriet Martineau rose early to write in secret.[119] Women who dared write publicly risked censure.[120]

As capitalism expanded the middle classes and increased free time, women became more avid readers and writers. For the first time, women could distance themselves from the physical work necessary to running a household (a lower-middle-class woman would have a servant; an upper-middle-class woman might have a dozen), and polite learning marked class membership.[121] Girls of means deigned not to prepare themselves for the workplace but rather for their role at home and in society. In such households, literacy and manners were closely linked, and girls studied courtesy manuals and language books that taught them

---

116 Joan Burstyn, *Victorian Education and the Ideal of Womanhood* (London: Croom Helm, 1980) 42.

117 "Feminine Wranglers," *Saturday Review* 18 (1864) 112; cited in Burstyn 42.

118 Dale Spender, *Women of Ideas* (London: Pandora, 1988) 449.

119 François Basch, *Relative Creatures: Victorian Women in Society and the Novel*, trans. Anthony Rudolf (New York: Schocken, 1974) 106.

120 Carol Poster and Linda C. Mitchell, eds., *Letter-Writing Manuals and Instruction from Antiquity to the Present* (Columbia: University of South Carolina Press, 2007).

121 In 1746, Eliza Haywood advised readers of *The Female Spectator* to learn only enough housekeeping to supervise the servants; more, she warned, might earn her "The reputation of a notable housewife, but not of *a woman of fine taste*, or in any way qualify her for polite conversation, or of entertaining herself agreeably when she is alone" (quoted in G. E. Fussell and K. R. Fussell, *The English Countrywoman: A Farmhouse Social History* [London: Andrew Melrose, 1953] 106, emphasis mine). Not long after, Hugh Blair would preach similar virtues for his young male students at Edinburgh.

the conventions of letter writing and other appropriate forms. Periodicals (some now edited and written by women) catered to the female at home, offering advice and entertainment, often in essay form. Less expensive periodicals (priced at about sixpence in 1800) targeted the women of the working classes.[122] Such entries served as models to be absorbed and emulated. One among many such organizations was the Edinburgh Essay Society (founded in 1865), "a galaxy of youthful maidens, eager for self improvement."[123] For all of the eighteenth century and most of the nineteenth, girls received a poor primary education that favored the domestic arts over academic ones—some girls received none at all. Even girls from well-off families received an inadequate education, for, as Joan Burstyn observes, "Schooling was considered a way for girls to obtain social rather than intellectual skills."[124] Parents chose schools accordingly, paying more attention to the other pupils' social backgrounds than to curricular matters. Girls were trained "to behave as contenders in the marriage market, and as social hostesses."[125] Any writing instruction they received—from their mother, governess, private tutor or private school—was suited to these purposes: letters of all kinds, meditations, and the like.

Girls of the lower classes, who attended the public elementary schools (as did six-sevenths of the working class, male and female), did not fare well.[126] According to Annmarie Turnball, before the 1870 Education Act, working-class children suffered much the same education: basic reading, perhaps some rudimentary writing, religion; they often left school at a young age, as soon as they could work or mind younger siblings. At those schools not under the auspices of the state—including **dame schools** (run by women) and charity schools—curriculums were more gendered, with most of the girls' time spent on sewing, needlework, and cleaning, the activities presumed to be most useful in their adult life.[127] During the closing decades of the nineteenth century, girls of all classes in England, Wales, and Ireland received free primary education from the state (Scottish girls had long enjoyed the benefit). For most of the poor, working, and lower-middle classes, the education was still inadequate and included minimal instruction in reading and writing. A significant portion of "writing" time was devoted to penmanship and to the most basic dictation skills; very little to composing original themes. Women philanthropists also recognized that their poorer sisters needed to be educated if they were to secure an honorable living. Some, like Jessie Boucherette, founded institutions like the Society for Promoting the Employment of Women (1859) to offer "a solid English education to young girls and teach older women to write a letter grammatically."[128] While poorer girls might be taught to read, they were rarely taught to write more than their

---

122 Anderson and Zinsser 139. See also Alison Adburgham, *Women in Print: Writing Women and Women's Magazines from the Restoration to the Accession of Victoria* (London: George Allen & Unwin, 1972).
123 Quoted in Avery 64.
124 Burstyn 22.
125 Ibid.
126 Avery 65.
127 Annmarie Turnball, "'So Extremely like Parliament': The Work of the Women Members of the London School Board, 1870–1904," in London Feminist History Group, ed. *Sexual Dynamics of History* (London: Pluto, 1983) 120–133, at 84.
128 Quoted in Anderson and Zinsser 185.

name. If, after 1870, attention to academic subjects increased somewhat for all children, the reading and writing assignments given girls and boys often remained gender-specific. Boys were to be independent (although obedient to authority) and brave; girls, submissive and meek.

The middle class did not fare much better. In response to Frances Buss's 1865 testimony, the Schools Inquiry Commission (i.e., the Taunton Committee) concluded:

> It cannot be denied that the picture brought before us of the state of middle-class female education is, on the whole unfavourable [. . .] want of thoroughness and foundation; want of system, slovenliness and showy superficiality; inattention to rudiments; undue time given to accomplishments, and these not taught intelligently or in any scientific manner; want of organisation [. . .] a very small amount of professional skill, an inferior set of school books, a vast deal of dry, uninteresting work, rules put into the memory with no explanation of their principles, no system of examination worthy of the name [. . .] a reference to effect rather than to solid worth, a tendency to fill rather than to strengthen the mind.[129]

Change came slowly.

Many girls of the upper-middle classes studied under governesses before being sent off to a finishing school. Girls were educated according to the changing whims and fortunes of their family. "Girls changed schools often, but the progression from one establishment to the next was not logical except in the social sense," writes historian Joyce Senders Pederson.[130] Toward the end of the nineteenth century, the education of female elites improved markedly. Pederson writes: "The public schools and colleges prepared women for public life most obviously in transmitting many of the intellectual skills required for effective functioning in the public sphere. In the old-fashioned, private schools even elementary skills often had been either badly taught (as with arithmetic) or taught so as to be of little use in public life (as was the case with the spiked, illegible handwriting favored by some school mistresses for its supposedly decorative effect). In the new public schools, on the other hand, the children routinely acquired at least the basic arithmetic and literary skills required in the conduct of virtually all sorts of public business, while in the upper school forms and in the women's colleges they were introduced to more arcane disciplines which they had to master were they to compete with men in academic and professional pursuits."[131] In order for women to participate effectively in public, they had to reject the affective ploys they had been taught to rely upon. Reforming headmistresses and college heads worked to instill independence in their

---

129 Frances Buss, "Evidence to the Schools Inquiry Commission (1865)," *The Education Papers: Women's Quest for Equality in Britain, 1850–1912*, ed. Dale Spender (New York and London: Routledge & Kegan Paul, 1987) 140–141.

130 Joyce Senders Pederson, *The Reform of Girls' Secondary and Higher Education in Victorian England: A Study of Elite and Educational Change* (New York: Garland, 1987) 48. Also see Margaret Bryant, *The Unexpected Revolution: A Study in the History of Women and Girls in the Nineteenth Century* (Windsor, UK: NFER, 1979).

131 Pederson 350–351.

charges.[132] Types of writing and topics for writing changed accordingly—from social forms to the professional, from the personal or light moral topics to serious often historical, economic, or political topics. At Kensington High School in 1873, girls were asked to write an essay on the following question: "Which does more for the promotion of industry and commerce, he who expends a given amount of wealth on his own direct personal enjoyments, or he who profitably invests the same, and why?" At Shrewsbury High, students competed every year for best essay on the British Empire. The first issue of North London Collegiate's *Our Magazine* contained essays on the Irish question.[133] Schools also formed debating and literary societies to foster the writing and speaking talents of their charges. Thus schooled, the female graduate of a public school thirsted for further academic training and showed a distinct interest in public affairs.

Thanks to the pioneering efforts of the Girls' Public Day School Trust, the education of upper-middle-class girls improved markedly in England and Wales.[134] Its standards were rigorous: schools under its supervision were staffed with teachers and a headmistress trained in high academic standards and teaching methodology; their curriculum was comparable to boys' public schools, although in addition to Latin, modern studies like French, German, and English (composition, grammar, and literature) were deemed important. The schools were inspected regularly. Its girls sat successfully for examinations, including the Oxford and Cambridge Local Examinations.

But not until the end of the century when two sisters, Emily Shirreff and Maria Shirreff Grey, "laid the foundation of a national education system for girls at the secondary level, a valid teacher-training pattern for that level of education, a revamped, in fact a new national system of early childhood education and the teacher-training structure to sustain it," did all British girls receive regular instruction in writing.[135] Until then the language education of girls and women was spotty, varying greatly by class and family. Of course, the pattern of improvement in female education was erratic and differed within a given city, and, of course, many women and men not mentioned here contributed to those efforts. In *The Best Type of Girl: A History of Girls' Independent Schools*, Avery observes that "English was traditionally a woman's subject and was despised on that account by boys' public schools, who would not recognize as a serious discipline something that they felt was part of the heritage of any well bred gentlemen."[136] Avery maintains that "until there was an abundance of specialist teachers for other subjects, it was probably the best one taught." Instruction was given in literature, composition, and in grammar, the latter being "the girls' substitute for the Latin complexities with which their brothers wrestled." The result, she maintains, was that "girls often emerged as far more fluent on paper than boys, though the content of their essays may not have been particularly apt or informative."[137] They learned to recite literature, and they frequently listened to it being recited.

---

132 Pederson 352.
133 Pederson 354.
134 Josephine Kamm, *Indicative Past: A Hundred Years of the Girls' Public Day School Trust* (London: George Allen & Unwin, 1971) 50.
135 Spender 454–455.
136 Avery 251.
137 Ibid.

Arguably, as students acquired an ear for the language, they became more able crafters of the vernacular. The institutionalized study of vernacular literature often required students to compose essays.

In the latter half of the nineteenth century, higher education gradually became available to women.[138] At North London Collegiate in 1883, students were drilled in French, which they had to translate painstakingly. Doing so was thought to improve their command of standard English. The teaching of English language was similarly uninspired: students "had to be word-perfect in the footnotes given in their texts, these consisting of the paraphrasing of lines thought to be obscure."[139] They also parsed, analyzed clauses, memorized poetry and prose, all in the service of mind training.[140]

In the nineteenth century, the gradual influx of women, first to instruction in universities, then to examinations, and finally at the end of the period to degrees, was perhaps inevitable and helped to bring political and economic recognition to women. The first women's college was Queen's in London, founded in 1848 thanks to the lobbying of the Governesses' Benevolent Institution, which recognized the grave need for competent teachers. Institutions like the Ladies' College (Bedford) followed soon after, mostly to provide teacher training. In 1858, Dorothea Beale, a graduate of Queen's College for Women, became principal of Cheltenham Ladies' College, founded several years earlier to provide middle-class women a rigorous education (but not one equal to that boys received in the public schools). Instruction in female "accomplishments" was replaced by serious training in language and science.[141] Other institutions followed the bold example. Beale also helped to found St. Hilda's College, Oxford, in 1893. Such institutions offered serviceable if not rigorous instruction in writing.

Another advancement in women's education came with the University Extension Lecture Movement, inspired by Anne Jemima Clough, born in Liverpool but receiving her childhood education in South Carolina before returning to her country of birth to teach, first in Ambleside in Westmorland (now Cumbria), then London and Liverpool. Frustrated by the poor quality of female education, she organized what became the University Extension Lecture movement and the North of England Council for Promoting the Higher Education of Women. The circuit ensured that girls from dozens of schools enjoyed high-quality lecturers.[142] Training in the vernacular—appreciation of the *belles lettres*, practice in elocution, instruction in composition—was featured.

---

138 In 1848–49, Queen's College and Bedford College for Women were founded in London, although examinations and degrees were still denied them. In 1865, Cambridge, Edinburgh, and Durham opened their local examinations to women, and the University of London followed in 1868. It was not until 1871, however, that a house of residence was opened for women at Cambridge, and, although in 1874 the University of Edinburgh issued a certificate for women, it was not until 1887 that Victoria University, formed from the union of colleges at Manchester, Liverpool, and Leeds, admitted women to degrees. The four Scottish universities followed suit in 1892 and the Federated University of Wales in 1893. Not until 1920 did Oxford grant women students full university status.

139 Avery 247.

140 Avery 248.

141 Dorothea Beale, *History of the Cheltenham Ladies' College, 1853–1904* (London, 1905).

142 Herbert Spencer, *Epitome of the Synthetic Philosophy of Herbert Spencer* (New York: Appleton, 1889) 449–450.

Salons

A consideration of women's writing instruction would be incomplete without a glance at salons.[143] Importing a tradition begun by the Marquise de Rambouillet in France (not unrelatedly, the birthplace of belletristic rhetoric), British city dwellers took to the salon as "a space in which talented and learned women could meet with men as intellectual equals." "By insisting on tastefulness, courtesy, and polite behavior," Rambouillet shaped "a genteel environment where aspiring authors of both sexes were encouraged to share their work, comment on each others' productions, and participate in elaborate discussions and conversational games."[144] The woman orchestrating such a circle did much to nurture the literary aspirations of the intellectual and social elites who met in their salon or drawing room. One such woman in mid-eighteenth-century London was Elizabeth Montagu, who, tired of trivialities like card playing, organized a salon at her home. Such groups became known as "bluestockings," an appellation that played off the white and black stockings that were de rigueur for Englishmen attending formal events.[145]

Indeed, women's entrée to writing was often through training in arts, either through manuals in rhetoric and belles lettres or courtesy manuals, which schooled them in the necessary social forms of writing, just as it taught them to discern and appreciate the moral virtues of beautiful style. The patronesses of the salon, the "salonières," also sponsored poor women like Elizabeth Carter, whose literary talents would have otherwise gone unrecognized and unsupported. The majority of women received no such opportunities, however, and society continued to deem them intellectually inferior. What's more, as hotbeds of culture, learning, and politics, salons became suspect in nineteenth-century Britain, especially for women.[146] Accordingly, "bluestocking" became a derogatory epithet for learned women who violated the norms of female domesticity.[147]

Middle-class women (viewed as guardians of culture by scholars from Cicero to modern linguist William Labov) constituted a significant portion of the audience in the popular city lectures in the eighteenth and nineteenth centuries. English literature was accessible to them as the classics were not. Their interest contributed to the illegitimacy of literature as an academic discipline, for as they filled lecture halls and (later) classes, women became, as Jo McMurtry points out, "an implicit liability when it came to demonstrating how hard the subject was."[148] Such forums did expand women's participation in literate culture and thus

---

143 Peter Quennell, ed., *Affairs of the Mind: The Salon in Europe and America from the 18th to the 20th Century* (Washington DC: New Republic, 1980) provides a useful overview of the salon movement.
144 Anderson and Zinsser 104.
145 Anderson and Zinsser 109. Feminist Mary Wollstonecraft observed, "[W]omen seem to take the lead in polishing the manners everywhere, that being the only way to better their condition" (*Letters Written during a Short Residence in Sweden, Norway, and Denmark* [Lincoln: University of Nebraska Press, 1976] 181; quoted in Anderson and Zinsser 110).
146 Anderson and Zinsser 114.
147 In 1825, *Ladies Magazine* opined, "Magazines, journals, and reviews abound with sarcastic comments upon the blue-stockings and their productions. Intellectual acquirement, when applied to a woman, is used as a term of reproach" (Cynthia L. White, *Women's Magazines: 1693–1968* [London: Michael Joseph, 1970] 39; quoted in Anderson and Zinsser 116).
148 McMurtry 13.

precipitated opportunities for writing. One final note: the charitable activities of Victorian women also contributed to their literacy skills. True, many women simply dabbled in philanthropy, but for others these projects became serious work. Letters of solicitation had to be written, as did speeches, reports and records. Such activity constituted a form of professional writing that merits further study.

Conclusion

Throughout our period, writing pedagogies in Great Britain varied greatly: some reproduced practices that had been done for many centuries; others went in new directions altogether; still others combined old and new. Although there is much we do not yet know about eighteenth- and nineteenth-century instructional practices in writing—in part because scholars have devoted more attention to studying reading practices than to writing practices[149]—we can make a few broad generalizations. At most schools, academies, and universities, precept guided intense practice in the form of examinations, exercises, and essays, and instruction in writing and speech often continued to be taught side by side within the same courses. In the most traditional grammar and high schools, in addition to exercises students wrote fables and stories and composed verse; at most university-level institutions, the students wrote essays and orations on a variety of subjects in addition to summaries of and responses to professors' lectures. Perhaps most important, just as when classics dominated the curriculum, pupils practiced their language skills as they studied the geography, history, and arts of the ancient world, so too as English became the language of instruction for studies across the curriculum, students wrote throughout most of the school day. In the best schools, then as now, instruction in writing was to some degree integrated into every subject, whether those subjects were taught by the same or different instructors. Although students were taught intensive lessons on writing by someone who claimed expertise, every instructor had the responsibility to have students write so that students wrote frequently in all courses and at all levels. Since Oxford, Cambridge, and Trinity universities and most grammar and public schools preserved the classical tradition until the end of the nineteenth century, and thus taught writing through the old rhetorical and grammatical methods, the dissenting academies, the Scottish universities, the redbrick universities, and other new educational institutions ushered in the beginnings of the modern tradition in English studies.

---

149   See for example the scope of the database that documents reading in Great Britain from 1450 to 1945: www.open.ac.uk/Arts/reading/UK/copyright_guide.php (accessed November 11, 2011).

Chapter 7

From Rhetoric to Rhetorics

An Interim Report on the History of American Writing Instruction to 1900

Suzanne Bordelon, Elizabethada A. Wright, and S. Michael Halloran

---

Key Concepts

Complicating previous narratives • Conservative oral vernacular curriculum • Rhetoric and "compositions" • Writing exercises at Princeton and Harvard • Orations and debates in literary societies • Belletristic rhetoric: Blair, Jamieson, Newman • "Taste" as new aesthetic criterion • Industrial Revolution and improved technologies for writing • Rise of the middle class • Larger numbers of university students • Schools for diverse students • Education for African Americans • Native Americans "educated to extinction" • Catholic women's schools • Normal schools • Influence of oratorical training at non-elite schools • Writing assignments • Literacy societies • Growth in availability of textbooks • Individualized, specialized knowledge • Sorting of students • Rhetorical propriety • Lyceum debates • New importance of "correct" English • Writing as bypasser of oratory forbidden to women • Women as teachers and public persuaders • Leadership in the public sphere • Current-traditional rhetoric • Emerging status of rhetoric as composition.

Local histories of composition test our theories about the influence of popular textbooks, innovative teachers, dominant pedagogies, and landmark curricular reforms. They challenge the dominant narrative of composition history, located in primarily elite research institutions, disrupting its apparent simplicity as the myth of origin and proposing alongside it a complicated and discontinuous array of alternative histories.

Gretchen Flesher Moon, *Local Histories:*
Reading the Archives of Composition

Ability in writing, whether for argumentation, instruction or entertainment, is here regarded as the crowning excellence of an education . . . and therefore great attention and earnest efforts are given to them [writing skills] in the rhetorical department of the college.

Saint Mary-of-the-Woods College (Indiana) 1864 Catalogue[1]

---

1 This catalogue information was reprinted in Kate Milner Rabb's "A Hoosier Listening Post." Undated newspaper article. Box 60, 1800 Sponsored Institutions 1810 WMW Academy/College. Archives of St. Mary-of-the-Woods.

The traditional narratives of the history of writing instruction in pre-twentieth-century America have tended to focus on prominent male rhetoricians who taught primarily at larger institutions. One noteworthy example is Albert R. Kitzhaber's *Rhetoric in American Colleges, 1850–1900* (1990), drawn from his groundbreaking 1953 dissertation.[2] Although it includes a broad survey of nineteenth-century textbooks, Kitzhaber's analysis highlights four rhetoricians and textbook authors, whom he refers to as the "big four": Adams Sherman Hill and Barrett Wendell of Harvard, John Franklin Genung of Amherst, and Fred Newton Scott of the University of Michigan. This narrative emphasis has revealed significant insight about the field, about early influential rhetoricians and textbooks, and about different conflicts that still have relevance today. However, in the last ten to fifteen years, historians have extended, challenged, and complicated these early stories through their investigation of the writing instruction of marginalized groups, and their focus on more local microhistories that complement more broad-scope narratives.[3] We, too, have contributed to these narratives and their extensions, with the first edition of this chapter focusing exclusively on all-male institutions and a revised second edition including discussion of the writing education of women and non-white students. This third edition embraces the periphery to include recent investigations of how writing was taught to students who previously have been largely overlooked in our histories. Some of the research complicates previous narratives, narratives such as the decline of oratorical culture in the nineteenth century and the liberating potential of rhetorical education.

In light of this new research, the concept of the movement from classical to vernacular and from scripted speech to silent prose, while it might have been useful for organizing earlier chapters on the history of writing instruction in nineteenth-century America, is insufficient in the twenty-first century. Explorations into far-flung archives have yielded understandings of pedagogical practices that were distant from the Harvard-influenced classroom, recognizing that pedagogical approaches are often linked to local needs and practices.[4] This diverse research includes investigations into non-school settings such as Sabbath

---

2   Albert R. Kitzhaber, *Rhetoric in American Colleges, 1850–1900* (Dallas: Southern Methodist University Press, 1990).

3   Although there are too many works to cite, some prominent examples include David Gold, *Rhetoric at the Margins: Revising the History of Writing Instruction in American Colleges, 1873–1947* (Carbondale: Southern Illinois University Press, 2008); Jessica Enoch, *Refiguring Rhetorical Education: Women Teaching African American, Native American, and Chicano/a Students* (Carbondale: Southern Illinois University Press, 2008); Shirley Wilson Logan, *Liberating Language: Sites of Rhetorical Education in Nineteenth-Century Black America* (Carbondale: Southern Illinois University Press, 2008); Patricia Donahue and Gretchen Flesher Moon, eds., *Local Histories: Reading the Archives of Composition* (Pittsburgh: University of Pittsburgh Press, 2007); Barbara L'Eplattenier and Lisa Mastrangelo, eds., *Historical Studies of Writing Program Administration: Individuals, Communities, and the Formation of a Discipline* (West Lafayette IN: Parlor Press, 2004); Cheryl Glenn, Margaret Lyday, and Wendy B. Sharer, eds., *Rhetorical Education in America* (Tuscaloosa: University of Alabama Press, 2004); Jacqueline Bacon, *The Humblest May Stand Forth: Rhetoric, Empowerment, and Abolition* (University of South Carolina Press, 2002); Susan Kates, *Activist Rhetorics and American Higher Education* (Carbondale: Southern Illinois University Press, 2001); and Thomas Miller, *The Formation of College English* (Pittsburgh: University of Pittsburgh Press, 1997).

4   Gold, op. cit. xi.

schools, mutual benefit societies, Civil War regiments, literary societies, and self-instruction. While our focus will be on writing instruction in formal educational settings, we will incorporate findings from these investigations, telling more about the wide groupings of students who began learning how to write. With this new focus, the old narratives of early American writing instruction must be amended. Although scholars previously saw the changes in nineteenth-century culture shifting the writing curriculum to one that focused on written, non-classical, and personal writing, a study of a larger body of American writing instruction suggests the changes were not as monolithic. While in the late nineteenth century many institutions may have encouraged more unimaginative writing lessons with repetitive drills, other schools (as well as individuals' instruction) actively promoted lessons in oral rhetoric and prepared people previously excluded from civic discourse to engage in it.

The remainder of this chapter, therefore, goes beyond the traditional understandings of the field and rhetorical education, yet it does not abandon them. This chapter first explains the nature of writing instruction in early America, overviewing the vast advancements in communication technologies that drastically altered writing education. It notes that these changes impacted different writing classes very differently. White men were affected differently from black men; people from low socioeconomic backgrounds desired and received different writing instruction than did those from elite backgrounds; women of all classes and races needed and used writing instruction very differently, and the differences and needs varied within each group. As Jasper Neel responds to the question, "What does it mean to teach writing?" with the answer, "It depends," so, too, is the answer to the question, "How did people teach writing in early America?" It depends.[5] Writing instruction was not monolithic, especially as more people began learning how to write. The needs of various people varied and often conflicted with each other. Some people wanted to engage in civic discourse; others sought to keep new people out of civic discourse. Some people desired a means to earn an income and rise to a higher class; others strove to control the newly educated working class. Some wanted knowledge and respect; some were in pursuit of credentials.

In an attempt to bring order to our understanding of this fluid period of writing instruction, we have fashioned our chapter, first explaining the forms of writing instruction that existed in early America. Forms existed for student bodies and purposes that had similar structures; however, as the country and its context evolved, the forms of writing instruction also evolved. Noting how the Industrial Revolution changed American society, we move to discuss how these changes affected writing instruction, most notably by bringing people to the classroom who had never been in it before and by providing means for people to learn how to write even outside the classroom. Finally, we conclude by noting how recent scholarship into writing instruction has changed the narratives of what American writing instruction has been since its origins.

---

5 Jasper P. Neel, *Aristotle's Voice: Rhetoric, Writing and Theory in America* (Carbondale: Southern Illinois University Press, 1994) 2.

Early American Writing Instruction

During the course of the eighteenth century, the writing of formal English gradually established itself as a primary concern in American colleges. In the period
immediately preceding the Revolution and extending into the early decades of
the nineteenth century, writing instruction was governed by assumptions and
methods drawn from the English derivation of classical rhetoric as filtered
through the theorists of the Scottish Enlightenment: oratory of the deliberative,
forensic, and ceremonial kinds was assumed to be the most important mode of
discourse. Students learned the *techne* or "art" of rhetoric by transcribing dictated
lectures and engaging in recitations. Writing instruction, then, was primarily the
scripting of an oral performance, part of what Gerald Graff terms an "oratorical
culture."[6]

The two most characteristic surviving examples of the art as taught in this
period are John Witherspoon's "Lectures on Eloquence" and "Lectures on Moral
Philosophy" (1802) and John Quincy Adams's *Lectures on Rhetoric and Oratory*
(1810). Witherspoon's lectures were read at Princeton, where he served as president from 1768 until his death in 1794. Adams presented his lectures as the first
Boylston Professor of Rhetoric and Oratory at Harvard from 1805 to 1809. We
call Witherspoon and Adams the two most characteristic American rhetorics of
the late eighteenth and early nineteenth centuries because they represent deliberate efforts to appropriate classical rhetoric for use in America. Also significant
were John Ward's *A System of Oratory* (1759) and Hugh Blair's *Lectures on Rhetoric
and Belles Lettres* (1783). Ward and Blair were British writers whose works
happened to be used there, yet they were very influential in the creation of
"American" rhetoric. For example, Ward's *System* was taught at Harvard prior to
Adams's professorship there. In fact, Ward's *System* was used to draw the statutes
for Harvard's Boylston Professorship.

Blair's *Lectures* was so influential that it eventually became the most widely
used rhetoric text in America. Published in 1783, it was adopted at Yale and other
American colleges shortly thereafter, Blair's text was an example of the increased
American interest in belletristic writing. Another example of America's interest
in belletristic notions is Witherspoon's inclusion of Blair's *Lectures* in his "Lectures
on Eloquence," particularly in the final lecture, which is devoted to principles of
taste and criticism that Witherspoon no doubt learned as a classmate of Blair at
the University of Edinburgh. Additionally, numerous other texts on the *belles
lettres*, such as Alexander Jamieson's *A Grammar of Rhetoric and Polite Literature* and
Samuel Phillips Newman's *A Practical System of Rhetoric*, also circulated throughout
the young United States.

In eighteenth- and nineteenth-century American schools, students of rhetoric
not only learned the art (or what we would call the theory) of rhetoric, but also
wrote "compositions" of various kinds, including orations that were supposed to
exhibit the full range of techniques described by the theory. Witherspoon
demanded his students be eloquent in the vernacular (as teachers of the early part
of the eighteenth century did not) and similarly expected students to know the

---

6 Gerald Graff, *Professing Literature: An Institutional History* (Chicago: University of Chicago Press, 1987)
   35–51.

classical languages, building their command of formally composed English upon that knowledge.[7] Witherspoon also included the study of English grammar in the Princeton curriculum—an important innovation for the time—and took the relatively modern and nonprescriptive view that the grammar of a language is "fixed" by its best writers. He especially recommends imitation as a compositional exercise, but cautions against devoting too much time to the imitation of any one author.

In practice, the writing exercises done at Princeton during the period of Witherspoon's presidency seem to have fallen into two broad categories: compositions and orations. The former were relatively brief pieces done on the short notice of no more than a few days for presentation in a recitation period, during which the class tutor and sometimes other students would offer critical comments. The latter were longer pieces written and performed before an audience of the entire college assembled in the main hall. Whether compositions or orations or whether at Princeton or other prominent colleges of the period, the topics on which students wrote tended to be political. For example, a list of some questions disputed at Harvard commencements in the decades leading to the Revolution illustrates the increasing focus on contemporary political affairs:

> Is unlimited obedience to rulers taught by Christ and his apostles? (1729)
> Is the voice of the people the voice of God? (1733)
> Does Civil Government originate from compact? (1743, 1747, 1761, and 1762)
> Is civil government absolutely necessary for men? (1758)
> Is an absolute and arbitrary monarchy contrary to right reason? (1759)
> Are the people the sole judges of their rights and liberties? (1769)[8]

The period spanned by this list coincides with the shift at Harvard from Latin to English as the primary focus of rhetorical instruction. When they were first introduced, the English language disputations and orations were assigned to the less accomplished students, but starting in the 1740s, they were more and more often assigned to the most capable ones.

In addition to their assigned work, students spent considerable effort on composing orations and debates for the student literary societies. Originating with the Spy Club founded at Harvard in 1719, the movement toward **student literary and debate societies** gathered momentum quickly around mid-century. By the closing decades of the nineteenth century, the typical college had at least two, and rivalry between them was a powerful motive for hard work on writing.[9] Students' tutors participated more or less as equals with the students in the rich oratorical activities of the college and could expect the same sort of

---

7 In this Witherspoon is in agreement with Quintilian, who prescribed translation as one means of making Roman students eloquent in Latin.

8 Samuel Eliot Morison, *Three Centuries of Harvard 1636–1936* (Cambridge MA: Harvard University Press, 1936) 90–91.

9 David Potter, "The Literary Society," *History of Speech Education in America. Background Studies*, ed. Karl R. Wallace (New York: Appleton, 1954) 238–258. See also Anne Ruggles Gere, *Writing Groups: History, Theory, and Implications* (Carbondale: Southern Illinois University Press, 1987) 9–16.

criticism of their own efforts as the students received from the tutors and each other. Neither the tutors nor anyone else graded students' work in the way we do today; the work was not done in the context of courses and credit hours and grade point averages. The audiences for which a student wrote regularly were his own class, his literary society, and the entire college assembled. It was the approval of these audiences that mattered, and the critical response of the tutor was valuable insofar as it helped a student achieve that end. Examination for the purposes comparable to what we call grading was done infrequently, usually in the form of oral disputation with the college president and perhaps the trustees judging the students' performances.

While students participated enthusiastically in this collegiate culture up through the opening decades of the nineteenth century, the oratorical culture was, as Nan Johnson argues, evolving toward a pragmatic hybridization of oratory, composition, and critical analysis.[10] Part of this evolution involved the emphasis on *belles lettres*—poetry, fiction, drama, essay—that had occupied a less prominent place in the older oratorical culture. In texts by Blair, Jamieson, and Newman, belletristic rhetoric incorporates some of the traditional concern for oratory in the classical genres and includes a classical pedagogy based upon the use of models, imitation, and graded practice, including translation into English from other languages. But the emphasis shifts somewhat from eloquence to the new ideal of "taste." As Barbara Warnick has illustrated, this shift can be understood as belletristic rhetoricians incorporating the empirical work of their contemporaries with their own.[11] For example, the new field of psychology was drawing conclusions about how the mind works and about human nature. The belletristic rhetoricians incorporated these new concepts into their instructions as to how an audience might be persuaded. A second implication of belletristic rhetoric's substitution of taste for eloquence is that it tends to make rhetoric an art of the audience more than of the speaker or writer. Taste is a quality that distinguishes readers of texts; eloquence is a virtue of the speaker or writer who makes them. Belletristic rhetoric thus set the stage for the elevation of interpretation and reading over invention and writing that would characterize the discipline of English studies.

At the same time that these evolutions were occurring, the Industrial Revolution was influencing the young United States. While the Industrial Revolution might seem quite separate from issues of writing instruction, it had a huge influence. Like the development of alphabetic literacy in ancient Greece, the invention and diffusion of the printing press during the Renaissance, and the development of electronic media in our own time, a revolution in writing technology coincided with the Industrial Revolution. While this revolution might be less considered than the other three, it was nonetheless important in its consequences for writing and writing instruction. Pens, ink, and pencils improved significantly, making it possible for people to write with less fuss and

---

10 Nan Johnson, *Nineteenth-Century Rhetoric in North America* (Carbondale: Southern Illinois University Press, 1991).

11 Barbara Warnick, *The Sixth Canon: Belletristic Rhetorical Theory and Its French Antecedents* (Columbia: University of South Carolina Press, 1993).

mess, and fewer pauses for blotting the ink and sharpening the pens. Paper decreased substantially in cost, making it economically feasible for people to write more, to use writing freely as a medium of exploration, to discard drafts and revise more extensively. Changes, too, occurred with the printing press. A process of making type from papier-mâché molds from set type and then converting the molds to metal plates, stereotyping, made books and periodicals easier to produce.[12] These developments, combined with dramatic changes in the postal system that made mailing rates affordable, meant many people who had no desire to read or write were suddenly learning to do both.[13] These changes also meant that more and more people were able to communicate at a distance. As David Kaufer and Kathleen Carley have observed, material components of writing can dramatically influence how and to what extent the average person could send and receive messages.[14] Egerton Ryerson, president of Canada's Victoria College, comments on the transformative power of these developments in his 1842 inaugural address:

> In an age of *printing and writing*—in all its varieties—to write well is of the last [i.e., most] importance. The power which an eloquent orator exerts over an assembly, an able writer exerts over a country. The "pen of a ready writer" has frequently proved an instrument of more potent power, than the sword of the soldier, or the sceptre of the monarch. The "heavens are his sounding board," and a nation, if not the world, his audience; and his productions will be listened to with edification and delight, by thousands and millions whom the human voice could never reach.[15]

12 Two excellent sources on the development of technology during the eighteenth and nineteenth centuries are Scott Bennett, "The Golden Stain of Time: Preserving Victorian Periodicals," *Investigating Victorian Journalism*, eds. Laurel Brake, Aled Jones, and Lionel Madden (New York: St. Martin's, 1990) 166–183; and Cynthia White, *Women's Magazines 1693–1968* (London: Michael Joseph, 1970). An interesting insight into the complexities of the fuss and mess of even the advanced nineteenth-century writing technologies can be found in Chapter 3 of Susan Warner's 1850 bestselling novel, *The Wide, Wide World* (New York: Feminist, 1987), which notes a young girl's extensive purchases of communication technologies so she can write letters to her mother in Europe. See also Lucille M. Schultz, "Letter-Writing Instruction in Nineteenth-Century Schools in the United States," *Letter Writing as a Social Practice*, eds. David Barton and Nigel Hall (Philadelphia: John Benjamins, 2000) 109–130.

13 A rich source of this information and much on changing technology is John W. Moore, compl., *Moore's Historical, Biographical, and Miscellaneous Gatherings, in The Form Of [Sel]ected Notes Relative To Printers, Printing, Publishing, and Editing of Books, Newspapers, Magazines, and Other Literary Productions, such as the early Publications of New England, the United States, and the World, from the Discovery of the Art, or from 1420 to 1886: With Many Brief Notices of Authors, Publishers, Editors, Printers, and Inventors* (1886; Detroit: Gale Research, 1968) 23–24. The importance of this change in postal rates to nineteenth-century Americans can be noted today in Cambridge, Massachusetts' Mount Auburn Cemetery, where people and their families comment on what they want posterity to remember them for: on the gravestone of one man, Barnabas Bates, is the inscription, "Father of Cheap Postage."

14 David S. Kaufer and Kathleen M. Carley, *Communication at a Distance: The Influence of Print on Sociocultural Organization and Change* (Hillsdale NJ: Erlbaum, 1993).

15 Cited in Henry A. Hubert *Harmonious Perfection: The Development of English Studies in Nineteenth-Century Anglo-Canadian Colleges* (East Lansing: Michigan State University Press, 1994) 164. Hubert's book also creates an interesting comparison between the teaching of writing in Canada and that in the United States, arguing that Canadian colleges' writing instruction has almost always come under the auspices of literature classes. Reading Ryerson's words, one cannot help but wonder what he would have thought of today's technologies, which allow rhetors to reach millions instantaneously.

Writing Instruction in the Second Half of the Nineteenth Century

Writing Instruction for (Mostly) White Men

The impact of this power wielded by the pen began to influence American colleges in a variety of different ways. First, the "thousands and millions" who had not been reached by the human voice started to recognize the potency of writing instruction and wanted it for themselves. This increased demand for instruction, with the growing population of the United States, meant that schools were inundated by people who wanted an education.[16] To satisfy the demand, new schools appeared on the landscape, including large institutions that began educating thousands. This increase in student body began creating many difficulties for schools. The larger numbers of students made the old system of oral recitation and disputation unworkable. Composition courses provided a means to teach larger numbers of students at once, assessing their success by measuring their adherence to prescribed standards.

Even with composition classes instead of lessons in oral recitation, schools had to find many new teachers to instruct the large numbers of new students, and there was continual concern over the quality of these new teachers. For example, Le Baron Russell Briggs of Harvard notes that "when the English of so many learned men is radically bad . . . the school gets out of the teacher all that it pays for."[17] New textbooks were mass produced for these students, often taking into consideration the dubious skills of potential teachers, making the textbooks what Thomas Miller calls "teacher-proof."[18]

Second, the "thousands and millions" who entered schools came from a variety of backgrounds; as David R. Russell notes, college was no longer a more homogeneous discourse community, nor were the colleges themselves part of the same discourse community.[19] No longer were schools solely the elite Princeton, Harvard, Yale, and others of similar prestige; instead, land grant, **normal**, co-ed, women's, Catholic, freedmen, and many other forms of schools appeared everywhere. With these diverse backgrounds, students had a variety of ways of expressing themselves, causing great consternation to many in the college and university setting. For example, Adams Sherman Hill commented on these vagaries that were created in response to a required English Composition course given to Harvard students:

> Some [students] . . . showed such utter ignorance of punctuation as to put commas at the end of complete sentences, or between words that no rational

---

16 David R. Russell. *Writing in the Academic Disciplines, 1870–1990* (Carbondale: Southern Illinois University Press 1991) 46.

17 "The Harvard Admission Examination in English," *The Origins of Composition Studies in the American College, 1875–1925*, ed. John C. Brereton (Pittsburgh: University of Pittsburgh Press, 1995) 73.

18 Thomas P. Miller, "Lest We Go the Way of Classics: Toward a Rhetorical Future for English Departments," *Rhetorical Education in America*, eds. Cheryl Glenn, Margaret M. Lyday, and Wendy B. Sharer (Tuscaloosa: University of Alabama Press, 2004) 25; Robert Connors. *Composition-Rhetoric: Backgrounds, Theory, and Pedagogy* (Pittsburgh: University of Pittsburgh Press, 1997) 84.

19 Russell, op. cit.

being would separate from one another, and a few began sentences with small letters, or began every long word with a capital letter.

Many . . . spelled as if starting a spelling reform, each for himself.[20]

To respond to this "utter ignorance" and multitude of reforms, many schools began instituting Freshman Composition classes that focused more on correctness than invention. For example, Harvard's course English A, initiated in the 1870s, focused less on traditional aspects of rhetoric and more on correctness and formulaic response. The concept of "discipline" had changed from moral and religious discipline, codes of conduct and virtue, to mental discipline, means of working with repetitive drills and exercises.[21] This shift fit the new competitive spirit of society, and the admission of so many new students gave a much greater importance to the business of sorting students, that is, of determining which were superior and which were merely adequate. Because written work could be evaluated more precisely, it allowed for a more meticulous sorting of the students.[22]

The Industrial Revolution affected the teaching of writing, not only by making paper plentiful and therefore making the power of the pen more readily available and more important to carefully supervise, but also by bringing in the need for specialized knowledge. No longer was the generalized knowledge of American eighteenth-century education sufficient for students who now needed to have complex understandings of very specific knowledge. The ideal of the German university, focusing on research, increasingly became a model for American colleges, thus altering the requirements of writing. While in earlier American classrooms, the goal of writing had been to display learning, learning that would be necessary in the pulpit, court, and deliberative bodies of society, the new model asked students to demonstrate original contributions.[23]

With this new focus, the rhetorical commonplace was eclipsed by individual, specialized knowledge. This loss may have led to an increase in personal writing. As Robert Connors points out, many of the topics for writing assignments advocated in the late nineteenth-century composition texts focused more sharply on the students' personal experience and feelings than had writing assignments typical of earlier times. In the traditional rhetoric classroom, students might have been asked to develop a broad and general topic such as "patriotism"; a late nineteenth-century text such as Reed and Kellogg's *Higher Lessons in English* would urge students to narrow the subject to something like "How Can a Boy Be Patriotic?" and consult their own experiences and feelings in developing it.

While there was much hand-wringing over the changes brought to writing instruction in the late nineteenth century, not all the changes were negative. As

---

20 Adams Sherman Hill, "An Answer to the Cry for More English," in Brereton, op. cit. 49–50.

21 Russell 36, op. cit.

22 Francis Wayland, then president of Brown, argued for a shift from oral to written examination in *Thoughts on the Present Collegiate System in the United States* (1842; rpt. New York: Arno Press and *the New York Times*, 1969) 99 ff.

23 Russell, op. cit.; Richard D. Brown, *Knowledge is Power: The Diffusion of Information in Early America, 1700–1865* (New York: Oxford University Press, 1989) 5, 70–80.

Cheryl Glenn notes, rhetoric's excellent training for leadership in the public sphere had been reserved for "only men of the upper class . . . at the expense of Others." She continues "the concerns of Others was not an issue until these Others made their way into the academy."[24] Though records of literacy in the eighteenth and nineteenth centuries reveal that surprising numbers of Americans could read,[25] prior to the nineteenth century, the only people who could hone their skills were elite white men. The many changes of the century both brought more students into the classroom and brought classroom texts, such as the *Columbian Orator*, to people outside the classroom, such as enslaved Frederick Douglass.[26]

Writing Instruction for (Mostly) White Women

One group who benefited from these many changes were white women. An increasing number of middle-class families were eager for their daughters to gain an education and help the family rise financially. In fact, from 1870 to 1920, the percentage of women among all college students more than doubled, burgeoning from 21 to 47 percent.[27] Technological developments made cheap paper and ink available, thus eliminating extravagance as an argument against teaching girls to write. The availability of inexpensive paper also encouraged letter-writing, an art applauded by theorists of belletristic rhetoric and considered very appropriate for the female sex. The popularity of belletristic rhetoric also helped advance women's education because of this rhetoric's focus on taste and literary style, rather than eloquence, an emphasis that fit well with the nineteenth-century notions of womanhood.[28] Theories of belletristic rhetoric considered women's

24 Cheryl Glenn, "Rhetorical Education in America (A Broad Stroke Introduction)," *Rhetorical Education in America*, eds. Cheryl Glenn, Margaret M. Lyday, and Wendy B. Sharer (Tuscaloosa: University of Alabama Press, 2004) vii–xvi.

25 "Literacy Instruction and Gender in Colonial New England," *Reading in America: Literature and Social History*, ed. Cathy N. Davidson (Baltimore: Johns Hopkins University Press, 1989) 53–80. Related to this rich but frequently overlooked history, Susan Miller, in *Assuming the Positions: Cultural Pedagogy and the Politics of Commonplace Writing* (Pittsburgh: University of Pittsburgh Press, 1998), makes the excellent point that we must resist the temptation to glorify nineteenth-century reformers of women's education by creating a mistaken history of education that ignores the extensive educational systems for women that existed before these women's reforms began.

26 See, for example, Ebenezer Porter's *The Rhetorical Reader, Consisting of Instructions for Regulating the Voice, with a Rhetorical Notation, Illustrating Inflection Emphasis, and Modulation* (1835). A copy from an antique shop claims on its title page to be the 220th edition.

27 Mabel Newcomer, *A Century of Higher Education for American Women* (New York: Harper, 1959) 45–46.

28 For an extensive discussion on the changing perceptions of womanhood and how these perceptions fostered women's education, see Ruth H. Bloch, "American Feminine Ideals in Transition: The Rise of the Moral Mother, 1785–1815," *Feminist Studies* 4 (June 1978): 101–27; Janet Carey Eldred and Peter Mortenson, " 'Persuasion Dwelt on Her Tongue': Female Civic Rhetoric in Early America," *College English* 60 (1998): 173–188; Catherine Hobbs, "Introduction: Culture and Practices of U.S. Women's Literacy," *Nineteenth-Century Women Learn to Write*," ed. Hobbs (Charlottesville: University Press of Virginia, 1995): 1–33; JoAnn Campbell, " 'A Real Vexation': Student Writing in Mount Holyoke's Culture of Service, 1837–1865," *College English* 59 (1997): 767–788; Sarah Delamont, "The Contradictions in Ladies' Education," *The Nineteenth-Century Woman: Her Cultural and Physical World*, ed. Sarah Delamont and Lorna Duffin (London: Croom Helm, 1978): 134–165; Barbara Welter, *Dimity Convictions: The American Woman and the Nineteenth Century* (Athens: Ohio University Press, 1976); and Linda K. Kerber, *Women of the Republic: Intellect and Ideology in Revolutionary America* (New York: Norton, 1980).

conversation to provide models of excellent prose, providing educators of young women with an additional justification for arguing that rhetoric was consistent with womanhood.[29]

Entrance to college was far from easy, however, for women. As Nan Johnson argues, during this period of time there were "popular constructions of rhetorical propriety" that attempted to define where women could and could not be and what women could do in locations where they were permitted. Of course, these constructions excluded women's discourse from public spaces, the space for which a thorough rhetorical education seemed to prepare students, and the constructions instead located women in private ones.[30] Thus, to provide women with an advanced education without running afoul of the many prohibitions still in place, educators adopted many Janus-faced strategies to legitimize their curriculum.[31] For example, while women typically could not deliver orations, it was considered socially appropriate for them to read aloud—so they did. P. Joy Rouse cites a story of a female student cooperating with this dictate by carrying her essay book to the stage, politely holding the written text, and boldly delivering it as an oration without glancing at it.[32] Schools such as Catharine Beecher's alma mater, the Litchfield Academy, could also provide women with the skills necessary for oratory by making school plays part of the curriculum, thereby forcing these women to work on various elements of delivery.[33] Martha Osborne Barrett, a student at a Massachusetts normal school, observes another important way women gained oratorical skills when she records in her diary her normal school's association with a **Lyceum** where women and men participated in debate, arguing such topics as "Advantages of Education and Disadvantages of Ignorance" and "Shall we be justified in assisting Ireland if she declares herself independent?"[34]

A part of this instruction was provided by Catholic educational institutions, some of which had existed since the eighteenth century. As demand for women's education grew, these schools, which had originated as institutes for primary and secondary education, expanded to include collegiate courses. While many students were not themselves Catholic, many were, and the collegiate education provided training to the many future nuns who were to teach in the growing number of Catholic primary and secondary schools. Although the writing curriculum at these Catholic schools varied enormously, the little research on them that is available suggests much of the curriculum was rigorous. For example, at Saint Mary's Academy in Indiana, now Saint Mary-of-the-Woods College, students

29 See Adam Smith, *Lectures on Rhetoric and Belles Lettres*, ed. J.C. Bryce (Oxford: Clarendon Press, 1983).
30 Nan Johnson, *Gender and Rhetorical Space in American Life, 1866–1910* (Carbondale: Southern Illinois University Press, 2002) 2.
31 Almost all scholars of women's nineteenth-century education have observed these strategies. For example, Carey Eldred and Mortenson (op. cit.) call the strategy "rhetoric of use," Delamont (op. cit.) "double conformity," and Campbell (op. cit.) "culture of service."
32 P. Joy Rouse, "Cultural Models of Womanhood and Female Education: Practices of Colonization and Resistance," *Nineteenth-Century Women Learn to Write*, ed. Catherine Hobbs (Charlottesville: University Press of Virginia, 1995) 230–247.
33 See Emily Noyes Vanderpoel, compil., *Chronicles of a Pioneer School from 1792 to 1833 Being the History of Miss Sarah Pierce and Her Litchfield School* (Cambridge: Cambridge University Press, 1903).
34 F. Mss. 13274. Env. 2, Fdr 2. Phillips Library, Peabody Essex Museum, Salem, MA.

studied composition, rhetoric, grammar, Latin, Greek, and literature; they wrote for exams, for daily exercises, and for ceremonies. Students wrote essays, poetry, and speeches. The writing was across the curriculum: for English and American literature as well as for "rhetoric, history and civil government." Additionally, students were engaged in various exercises, from analysis of speeches to questions, and these in logic and metaphysics. One student, May Wilkin, kept a notebook with these various exercises, which included an outline of an essay in the form of "points" and "hints," and then composed the essay from this outline. One such essay, marked "very good" by the instructor, discussed the value of wisdom:

> Their [sic] are many poor persons who can not be the possessors of wisdom simply because they have not the opportunity or means for obtaining it nor the means for buying books or the time for study.
> Their [sic] are some persons who have great advantage that is they have good teachers but do not appreciate them, where as their [sic] are others who would greatly appreciate a good teacher could they only have one.
> Wisdom when once gained is preferable to wealth, for it can never be taken from us, but that can not be said of money, for a man may have plenty of money and be wealthy to-day; but be a poor penniless man to-morrow, for in a thousand of ways money can be lost.
> Wisdom is, indeed, valuable, and it can not be given to us; but it must taste the sweets of one's own labor and exertion.[35]

The instructor's apparent focus on the content of Wilkin's essay, not on her misuse of "their," her misspellings, and her at times awkward prose, suggests not all nineteenth-century instruction focused on correctness. An alumna's 1891 essay on the importance of women's education suggests these schools continued to teach women the elements of argument so that women could defend their faith.[36]

The Catholic schools' maintenance of the traditional rhetorical education, creating graduates ready to defend Catholicism, may have been what prompted the rigorous education at many Protestant women's colleges. Carol Mattingly's recent research on Catholic women's schools argues that many of the women's nineteenth-century schools better known to us today, schools such as the Hartford Female and Ipswich Female seminaries as well as Mount Holyoke Female Seminary (later Mount Holyoke College), were founded out of a fear of the Catholic schools' influence on American society. With Sarah Josepha Hale, an influential editor and advocate of women's education, repeatedly calling for public funding of non-Catholic seminaries "to counter the proliferation of Catholic academies," Protestant female seminaries grew in number throughout the United States.[37]

35 May Wilkin, unpublished document. Archives at Saint Mary-of-the-Woods College.
36 Frances R. Howe. "Higher Education for Women and its True Use." Vico County, Indiana: Saint Mary-of-the-Woods, 1891. Archives of Saint Mary-of-the-Woods College.
37 Carol Mattingly. "Uncovering Forgotten Habits: Anti-Catholic Rhetoric and Nineteenth-Century American Women Literacy," *College Composition and Communication* 58 (2006): 170; Mary Ewens, *The Role of the Nun in Nineteenth-Century America: Variations on the International Theme. A Thesis Submitted to the Faculty of the Graduate School of the University of Minnesota, March 1971* (New York: Arno Press, 1978).

Although these **female seminaries** were often criticized for the shallowness of their curriculum, others, including Mount Holyoke, shared a similar emphasis on rigor as the Catholic academies.[38] For instance, Mary Lyon, who established Mount Holyoke in 1837, supported the idea of "providing rigorous education for women in a structured setting."[39] Early rhetoric courses drew on the texts of Blair, Newman and Whately, while classes later in the century drew on the texts of Genung and Hill. These textbooks were similar to those used in the rhetoric courses offered at Mount Holyoke's nearby "brother" institutions of Harvard and Amherst. In addition, like many schools of this period, rhetoric at Mount Holyoke extended well beyond writing instruction, including study in oratory, declamation, and debate.[40] This emphasis on debate was also evident at the other Seven Sisters colleges in the late nineteenth century.

In fact, the training women received in argumentation and debate helped them develop a public voice.[41] At Smith College, Mary August Jordan viewed the study of argument as central to students' abilities "to think critically and conscientiously."[42] At Vassar College, Gertrude Buck authored and coauthored textbooks on argumentation and debate that encouraged Vassar students to reflect on women's issues and emphasized "action, communal interests, free inquiry, and equality."[43] And after college, many women at the Seven Sisters "put their education to work as pro- and anti-suffrage speakers."[44] Although these institutions weren't without their contradictions, women's colleges were important in helping women to gain a civic identity and in fostering their intellectual independence. From the 1890s until 1920, when women received national suffrage, these schools served as "political backgrounds" both in articulating women's rights and in redefining traditional assumptions about women.[45]

Normal School Writing Instruction

Besides female seminaries and colleges, normal schools—the teacher-training institutions of the period—also benefited many women. Many founders of normal and public schools argued that women were best suited to supply the increasing demand of teachers, since teachers dealt mostly with children and women were innately talented in this area. The normal school also subscribed to

---

38 Thomas Woody, *A History of Women's Education in the United States*, vol. 1 (1929; rpt., New York: Octagon, 1974) 441.

39 Lisa S. Mastrangelo, "Learning from the Past: Rhetoric, Composition, and Debate at Mount Holyoke College," *Rhetoric Review* 18 (1999): 49.

40 Ibid., 49–50.

41 For relevant research, see Kathryn M. Conway, "Woman Suffrage and the History of Rhetoric at the Seven Sisters Colleges, 1865–1919," *Reclaiming Rhetorica: Women in the Rhetorical Tradition*, ed. Andrea A. Lunsford (Pittsburgh: University of Pittsburgh Press, 1995) 203–226; Mastrangelo, "Learning from the Past," 46–63; and Suzanne Bordelon, *A Feminist Legacy: The Rhetoric and Pedagogy of Gertrude Buck* (Carbondale: Southern Illinois University Press, 2007).

42 Susan Kates, *Activist Rhetorics and American Higher Education: 1885–1937* (Carbondale: Southern Illinois University Press, 2001) 28.

43 Bordelon, op. cit., 11.

44 Conway, op. cit. 203.

45 Vickie Ricks, " 'In an Atmosphere of Peril': College Women and Their Writing," *Nineteenth-Century Women Learn to Write*, ed. Catherine Hobbs (Charlottesville: University Press of Virginia, 1995) 81.

this rationale. Though not exclusively for women, normal school classrooms often were dominated by women. Developing out of the common school revival during the decades before the civil war, normal schools provided the vehicle for many middle- and working-class women to enter the teaching profession.[46] During the second half of the nineteenth century, more than fifty percent of women seeking education beyond the secondary level attended normal schools and teachers' colleges.[47] According to Kathryn Fitzgerald, state normal schools "democratized and expanded educational and vocational opportunity far beyond any existing institution, in terms of both class and gender."[48]

The "writing" aspect of the normal school education is difficult to clearly identify. Mixing theory with practice, the normal school education taught pedagogy, mixing writing in with its theory but also working to make sure future teachers themselves could do what they would teach.[49] It can be difficult and perhaps even a bit reductive to tease out writing as a separate academic endeavor, especially since departmentalization didn't occur at many schools on the educational periphery until after the nineteenth century. As Jane Donawerth explains, during the late nineteenth century elocutionary training often was "intermingled" with "English composition, public speaking, rhetoric, dramatic acting, and physical education."[50] Although Donawerth is discussing elocutionary training, the same can be said of writing instruction. Essays were often written for recitation and oral delivery.

What we can determine from the archives about the writing instruction at normal schools is that there were thriving and diverse rhetorical practices. For example, the faculty at Westfield State Normal School in Massachusetts supported a curriculum and extracurriculum "meant to produce teachers who, regardless of gender, could sway public sentiment on matters of civic concern."[51] Thus, although Westfield's early program stressed "drill" in the subjects students would teach—reading, arithmetic, geography—students also were required to complete advanced studies "in subjects such as rhetoric, philosophy, and the natural sciences."[52] In addition, Westfield students were active in the school's literary societies. Although from the 1850s through the 1870s female students were less likely to participate in formal debates and extemporaneous speech, they did

---

46 As Shirley Wilson Logan and Jessica Enoch point out, many of these women were African American women. Noting that women such as Frances Harper and Ida B. Wells were public school teachers, Enoch suggests the efforts of these and other black women who served as teachers "should inspire further investigation and recovery of their educational work" (69). See Logan, " 'When and Where I Enter': Race, Gender, and Composition Studies," *Feminism and Composition Studies: In Other Words*, ed. Susan C. Jarratt and Lynn Worsham (New York: MLA, 1998) 45–57; and Enoch, op. cit.

47 Newcomer, *A Century of Higher Education for Women*, 88.

48 Kathryn Fitzgerald, "A Rediscovered Tradition: European Pedagogy and Composition in Nineteenth-Century Midwestern Normal Schools," *College Composition and Communication* 53 (2001): 228.

49 See Merle Borrowman, ed., *Teacher Education in America: A Documentary History* (New York: Teachers College Press, 1965).

50 Jane Donawerth, ed., *Rhetorical Theory by Women Before 1900* (Lanham MD: Rowman & Littlefield, 2002) xxvii.

51 Beth Ann Rothermel, "A Sphere of Noble Action: Gender, Rhetoric, and Influence at a Nineteenth-Century Massachusetts State Normal School," *Rhetoric Society Quarterly* 33 (2001): 36.

52 Ibid. 40–41.

write for the society's literary magazine and gave recitations. In their magazine writing, female students produced essays on socially acceptable topics, but they also wrote powerful arguments on issues related to their future careers as teachers and used this writing "to voice views on various political issues."[53] In the early years, both male and female students also displayed their rhetorical skills before the community and school officials in teaching demonstrations and oral examinations, and after 1856, they presented graduation addresses before the community.[54] Similarly, William Leonidas Mayo, the founder of East Texas Normal College, a private teacher-training school in rural northeast Texas, provided his students with a "rich rhetorical environment, in which literature, drama, oratory, debate, and writing were woven into the daily fabric of campus life."[55] Although Mayo was a strict disciplinarian and emphasized correctness, he stressed "practical production" more than teaching grammar.[56] Mayo and his faculty also tried to use material that would be relevant to their students' interests and encourage achievement. Furthermore, instead of using textbooks to teach writing, Mayo drew on "model orations on cultural and political topics."[57] On the West Coast at California State Normal School in San Jose, students also were exposed to flourishing and diverse rhetorical practices. In fact, in their coeducational societies and debating clubs, women and men at California Normal participated on a relatively equal basis. In these organizations women directly argued against men in weekly society gatherings, in broader public meetings, and in internormal debating competitions. These activities not only strengthened their academic endeavors, but they also "enhanced their leadership abilities, broadened their intellectual life, and ultimately prepared women for more vocal and public social roles."[58]

However, all normal school writing pedagogy may not have shared such a democratic impetus. For instance, Kenneth Lindblom, Will Banks, and Risë Quay have argued that during the 1860s the Illinois State Normal School (ISNU) "largely reproduced the elitist attitudes about grammar and composition prominent at northeastern academies."[59] Although aspects of his pedagogy seem progressive, ISNU teacher Albert Stetson believed that "working-class 'habits' must be 'unlearned' " when it came to grammar instruction.[60] This notion is particularly evident in Stetson's spelling instruction, in which students were assigned twenty-five words each day and misspelling more than one word a term meant retaking spelling. Typically, it took students five terms to clear the spelling requirement.[61] In their analysis, Lindblom, Banks, and Quay reveal how, over

53 Ibid. 50.
54 Ibid. 44, 50.
55 Gold, op. cit. 133.
56 Ibid. 145.
57 Ibid. 138.
58 Suzanne Bordelon, "Participating on an 'Equal Footing': The Rhetorical Significance of California State Normal School in the Late Nineteenth Century," *Rhetoric Society Quarterly* 42 (2011): 187.
59 Kenneth Lindblom, William Banks, and Risë Quay, "Mid-Nineteenth-Century Writing Instruction at Illinois State Normal University: Credentials, Correctness, and the Rise of a Teaching Class," *Local Histories: Reading the Archives of Composition*, eds. Patricia Donahue and Gretchen Flesher Moon (Pittsburgh: University of Pittsburgh Press, 2007) 95.
60 Ibid. 100.
61 Ibid. 101.

time, some students' attitudes about writing transitioned from excitement about writing to eventual dread of both school compositions and letters home to the family.

Writing Instruction for Students of Color and/or Low Socioeconomic Status

Not only was there an upsurge in the educational opportunities for white women, but the opportunities for African Americans to learn to write also increased as the nineteenth century progressed. Only considered citizens with the Fourteenth Amendment, many of these new citizens rushed to advance their education, an education some had already begun independent of any formal school setting, often covertly or illegally. Yet African Americans' formal education prior to this time was not non-existent. Though many Southern laws forbade writing instruction to them, many African Americans went to school in Northern states, learning to read and write. For example, in New Hampshire, Dinah Whipple, a woman born into slavery but freed when she was twenty-one, had such a command of reading and writing that she was able to support herself with her school, the Ladies Charitable African School. Northern public schools, too, often educated black students in writing.[62] Even in the South, there had been formal schools for African Americans, most of which were run by Catholic orders of women, until public pressure forced these schools to close.[63]

Nevertheless, with the end of slavery, demand for schools for African Americans increased significantly. To meet this demand in the South, schools began appearing in many places. Run by the government, charitable organizations, missionaries, churches, and freedmen themselves, these schools taught a range of subjects. New colleges for African Americans, including Howard, Berea, Hampton, and others offered "good classes in the English branches" and "elements of an English education," while having their students engage in recitations in "mathematics, latin and greek [sic] composition, and other higher branches . . . [of] instruction."[64] However, like the women's colleges, many of these schools adopted Janus-faced strategies; for example, Hampton put an emphasis on its trade school education, thus masking its rigorous program.[65]

As David Gold and Susan C. Jarratt have demonstrated, this focus on the classical liberal arts curriculum, including an emphasis on Latin and Greek as well as oratory, was required at many black colleges up through the 1920s.[66] As Jarratt asserts in her analysis of student periodicals from 1878 to 1912, at Fisk, Atlanta, and Howard universities, classical learning for these students "serves not merely as a superficial measure of cultural attainment, but as a lifeline for blacks in the

---

62 Mark J. Sammonds and Valerie Cunningham. *Black Portsmouth: Three Centuries of African-American Heritage* (Durham: University of New Hampshire Press, 2004) 91–94.
63 Ewens, op. cit.
64 J. W. Alvord, *Letters From the South Relating to the Condition of the Freedman Addressed to Major General O. O. Howard* (Washington DC: Howard University Press, 1870) 13, 32, 38.
65 James D. Anderson. *The Education of Blacks in the South, 1860–1935* (Chapel Hill: University of NC Press, 1988) 34.
66 See Gold, op. cit., Chapter 1; and Susan C. Jarratt, "Classics and Counterpublics in Nineteenth-Century Historically Black Colleges," *College English* 72 (2009): 134–159. Jarratt, op. cit. 140.

post-war South, as a link between blacks and whites, as a resource for thinking through historical change and political struggle, and as a ground of public debate about the future of a people."[67] The classically based course of study for these African American students ultimately "was a mark of acceptance into full personhood."[68]

Although college was beyond reach for many students, this did not necessarily mean lessons in writing were over for them. Literary societies offered advanced forms of writing instruction for many people, particularly African American men and women. These societies provided libraries, practice in public speaking and debate, and critique of written work. More significantly, African American societies fostered the rhetorical education of their members, and these members reinvented this education to serve their own purposes, namely as a tool to help them gain freedom and resist oppression. For instance, Jacqueline Bacon and Glen McClish have demonstrated that discussions of rhetorical principles are apparent in documents dating from 1818 to 1832 from African American literary societies in Philadelphia. In particular, these societies seem to have drawn on the principles of Scottish theorists such as Blair, Campbell, and Smith. However, these principles weren't merely "borrowed," but were "infused with new purposes; deployed for radical ends."[69] Eighteenth-century Scottish rhetorical pedagogy, for instance, tended to be "conservative and assimilationist."[70] Within these societies, though, some members refashioned this pedagogy to become a "form of resistance for the oppressed."[71] In addition to fostering rhetorical education, black literary societies were significant because "they enabled communal involvement," motivating and training several prominent nineteenth-century African American speakers, including Frederick Douglass, Mary Church Terrell, and Anna Julia Cooper.[72]

Additionally, individuals without access to literary societies or schools could improve their reading and writing skills without entering any schools. The work of Jean Ferguson Carr, Stephen L. Carr, and Lucille M. Schultz illustrates the growth of the genre of the textbook as a result of the developments of eighteenth- and nineteenth-century technologies, discussing the importance and value of self-instruction made possible by these textbooks.[73] These and other books helped to promote the study of popular rhetoric and elocutionary skills by

67 Ibid. 144.
68 Ibid. 142.
69 Jacqueline Bacon and Glen McClish, "Reinventing the Master's Tools: Nineteenth-Century African-American Literary Societies of Philadelphia and Rhetorical Education," *Rhetoric Society Quarterly* 30 (2000): 20–21.
70 Ibid. 27.
71 Ibid. 39. For more on these societies, see Shirley Wilson Logan, *Liberating Language: Sites of Rhetorical Education in Nineteenth-Century Black America* (Carbondale: Southern Illinois University Press, 2008) Chapter 3; and Elizabeth McHenry, *Forgotten Readers: Recovering the Lost History of African American Literary Societies* (Durham: Duke University Press, 2002) and "Rereading Literary Legacy: New Considerations of the 19th-Century African American Reader and Writer," *Callaloo* 22 (1999): 477–82.
72 Logan, *Liberating Language* 84–90.
73 Jean Ferguson Carr, Stephen L. Carr, and Lucille M. Schultz. *Archives of Instruction: Nineteenth-Century Rhetorics, Readers, and Composition Books in the United States* (Carbondale: Southern Illinois University Press, 2005).

individual learners. As Nan Johnson asserts, public demand and interest in rhetorical education encouraged "a burgeoning of popular education in rhetoric between 1850 and 1910."[74] This interest may have been furthered by the view, advocated by the popular rhetoric movement, that rhetoric was a key skill in the professional and social arenas. Likewise, popular elocutionists supported the notion that the study of elocution had "far-reaching intellectual and moral implications" that also likely encouraged individual learners.[75]

Although textbooks were important for many, some learners drew on other available means. For example, African Americans developed their rhetorical skills in various settings. Drawing on novelist Ralph Ellison's terminology, Shirley Wilson Logan explores these sites of "free floating literacy," or places of learning located within and outside the community.[76] These sites included "bush harbors" built to conceal meetings in places such as woods and plantations, churches, Civil War battlefield camps, political settings, and workplace venues.[77] African Americans' rhetorical education also was fostered through the rhetorical principles presented in black periodicals.[78] The variety of sites available demonstrates the depth of literacy learning that occurred in the African American community.

However, not all writing education was so empowering. For example, because Native Americans were not entirely given United States citizenship with the Fourteenth Amendment,[79] government policies continued to treat them as less than human, and the writing instruction that existed from this group of Americans reflected this perspective. As David Wallace Adams has shown, Native Americans were "educated to extinction" through classes that taught students to be passive conveyors of language. For example, though the Cherokee Female Seminary in what is now Oklahoma offered its students rich training, including opportunities to write in a literary magazine, it was essentially a "white" education, at the conclusion of which "the bow and arrow have been laid aside."[80] Likewise, Jessica Enoch's analysis of the **Carlisle Indian School** and the writing of Zitkala-Sa, a Sioux and former teacher at Carlisle at the turn of the twentieth century, demonstrates the ways the school viewed the Indians as "savages who must be civilized."[81] Thus, students were removed from their reservations, brought to Carlisle, and cleansed of any tribal attributes. A goal of the school was to purge students of their tribal languages and to teach them English.

---

74 Nan Johnson, "The Popularization of Nineteenth-Century Rhetoric: Elocution and the Private Learner," *Oratorical Culture in Nineteenth-Century America: Transformations in the Theory and Practice of Rhetoric*, eds. Gregory Clark and S. Michael Halloran (Carbondale: Southern Illinois University Press, 1993) 140–141.

75 Ibid. 148.

76 Logan, *Liberating Language*, 11.

77 Ibid.

78 Logan, *Liberating Language*, 96–134.

79 See Earle M. Maltz, "The Fourteenth Amendment and Native American Citizenship," *Constitutional Commentary* 17.3 (2000), 555.

80 Devon A. Mihesuah. "Let Us Strive Earnestly to Value Education Aright: Cherokee Female Seminarians as Leaders of a Changing Culture," *Nineteenth-Century Women Learn to Write*, ed. Catherine Hobbs (Charlottesville: University Press of Virginia, 1995) 107, 111.

81 Enoch, op. cit. 96.

By drawing on Zitkala-Sa's stories published in the *Atlantic Monthly*, Enoch reveals the ways she contested such educational practices by using her autobiographical essays to reach out to white readers and to expose the devastating "civilizing" process practiced at Carlisle. Students at many Native American schools did learn writing skills that allowed them to succeed—albeit not in their indigenous environment but in the white world.[82]

Concluding Remarks: Continuing the Project of Revising Our Stories

American writing instruction evolved with America. Beginning with a focus on training leaders of the young nation, writing classes grew as the nation grew. The growth of the middle-class spirit placed a new burden on the colleges, both in sheer numbers of students and in new responsibilities. Students who came to college as a means of rising on the socioeconomic ladder swelled institutions of higher education far beyond anything known during the seventeenth and eighteenth centuries.[83] Without cheap textbooks, paper and ink, colleges would never have been able to meet these demands, and less affluent students would never have been able to have such lofty goals. With the increasingly large numbers of students, graded work became a reality; credentialing became a function of schools. Thus, these changes, so the narrative goes, led to the formulaic, unimaginative lessons and rigid grammatical prescriptions that have come to be understood as part of the so-called **current-traditional rhetoric**.[84]

Yet research that has been conducted during the past decade illustrates that this picture is not fully accurate. Just as Gold's and Jarratt's research reveals the classical liberal arts curriculum at many nineteenth-century Historically Black Colleges and Universities, so, too, does emerging scholarship suggest that a rich classical liberal arts curriculum existed at many women's Catholic schools.[85] Oratory may not have disappeared as has previously been assumed. For example, normal schools, Catholic schools, and women's Protestant schools may also have included more work in oratory than is at first apparent. Research on normal schools has revealed the diverse rhetorical training students received, including curricular and extracurricular training in oratory. Similarly, women's colleges

---

82 Mihesuah, op. cit.

83 At Harvard, class size first reached 100 in 1860, then went to 200 in 1877, to 300 in 1892, to 400 in 1896, to 500 in 1904, and to 600 in 1906, and remained at about that level until shortly before World War I. Morison, op. cit. 415–46.

84 Although current-traditional rhetoric has become a general label for virtually any theory that current practitioners view as negative, it typically has been used to characterize dominant approaches to pedagogy and rhetorical theory in the late nineteenth century. The term is primarily based on historians' analyses of rhetoric and grammar textbooks to understand the teaching of writing at men's eastern colleges such as Harvard, Yale, Amherst, and Michigan (see JoAnn Campbell, *Toward A Feminist Rhetoric: The Writing of Gertrude Buck* [Pittsburgh: University of Pittsburgh Press, 1996] xl). For early references to the term, see Daniel Fogarty, *Roots for a New Rhetoric*. 2nd ed. (New York: Russell and Russell, 1968), and Richard Young's "Paradigms and Problems: Needed Research in Rhetorical Invention," *Research and Composing: Points of Departure*, ed. Charles R. Cooper and Lee Odell (Urbana IL: NCTE, 1978) 29–47.

85 Scholars such as Elizabethada A. Wright, Nan Johnson, and Carol Mattingly are currently completing research on women's Catholic schools in the nineteenth and early twentieth centuries.

provided the rhetorical education necessary to help women gain a civic identity and foster their intellectual independence.

The story of much Native American writing instruction illustrates how such instruction may limit individuals' engagement in the public sphere—or prescribes how they must engage. Yet, writing instruction's disempowering abilities did not originate in the nineteenth century. The work of Tamara Plakins Thornton shows that in early America, when people discussed learning to write, they were usually referencing handwriting. For example, in 1684, Boston's secondary education was separated into two writing tracks: one for Harvard-bound scholars focusing on the classical languages, and another for boys entering the world of commerce. In the latter case, though, writing focused on "acquiring and perfecting . . . penmanship skills."[86]

Still, despite twentieth-century traditional narratives that America's writing instruction evolved to disempowering current-traditional rhetoric, much recent research illustrates that many students throughout early America received a writing education that allowed them to participate in the public sphere. These new students range from African American Revolutionary War veteran Prince Hall, who believed schools for young African Americans could provide them with the means to success,[87] to the women at the western normal schools, who learned how to negotiate restrictions on women with their participation in the public sphere.

Certainly, in the first years of the North American British colonies, white male students sought the instruction necessary for their careers as lawyers and ministers and for their anticipated leadership in the civic arena. And with the shifts that occurred in the nation and in writing instruction, some nineteenth-century white male students remained concerned with prestige and income, and others continued to gain knowledge necessary for participation in the public sphere. Yet with these shifts, many people who hadn't participated in writing education when the colonies were just beginning began going to school. African American students, too, pursued writing instruction for all the above varying reasons, plus they desired the respect associated with the knowledge that had been denied to them since the beginnings of the nation. Women, too, wanted the instruction for various reasons; some wanted to use their writing for civic engagement; others, to advance their knowledge in sciences ranging from botany to the domestic sciences. Teachers of writing also had varying goals. Some, such as those discussed by Susan Kates, were concerned with ensuring citizen participation in the democratic nation; others worked to carefully sort students to ensure only certain students could participate.[88] While the research of twenty years ago may have assumed the end of writing instruction came in the late nineteenth century, recent research shows early American writing instruction was much more complex and varied.

With this narrative of American writing instruction before 1900, we know we have omitted information, as our essays in the first and second editions did. Akin to what James Murphy writes in his introduction to this book, our summary undoubtedly results "in a kind of unconscious misrepresentation." Nevertheless,

---

86 Tamara Plakins Thornton, *Handwriting in America: A Cultural History* (New Haven: Yale University Press, 1996) 8–9.
87 Dorothy Porter, *Early Negro Writing, 1760–1837* (Baltimore: Black Classic Press, 1995) 79.
88 Kates, op. cit.

the main point that we intend to make in this brief history is that, as technology and the young United States changed together, the model of writing instruction grew increasingly complex. Because gatekeepers continued to exclude some students from certain schools, the models of instruction became increasingly varied as those excluded tried to figure out how to teach others (and themselves) how to write. Sometimes this instruction was done in schools; sometimes, because of prohibitions of law, finance, or location, the instruction was done outside schools. Although Lucille M. Schultz is talking specifically about school-based writing instruction, her words echo our sentiment; we, too, hope that this chapter reveals the diversity and textured nature of writing instruction in the nineteenth century, and "will spark others to visit the still-unexplored libraries, museums, historical societies, and private collections in order that we might continue to construct and revise our stories . . ."[89]

Appendix A
Assignment from notebook of May E. Wilkin

[Wilkin, May E. Unpublished Writing Book. Box 6, 1800 Sponsored Institutions 1810 WMW Academy/College. Archives of St. Mary-of-the-Woods.]

Music

Point 1st	*Definition*
" 2nd	Antiquity of Music.
Hint 1st	Mentioned in old testaments.
" 2nd	Mentioned in ancient literature.
" 3rd	Cultivated from the earliest ages in Grecian Rome.
Point 3rd	Music universally loved and cultivated.
Hint 1st	Every nature has music of some from even the most barbarous.
Hint 2nd	In civilized countries we find music cultivated is one of the most brilliant and refined accomplishments.
Hint 3rd	It is accepted as a form of worship in every part of the world.
Point 4th	The influence of music.
Hint 1st	The favorite recreation of the most refined intellect and most cultivated minds.
Hint 2nd	The power and charm of a home circle.
Hint 3rd	It can not be degraded.
" 4th	It sooths the weary.
" 5th	It comforts the suffering.
" 6th	It cheers the afflicted.
Point 5th	Valuable as a study.
Hint 1st	It requires patience, perseverance, taste, and talent in its cultivation.
Hint 2nd	It trains at once the mind—the eye—the fingers and the voice.
Hint 3rd	It is an unfailing source of pleasure in one selves.
Hint 4th	It gives us the power to impart pleasure to others.
Point 6th	Conclusion.
Hint 1st	No accomplishment is so graceful so universally popular as a good musical education.

89 Schultz, op cit. 8.

Music is a succession of sounds so modulated as to please the ear.

Many Piano-Forte players professional as well as amateurs, endeavor to escape a thorough study of their instrument. to [sic] be good players should be the aim of every pianist, so far as circumstances will allow. The most thorough method is after all, the shortest; and to devote four or five hours daily to the Piano must surely be possible for every musician, without intruding upon his study in counterpoint and composition. He who makes the Piano-Forte his chief study must, of course, give it the most time. The main point is, to employ this time well, and to devote it to serious, systematic study instead of with trifling music, and wandering about without plan or method. All that a player may desire, is to perform a composition with feeling and taste. [This entire paragraph is crossed out with the note written on the side: "This is a deviation."]

One of the main points in music is the touch, and the main point to be considered in regard to touch is the smooth connection of the successive tones.

There are two kinds of touch: Legato and Stacato. The Legato touch is the most important because it occurs oftenest, and it is the one universally to be employed; where none other is marked.

As soon as a performer feels fatigued he should at once discontinue practice, until he has entirely regained his strength, for unless he can readily give practice his undivided attention, it will do him more harm than good. [These two paragraphs are crossed out with the comment "Please re-write and follow your outline." The next page begins the rewrite.]

Music is the science which teaches the propertier [?], dependences, and relations of melodious sounds, an art over which muses presided, especially music of the art of producing harmony and melody by the due combinations and arrangements of these sounds; the science of harmonical [sic] sounds.

The pleasure derived from music arises from its exciting agreeable sensations, and raising pleasing mental images and emotions. Apart from words, it expresses passions and sentiment, and linked to words, it loses its vagueness; and becomes a beautiful illustration of language.

Music seems to have existed in all countries and at all times. Instrumental music is of a very early date: representations of musical instruments occur on the Egyptian obelisks and tombs. The music of the Hebrews is supposed to have a defined rhythm and melody.

The Greeks numbered music among the sciences, and studied the mathematical proportions of sounds. The Romans borrowed their music from the Etruscans and Greeks, and had both stringed instruments and wind instruments.

The early music of the Christian Church was probably in part of Greek and in part of Hebrew origin. St Ambrose and Gregory the Great directed their attention to its improvement, and under them some sort of harmony or counterpoint seems to have found its way into the service of the church.

Franco of Cologne, in the thirteenth century first indicated the duration of notes by diversity of form. Music in some form either is found in every nation even the most barbarous. In civilized nations music is cultivated as one of the most brilliant and refined accomplishments. [There is a note at the end of this line: "Please finish this." There is no evidence of completion.]

Appendix B
Minutes of the Erosophian Society of California State Normal School, Feb. 13, 1874, featuring a union meeting and a public debate, with teams comprised of men and women

[Erosophian Society, p. 35. SJSU University Archives: Normal School [MC 327]. Courtesy of San Jose State University Special Collections and Archives, Dr. Martin Luther King, Jr. Library.]

The officers and members of the Philomathian and Erosophian Societies met this day in the chapel of the State Normal School at 2 p.m. The Emendian, Rhizomian, Archanian Platonic, and Santa Clara Literary Societies of Santa Clara valley were also present by invitation.

Capt. Wash was appointed president for the day. The usual business of the meeting was postponed for today.

President appointed Prof. Allen [principal of California State Normal School] critic for the day. Instrumental music Miss Allen. After which Capt. Wash introduced Mr. G. W. Henning to the Societies, who delivered a speech to the societies the subject of which was "The Grangers." Miss E. Hammond followed with an essay, subject "Why." Quartette by Misses Holloway, Singletary and Hammond and Mr. Jewell. Mr. Johnson introduced to the society Mr. White commonly known as "Humorous White" who took his place in delivering an oration, title "Marmion and Douglass." An original poem by Mrs. Miller, title "Cupid and Psyche." Select reading Miss M. E. Wilson, title "Coronation of Inez De Castro." Solo, "I can not sing tonight." Miss Singletary. After which three minutes was allowed the societies for recess, during the time Mr. White favored us with some humorous anecdotes.

Societies being called to order the following resolution was then offered for debate and decision. "Resolved, that the present social and political conditions of the United States demands the action of the Grangers." The following ladies and gentlemen were appointed on the Aff. and Neg. of the question. Aff. Miss Crumry and Mr. Farnham. Neg. Mr. E. R. Brooks and Miss Intermille.

President left the decision to the Societies.

Secretary received notes from Miss Gallimore Sec. of the Emendian Lit. So. And Mr. May Sec. of Rhizomian Lit. So. thanking both societies for the honor conferred on them, by the invitation to our Union meeting.

A motion carried to the effect that a vote of thanks be given to Mrses. [sic] White and Henning for adding so much to the pleasure of the day.

Critic not being present no report was given.

Exercises closed with a hymn by the societies
"Oh! Praise the Lord."

Capt. Wash President Pro. Tem.
Ida M. Clayton Sec.

Chapter 8

Writing Instruction in School and College English

The Twentieth Century and the New Millennium

David Gold, Catherine L. Hobbs, and James A. Berlin[1]

Key Concepts

Introduction: writing as a site of contestation • **Twentieth Century Beginnings**: Committee of Ten; current-traditional rhetoric; the liberal culture ideal; methods of instruction in the schools • **1900–1917**: social efficiency; alternative social rhetorics; reorganization of English • **Between the Wars**: self-expression and creative writing; challenges from behaviorism; challenges from social rhetorics; NCTE curriculum projects • **1945–1960**: social adjustment, language arts, and communication; literature and composition; linguistics and composition; historical rhetorics • **1960–1975**: English studies responds; cognitive processes and composing; processes of personal and linguistic growth; social-epistemic theories • **1975–2000**: high school writing and the literacy "crisis"; teacher initiatives; college writing becomes a discipline; divergent approaches to teaching writing; the turn to literacy; cultural studies, critical pedagogy, and composition; feminism and diversity; continuing language issues; computers and technological change; professional issues • **The New Millennium**: attending to the local; civic engagement; digital literacy and multimodal composing; rhetoric, grammar, and style; empirical research • **Conclusion**: over a century of change.

---

1 This chapter cannot help but retain the imprint of the article prepared by the late James A. Berlin (1942–94) for the first edition of this book. His pioneering monographs, *Writing Instruction in Nineteenth-Century American Colleges* (Carbondale: Southern Illinois University Press, 1984) and *Rhetoric and Reality: Writing Instruction in American Colleges, 1900–1985* (Carbondale: Southern Illinois University Press, 1987), inspired a wave of historiographic research in writing studies and continue to influence the field, particularly in their insistence on examining the socioeconomic factors influencing pedagogies and the competing visions of literacy—and society—they enact. If his ideological commitments to liberatory pedagogies led him to at times downplay the contributions of other approaches, his understanding of writing as social and his commitment to social justice remain resonant. Among Berlin's major contributions was the articulation of a taxonomy of historical approaches to teaching writing, which he termed "rhetorics"—primarily the product-oriented current-traditional, the liberal-culture expressivist, and the civic social-epistemic—each differing not only in praxis but in ideology and epistemology. While these categories remain useful, we treat them here as somewhat less deterministic and discrete and more fluid and interdependent, a direction Berlin himself perhaps prefigures in his final, posthumously published work, *Rhetorics, Poetics, and Cultures: Refiguring College English Studies* (Urbana, IL: NCTE, 1996).

This is, of course, an impossible title and an impossible assignment. To write a history of anything requires data, records that document what occurred in the past, so that an author can construct a narrative of events. Even acknowledging that histories are always interpretations, that they do not report what actually happened in the past but are simply records of what writers say happened, even this does not make it possible to write a history of writing instruction. The problem is that instruction, especially instruction in writing, remains largely invisible . . . [A]n instructor goes into a room with a group of students and closes the door. . . . Then, too, writing instruction is not limited to what happens inside classrooms.

Anne Ruggles Gere[2]

Everyone teaches the process of writing, but everyone does not teach the same process.

James A. Berlin[3]

Introduction: Writing as a Site of Contestation

Writing instruction in school and college English programs has been a scene of struggle over the last century. Even before the late-twentieth-century attention to language as a creator of meaning and experience, educators and policy shapers realized that the study of language and literature was an integral part of learning rather than a superficial acquirement. If education in a democratic society is a site of contest over the kind of economic, social, and political formations we want schools to endorse, it is no wonder that English studies, with its concern for the literary and rhetorical texts students are to read and to write, remains near the center of curricular decisions. Perhaps more than with any other subject, decisions about writing pedagogy put into material practice our beliefs about the purpose education should serve in society.

In the nineteenth century, when English studies was first taking shape, literature was primarily studied in classical texts, in Latin or Greek, leaving more curricular space for the development of written composition or public speech in the vernacular. Centering the English curriculum on literary texts is a "modern" phenomenon that only occurred as language studies moved into the twentieth century; as late as 1884, Harvard President Charles W. Eliot could complain of the lack of "equal rank" accorded English by classics-centered colleges.[4] The founding of the Modern Language Association (MLA) in 1883 did much to improve the professional status of English studies, but as the organization grew it turned away from pedagogical issues in favor of literary research, disbanding its pedagogical section in 1903. Yet instruction in writing always remained central to English studies, even if histories of the profession have not always done it justice. With the professionalization of composition in the late twentieth century, the field's historians have been laboring to tell stories of this uninterrupted

---

2 Anne Ruggles Gere, "The Teaching of Writing, 1912–2000," in *Reading the Past, Writing the Future: A Century of American Literacy Education and the National Council of Teachers of English*, ed. Erika Lindemann (Urbana, IL: NCTE, 2010), 93–94.

3 James A. Berlin, "Contemporary Composition: The Major Pedagogical Theories," *College English* 44.8 (1982): 777, itals. orig.

4 Charles W. Eliot, "What Is a Liberal Education?" *The Century*, June 1884, 205.

activity of instruction in writing.[5] They are confirming that writing pedagogy has been a site of contestation and that no classroom pedagogy can long survive without in some way responding to its historical conditions.

The modern high school and comprehensive university took their shapes as part of an economic shift from a largely laissez-faire market economy to a managed one of corporate and government alliances and planning. Education, particularly the new formation of English, played a central role in this transition. For most of the nineteenth century, higher education served to prepare an elite for leadership in society. General education was common to all students able to earn a higher education: rhetoric, classical languages and literature, moral philosophy, and some mathematics and science. Specialized training in the professions, primarily law, the ministry, and medicine, was carried out primarily through apprenticeship programs, although a few professional schools were available.

The rise of the German research university model, with its specialized disciplines and rigorous research mission, joined with economic and social forces in the United States to produce the new comprehensive university. This momentous transformation was signaled early on by the passing of the federal Morrill Land Grant Act of 1862, which supported states in establishing agricultural and technical institutions designed to apply the findings of science to the managing of economic and social affairs. In the new university, the curriculum was to be elective, not prescribed, specialized rather than general, and its purpose was to train certified experts in the new sciences to produce the knowledge that would move the economy and society forward.

When the act was renewed in 1890, a provision ensured that funds would go to both races, improving black institutions or, as happened in the South, establishing separate black colleges. The commitment of public funds from both Morrill Acts also put pressure on institutions to accept women, where again in the South reluctance to fully admit women to these institutions produced several public women's colleges. But generally, colleges, especially state institutions, began to open their doors to more diverse people of talent—women as well as men, black as well as white—although genuine equality remained more an ideal than a reality. The change in higher education also brought about changes in the high schools. While virtually all states outside the South by the time of the Civil War provided some form of common school for the lower grades, many secondary schools were private and were designed as places for college preparation. The same sort of political pressures that encouraged colleges to become places of scientific training for a more productive workforce were effective in arguing that

5   In the preface to 2007 edition of his influential 1987 *Professing Literature: An Institutional History*, Gerald Graff acknowledges this gap in the previous work (twentieth anniversary ed., Chicago: University of Chicago Press, 2007), xvii. Among works that attempt to do justice to rhetoric and composition's history as part of English studies are Sharon Crowley, *The Methodical Memory: Invention in Current-Traditional Rhetoric* (Carbondale: Southern Illinois University Press, 1990); John C. Brereton, ed., *The Origins of Composition Studies in the American College, 1875–1925: A Documentary History* (Pittsburgh: University of Pittsburgh Press, 1995); Thomas P. Miller, *The Formation of College English: Rhetoric and Belles Lettres in the British Cultural Provinces* (Pittsburgh: University of Pittsburgh Press, 1997); W. Ross Winterowd, *The English Department: A Personal and Institutional History* (Carbondale: Southern Illinois University Press, 1998). For recent historical studies, see the sections "Current-Traditional Rhetoric" (p. 237) and "Attending to the Local" (p. 263) in this chapter.

high schools, where attendance was then increasing, should serve the same purposes.

In the U.S. in 1890, there were approximately 298,000 students enrolled in high school; this figure jumped to 630,000 by 1900 and to 4.7 million in 1930; school enrollment rates among 14- to 17-year-olds during this period increased from 5.6 percent in 1890 to 10.2 percent in 1900 to 50.7 percent in 1930. Increased attendance in colleges was almost as dramatic, from approximately 157,000 students in 1890 to 238,000 in 1900 to 1.1 million in 1930, with an enormous expansion due to baby boomers coming about just as composition studies was aspiring to disciplinary status, from approximately 2.4 million in 1950 to more than 8 million in 1970. By 2009, more than 19.1 million students were in college, with 41.3 percent of all 18- to 24-year-olds enrolled, and among high school graduates of the same age group, 48.8 percent.[6] Thus, high schools became an institution serving the majority of American youth only in the early twentieth century; it appears that colleges are crossing this line early in the twenty-first century.

The role of gender in these revised educational arrangements is crucial. More girls than boys graduated from high school at the start of the twentieth century, but few could go to college, although the number enrolled had grown from approximately 1,100 in 1870 to 85,000 in 1900. But women persisted in gaining higher education, so that later in the century, much of the increase in college enrollment would be made up of women, who would comprise 51.4 percent of college students by 1980 and 57.1 percent by 2003.[7] Many of the new college composition positions, both adjunct and tenure-line, were also being filled by women, who earned doctorates at a sharply increasing rate beginning in the 1970s.[8] It should be noted, however, that throughout the twentieth century across the profession of teaching, women have dominated at the primary level, demonstrated a clear majority at the secondary level, and been a minority at the college level. The percentage of women in public school teaching remains high, while men continue to dominate at the college level. Moreover, women college faculty tend to teach in lower-paying areas such as education and the humanities; a 2008 survey of College Composition and Communication Conference members found that women made up 60.3 percent of writing program directors and 63.8 percent of composition instructors.[9] Overall, salaries for women, especially in college English and in the schools, remain at less than those for men doing the same work. This pattern of inequality should be kept in mind in discussing the activity of a profession in which women have played so prominent and successful a role.

---

6 Thomas D. Snyder and Sally A. Dillow, *Digest of Educational Statistics 2010* (Washington, DC: National Center for Education Statistics, 2011), 87, 290, 308.

7 Snyder and Dillow, *Digest 2010*, 290–91. Women's percentage of total enrollment has remained relatively stable since 2003, though their absolute numbers continue to increase.

8 Sue Ellen Holbrook, "Women's Work: The Feminizing of Composition," *Rhetoric Review* 9.2 (1991): 201–29.

9 Anne Ruggles Gere, "Initial Report on Survey of CCCC Members" (2009), http://www.ncte.org/library/NCTEFiles/Groups/CCCC/InitialReportSurveyCCCCMembers.pdf (accessed November 15, 2011).

Twentieth Century Beginnings

Committee of Ten

By the turn of the twentieth century, the required classical course was generally abandoned, though not without a struggle.[10] Because high schools had seen their mission as preparing students for college, they had emphasized classical language and literature. In contrast, the new high school and college would organize around the study of English. By the nineteenth century, the rhetoric course had come to be taught in English. As a result, the original courses in the emerging English department at the college level, most conspicuously at Harvard, were in composition. In 1874, Harvard became the first to introduce a new entrance exam in writing—one destined to replace the classical language requirement—asking each candidate for admission to write "a short English Composition, correct in spelling, punctuation, grammar, and expression, the subject to be taken from such works of standard authors as shall be announced from time to time." The essay, as Applebee has indicated, was designed to test writing ability, not knowledge of literature.[11]

The prestige of Harvard, the fact that secondary schools had previously based the curriculum on college preparation, and the absence of a new curricular model for the new high school all conspired to make the new entrance policy decisive in shaping secondary English courses. Since Harvard's reading list, as well as the lists of those colleges emulating its example, changed from year to year, it was difficult for high school teachers to know what literary works to teach. As a result, regional organizations were established to provide uniform reading lists, and these groups were finally replaced in 1894 by the National Conference on Uniform Entrance Requirements.

Toward this end, in 1892 the National Educational Association (NEA) appointed a group known as the Committee of Ten, with Harvard president Charles W. Eliot as chair, for the purpose of examining and reforming the U.S. secondary school curriculum. In what would become an important policy statement, its Conference on English in its final report outlined two primary objectives in teaching English: "(1) to enable the pupil to understand the expressed thoughts of others and to give expression to thoughts of his own; and (2) to cultivate a taste for reading, to give the pupil some acquaintance with good literature, and to furnish him with the means of extending that acquaintance." The elaboration of the first is crucial to composition history. The document encouraged the student in the elementary school "to furnish his own material, expressing his own thoughts in a natural way" and relying on his own "observation or personal experience." This represented a concession to student interest and innovation that was that hallmark of the newly emergent child-centered progressive elementary education. These methods, however, were to be abandoned by the secondary school, where the emphasis was to be on the more rigorous "study of literature and training in the expression of thought."[12] Here

10 Frederick Rudolph, *The American College and University: A History* (New York: Vintage, 1962), 196, 214.
11 Harvard University, *Catalogue* (1873–74), 53; Arthur N. Applebee, *Tradition and Reform in the Teaching of English: A History* (Urbana: NCTE), 1974, 30.
12 National Educational Association, *Report of the Committee of Ten on Secondary School Studies* (New York: American Book Co., 1894), 86–90.

the orientation was provided by the tenets of mental discipline and faculty psychology, now offered in the service of the scientific values of precision, clarity, and conciseness. Indeed, given that the members of the Conference on English were appointed by Eliot and that it included Harvard's George Lyman Kittredge, it is perhaps not unexpected that the method of writing instruction for high schools recommended was the one later characterized by writing scholars as "current-traditional" rhetoric, a method that had one of its origin points in Harvard's English department.

Current-Traditional Rhetoric

In the early twentieth century, Harvard was one of the founding centers of what has since come to be termed current-traditional rhetoric,[13] particularly through the textbooks of Adams Sherman Hill and Barrett Wendell (although those of Amherst's John Franklin Genung were popular as well). According to Berlin, its epistemological base, derived from eighteenth-century faculty psychology and a nineteenth-century faith in science and progress, is positivistic and rational, offering writing as an extension of the scientific method. Since the basis of reliable knowledge is sense impression, the writer is to use inductively derived data whenever possible, and to try to convey thoughts as transparently as possible to let reality show through. Moreover, the mind's faculties give rise to the forms of rhetorical discourse, "modes" such as exposition and argument, corresponding to the faculty of reason, or description and persuasion, arising from the emotions and will. The latter are particularly suspect since the feelings can distort reality.

Current-traditional rhetoric, argues Berlin, shifts attention from the rhetorical canon of invention—the search for the right line of argument to persuade a given audience in a contingent situation—to arrangement and style, with instruction emphasizing the modes of discourse, clarity, and correctness. Moreover, in this more objective, scientific rhetoric, social problems are reduced to technical problems; questions formerly in the realm of public discourse and participatory democracy are relegated to professional experts, such as engineers and technical specialists.

Though current-traditional rhetoric has long been maligned within rhetoric and composition studies, as recent scholars have revisited this period, they have found it to be not as easily characterized and categorized as Berlin sets forth. Charles M. Paine, for example, has found that Hill and Wendell had social concerns and wanted to "inoculate" students against the ills of mass culture; Susan Kates and others have found wider presence of socially activist rhetorics during this period; and David Gold has found that, for some student populations,

---

13 Coined by Daniel Fogarty in the 1959 *Roots for a New Rhetoric* (New York: Teachers College, Columbia University), the term was popularized in composition studies by Richard E. Young and Berlin. For treatments, see Young, "Paradigms and Problems: Needed Research in Rhetorical Invention," in *Research on Composing: Points of Departure*, ed. Charles R. Cooper and Lee Odell (Urbana, IL: NCTE, 1978), 29–47; Berlin, *Rhetoric and Reality*; Crowley, *Methodical Memory*. Robin Varnum's *Fencing with Words: A History of Writing Instruction at Amherst College during the Era of Theodore Baird, 1938–1966* (Urbana: NCTE, 1996) criticizes the concept of "current-traditional" in part for causing historians to neglect the mid-twentieth century through its homogeneously negative characterizations of writing instruction.

an emphasis on prescription was welcomed as study that could potentially offer economic, social, and political advancement, arguing that "what we have dismissed as current-traditional rhetoric" may in fact represent a network of "interwoven practices, both conservative and radical, liberatory and disciplining, and subject to wide-ranging local and institutional variations."[14] Although some scholars have continued to read the period through Berlin's original lens, these revisionist views are becoming increasingly accepted.

The Liberal Culture Ideal

Of course, current-traditional rhetoric was not the only model of writing instruction in the new college and university. At Yale and other established Atlantic seaboard colleges, faculty promoted what James Berlin has termed the **"liberal cultural"** ideal. The proponents of liberal culture argued that the literary text was the expression of the highest potential of human nature. If Harvard's response to the perceived literacy crises brought on by the rise in college enrollment and new constituencies of students was to attempt to inculcate in every student, no matter their talent or ability, the "habitual use of correct and intelligent English,"[15] at Yale, if writing was to be taught at all, it ought to be to the few who were gifted, and then in order to encourage the creation of literature, not rhetoric. From this perspective, the claims of current-traditional rhetoric were too democratic, arguing mistakenly that writing, like engineering or farming or pharmacy, could be taught. Liberal culture thus represented the reaction of the old, elite colleges to the new meritocratic university, its proponents generally agreeing that the business of higher education was to train the leaders of society and that the best way to offer such training was through a literary education.

Summing up the tenor of this contentious debate for the *English Journal* in 1912, the University of Kansas's Glenn E. Palmer observed, "The one would develop a few geniuses by the systemic treatment of enriching thoughts and broadening experiences. The other would train a class full of Philistines prepared for the everyday needs of democracy, by enforcing good language habits, and increasing expressiveness."[16] In contrast, Palmer sought a compromise between these ideals of "culture" and efficiency"; while his sentiments were no doubt shared by many instructors in the newly formed National Council of Teachers of English, the Arnoldian ideal represented by liberal culture that literature represented the best thought of the best minds and was the appropriate basis for educating each new generation would become the model for newly emerging literature-centered English departments.

---

14 Charles M. Paine, *The Resistant Writer: Rhetoric as Immunity, 1850 to the Present* (Albany: State University of New York Press, 1999); Susan Kates, *Activist Rhetorics and American Higher Education, 1885–1937* (Carbondale: Southern Illinois University Press, 2001); David Gold, *Rhetoric at the Margins: Revising the History of Writing Instruction in American Colleges, 1873–1947* (Carbondale: Southern Illinois University Press, 2008), 5.

15 C. T. Copeland and H. M. Rideout, *Freshman English and Theme-Correcting in Harvard College* (New York: Silver, Burdett and Co., 1901), 2.

16 Glenn E. Palmer, "Culture and Efficiency Through Composition," *English Journal* 1.8 (1912): 488.

Methods of Instruction in the Schools

The divisions in these two conceptions of writing instruction are fairly transparent in the debates taking place at the college level during this time. When we turn to the practices of high school teachers, however, the methods called upon in teaching writing are not nearly so clear-cut. Despite the fact that, as high school enrollments increased, the absolute numbers of students not going on also to college increased, the curriculum remained tied to the needs of the college-bound. This meant that most of the writing a student attempted focused on literary texts. This writing, however, varied greatly depending on the nature of the literary study undertaken.

The philological method that emphasized responding to the text as a historical artifact to be studied scientifically lent itself to the composing processes of current-traditional rhetoric. Thus, the text could be used to demonstrate certain rhetorical principles, or the student could be asked to write about certain historical features of the text's production. A reading, on the other hand, that insisted on the unique ability of the literary text to provide a rare experience of truth and beauty would be more inclined to use the rhetoric of liberal culture. The liberal culture classroom encouraged students to offer an appreciative reading of the text, sometimes a unique response to the text in unique language, or occasionally an original literary production. The point was to develop literary taste in students, which would equip them for a better life both morally and aesthetically, and to discover those with the talent for creative effort if any were in fact in the classroom. As is indicated by some of the high school textbooks at the turn of the century, sometimes the two methods appeared in the same classroom.

1900–1917

During the first two decades of the century, the teaching of English in high schools and colleges attained professional standing. English teachers now were more confident about the special materials of their discipline and of the methods for teaching them. A number of social and political developments at this time encouraged the new stability and status of English studies.

Social Efficiency

During these decades of economic extremes such as the robber barons and monopolies, the effects of unregulated capitalism became unacceptable to many, and the federal government began to intervene to make the economy more efficient and fair. A parallel concept of "**social efficiency**" was extended to the public schools. As Joel Spring explains, "social efficiency" meant that schools were to provide curricula that met "the future social needs of the student," taught "cooperation as preparation for future social activities," and provided for "the future social destination of the student."[17] Students were now to be prepared for work—primarily for life in the large-scale organizations where cooperation

17 Joel Spring, *The American School, 1642–1985* (New York: Longman, 1986), 198.

(as well as conformity) was valued over competition. School and work were also regarded as places of equal opportunity where the best, brightest, and hardest working were to be rewarded in accordance with meritocratic principles, an ideal that, if never quite realized, was widely shared. To address concerns about potential social fragmentation in the new comprehensive high school, English teachers were also recruited to teach "the mother tongue,"[18] providing through literature and composition the means for a common culture that would increase social cohesion. After World War I, this function would be further encouraged through the "Americanization" programs provided for the new wave of immigrants.

Teachers of English were generally supportive of these trends. In fact, the National Council of Teachers of English (NCTE) was formed in 1911 in protest at uniform reading lists. A coalition made up primarily of teachers from the Midwest and New York City, the NCTE argued that teachers, not the colleges, should set reading and writing requirements for their students, taking into account their special needs. Their resolve was intensified by their concern for the learning problems of the many students not going on to college, particularly the increasing numbers of immigrant students.

The effects on classroom practices of this movement to prepare students for economic and social life were in no way monolithic. The new emphasis on vocational education often led to pragmatic-minded English courses, offering, for example, "units on salesmanship, advertising, and printing."[19] But the emphasis on the high school as a place of training for work could also restrict writing instruction to the strictly utilitarian and vocational, without regard for the personal or political life of the student. At its best, however, the drive for social efficiency promoted a democratic rhetoric that responded to the progressive agenda of John Dewey's full educational experience: self-development within a democratic environment, a concern for social reform and harmony, and the preparation for economic integration. This rhetoric is seen in the work of Fred Newton Scott of the University of Michigan, Joseph Villiers Denney of Ohio State, and Gertrude Buck of Vassar.[20] Scott is particularly worth examining as an example of this social rhetoric because of his considerable influence in both public schools and colleges.

Alternative Social Rhetorics

Fred Newton Scott's rhetoric was consciously formulated as an alternative to both current-traditional rhetoric, with its emphasis on the efficient, the scientific and practical, and to the rhetoric of liberal culture, with its privatization of experience and elitism. For the socially minded Scott, argues Berlin, reality was neither exclusively sensory nor exclusively subjective, but was a product of the interaction of the private and public in a social setting. Scott's pedagogy was

---

18 Spring, *American School*, 203.
19 Applebee, *Tradition and Reform*, 60.
20 See Donald C. Stewart and Patricia L. Stewart, *The Life and Legacy of Fred Newton Scott* (Pittsburgh: University of Pittsburgh Press, 1997); Suzanne Bordelon, *A Feminist Legacy: The Rhetoric and Pedagogy of Gertrude Buck* (Carbondale: Southern Illinois University Press, 2007).

intent on providing for public discourse in a democratic and heterogeneous society. "The value of any piece of discourse, or mode of communication," he wrote, "is to be measured by its effect upon the welfare of the community."[21] Scott thus proposes a rhetoric of public service, a commitment to using discourse for the public good.

His popular textbooks, such as the elementary composition text he wrote with Denney, sought to offer students what Berlin termed "a complete rhetorical situation," one that was thoroughly social without denying the importance of the individual.[22] As Denney explains elsewhere, in leading students to topics, it is necessary to choose "a typical situation in real life," express the topic so as to suggest to the student "a personal relationship to the situation," and provide "a particular reader or set of readers who are to be brought into vital relationship with the situation."[23] Although it is difficult to determine exactly how these textbooks were used in the classroom, Scott remains a pivotal figure. As Anne Ruggles Gere suggests, by "identifying social causes of problems in writing instruction, rather than advocating for social efficiency or a focus on the individual writer,"[24] Scott prefigures later socially grounded approaches that would become increasingly important to writing studies.

Reorganization of English

The larger effects of the social efficiency effort on English studies were presented in a 1917 report, *Reorganization of English in Secondary Schools*, sponsored by a joint committee of the NEA and the NCTE. It argued that English courses should emphasize personal and social needs of students and society rather than college requirements. As for writing, there was to be, as in the Committee of Ten report, a progression from creative and individual activities at the lowest grades to social and more practical activities at the upper levels. Thus students in the seventh, eighth, and ninth grades were to engage in creative writing, such as stories about their experiences, sensory descriptions of memorable scenes, accounts of imaginary journeys, and fictional conversations. In the upper grades, however, writing was to be functional, growing out of the experiences of students, but focusing on social exigencies. The student should write for a clearly designated audience, not "with the vision of a teacher, blue pencil in hand, looking over his shoulder." Despite its attention to the social the report was, in general, a conservative document, emphasizing the utilitarian and social nature of mature discourse but saying little about the uses of writing in preparing students for citizenship in a democracy or in enabling them to arrive at personal fulfillment. The strongest impulse for writing instruction is to prepare the student to be an efficient worker.[25]

21 Berlin, *Rhetoric and Reality*, 46–50; Fred Newton Scott, "Rhetoric Rediviva," *CCC* 31.4 (1980): 415.

22 Berlin, *Writing Instruction*, 83.

23 Joseph Villiers Denney, "Two Problems in Composition-Teaching," *The Inlander*, April 1897, 297.

24 Gere, "Teaching of Writing," 101–02.

25 James Fleming Hosic, ed., *Reorganization of English in Secondary Schools*, Bulletin 1917, no. 2 (Washington, DC: GPO, 1917), 57; Applebee, *Tradition and Reform*, 66.

Between the Wars

Self-Expression and Creative Writing

World War I served to establish beyond doubt the value of English studies to the nation as a whole. While English teachers in the schools organized courses around patriotic themes, their counterparts in the universities turned their prewar training in German universities to the national interest, especially in the postwar occupation. The years immediately following the war were a time of relative prosperity and optimism for the schools. In English studies, the most notable turn was the concern for the unique individuality and creative potential of each student. The center of composition activities for an increasing number of school and college teachers became expressive writing about personal experience, and occasionally creative writing. As Berlin suggests, the insistence of liberal culturists on genius as the essential element of writing at its best was now given a democratic application. Each and every individual was seen to possess creative potential, a potential the proper classroom environment could unlock and promote.[26]

This movement—at first termed "**expressionistic rhetoric**" by Berlin, though "expressivist" has become more common—had a number of influences: progressive educational ideals, particularly the emphasis on instrumental value and democratic ends; child-centered developmental theories inspired by Froebel and Pestalozzi; popularizations of Freud that emphasized the inner self; anti-corporatism; and strains of American Romanticism that celebrated both the individual and the larger democratic society.[27] This description well fits the pedagogy of Theodore Baird, whose influential leadership of the writing program at Amherst spanned nearly forty years, beginning in 1938.[28]

In his historical treatment of creative expression in the school English curriculum, Kenneth J. Kantor offers an overview of the various features of the movement between the wars.[29] One form it took was to argue that English is an art subject like painting or music—not preparation for the more efficient uses of language. Proponents such as Hugh Mearns, Harold Rugg, and John T. Frederick argued that traditional English courses had encouraged conformity and imitation rather than self-expression and that creative writing could enable the student to recognize the dignity of his own experience. Numerous other claims for the benefits of expressive writing were also made: it could promote fully rounded individuals; advance cultural values; improve the mechanical elements of writing as students strove to communicate a message that really matters to them; and enhance students' enjoyment of literature as they discovered for themselves the values of literary discourse through their attempts to produce it.

These approaches were not unproblematic. As Kantor points out, the values most commonly promoted by creative expression were those of the comfortable

---

26 Berlin, *Rhetoric and Reality*, 73. See also D. G. Myers, *The Elephants Teach: Creative Writing Since 1880* (Englewood Cliffs, NJ: Prentice-Hall, 1996).

27 Berlin, *Rhetoric and Reality*, 73–81; see also Berlin, *Writing Instruction*, 42–57.

28 See Varnum, *Fencing with Words*.

29 Kenneth J. Kantor, "Creative Expression in the English Curriculum: An Historical Perspective," *Research in the Teaching of English* 9.1 (1975): 5–29; see also Myers, *Elephants Teach*, 101–45.

white middle class, ignoring, for example, the experiences of African Americans and other minorities. Moreover, James Berlin has critiqued expressivist rhetoric, particularly in its later manifestations, for what he considered its subjectivist epistemology, privileging the private and personal vision of the author at the expense of the public and the social. Although he supported expressivism's anti-conformist and anti-corporatist impulses, he was less confident of its ability to promote social change: "for expressionistic rhetoric, the correct response to the imposition of current economic, political, and social arrangements is . . . resistance, but a resistance that is always construed in individual terms."[30] A resurgence in expressivist and creative approaches would occur during the 1960s and 1970s.

Challenges from Behaviorism

This enthusiasm for expressive, creative writing did not go unchallenged. Between the wars, the turn to quantitative measurement in psychology inspired by Edward L. Thorndike and the efficiency movement in business inspired by Frederick Taylor combined to create a drive for measurement of student abilities and achievement in schools and colleges. In English studies, this rage for quantification produced a variety of activities, some salutary, others unfortunate. For example, the testing of student abilities led to tracking in English courses at both the high school and college levels. A joint survey conducted by the MLA and the NCTE found that high school students wrote on average 400 words per week while college freshmen averaged 650. The study revealed just how "efficient" English studies was, the course clearly overworking teachers to an appalling degree. The report argued convincingly for reform, although none was forthcoming.[31]

Challenges from Social Rhetorics

Another challenge to the dominance of expressive writing came in the form of socially based rhetorics. These were found in courses inspired by Dewey and Scott, and were especially apparent during the Depression years. The insistence that writing is a social act performed through a complex interaction of writer, audience, subject, and language appeared at colleges in every geographical region.[32] These offerings tended to be specifically political in their orientation, addressing the economic crisis at home and the international crises abroad as failures of the total community, not of the individual. Many advocates of social rhetoric laid the blame for these disorders at the feet of the social and political arrangements generated by capitalism, a diagnosis in which they were led by strong factions in the American Historical Association and the Progressive Education Association.[33] While the expressionists looked to the individual to address the horrors of the 1930s and 1940s, the sponsors of social reform looked to collective solutions.

30 James A. Berlin, "Rhetoric and Ideology in the Writing Class," *College English* 50.5 (1988): 487.
31 John Michael Wozniak, *English Composition in Eastern Colleges, 1850–1940* (Washington, DC: University Press of America, 1978), 169–70.
32 Berlin, *Rhetoric and Reality*, 81–90.
33 Applebee, *Tradition and Reform*, 115–16.

NCTE Curriculum Projects

All of these conflicting positions on the most effective method for teaching writing are reflected in two NCTE-sponsored reports led by Ruth Mary Weeks. The first of these was the 1935 *An Experience Curriculum in English*. Encouraged by the social efficiency movement and certain strands of progressive education, the report promoted a "body of guided experiences" in reading, writing, and speaking that would parallel those that students would engage with in their lives outside of school.[34] Implying that both privatized expression and public discourse were to be encouraged in the classroom, the report also came out against mechanistic and formulaic methods of teaching writing, most controversially in its recommendation that formal grammar instruction be abandoned in favor of teaching grammar as a part of composing.

Building on this work, the next year, Weeks and a committee published *A Correlated Curriculum*, a monumental interdisciplinary project to integrate writing across the curriculum. This innovative and ambitious curriculum failed to take hold, in part because, even at this early date, a backlash was forming against Progressive-era theories and practices. Yet, as Suzanne Bordelon notes, Weeks's efforts "to open education to broader classes of students, to promote learning as a collaborative process, [and] to prepare all students to meet the demands of transforming social and industrial circumstances" remain resonant themes with contemporary composition scholars and teachers.[35]

1945–1960

The mid-century saw an enormous expansion of education, with both high school and college enrollments roughly doubling between 1930 and 1950, and the percentage of 14- to 17-year olds enrolled in school increasing from 50.7 to 76.1 percent.[36] In both schools and colleges, English instructors were being asked to take an increasing role in preparing students for modern life. At the college level, writing instructors began drawing on a widening scope of scholarship as they coordinated their efforts around the growing composition course, establishing a burgeoning sense of professional identity.

Social Adjustment, Language Arts, and Communication

In the schools, the **"life adjustment"** movement, fostered in part by the Progressive Education Association's 1944 report, *Education for All American Youth*, became an important part of postwar education. As Kantor explains, "Personal

---

34 W. Wilbur Hatfield, chair, *An Experience Curriculum in English: A Report of the Curriculum Commission of the National Council of Teachers of English* (New York: Appleton-Century, 1935), 9. Though Hatfield chaired the report, Weeks, NCTE President in 1929–30, initiated this project. Only recently have her contributions to the field been recognized; for a treatment, see Suzanne Bordelon, "Restructuring English and Society through an Integrated Curriculum: Ruth Mary Weeks's *A Correlated Curriculum*," *Rhetoric Review* 29.3 (2010): 257–74.

35 Ruth Mary Weeks, chair, *A Correlated Curriculum: A Report of the Committee on Correlation of the National Council of Teachers of English* (New York: Appleton-Century, 1936); Bordelon, "Restructuring English," 257.

36 Snyder and Dillow, *Digest 2010*, 87, 290.

and social 'adjustment' . . . sought to provide a new security for those whose lives had been disrupted by the war." Drawing on themes earlier articulated by the social efficiency movement, proponents of life adjustment sought to make language instruction—which they viewed "as contributing primarily to citizenship in a democracy"—relevant to students' daily lives, emphasizing both practical skills such as letter writing and conversation and an "appreciation" of the arts.[37]

English instructors' reactions to the movement were varied, some seeing it as a watering down of the curriculum that neglected basic skills and "mastery" of the subject, others as an extension of socially minded approaches to reading and writing already in play, such as the experience curriculum. The NCTE's own contributions during this period, most notably the 1952 *The English Language Arts* and the 1956 *The English Language Arts in the Secondary School*, sought a middle ground, emphasizing the "growth of young people as individual persons, as members of social groups, as citizens, and as workers," while maintaining a research-based approach to developing students' skills in reading, speaking, listening, and writing, and calling for the teaching of grammar and vocabulary in context. Though popular, the guides did generate conflicting responses among English teachers, suggesting both the diversity of approaches in the schools and the increasing sense of curricular stakes in the postwar era.[38] However, their comprehensive approach to the "language arts" would be influential.

Along these lines, in colleges the **communications course** became popular, gaining widespread appeal after the army adopted it in its officer training programs during the war. Influenced by the general education movement, the general semantics school of linguistics, and the life-adjustment movement, the communications course offered a combination of reading, writing, speaking, and listening activities designed to offer practical skills in communication. As an experimental course, it varied widely in form, often resulting in a current-traditional emphasis, a deficit model of student skills, and an approach to social "adjustment" that enforced rigid social norms rather than individual development. At the same time, it attempted to be forward-looking in its integrated approach, concern for student development, emphasis on the social ends of communication, and goal of preparing students for civic and professional life. In examining curricula, Berlin found both "remarkable . . . innovation" and "unfortunate excesses," though he ultimately judged it as encouraging a "fresh and worthy set of ideas" that made "a substantial contribution" to writing studies.[39]

Though the communications course declined during the 1950s, it did, however, for a brief time bring members of speech and English departments together again, leading to an enrichment of rhetorical studies among English

37 Kantor, "Creative Expression," 21.

38 Dora V. Smith, "*The English Language Arts*: A Link between Yesterday and Tomorrow," *English Journal* 42.2 (1953): 76–77. See also W. M. Bedell, Lois Anne Dilley, Joseph Gallant, Eula Phares Mohle, H. C. Newton, and E. Louise Noyes, "Varied Views of *The English Language Arts*," *English Journal* 41.7 (1952): 362–69; Angela M. Broening, "*The English Language Arts in the Secondary School*: An Overview," *English Journal* 45.7 (1956): 406–09; Jean L. B. Christison, Edward J. Gordon, Paul Farmer, and Robert W Mitchner, "The Significance of *The English Language Arts in the Secondary School*: A Symposium," *English Journal* 46.5 (1957): 286–93.

39 Berlin, *Rhetoric and Reality*, 93–104.

teachers and bringing about the formation of the Conference on College Composition and Communication (CCCC) in 1949 and the founding of the journal *College Composition and Communication (CCC)* the following year.[40] The formation of the CCCC signaled a renewed interest in composition at the college level, motivated in part by the large number of veterans attending college on the G.I. Bill. The pages of *CCC* and *College English* during this time attest to this new activity.[41]

Literature and Composition

Using literature texts as materials for analysis in order to teach writing had of course been commonplace throughout the century. The literary emphasis, however, gained new energy with the advent of New Critical approaches and an increasing sense of professional identity among teachers of literature following the war. Arguments offered in defense of this view came directly from the tradition of liberal culture, still alive in literary studies, which held that reading literary texts and writing about them provided the knowledge and stimulation that the student needed to become liberally educated. Literature in this view also preserved the integrity of the individual against the tyranny of the mob and could thus promote democracy. Writing about literature was also offered in service of professional interest: after all, it was literature that scholars knew best, and if they were to teach writing they ought to do so by focusing on their own area of expertise. These arguments for placing literature at the center of English studies and marginalizing writing instruction were to prove extremely successful during the 1960s and 1970s when, as Applebee explains, "an academic revival . . . wrested the initiative in educational reform away from progressive education and returned it to college faculties of liberal arts."[42] This influence of college English teachers in curriculum formation eventually had serious consequences for writing instruction in the schools, as the study of literature became privileged over writing for many teachers, despite the conceptualization of English as "language arts."

Linguistics and Composition

The advent of **structural linguistics** during the 1950s seemed for many to offer a panacea for writing instruction. It was hoped that learning about the structure of language would enable students to learn about the structure of discourse, not to mention mastering grammar, making them better writers. In the 1950s and early 1960s, the most frequently cited authors in *CCC* articles were linguists.[43] In the 1960s through the 1980s, this attention would give rise to

---

40 For an overview on composition's relationship with communication, see Diana George and John Trimbur, "The Communication Battle, or Whatever Happened to the 4th C?," *CCC* 50.4 (1999): 682–98.

41 *College English* was founded in 1939 as an offshoot of the NCTE's then-organ, the *English Journal*, which thereafter concentrated on English in secondary schools.

42 Berlin, *Rhetoric and Reality*, 107–11; Applebee, *Tradition and Reform*, 140; see also Richard Ohmann, *English in America: A Radical View of the Profession* (New York: Oxford University Press, 1976).

43 Donna Burns Phillips, Ruth Greenberg, and Sharon Gibson, "College Composition and Communication: Chronicling a Discipline's Genesis," *CCC* 44.4 (1993): 443–65.

research in sentence combining, discourse and semiotic analysis, and sociolinguistics. It would also promote a strong interest in style, particularly in the work of Edward P. J. Corbett and Winston Weathers.[44]

Perhaps most radically from the late-century viewpoint, the linguistics emphasis encouraged the important 1972 executive committee CCCC position statement (membership-ratified in 1974), **"Students' Right to Their Own Language,"** a document that resisted class and race discrimination in teaching language.[45] Grounded in both sociolinguistics and the civil rights movement, the Students' Right resolution sought to enlighten on language attitudes, promote the value of linguistic diversity, and convey information on language and language variation that would enable teachers to teach more effectively.

Historical Rhetorics

The attention to historical rhetorics, like that paid to linguistics, was part of the rediscovery of the complexity of language in all its manifestations. Among the pioneers renewing attention to rhetoric important to rhetoric and composition studies were Richard McKeon, Richard Weaver, Chaim Perelman and Lucie Olbrechts-Tyteca, Kenneth Burke, Walter Ong, and Wayne Booth. Within rhetoric and composition studies proper, the historical recovery work of scholars such as James J. Murphy and Edward P. J. Corbett reminded English teachers of the central place that the production of speech and writing had occupied in the educational institutions of the past—and suggested new paths for the future.[46] These and others advocating the "New Rhetoric" such as Janice Lauer, Richard Young, Frank D'Angelo, Richard Larsen, James Kinneavy, and George Yoos would in the next decade work to establish rhetoric and composition as a discipline, and it continues to impact theorists and practitioners today.

1960–1975

One of the major concerns after World War II was the continued provision of talented and trained workers to serve the economic growth of the nation as a means to prosperity and national security. During the 1950s, the student-centered orientation of life adjustment came under attack from a variety of politically conservative critics of the schools. The major charge made was anti-intellectualism and a failure to provide the educated experts needed for a strong economy and a strong nation; public schools, this argument went, should be subject-centered, not student-centered, emphasizing the scientific and

---

44 Edward P. J. Corbett, "The Theory and Practice of Imitation in Classical Rhetoric," *CCC* 22.3 (1971): 243–50; Winston Weathers, *An Alternate Style: Options in Composition* (Rochelle Park, NJ: Hayden, 1980).

45 Committee on CCCC Language Statement, "Students' Right to Their Own Language," *College English* 36.6 (1975): 709–26. For a history of the resolution and movement from one of its key leaders, see Geneva Smitherman, "CCCC's Role in the Struggle for Language Rights," *CCC* 50.3 (1999): 349–76. Also important to the effort was James Sledd; see his "In Defense of the Students' Right," *College English* 45.7 (1983): 667–75.

46 See Edward P. J. Corbett, "What Is Being Revived?," *CCC* 18.3 (1967): 166–72.

scholarly disciplines around which the college is organized. This note was sounded in many popular critiques by figures such as Mortimer Adler and Mark Van Doren. The Russian launch of Sputnik in 1957 gave instant credibility to these charges, providing concrete evidence to many that the United States' technological dominance was being eclipsed.

English Studies Responds

A number of measures by government agencies and by private foundations to address this crisis were quickly undertaken, in particular the 1958 National Defense Education Act (NDEA). This measure was at first designed to improve school instruction in math and the sciences, but by 1964 also included the study of literature, language, and composition. Efforts to consider English studies specifically included the 1958 "Basic Issues" conference, funded by the Ford Foundation, with representatives from the MLA, NCTE, American Studies Association, and the College English Association. Designed to address the English curriculum of the public schools, the conference recommended a cultural traditions ideal organized around language, literature, and composition.

Among the most influential of the curricular efforts for composition was Jerome S. Bruner's 1960 *The Process of Education*,[47] a document that served as an account of the new spiral curriculum. This plan organized the school curriculum around the structure of an established academic discipline which was then to be presented sequentially to students according to their level of cognitive development. Bruner's recommendation for the organization of a sequenced curriculum was influential in other curriculum studies, including the College Examination Board's 1965 *Freedom and Discipline in English*, and was central in the policies of Project English, a program for funding research founded in 1962 by the U.S. Office of Education, and the NDEA when it began granting money to English studies in 1964.

Cognitive Processes and Composing

Bruner encouraged the use of cognitive psychology in discussions of educational matters. His emphasis was on learning as "process," a concept that had been an important part of progressive education. Bruner, however, conceived of the learning process in terms of the cognitive level of the student and its relation to the structure of the academic discipline being studied. Nonetheless, Bruner emphasized the role of discovery in learning, arguing that students should use an inductive approach in order to discover on their own the structure of the discipline under consideration. The student was to engage in the act of doing physics or math or literary criticism, and was not simply to rely on the reports of experts. Bruner believed that students learned the structure of a discipline through engaging in research as a practitioner of the discipline.

The implications of Bruner's thought for writing instruction are not difficult to deduce. Students should engage in the process of composing, not in the study of someone else's process of composing. Teachers may supply information about

---

47 Jerome S. Bruner, *The Process of Education* (Cambridge, MA: Harvard University Press, 1960). The work originated out of the 1959 National Academy of Sciences-sponsored Woods Hole Conference.

writing or direct students in its structural stages, but their main job is to create an environment in which students can learn for themselves the behavior appropriate to successful writing. The product of student writing, moreover, is not as important as engaging in the process of writing. Writing involves discovery, a practice requiring intuition and pursuing hunches—in short, acting in the way mature writers do.

Teaching writing as a cognitive process was immediately encouraged by a number of researchers and teachers, among them Janet Emig, whose 1971 *Composing Process of Twelfth Graders* provided research evidence supporting the description of composing being forwarded by cognitivists, and James Britton, whose 1975 *Development of Writing Abilities* furthered the cognitivist agenda.[48] The use of the **cognitive model** of composing was also found at numerous summer workshops for high school teachers sponsored by the College Entrance Examination Board's Commission on English in the 1960s.

Processes of Personal and Linguistic Growth

The cognitive version of the composing process was not the only alternative to be forwarded at this time. A related though divergent ideal of personal growth was endorsed by the Dartmouth Conference of 1966. This meeting brought together approximately fifty English teachers from Britain and the United States to consider their common problems. The result was a revelation to the American representatives. Contrary to the emphasis on English as an academic discipline which emerged in the U.S. after the rejection of the child-centered approaches of the progressives, the British offered, as Applebee explains, "a model for English instruction which focuses not on the 'demands' of the discipline but on the personal and linguistic growth of the child." Though the British, too, emphasized process, unlike the cognitivists, the emphasis was not on mastering the composing process because of its value in solving writing problems, but because of its value to the personal development of the student.[49]

The result of the Dartmouth Conference was to reassert for United States teachers the value of the expressive model of writing, which, though never fading completely had been de-emphasized in most curricular recommendations in the early 1960s. The political activism of the late 1960s and early 1970s also helped give it new life. Once again, the highly personal and individual process of composing became conspicuous at the high school and college level, through the work of scholars such as Ken Macrorie, Donald Murray, Elizabeth Cowan, and Peter Elbow.[50] Expressivism was also at the center of D. Gordon Rohman and

---

48 Janet Emig, *The Composing Processes of Twelfth Graders* (Urbana: NCTE, 1971); James Britton, *The Development of Writing Abilities (11–18)* (London: Macmillan, 1975). At the college level, those concerned with cognitive processes during this time were represented by Janice Lauer, Richard Young, Richard Larson, and Frank D'Angelo, all of whom worked with concepts of inventional arts from classical rhetoric.

49 Applebee, *Tradition and Reform*, 229–30; see also John Dixon, *Growth Through English: A Report Based on the Dartmouth Seminar 1966* (Reading, UK: NATE, 1967); Joseph Harris, *A Teaching Subject: Composition Since 1966* (Upper Saddle River, NJ: Prentice-Hall, 1997), 1–17.

50 Varnum's *Fencing with Words* provides a genealogy of expressivists influenced by the Theodore Baird-led Amherst program, including Walker Gibson, Roger Sale, and William Coles.

Albert O. Wlecke's influential 1964 study, *Pre-Writing*, which helped launch the process movement in the schools.[51] The expressionist process was frequently taught in classes organized around resistance to dominant political formations, particularly during the 1960s, in the interest of preserving the integrity of the individual.

Social-Epistemic Theories

The central place of language in rhetoric was the distinguishing feature of proponents of what would come to be known as **social–epistemic rhetoric**, a group including Richard Ohmann, Richard Young, Ann E. Berthoff, Kenneth Bruffee, and W. Ross Winterowd. These diverse approaches agreed that language is constitutive rather than simply reflective of material and social realities. These rhetorics, then, are preeminently social in their orientation, since they argue for the public and communal nature of language, a system of differences which is formed not by individuals or even by the system as a whole but by interaction among people. In their most extreme form, these rhetorics argue that we exist in a prison house of language, never reaching contact with any externally verifiable realities. More commonly, however, these rhetorics argue for a dialectical relationship among the elements of the rhetorical context.

The early conceptions of composing that placed writing in a social context were most commonly found in college classrooms rather than in the public schools, among them Edward P. J. Corbett's 1965 *Classical Rhetoric for the Modern Student* and James L. Kinneavy's 1971 *A Theory of Discourse*, which emphasized the aims in writing, contrasting with traditional school approaches that tended to treat the "modes" of discourse arhetorically.[52] Both authors emphasized writing as a response to public discourse politically conceived, themes which would become increasingly important to college writing studies as the century progressed.

1975–2000

The last quarter of the twentieth century was a period of major growth and change in the field of writing instruction, with rhetoric and composition solidifying as a discipline of study in colleges and responding to numerous social forces.

High School Writing and the Literacy "Crisis"

The 1968 NCTE survey *High School English Instruction Today* discovered that, while students were writing in the advanced tracks of schools, students in "terminal" tracks were writing little, if at all, and, the authors lamented, across all tracks virtually no actual instruction in writing was taking place. What little

---

51 D. Gordon Rohman and Albert O. Wlecke, *Pre-Writing: The Construction and Application of Models for Concept Formation in Writing* (East Lansing: Michigan State University Press, 1964).

52 Edward P. J. Corbett, *Classical Rhetoric for the Modern Student*, now in a fourth edition with Robert J. Connors (New York: Oxford University Press, 1998); James L. Kinneavy, *A Theory of Discourse: The Aims of Discourse* (Englewood Cliffs, NJ: Prentice-Hall, 1971).

there was suggested the prevalence of current-traditional approaches, ignoring the writing process and emphasizing usage and mechanics: "For most instructors, correcting papers is synonymous with teaching writing." As Miles Myers notes, while a few schools through the 1960s and 1970s adopted Dartmouth's personal growth model, most continued to use the older "decoding/analytical" model of literacy "in which 'low-track students' were given slot-filling exercises; the 'college-bound' were taught the forms of the triad–language, literature, and composition; and the 'general students' got a mixture of both." The neglect of writing and writing instruction throughout the high schools during the 1970s was further confirmed in the 1981 NCTE research report *Writing in the Secondary School.*[53]

In response to the proliferation of conflicting pedagogies for reading and writing, George Hillocks, Jr., a pioneering researcher in English education, inquired into the best pedagogical models. Through a number of independent and meta-analytical studies, he found that what he termed "environmental" teaching, in which instructors engage students with problems that model and promote the skills they wish them to learn, produced more learning than "presentational" teaching, in which instructors see their role as delivering information, usually through lectures and directed discussions. Along these lines, stressing rhetorical concerns in writing produced better results than emphasizing formal grammar and mechanics. His findings, but especially the concept at their heart of "reflective practice," continue to have wide influence, in both secondary and post-secondary institutions.[54]

Public discourse about education in the United States has long been marked by a recurring, intermittent theme of crisis.[55] In 1975, the state of writing in the schools received national attention in a *Newsweek* cover story, "Why Johnny Can't Write," helping to initiate a widely reported literacy "crisis" culminating in the 1983 *A Nation at Risk* report by President Ronald Reagan's National Commission on Excellence in Education.[56]

While there was little evidence students wrote more poorly than they used to, especially given the vast expansion of secondary and higher education in the

---

53 James R. Squire and Roger K. Applebee, *High School English Instruction Today: The National Study of High School English Programs* (New York: Appleton-Century-Crofts, 1968), 121–38; Miles Myers, *Changing Our Minds: Negotiating English and Literacy* (Urbana, IL: NCTE, 1996), 5; Arthur N. Applebee, Anne Auten, and Fran Lehr, *Writing in the Secondary School: English and the Content Areas* (Urbana, IL: NCTE, 1981).

54 George Hillocks, Jr., *Research on Written Composition: New Directions for Teaching* (Urbana, IL: ERIC, 1986); Hillocks, *Teaching Writing as Reflective Practice: Integrating Theories* (New York: Teachers College Press, 1995); Hillocks, *Ways of Thinking, Ways of Teaching* (New York: Teachers College Press, 1999). See also Thomas M. McCann, Larry R. Johannessen, Elizabeth A. Kahn, Peter Smagorinsky, and Michael W. Smith, eds., *Reflective Teaching, Reflective Learning: How to Develop Critically Engaged Readers, Writers, and Speakers* (Portsmouth, NH: Heinemann, 2005).

55 See Harvey A. Daniels, *Famous Last Words: The American Language Crisis Reconsidered* (Carbondale: Southern Illinois University Press, 1983); John Trimbur, "Literacy and the Discourse of Crisis," in *The Politics of Writing Instruction: Postsecondary*, ed. Richard Bullock and John Trimbur (Portsmouth, NH: Heinemann, 1991), 277–95.

56 Merrill Sheils, "Why Johnny Can't Write," *Newsweek*, Dec. 8, 1975, 58–65; National Commission on Excellence in Education, *A Nation at Risk: The Imperative for Educational Reform* (Washington, DC: GPO, 1983).

second half of the twentieth century—a 1988 empirical study by Robert J. Connors and Andrea A. Lunsford would find little change in students' error rates between 1917 and 1986—what mattered was perception. As Lester Faigley and Thomas P. Miller have noted, while there was little evidence students wrote more poorly than they used to, especially given the vast expansion of secondary and higher education in the second half of the twentieth century, "many people *believed* that high-school and college students didn't write as well as they used to."[57]

Part of a backlash against 1960s-inspired progressive educational movements—Sheils in particular indicted the CCCC's "Students' Right to Their Own Language" statement[58]—the literacy crisis and the "back to the basics" movement it engendered came at a time when education and literacy researchers were suggesting that such education often promoted social stratification and a reductive view of literacy.[59] While these conclusions would not gain wide public acceptance, in the 1980s a number of teacher initiatives would try to foster approaches to teaching writing that made use of a growing body of research in education, literacy, and the burgeoning field of rhetoric and composition.

Teacher Initiatives

Teachers themselves took the initiative in filling a leadership vacuum and gap between those interested in writing and the older status quo. Three efforts are particularly worth noting: the **National Writing Project**, the teacher-as-researcher movement; and the **whole language** approach, the last of which would come under especially heavy attack from advocates of the "back to the basics" movement.

The National Writing Project (NWP) was organized in 1974 as the Bay Area Writing Project. The NWP has established teacher-training centers to improve the teaching of writing in schools in virtually every state. The unique feature of this effort is that its work is almost exclusively conducted by teachers in the schools. Although each site is usually situated at a university, the training programs are run by teachers and for teachers. Successful teachers of writing from all levels themselves design the instructional materials during a summer workshop, and then share them with other teachers in in-service workshops throughout the school year. It should be noted that the NWP has had no party affiliation insofar as theory is concerned. It can, however, best be characterized as student-centered and expressive in its orientation. In its first twenty-five years, the NWP served more than two million teachers, and today reaches approximately 130,000 teachers and 1.4 million students a year.[60] Nonetheless, in 2011,

---

57 Robert J. Connors and Andrea A. Lunsford, "Frequency of Formal Errors in Current College Writing, or Ma and Pa Kettle Do Research," *CCC* 39.4 (1988): 395–409; Lester Faigley and Thomas P. Miller, "What We Learn from Writing on the Job," *College English* 44.6 (1982): 557, itals. orig.

58 See the section "Linguistics and Composition" in this chapter (p. 246).

59 See, for example, Jean Anyon, "Social Class and School Knowledge," *Curriculum Inquiry* 11.1 (1981): 3–42; Martin Haberman, "The Pedagogy of Poverty versus Good Teaching," *Phi Delta Kappan* 73.4 (1991): 290–94.

60 National Writing Project, "2009 Annual Report," and "1999 Annual Report," http://www.nwp.org/cs/public/print/doc/about/annual_reports.csp (accessed November 15, 2011). See also Anne Ruggles Gere, *Writing Groups: History, Theory and Implications* (Carbondale: Southern Illinois University Press, 1987).

cuts were made to the federal secondary education budget that would end the program if not rescinded, and a fierce political battle was being fought.

The second initiative, the teacher-as-researcher phenomenon, was early on described in the 1987 essay collection *Reclaiming the Classroom*.[61] Its proponents worked to return control of the classroom to the teacher. Partly an attempt to resist narrow state- and district-mandated curricula, this approach to pedagogy encourages teachers to study the unique features of their students in order to design appropriate teaching strategies. The Bread Loaf School of English has been a leader in forwarding these methods, calling on the work of a broad range of researchers, including Garth Boomer, James Britton, Anne E. Berthoff, Donald Graves, Shirley Brice Heath, Ken Macrorie, Janet Emig, Mina Shaughnessy, Nancy Atwell, Lucy Calkins, and others. Attention to ethnographic techniques in studying cultural contexts made this approach to writing instruction sensitive to the social dimensions of learning and writing, especially issues of class, race, and gender. Particularly influential among classroom instructors was the work of Nancy Atwell, whose 1987 *In the Middle* remains a popular work.[62] Although teacher research continued, teachers lost power and influence over the years with the coming of the No Child Left Behind era, and attacks on teacher unions and quality lessened incentives for such work.

The third teacher initiative, the spread of the whole language approach to English studies in the schools, was closely related to the teacher-as-researcher movement in that a number of the same researchers and techniques were often invoked. Whole language teachers, however, were often less interested in cognitive and emotional processes and more interested in the social nature of learning. They also insisted on the integrated nature of reading, writing, speaking, and listening in all experience and argued the need to create learning activities that brought them together in a social environment. In the 1980s, whole language theory became an international phenomenon, appearing in New Zealand, Great Britain, and Canada, as well as the United States, and by the end of the decade, a clear consensus in college writing instruction developed that paralleled the values of whole language approaches.[63] However, with the national turn to conservativism, the whole language practices so abundant in the schools came under serious attack. Whole language teaching was opposed by proponents of "back to basics" methods such as phonics or traditional grammar instruction, although many teachers continued introducing such fundamentals in context while using a process approach to composing. One outcome of whole language

---

61 Dixie Goswami and Peter R. Stillman, eds., *Reclaiming The Classroom: Teacher Research as an Agency of Change* (Upper Montclair, NJ: Boynton/Cook, 1987). See also Donald A. Daiker and Max Morenberg, eds., *The Writing Teacher as Researcher: Essays in the Theory and Practice of Class-based Research* (Portsmouth, NH: Boynton/Cook, 1990); Ruth E. Ray, *The Practice of Theory: Teacher Research in Composition* (Urbana, IL: NCTE, 1993).

62 Nancy Atwell, *In the Middle: Writing, Reading and Learning with Adolescents* (1987; 2nd ed., Portsmouth, NH: Boynton/Cook, 1998).

63 See Judith M. Newman, ed., *Whole Language: Theory in Use* (Portsmouth, NH: Heinemann, 1985); Ken Goodman, *What's Whole in Whole Language* (1986; 20th anniversary ed.; Berkeley, CA: RDR Books, 2005); Kathryn F. Whitmore and Yetta M. Goodman, eds., *Whole Language Voices in Teacher Education* (York, ME: Stenhouse, 1995).

theory in both school and college was the increasing shift to portfolio **assessment** of writing. This was pioneered by expressionists such as Peter Elbow and Pat Belanoff and spread into both school and college writing assessment.[64]

College Writing Becomes a Discipline

Rhetoric and composition studies at the college level in the last quarter of the twentieth century dramatically changed as the field attained disciplinary status, complete with major conferences, journals, and indexes.[65] The encouragement of composition studies by college administrations was a response both to the literacy "crisis" and demands of the workplace, where changing technologies began to require writing ability to a greater extent than ever before, as well as rising college enrollments along with increasingly diverse student bodies. The 1980s in particular saw the expansion and strengthening of freshman composition programs, undergraduate college writing programs, and graduate composition programs, the last of which in turn began to train specialists in writing instruction. These programs, including those at Penn State, Purdue, Ohio State, Rensselaer, Carnegie Mellon, the University of Texas, and the University of Pittsburgh, would grow nationwide, producing writing specialists to fill a burgeoning number of faculty jobs, as well as administrative positions in writing programs and university writing centers.

Divergent Approaches to Teaching Writing

By the end of the 1980s, the maturing field of rhetoric and composition widely recognized three major paradigms or approaches to writing instruction: cognitive, expressivist, and social-epistemic rhetoric. Though scholars and instructors frequently identified themselves with various camps and were at times at odds, actual classroom practice, then and now, likely blended approaches, and each strain continues to inform contemporary scholarship and instruction.

A particularly important paradigm during the 1980s was cognitive rhetoric. This paradigm advanced the primacy of cognitive structures in composing, arguing that any study of the process must consider an analysis of these structures. Relying on the methods of qualitative research, cognitive researchers offered empirical data toward understanding composing behavior by studying the actual composing processes of both experienced and inexperienced writers. Among their discoveries were that, for successful writers, composition was a recursive process—not a linear or stage-model one—in which they constantly shifted from planning to drafting to revising in the act of composing. Successful writers also did a great deal of planning and revising relative to drafting, particularly at the macro or global level, and typically wrote and revised with rhetorical

---

64 See Kathleen Blake Yancey, ed., *Portfolios in the Writing Classroom: An Introduction* (Urbana, IL: NCTE, 1992); Yancey and Irwin Weiser, eds., *Situating Portfolios: Four Perspectives* (Logan: Utah State University Press, 1997).

65 For a treatment of this period, see Stephen M. North, *The Making of Knowledge in Composition: Portrait of an Emerging Discipline* (Upper Montclair, NJ: Boynton/Cook, 1987).

purposes such as audience in mind.[66] Though cognitive research offered many insights into the writing process and advances in writing instruction, it was also criticized for ignoring social, ethical, or political factors in writing.[67] Some of the objection to cognitive research was also due to the discomfort of humanities scholars with research methods—and, ostensibly, epistemologies and ideologies—drawn from the sciences.

The expressivist approach was also a force in rhetoric and composition studies during this period. Such figures as Peter Elbow, Donald M. Murray, Ken Macrorie, and others continued to emphasize and advocate for the personal, original, authentic, and unique voice of the writer. Expressivists tended to treat composing not as a universal cognitive process but as a probe for the discovery and formation of the self, and writing instruction as a means for writers to articulate that self, often in resistance to the demands of institutional conformity. Elbow, for example, contra the advice of more cognitively and socially oriented approaches, advocated ignoring audience in the initial stages of writing, seeing it as a potentially constraining force: "[E]ven though much dead student writing comes from students' not really treating their writing as a communication with real readers . . . we often do not really develop a strong, authentic voice in our writing till we find important occasions for *ignoring* audience—saying, in effect, 'To hell with whether they like it or not. I've got to say this the way *I* want to say it.' "[68]

Expressivist scholars and instructors also emphasized the centrality of the student in the classroom, the importance of revision and self-reflection, and the inherent potential for all individuals to learn to write; their legacy can be seen in the continuing importance of these tropes in contemporary writing classrooms as well as the lasting popularity of their work with the lay public; Elbow's *Writing Without Teachers*, first published in 1973, and Murray's *A Writer Teaches Writing*, first published in 1968, both remain in print in revised editions, as do many of their other works.[69]

With a growing concurrence about the primacy of the social and writing, the group of rhetorics variously labeled social-constructivist or social-epistemic constituted a third, increasingly influential paradigm at the end of the 1980s. These rhetorics started with the social as the foundation of subject formation and so tended to call on neo-pragmatist, Marxist, and soon poststructuralist theory in

66 See Linda Flower, "Writer-Based Prose: A Cognitive Basis for Problems in Writing," *College English* 41.1 (1979): 19–37; Nancy Sommers, "Revision Strategies of Student Writers and Experienced Adult Writers," *CCC* 31.4 (1980): 378–88; Carl Bereiter and Marlene Scardamalia, *The Psychology of Written Composition* (Hillsdale, NJ: Lawrence Erlbaum, 1987). Of particularly influence was the work of Linda Flower and John R. Hayes, whose "A Cognitive Process Theory of Writing," *CCC* 32.4 (1981): 365–87, provided a model of the writing process that inspired both research and critique. Flower has since turned toward more public approaches; see the section "Attending to the Local" in this chapter (p. 263).

67 See Patricia Bizzell, "Cognition, Convention, and Certainty: What We Need to Know about Writing," *Pre/Text* 3.3 (1982): 213–43; Lester Faigley, "Competing Theories of Process: A Critique and a Proposal," *College English* 48.6 (1986): 527–42; Berlin, "Rhetoric and Ideology."

68 Peter Elbow, "Closing My Eyes as I Speak: An Argument for Ignoring Audience," *College English* 49.1 (1987): 55, itals. orig.

69 Peter Elbow, *Writing Without Teachers* (1973; 2nd ed., New York: Oxford University Press, 1998); Donald M. Murray, *A Writer Teaches Writing*, (1968; rev. 2nd ed., Boston: Thompson/Heinle, 2004). See also Ken Macrorie, *Telling Writing* (1970; 4th ed., Upper Montclair, NJ: Boynton/Cook, 1985).

presenting their case. All emphasized, to a greater or lesser degree, the constitutive power of language in human activity. Sometimes the focus was the social nature of composing, seeing the writer as always already socially situated, such as W. Ross Winterowd and Charles Bazerman. Another group bore the marks of poststructuralist and Marxist elements, seeing composing as vehicle for political critique or transformation, such as Ira Shor, Linda Brodkey, and John Trimbur. Others emphasized the role of discourse communities and the importance of assisting students in negotiating and joining them, such as Patricia Bizzell and David Bartholomae.[70] In terms of effect on writing pedagogy, this last approach has been perhaps the most influential and long-lasting strain; in a recent interview with Bartholomae on the occasion of the twenty-fifth anniversary of his landmark 1985 essay, "Inventing the University," *College English* editor John Schilb cited the work as "perhaps the most often cited and discussed essay in composition studies."[71]

The Turn to Literacy

Tensions over escalating demands for literacy continued to increase toward the end of the twentieth century, showing up in numerous assessments of literacy and writing. Both the 1986 report *Literacy: Profiles of America's Young Adults*, sponsored by the National Assessment of Educational Progress (NAEP), and the 1993 *Adult Literacy in America*, sponsored by the National Center for Education Statistics (NCES), found that although strict "illiteracy" was not a major problem, a disturbing number of students and adults lacked the higher-level literacy skills to be able to function as citizens and workers in a complex society. The 1986 NAEP report, *Writing: Trends Across the Decade*, found little improvement in student writing skills or increase in time spent writing, and the *NAEP 1992 Writing Report Card* similarly reported that students across grade levels "continue[d] to have serious difficulty in producing effective informative, persuasive, or narrative writing."[72] The turn to literacy served to draw together government, schools, colleges, and communities in joint efforts to improve literacy through reading and writing instruction, often by volunteers working with both younger and older adults in high school extension programs or libraries.

70 W. Ross Winterowd, *The Culture and Politics of Literacy* (New York: Oxford University Press, 1989); Charles Bazerman, *Constructing Experience* (Carbondale: Southern Illinois University Press, 1994); Ira Shor, *Critical Teaching and Everyday Life* (Chicago: University of Chicago Press, 1980); Linda Brodkey, *Writing Permitted in Designated Areas Only* (Minneapolis: University of Minnesota Press, 1996); John Trimbur, "Composition and the Circulation of Writing," *CCC* 52.2 (2000): 188–219; Patricia Bizzell, *Academic Discourse and Critical Consciousness* (Pittsburgh: University of Pittsburgh Press, 1992); David Bartholomae, *Writing on the Margins: Essays on Composition and Teaching* (Boston: Bedford/St. Martins, 2005).

71 David Bartholomae and John Schilb, "'Inventing the University' at 25: An Interview with David Bartholomae," *College English* 73.3 (2011): 260.

72 Irwin S. Kirsch and Ann Jungeblut, *Literacy: Profiles of America's Young Adults* (Princeton, NJ: NAEP, Educational Testing Service, 1986); Irwin S. Kirsch, Ann Jungeblut, Lynn Jenkins, and Andrew Kolstad, *Adult Literacy in America: A First Look at the Findings of the National Adult Literacy Survey* (Washington DC: U.S. NCES, 1993); Arthur N. Applebee, Judith A. Langer, and Ina V. S. Mullis, *Writing: Trends Across the Decade, 1974–84* (Princeton, NJ: NAEP, Educational Testing Service, 1986); Arthur N. Applebee, Judith A. Langer, Ina V. S. Mullis, Andrew S. Latham, and Claudia A. Gentile, *NAEP 1992 Writing Report Card* (Washington, DC: GPO, 1994), 3.

Despite this work, literacy remained poorly understood by the public, fueled in part by the "culture wars," a loose movement of largely conservative critics that emphasized content delivery of information and canonical works of Western culture as a palliative against the perceived ills of progressive education and post-1960s culture.[73] In contrast to these at-times well-meaning but often simplistic narratives, literacy scholars during this period were concluding that literacy was not a universal, portable skill but rather a socially embedded, culture- and context-dependent complex of practices.[74] In particular, scholars were concerned with both how home and school literacies were acquired and improving school instruction. Among them were Shirley Brice Heath, who examined literacy practices among white and black working-class communities in the Piedmont Carolinas; Mike Rose, who described the effects of schooling on economically disadvantaged, largely minority students in Southern California; and Deborah Brandt, who examined the acquisition and uses of literacy during the twentieth century among several generations of ordinary Americans.[75]

Cultural Studies, Critical Pedagogy, and Composition

While school writing has long been tied to social and cultural concerns, in the 1980s and especially 1990s, scholars and teachers felt an increasing sense of urgency regarding the cultural impact of writing instruction, as the rise of literary **cultural studies** and critical pedagogy converged with ongoing, parallel social-epistemic tropes in composition studies.[76] Of particular importance to writing studies was the work of Brazilian educator Paulo Freire, whose liberatory theories of teaching inspired a wave of like-minded pedagogies in the composition classroom; Michel Foucault, whose analyses of the discourse of power inspired many instructors to reflect on the ways that writing instruction might reinforce dominant hegemonies; and Berlin, whose theory of social-epistemic rhetoric challenged composition scholars to consider the implicit ideologies their pedagogies were enacting and adopt more socially enlightened

---

73 See, for example, E. D. Hirsch, *Cultural Literacy: What Every American Needs to Know* (Boston: Houghton Mifflin, 1987); Allan Bloom, *The Closing of the American Mind: How Higher Education Has Failed Democracy and Impoverished the Souls of Today's Students* (New York: Simon and Schuster, 1987).

74 Of particular influence was Brian V. Street's challenging of the "autonomous" model of literacy and James Paul Gee's notion of literacy as the ability to function in a given discourse community. See Street, *Literacy in Theory and Practice* (New York: Cambridge University Press, 1984); Gee, *Social Linguistics and Literacies: Ideologies in Discourses* (1990; 3rd ed., New York: Routledge, 2008).

75 Shirley Brice Heath, *Ways with Words: Language, Life, and Work in Communities and Classrooms* (New York: Cambridge University Press, 1983); Mike Rose, *Lives on the Boundary: A Moving Account of the Struggles and Achievements of America's Educationally Underprepared* (1989; New York: Penguin, 2005); Deborah Brandt, *Literacy in American Lives* (New York: Cambridge University Press, 2001). See also Ellen Cushman, Eugene R. Kintgen, Barry Kroll, and Mike Rose, eds., *Literacy: A Critical Sourcebook* (Boston: Bedford/St. Martin's, 2001).

76 Influenced by the work of French poststructuralist language theorists such as Foucault and Jacques Derrida, Marxist literary theorists such as Terry Eagleton, American neo-pragmatist philosophers such as Richard Rorty, and cultural critics such as Henry A. Giroux and Jean Baudrillard, cultural studies approaches argued that language is at the center of the formation of consciousness. From this perspective, culture is made up of an assortment of competing linguistic codes that "write" individual subjects; under this rubric, an important part of the work of English studies was to learn how these codes operate.

ones: "a rhetoric," he wrote, "can never be innocent, can never be a disinterested arbiter of the ideological claims of others because it is always already serving certain ideological claims."[77]

Such work inspired much debate, often rancorous, over the proper ends of writing instruction. Some scholars indicted composition for its work in disciplining student subjectivities while others sought an emancipatory pedagogy that would liberate students from hegemonic ideologies. In contrast, some scholars expressed concern over the seeming insertion of politics into the classroom and the possibility of indoctrinating students in the name of liberating them, while others sought to sidestep the controversy by reaffirming the field's commitment to writing pedagogy. While conflicts over the political ends of the composition classroom would continue to engender debate, tensions in the field as a whole would wane as many scholars sought pedagogies that, as Richard E. Miller suggested, could teach students "how to work within and against discursive constraints simultaneously." Moreover, many instructors continue to find value in the reflective pedagogies that cultural and critical approaches engendered, even if they do not hold to all their tenets.[78]

Feminism and Diversity

By the end of the 1980s, feminists in college composition were strongly articulating the impact of feminist theories on their teaching practices. In particular, this period opened the publishing floodgates to work on women in the history of rhetoric and writing and on effects of gender on composing.[79] By the turn of the twentieth century, feminist theory and practice had become an established part of composition studies, with two important edited collections articulating its theory and practice: Susan Jarratt and Lynn Worsham's *Feminism and Composition Studies* and Gesa E. Kirsch et al.'s *Feminism and Composition: A Critical*

---

77 Berlin, "Rhetoric and Ideology," 477.

78 See, for example, Maxine Hairston, "Diversity, Ideology, and Teaching Writing," *CCC* 43.2 (1992): 179–93, and "Responses to Maxine Hairston, 'Diversity, Ideology, and Teaching Writing' and Reply" *CCC* 44.2 (1993): 248–56; Denise David, Barbara Gordon, and Rita Pollard, "Seeking Common Ground: Guiding Assumptions for Writing Courses," *CCC* 46.4 (1995): 522–32; Ellen Cushman, "Critical Literacy and Institutional Language," *Research in the Teaching of English* 33.3 (1999): 245–74; Richard Fulkerson, "Composition at the Turn of the Twenty-First Century," *CCC* 56.4 (2005): 654–87, and "Responses to Richard Fulkerson, 'Composition at the Turn of the Twenty-First Century,'" *CCC* 57.4 (2006): 730–62; Richard E. Miller, "The Arts of Complicity: Pragmatism and the Culture of Schooling," *College English* 61.1 (1998): 27.

79 Key discussions of theory and teaching in this period include Elizabeth Flynn, "Composing as a Woman," *CCC* 39.4 (1988): 423–35; Cynthia L. Caywood and Gillian R. Overing, eds., *Teaching Writing: Pedagogy, Gender, and Equity* (Albany: State University of New York Press, 1987); Dale M. Bauer, "The Other 'F' Word: The Feminist in the Classroom," *College English* 52.4 (1990): 385–96; Susan Miller, "The Feminization of Composition," in Bullock and Trimbur, *Politics of Writing Instruction*, 39–53. Key early books on women in rhetoric and writing history include Andrea A. Lunsford, ed., *Reclaiming Rhetorica: Women in the Rhetorical Tradition* (Pittsburgh: University of Pittsburgh Press, 1995); Louise Wetherbee Phelps and Janet Emig, eds., *Feminine Principles and Women's Experience in American Composition and Rhetoric* (Pittsburgh: University of Pittsburgh Press, 1995); Catherine Hobbs, ed., *Nineteenth-Century Women Learn to Write* (Charlottesville: University of Virginia Press, 1995); Cheryl Glenn, *Rhetoric Retold: Regendering the Tradition from Antiquity through the Renaissance* (Carbondale: Southern Illinois University Press, 1998).

Sourcebook.[80] Among its wide interests, feminist and gender work focused on theory and critical pedagogy, feminist ethics, and gender roles and educational institutions, seeking, as Kirsch et al. summarized in the dedication to their work: "to 'take our women students seriously' (to borrow Adrienne Rich's much cited phrase); to experiment with new forms of writing; to develop interactive pedagogies; to conduct reflective, feminist research and scholarship; and to begin improving working conditions for women (where much more remains to be done)."[81] Over time, women's historical work would move from more general description and recovery to more local and site-specific contexts, broadening concepts of rhetoric all the while, exemplified by Shirley Wilson Logan's 2008 *Liberating Language*.[82]

The civil rights movement of the 1960s had made diversity a familiar issue in the composition class, and this theme intensified as minorities entered colleges in larger numbers. But as Jacqueline Jones Royster has pointed out, composition itself could function as an elite guild.[83] Nonetheless, despite some resistance, diverse groups, and women in them, made progress in the profession at the century's end and served as exemplars for students in schools and colleges. The recovery of historical voices of scholars and rhetors and the rethinking of difference remained pivotal among many researchers, including Logan, Royster, Anne Ruggles Gere, Keith Gilyard, Molly Meijer Wertheimer, Suzanne Bordelon, and Cheryl Glenn.[84]

At century's end, the trend towards inclusivity and diversity in the field intensified. At times our professional worlds, both in schools and colleges, seemed to remain far less diverse than our classrooms, but this was transforming with the new millennium. The work done by scholars in this area shed light on institutional as well as student and faculty diversity and helped change pedagogies, in particular calling attention to the need for more knowledge about difference and less colonizing pedagogies and offering curricular guidance for diverse populations. For example, major work on teaching students with disabilities was published by Cynthia Lewiecki-Wilson and Brenda Brueggeman; attention was

---

80 Susan C. Jarratt and Lynn Worsham, eds., *Feminism and Composition Studies: In Other Words* (New York: MLA, 1998); Gesa E. Kirsch, Faye Spencer Maor, Lance Massey, Lee Nickoson-Massey, and Mary. P. Sheridan-Rabideau, eds., *Feminism and Composition: A Critical Sourcebook* (Boston: Bedford/St. Martins, 2003).

81 Kirsch et al., *Feminism and Composition*, v. See also Suzanne Clark, "Review: Women, Rhetoric, Teaching," *CCC* 46.1 (1995): 108–22.

82 Shirley Wilson Logan, *Liberating Language: Sites of Rhetorical Education in Nineteenth-Century Black America* (Carbondale: Southern Illinois University Press, 2008).

83 Jacqueline Jones Royster, "In Search of Ways in: Reflection and Response," in Phelps and Emig, *Feminine Principles*, 385–91.

84 Shirley Wilson Logan, *"We Are Coming": The Persuasive Discourse of Nineteenth-Century Black Women* (Carbondale: Southern Illinois University Press, 1999); Jacqueline Jones Royster, *Traces of a Stream: Literacy and Social Change among African American Women* (Pittsburgh: University of Pittsburgh Press, 2000); Anne Ruggles Gere, *Intimate Practices: Literacy and Cultural Work in U.S. Women's Clubs, 1880–1920* (Urbana: University of Illinois Press, 1997); Keith Gilyard, *Voices of the Self: A Study of Language Competence* (Detroit: Wayne State University Press, 1991); Gilyard, ed., *Rhetoric and Ethnicity* (Portsmouth, NH: Boynton/Cook, 2004); Molly Meijer Wertheimer, ed., *Listening to Their Voices: The Rhetorical Activities of Historical Women* (Columbia: University of South Carolina Press, 1997); Bordelon, *A Feminist Legacy*; Glenn, *Rhetoric Retold*.

brought to the history and current issues in teaching Native American students by scholars such as Scott Lyons and Malea Powell; and issues pertinent to the growing Latino/a population in higher education have been addressed by scholars including Victor Villanueva and Jaime Mejía. Chinese and global rhetorics became more frequent research topics in our journals, and full-length monographs such as LuMing Mao's *Reading Chinese Fortune Cookie* appeared that were helpful not only in TESOL classes but in reconsiderations of composition theory and practice in general. Cultural approaches and postcolonial theory were brought into the field by scholars such as Nedra Reynolds to prise out larger cultural issues in the teaching of diverse populations that had been unattended to and not well understood. Queer theories and social action rhetoric as well provided new windows through which to address diversity.[85]

Continuing Language Issues

Despite the increasing attention to diversity and more complex understanding of literacy within the field of writing studies, wider social pressures continued to be a challenge. In response to increases in immigration, the "English Only" blow struck by California in its English Language Amendment of 1986, declaring English the official state language, subsequently broadened to a national cause. In response, along with other organizations, CCCC took a stand, passing its National Language Policy in 1988, calling for resources and programs to "enable native and nonnative speakers to achieve oral and literate competence in English . . . assert the legitimacy of native languages and dialects . . . [and] foster the teaching of languages other than English." The policy, wrote one of its architects, Geneva Smitherman, "stresses the need not just for marginalized Americans but for all Americans to be bi- or multi-lingual in order to be prepared for citizenship in a global, multicultural society."[86]

But by the mid-1990s, CCCC was swimming against the tide as a new language issue claimed the public's attention, this time over the teaching of "Ebonics" in the Oakland, California schools. Both blacks and whites nationally seemed to lack an understanding of the educational values of bi-dialecticism, intensifying a nationwide commitment to the teaching of Standard Written English. Thus, public sentiment at century's end was far different from that of English teachers' of the 1970s, with their radical statement of "students' right to their own language." In part, such attitudes belied anxiety about future

85 Cynthia Lewiecki-Wilson and Brenda Brueggeman, eds., *Disability and the Teaching of* Writing: *A Critical Sourcebook* (Boston: Bedford/St. Martin's, 2008); Scott Richard Lyons, *X-Marks: Native Signatures of Assent* (Minneapolis: University of Minnesota Press, 2010); Malea Powell, "Rhetorics of Survivance: How American Indians Use Writing," *CCC* 53.3 (2002): 396–434; Victor Villanueva, Jr., *Bootstraps: From an American Academic of Color* (Urbana, IL: NCTE, 1993); Jaime Armin Mejía, "Arts of the U.S.–Mexico Contact Zone," in *Crossing Borderlands: Composition and Postcolonial Studies,* ed. Andrea A. Lunsford and Lahoucine Ouzgane (Pittsburgh: University of Pittsburgh Press, 2004), 171–98; LuMing Mao, *Reading Chinese Fortune Cookie: The Making of Chinese American Rhetoric* (Logan: Utah State University Press, 2006); Nedra Reynolds, *Geographies of Writing: Inhabiting Places and Encountering Difference* (Carbondale: Southern Illinois University Press, 2004); William P. Banks, "Written through the Body: Disruptions and 'Personal' Writing," *College English* 66.1 (2003): 21–40.
86 Smitherman, "CCCC's Role," 369.

employment security despite a strengthening economy, and, to some degree, loss of white majority power.

Computers and Technological Change

The introduction of computers into writing classrooms and, subsequently, networked forums and information sources challenged writing teachers across schools and colleges to further transform their classroom practices. The first dissertation to examine the use of computers in teaching writing was published in 1979.[87] *Computers and Composition*, founded as a newsletter in 1983, was by the end of the decade an established journal focusing on a growing body of research that explored the uses of technology in teaching writing. By the 1990s, the importance of work on computers and writing was widely recognized, with at least three CCCC chairs during that decade known for their work in the field, Lillian Bridwell-Bowles (1994), Lester Faigley (1996), and Cynthia L. Selfe (1998). Among the many concerns of pioneering scholars and instructors were the effective integration of technology in the classroom, the effects of computers on composing processes, the widening "technology gap" between those students and schools with and without access to the latest technology, and the effects of the "digital revolution" on communication and culture, particularly in the wake of the spread of personal computers and the advent of the World Wide Web and other networked social communication environments.[88]

These changes challenged writing scholars and instructors not simply to deliver effective writing instruction with the assistance of technology but to reconsider what it meant to read, write, and be literate in an era demanding increasingly complex literacy skills, particularly those providing access to high-paying jobs that President Clinton's Labor Secretary Robert B. Reich said would increasingly be held by "symbolic-analysts."[89] In her 1998 CCCC Chair's Address, Selfe enjoined the conference to start "paying attention" to technology. Compositionists, trained as humanists, she noted, prefer their technologies and the material conditions associated with text production to remain invisible, a short-sighted attitude. She observed that technological literacy has been a primary governmental goal, with billions of dollars being spent on educational technology, yet with little input from literacy professionals or composition

---

87 Hugh Lee Burns, "Stimulating Rhetorical Invention in English Composition through Computer-assisted Instruction" (PhD diss., University of Texas, 1979). Burns remains active in the area of rhetoric, writing, and technology.

88 See, for example, Gail E. Hawisher and Cynthia L. Selfe, eds., *Critical Perspectives on Computers and Composition Instruction* (New York: Teachers College Press, 1989); Lester Faigley, *Fragments of Rationality: Postmodernity and the Subject of Composition* (Pittsburgh: University of Pittsburgh Press, 1992); Selfe and Susan Hilligos, eds., *Literacy and Computers: The Complications of Teaching and Learning with Technology* (New York: MLA, 1994). For a history of this period, see Hawisher, Paul LeBlanc, Charles Moran, and Selfe, *Computers and the Teaching of Writing in American Higher Education, 1979–1994: A History* (Norwood, NJ: Ablex, 1996). Hawisher and Selfe, pioneers in the field, have co-edited *Computers and Composition* since 1988.

89 In *The Work of Nations: Preparing Ourselves for 21st-Century Capitalism* (New York: Knopf, 1991), Reich outlines three categories of work: routine production services, in-person services, and symbolic-analytic services, the latter entailing the solving, identifying, and brokering of problems through the manipulation of symbols and requiring the most complex literacy skills.

organizations. Paying attention to technology and the human issues they raise can make us better humanists, she argued.[90]

Professional Issues

By the end of the twentieth century, rhetoric and composition studies, sometimes now called writing studies, had in one sense progressed from being overshadowed by literary studies to holding pride of place in addressing society's need for new literacies associated with competitive global capitalism and new information technologies. Throughout the 1990s, consensus emerged about some of the broader issues of writing instruction, while pedagogies emerged to flesh out and refine some significant theorizing from the 1980s. Expressive and cognitive rhetorics continued in both school and college programs, but a widespread emphasis on socially cognizant pedagogies blurred in practice some of the theoretical boundaries that had previously divided some scholars. By 2000, college rhetoric and writing programs had expanded to the point where roughly a quarter of all English studies jobs listed in the annual MLA job bulletin were for rhetoric and composition or technical writing.[91]

Despite professional growth and success, rhetoric and composition remained in a hybrid position in many higher educational institutions, with an often tenuous or still subordinate relationship to literary studies in many English departments, where it was still typically housed. Moreover, issues such as the "feminization" of composition studies and the reliance by colleges on contingent labor increasingly became topics of professional concern, as did awareness of the need to speak out on public issues of shared concern regarding literacy education. When, for example, New York City Mayor Rudolph W. Giuliani spearheaded efforts to ban "remedial" courses at the city's eleven senior colleges in 1998, open admissions policies established in 1970 disappeared, and public understanding of knowledge gained by writing specialists was revealed to be thin or even nonexistent. Such events are why composition was now said to be on a "professional faultline, a site where contradictions meet."[92]

Nonetheless, as the twentieth century ended, colleges and secondary schools were paying serious attention to writing, leaving many writing specialists with a sense of both challenge and satisfaction. In the face of contestation and change, the field had transformed in multiple ways to respond to the pluralistic demands of its increasingly diverse constituencies.

The New Millennium

Writing instruction in the first decade of the twenty-first century has seen an acceleration of both the changes and the challenges wrought in the last decades of

---

90 Cynthia L. Selfe, "Technology and Literacy: A Story About the Perils of Not Paying Attention," *CCC* 50.3 (1999): 411–36.

91 David Laurence, "Count of Listings in the October 2000 MLA Job Information List," *ADE Bulletin* 128 (2001): 7.

92 Cynthia Lewiecki-Wilson and Jeff Sommers, "Professing at the Fault Lines: Composition at Open Admissions Institutions," *CCC* 50.3 (1999): 439.

the twentieth, with particular key emerging areas of research and practice gaining the attention of scholars and teachers. Of especial note is the overlap between various lines of research as scholars increasingly bridge former theoretical divides.

Attending to the Local

The increasing interest in linguistic and cultural diversity in the late twentieth century, manifested in attention to minority discourses, multiliteracies, and global Englishes, has taken on new energy in the twenty-first century, as scholars have increasingly called attention to the challenges of teaching local constituencies, particularly previously under-examined communities such as religious, rural, urban, and Latino/a students. Recently James M. Cahalan has examined the value of hometown literature in promoting student engagement; Shannon Carter, the connections between home and school literacies among evangelical students in rural North Texas; and Nathan Shepley, the effect of place on literacy acquisition among students in Appalachian Ohio. Also exploring these intersections are Kim Donehower, Charlotte Hogg, and Eileen E. Schell's collaborative and multivoiced work on rural literacies; and edited collections by Beth Daniell and Peter Mortensen on women's literacies; Michelle Hall Kells, Valerie M. Balester, and Victor Villanueva on Latino/a discourses; and Cristina Kirklighter, Diana Cárdenas, and Susan Wolff Murphy on teaching writing at Hispanic-serving institutions.[93]

Three distinct yet overlapping strains of research have contributed to this move: historical research into rhetoric and writing instruction that has increasingly emphasized local locations, conditions, and communities, including work by Susan Kates, Jessica Enoch, and David Gold, and an edited collection by Patricia Donahue and Gretchen Flesher Moon;[94] local service learning and other community interaction projects by scholars such as Linda Flower, David Jolliffe, and Paula Mathieu;[95] and ethnographic work on literacy acquisition, including

---

93 James M. Cahalan, "Teaching Hometown Literature: A Pedagogy of Place," *College English* 70.3 (2008): 249–74; Shannon Carter, "Living inside the Bible (Belt)," *College English* 69.6 (2007): 572–95; Nathan Shepley, "Places of Composition: Writing Contexts in Appalachian Ohio," *Composition Studies* 37.2 (2009): 75–90; Kim Donehower, Charlotte Hogg, and Eileen E. Schell, *Rural Literacies* (Carbondale: Southern Illinois University Press, 2007); Beth Daniell and Peter Mortensen, eds., *Women and Literacy: Local and Global Inquiries for a New Century* (New York: Routledge, 2007); Michelle Hall Kells, Valerie M. Balester, and Victor Villanueva, *Latino/a Discourses: On Language, Identity and Literacy Education* (Portsmouth, NH: Boynton/Cook, 2004); Cristina Kirklighter, Diana Cárdenas, and Susan Wolff Murphy, eds., *Teaching Writing with Latino/a Students: Lessons Learned at Hispanic-Serving Institutions* (Albany: State University of New York Press, 2007).

94 Kates, *Activist Rhetorics;* Jessica Enoch, *Refiguring Rhetorical Education: Women Teaching African American, Native American, and Chicano/a Students, 1865–1911* (Carbondale: Southern Illinois University Press, 2008); Gold, *Rhetoric at the Margins;* Patricia Donahue and Gretchen Flesher Moon, eds., *Local Histories: Reading the Archives of Composition* (Pittsburgh: University of Pittsburgh Press, 2007). Beginning with Varnum, rhetoric and composition historiographers have increasingly challenged and complicated the more general histories of the 1980s; for an overview of this development, see Gold, 1–13.

95 Linda Flower, *Community Literacy and the Rhetoric of Public Engagement* (Carbondale: Southern Illinois University Press, 2008); David Jolliffe, "Writing Democracies: Community Arts and Community Literacy as an Antidote to 'Co-Curricular Poverty'" (Writing Democracy Conference, Commerce, TX, Mar. 9–11, 2011); Paula Mathieu, *Tactics of Hope: The Public Turn in English Composition* (Portsmouth, NH: Boynton/Cook, 2005).

that of Ellen Cushman, Deborah Brandt, and Patrick J. Finn.[96] Together these scholars call attention to the various ways academic discourses are acquired and remind us that, in effect, all literacies are local; they also suggest the importance of connecting the local to wider scholarly conversations.

Civic Engagement

Closely tied to attending to the local in writing instruction is an emphasis on promoting civic engagement through writing instruction. Rhetorically informed writing instruction has, of course, long emphasized the public nature of writing. Scott and Denney in 1911 asserted composition to be "a social act,"[97] and numerous scholars have pointed to the civic ends of classical rhetorical education. While the public or social turn of the late twentieth century, inspired in large part by the recovery of the classical rhetorical tradition and James Berlin's notion of social-epistemic rhetoric, stressed the importance of teaching writing as public argument and encouraging civic participation, publicly engaged instruction in the new century has begun to explore and appreciate just how complicated that directive is. As Lester Faigley foreshadowed in his 1996 CCCC Chair's Address, "providing venues for the discussion of public issues does not necessarily lead to a more informed public, increased civic engagement, or enhanced democracy."[98]

Two essays by one author nearly a decade apart illustrate the field's growing sense of the challenge. In her 1997 "Encouraging Civic Participation," Elizabeth Ervin confidently reports encouraging students to represent themselves as citizens and participate in public discourse through an intense group exploration of a local community issue. By her 2006 "Teaching Public Literacy," she voices the widespread recognition among writing instructors that students may be turned off by classes that emphasize public issues. As a workable compromise, she proposes what she terms "publicist rhetorical strategies," allowing students to write highly personal, interest-based arguments, but requiring them to consider and develop successful rhetorical strategies within that context.[99]

As the field of composition and rhetoric coalesces around what Richard Fulkerson has called "procedural rhetoric,"[100] which judges writing by suitability of context, and as it expands the scope of that context from writing for the academy to writing for wider publics, teachers and scholars have become increasingly concerned with how to provide for models of civic engagement and public discourse, particularly in light of heightened contemporary concerns about the fragmentary nature of the public sphere and the limits of classical rhetoric and

96 Ellen Cushman, *The Struggle and the Tools: Oral and Literate Strategies in an Inner City Community* (*Albany*: State University of New York Press, 1998); Brandt, *Literacy in American Lives*; Patrick J. Finn, *Literacy with an Attitude: Educating Working-Class Children in Their Own Self-Interest* (2nd ed., Albany: State University of New York Press, 2009).

97 Fred Newton Scott and Joseph Villiers Denney, *The New Composition-Rhetoric* (Boston: Allyn and Bacon, 1911), iii.

98 Lester Faigley, "Literacy after the Revolution," *CCC* 48.1 (1997): 36.

99 Elizabeth Ervin, "Encouraging Civic Participation among First-Year Writing Students; or, Why Composition Class Should Be More Like a Bowling Team," *Rhetoric Review* 15.2 (1997): 382–99; Ervin, "Teaching Public Literacy: The Partisanship Problem," *College English* 68.4 (2006): 407–21.

100 Fulkerson, "Composition at the Turn."

liberal rhetorical models. Patricia Roberts-Miller has criticized writing instructors for not thinking through the various models of the public sphere they are implicitly offering to students when they teach argument. In a similar vein, Sharon Crowley has criticized liberal rhetorical theory for discounting the roles of emotion and values in persuasion.[101] Scholars have also expressed concern about the complicity of educational institutions and in particular literacy instruction in promulgating social inequities.[102] Finally, as Wendy B. Sharer notes, the expanding scope of composition instruction has generated institutional tensions in balancing civic engagement with the more traditionally understood goals of academic and professional preparation.[103]

Despite these concerns, many scholars remain optimistic about promoting civic engagement through rhetoric and writing instruction.[104] Though exhibiting a diversity of approaches and ideological attachments, they are largely linked by the conviction that student writing matters; that instruction should, as Ann M. Feldman suggests in her own case study of community-based writing, "[position] students as rhetors" who write "to make a material difference in a situation."[105]

Digital Literacy and Multimodal Composing

In his 1996 CCCC Chair's Address, Lester Faigley predicted the rise of self-sponsored writing engendered by online digital forums; access to the internet, he declared, had encouraged a "new medium of literacy" that for many inspirited "writing for purposes other than work."[106] The advent of what has been termed **Web 2.0**, which marked a shift in energy from centralized, single- or institutionally authored websites delivering content to interactive and collaborative spaces such as individual and community blogs, web forums, wikis, and social networking and file-sharing sites, has only increased this trend. A central concern of writing instructors in the new century is understanding these emerging forums and the literacies they require. In the 1980s and 1990s, it was common for instructors

---

101 Patricia Roberts-Miller, *Deliberate Conflict: Argument, Political Theory, and Composition Classes* (Carbondale: Southern Illinois University Press, 2004); Sharon Crowley, *Toward a Civil Discourse: Rhetoric and Fundamentalism* (Pittsburgh: University of Pittsburgh Press, 2006).

102 See J. Elspeth Stuckey, *The Violence of Literacy* (Portsmouth, NH: Boynton/Cook, 1991); Sharon Crowley, *Composition in the University: Historical and Polemical Essays* (Pittsburgh: University of Pittsburgh Press, 1998); Henry A. Giroux, *Schooling and the Struggle for Public Life: Democracy's Promise and Education's Challenge* (2nd. ed., Boulder: Paradigm, 2005); Harvey J. Graff, *Literacy Myths, Legacies, and Lessons: New Studies on Literacy* (New Brunswick, NJ: Transaction, 2011).

103 Wendy B. Sharer, "Civic Participation and the Undergraduate Classroom," in *The SAGE Handbook of Rhetorical Studies*, ed. Andrea A. Lunsford (Los Angeles: SAGE, 2009), 382. See also Lynée Lewis Gaillet's review essay, "The Rhetoric of Social Movements Revisited," *CCC* 62.2 (2010): 379–92.

104 See, for example, Rosa A. Eberly, "Rhetoric and the Anti-Logos Doughball: Teaching Deliberating Bodies the Practices of Participatory Democracy," *Rhetoric & Public Affairs* 5.2 (2002): 287–300; Donald Lazere, "A Core Curriculum for Civic Literacy," *Chronicle of Higher Education*, February 5, 2010, B4, and *Reading and Writing for Civic Literacy: The Critical Citizen's Guide to Argumentative Rhetoric* (brief ed., Boulder: Paradigm, 2009); John M. Ackerman and David J. Coogan, eds., *The Public Work of Rhetoric: Citizen-Scholars and Civic Engagement* (Columbia: University of South Carolina Press, 2010).

105 Ann M. Feldman, *Making Writing Matter: Composition in the Engaged University* (Albany: State University of New York Press, 2008), 4.

106 Faigley, "Literacy after the Revolution," 37.

to introduce and offer direct instruction in the use of writing technologies such as networked writing environments and even word-processing software. Now, they are more likely to take advantage of students' existing familiarity with online writing spaces to promote better critical understanding and more successful rhetorical strategies within these environments. Attendant with this move is an increasing interest in collaboratively written assignments that take advantage of technologies that promote group writing and editing, such as Microsoft Word's "track changes" feature and wiki software. Though some observers have expressed concern about reaching so-called "digital natives," young students who grew up in a richly technologically mediated environment,[107] most scholars in the field maintain that students still require—and without instruction often lack—the analytic and rhetorical skills to allow them to be fully (and critically) literate in this environment, particularly when negotiating corporate-sponsored and public spaces. Indeed, many of the traditional concerns of writing instructors—promoting critical reading, rhetorical dexterity, a sense of purpose and audience, a reason for writing, information literacy, and civic engagement—have taken on new exigence.

In her 2004 CCCC Chair's Address, Kathleen Blake Yancey, noting that our writing practices as scholars, teachers, students, and citizens are already largely multimodal and often self-sponsored, called for new forms of instruction that ask students to consider how texts now circulate—and how they might participate in their circulation. "[I]f we believe that writing is social, shouldn't the system of circulation . . . extend beyond and around the single path from student to teacher?"[108] Taking up her call, scholars have examined subjects ranging from the effective use of new media in the writing classroom, including blogs, fan forums, and video games,[109] to the political and civic potentials of online discourses and publics.[110] Such work is likely to continue to transform and become increasingly a part of writing courses and pedagogies.

107 See Marc Prensky, "Digital Natives, Digital Immigrants," On the Horizon 9 (2001): 1–6; Sue Bennett, Karl Maton, and Lisa Kervin, "The 'Digital Natives' Debate: A Critical Review of the Evidence," British Journal of Educational Technology 39.5 (2008): 775–86; Marisa A. Klages and J. Elizabeth Clark, "New Worlds of Errors and Expectations: Basic Writers and Digital Assumptions," Journal of Basic Writing 28.1 (2009): 32–49.

108 Kathleen Blake Yancey, "Made Not Only in Words: Composition in a New Key," CCC 56.2004: 310–11.

109 See Cynthia L. Selfe, ed., Multimodal Composition: Resources for Teachers (Cresskill, NJ: Hampton Press, 2007); James Paul Gee, What Video Games Have to Teach Us about Learning and Literacy (2003; rev. ed., New York: Macmillan, 2008); Jeremiah Dyehouse, Michael Pennell, and Linda K. Shamoon, "'Writing in Electronic Environments': A Concept and a Course for the Writing and Rhetoric Major," CCC 61.2 (2009): W330–50; Anne Herrington, Kevin Hodgson, and Charles Moran, eds., Teaching the New Writing: Technology, Change, and Assessment in the 21st-Century Classroom (New York: Teachers College Press, 2009); Cheryl E. Ball and James Kalmbach, eds., RAW (Reading and Writing) New Media (Cresskill, NJ: Hampton Press, 2010); Steven Fraiberg, "Composition 2.0: Toward a Multilingual and Multimodal Framework," CCC 62.1 (2010): 100–26; J. Elizabeth Clark, "The Digital Imperative: Making the Case for a 21st-Century Pedagogy," Computers and Composition 27.1 (2010): 27–35. Also of use is the "Virtual Classroom" section of Computers and Composition Online, http://www.bgsu.edu/cconline/virtualc.htm (accessed November 15, 2011).

110 See Jonathan Alexander, Digital Youth: Emerging Literacies on the World Wide Web (Cresskill, NJ: Hampton Press, 2006); Barbara Warnick, Rhetoric Online: Persuasion and Politics on the World Wide Web (New York: Peter Lang, 2007); Michele W. Simmons and Jeffrey T. Grabill, "Toward a Civic Rhetoric for Technologically and Scientifically Complex Places: Invention, Performance, and Participation," CCC 58.3 (2007): 419–48.

Rhetoric, Grammar, and Style

Although attention to style, the third canon of rhetoric, has always been important to writing instruction, professional discourse on the subject, particularly regarding sentence-level concerns, somewhat receded in the last decade of the twentieth century. This neglect had several sources: an increasing emphasis on public argument and civic ends in writing, derived from the social turn in composition and a renewed interest in classical rhetoric; a desire to instruct students in the higher-order or macro-level revising strategies that mark the processes of sophisticated writers, derived from cognitive research; and, perhaps, a wish to distance the field from reductive forms of current-traditional and expressivist instruction that emphasized, respectively, prescriptive grammar at the expense of rhetorical purpose, and the private at the expense of the public.

Yet it never truly disappeared as a topic of concern, particularly in the writing classroom, where style handbooks remain brisk sellers. As Paul Butler, who has been influential in renewing attention to the subject, has argued, "style in its dispersed form is often not *called* style but instead is named something else within the field"; it invisibly animates the work of rhetorical analysis, which considers a rhetor's effectiveness in addressing specific audiences for specific purposes, and is an integral component of classically inspired contemporary textbooks.[111]

Concerns about grammatical prescriptivism have especially made scholars reluctant to explore writing at the sentence level. The conclusions of the 1963 NCTE *Research in Written Composition* report that instruction in the rules of "formal" grammar has a "negligible or . . . even a harmful effect" on student writing are still widely shared—and largely borne out by empirical research.[112] Beginning in the 1980s, some scholars began to call for a more robust and nuanced interrogation of the subject, grounded in recent advances in sociolinguistics and language learning.[113] In 1991, Martha Kolln published *Rhetorical Grammar*, now in its sixth edition, which by closely examining how rhetorical purposes can be addressed through attention to linguistic structures, word-level phrasing, and even punctuation, helped reanimate interest in exploring the links between grammar, style, and rhetoric. In a 2004 call for more attention to the

---

111 See, for example, Joseph M. Williams' 1981 *Style: Lessons in Clarity in Grace*, now in its tenth edition with co-author Gary G. Colomb (Boston: Longman, 2010). Paul Butler, "Style in the Diaspora of Composition Studies," *Rhetoric Review* 26.1: 5, itals. orig. See, for example, Corbett and Connors, *Classical Rhetoric*; Sharon Crowley and Debra Hawhee, *Ancient Rhetoric for Contemporary Students* (4th ed., New York: Longman, 2008).

112 Richard Braddock, Richard Lloyd-Jones, and Lowell Schoer, *Research in Written Composition* (Champaign, IL: NCTE, 1963), 37–38; George Hillocks, Jr., "What Works in Teaching Composition: A Meta-Analysis of Experimental Treatment Studies," *American Journal of Education* 93.1 (1984): 133–70; English Review Group, *The Effect of Grammar Teaching (Syntax) in English on 5 to 16 Year Olds' Accuracy and Quality in Written Composition* (London: Research Evidence in Education Library, EPPI-Centre, 2004), http://eppi.ioe.ac.uk/cms/Default.aspx?tabid=230 (accessed November 15, 2011).

113 See Patrick Hartwell, "Grammar, Grammars, and the Teaching of Grammar," *College English* 47.2 (1985): 105–27; Lester Faigley, "The Study of Writing and the Study of Language," *Rhetoric Review* 7.2 (1989): 240–56; Marcia Farr, "Language, Culture, and Writing: Sociolinguistic Foundations of Research on Writing," *Review of Research in Education* 13 (1986): 195–223; and the work of M. A. K. Halliday, *An Introduction to Functional Grammar* (London: Arnold, 1985).

subject, Laura R. Micciche argued that "rhetorical grammar instruction can demonstrate to students that language does purposeful, consequential work in the world—work that can be learned and applied."[114] The past decade in particular has seen renewed interest in various aspects of style, as evidenced by a growing body of work aimed at both writing instructors and students.[115]

Empirical Research

Since the publication of Janet Emig's *The Composing Processes of Twelfth Graders* in 1971, empirical research on writing processes and writing instruction has been a key component of college writing studies, though its perceived centrality to the field has varied over the years. With the rise of cultural studies approaches in English studies and the concomitant social turn in rhetoric and composition in the 1980s and 90s, many scholars looked warily upon the employment of scientific methods in writing research; responding to this trend, in 1996, empirical researcher Davida Charney felt compelled to declare that empiricism was "not a four-letter word."[116]

Empirical research in writing studies has long had a home in the journals *Research in the Teaching of English* (*RTE*) and *Written Communication*, as well as technologically oriented journals such as *Computers and Composition* and pedagogically oriented ones such as the *Journal of Basic Writing*. In the last decade, driven in part by the increasing impact of and interest in technology, the field has expanded.[117] In 2008, an international open-access publication, the *Journal of Writing Research*, was launched, and in 2010, Kathleen Blake Yancey, in assuming the editorship of *College Composition and Communication*, renewed the journal's commitment to a multimodal research approach that includes empirical research and discussion of research methodologies.[118]

In 2010, the compilers of *RTE* annotated annual bibliography noted four expanding areas of research over past decade: digital technologies; second language and multicultural literacy; teacher education and professional development; and literacy practices across multiple domains. Inspired in part by

---

114 Martha Kolln and Loretta Gray, *Rhetorical Grammar: Grammatical Choices, Rhetorical Effects* (6th ed., New York: Longman, 2010); Laura R. Micciche, "Making a Case for Rhetorical Grammar," *CCC* 55.4 (2004): 719.

115 See T. R. Johnson and Thomas Pace, eds., *Refiguring Prose Style: Possibilities for Writing Pedagogy* (Logan: Utah State University Press, 2005); Tim Mayers, *(Re)Writing Craft: Composition, Creative Writing, and the Future of English Studies* (Pittsburgh: University of Pittsburgh Press, 2005); Paul Butler, *Out of Style: Reanimating Stylistic Study in Composition and Rhetoric* (Logan: Utah State University Press, 2008); Butler, ed., *Style in Rhetoric and Composition: A Critical Sourcebook* (Boston: Bedford/St. Martin's, 2010); Chris Holcomb and M. Jimmie Killingsworth, *Performing Prose: The Study and Practice of Style in Composition* (Carbondale: Southern Illinois University Press, 2010).

116 Janet Emig, *The Composing Processes of Twelfth Graders* (Urbana, IL: NCTE, 1971); Davida Charney, "Empiricism Is Not a Four-Letter Word," *CCC* 47.4 (1996): 567–93.

117 Between 2004 and 2011 the annual CCCC convention saw a doubling in the number of panels self-identifying under the cluster heading "Research," and between 2003 and 2010 *RTE's* annotated bibliography increased from 15 to 88 pages. See Richard Beach et al., "Annotated Bibliography of Research in the Teaching of English," *Research in the Teaching of English* 45.2 (2010): AB1, http://www.ncte.org/journals/rte/issues/v45-2 (accessed November 15, 2011).

118 "From the Editor," *CCC* 61.3 (2010): 405–13.

ethnographic and linguistic research on literacy, qualitative research in all areas has increasingly considered the socially situated nature of writing and literacy, implicitly responding to some of the concerns of earlier social-epistemic criticism. It has also begun to update and revise earlier understandings of the composing process as well as defining assessment more broadly.[119] Among recent research strands of particular interest to writing scholars and instructors have been examinations of the effects of emerging writing technologies on literacy and pedagogical practices on student writing. Christina Haas and Pamela Takayoshi have examined the paralinguistic strategies in students' instant messaging; Anish M. Dave and David R. Russell, the changing meaning of drafts and revisions in contemporary composing environments; Laura Wilder and Joanna Wolfe, the effects of explicit instruction in rhetorical discourse conventions on student writing; Melissa M. Nelson and Christian D. Schunn, the features of peer review feedback that inspire student revision; and Maria O. Treglia, the effects of teacher commentary on revision. After the 2008 Writing Research Across Borders conference, Charles Bazerman et al. published *Traditions of Writing Research*, an edited collection on quantitative and qualitative composition research from around the world.[120]

Conclusion: Over a Century of Change

College-level writing instruction has changed dramatically since the beginning of the twentieth century. In 1900, writing instruction was often limited to a single freshman course, with the standard assignment a daily or fortnightly "theme"—a brief narrative, descriptive, or expository sketch—graded with an eye toward form and correctness by an instructor with little pedagogical training.[121] Today, writing instruction is more commonly delivered at multiple points across the university, with supplemental instructional support for both

---

119 Beach et al.,"Annotated Bibliography," 1–3; Katherine Schultz, "Qualitative Research in Writing," in *Handbook of Writing Research*, ed. Charles A. MacArthur, Steve Graham, and Jill Fitzgerald (New York: Guilford, 2006); Brian Huot and Peggy O'Neil, eds., *Assessing Writing: A Critical Sourcebook* (Boston: Bedford/St. Martin's, 2009).

120 Christina Haas and Pamela Takayoshi, with Brandon Carr, Kimberley Hudson, and Ross Pollock, "Young People's Everyday Literacies: The Language Features of Instant Messaging," *Research in the Teaching of English* 45.4 (2011): 378–404; Anish M. Dave and David R. Russell, "Drafting and Revision Using Word Processing by Undergraduate Student Writers: Changing Conceptions and Practices," *Research in the Teaching of English* 44.4 (2010): 406–34; Laura Wilder and Joanna Wolfe, "Sharing the Tacit Rhetorical Knowledge of the Literary Scholar: The Effects of Making Disciplinary Conventions Explicit in Undergraduate Writing about Literature Courses," *Research in the Teaching of English* 44.2 (2009): 170–209; Melissa M. Nelson and Christian D. Schunn, "The Nature of Feedback: How Different Types of Peer Feedback Affect Writing Performance," *Instructional Science* 37.4 (2009): 375–401; Maria O. Treglia, "Teacher-Written Commentary in College Writing Composition: How Does It Impact Student Revisions?," *Composition Studies* 37.1 (2009): 67–86; Charles Bazerman, Robert Krut, Karen Lunsford, Susan McLeod, Suzie Null, Paul Rogers, and Amanda Stansell, eds., *Traditions of Writing Research* (New York: Routledge, 2010).

121 For contemporary assignments and complaints, see Copeland and Rideout, *Freshman English*; Charles Francis Adams, Edwin Lawrence Godkin, and Josiah Quincy, *Report of the Harvard Committee on Composition and Rhetoric* (Cambridge, MA: Harvard University, 1892); Adams Sherman Hill, Le Baron Russell Briggs, and Byron Satterlee Hurlbut, *Twenty Years of School and College English* (Cambridge, MA: Harvard University, 1896).

students and instructors offered through campus writing centers and writing program offices. A typical freshman writing assignment is much more complex and demanding than a century prior, typically argument based, grounded in a rhetorical context, and asking students to engage in research, consider audience and purpose, and address counter-arguments.

Charting these trends, Andrea A. Lunsford and Karen J. Lunsford found that the average freshman writing assignment in 1917 was 162 words; in 2006, 1,038; examining 877 assignments collected in a national survey, they found that 54 percent asked for argumentative writing, commonly involving research; 27 percent analysis of texts, such as a close reading, comparison/contrast essay, or rhetorical analysis; and only 13 percent the historically traditional expository categories of personal narrative, description, or definition. As they note, these findings concord with Kathleen Blake Yancey et al.'s 2005 survey of 1,861 faculty, which found 57 percent citing academic writing and 41 percent argument as their most important approaches, and the writing process, revision, and peer review as their most common teaching practices; and offer empirical support for Richard Fulkerson's recent survey of the field, based on a descriptive reading of textbook and journal trends.[122]

The value of writing and writing instruction is also more routinely recognized than a century ago. In a recent survey of freshman writing at Harvard, the institution long disparaged as one of the origin points of current-traditional rhetoric, Nancy Sommers and Laura Saltz found wide campus support and opportunities for writing, with both instructors and students seeing writing as a means for students "to engage . . . with their learning."[123] The nationwide increase in campus writing across the curriculum and writing in the disciplines programs, undergraduate concentrations and majors, and graduate programs in rhetoric and writing has also raised the visibility of writing as a subject. As of 2011, the CCCC Committee on the Major in Writing and Rhetoric lists 68 undergraduate programs offering majors in rhetoric and composition and the Consortium of Doctoral Programs in Rhetoric and Composition 70 members.[124] In the schools, partly in response to new SAT and AP exams that emphasize writing, increasing attention is being given to writing instruction. The most recent California K–12 language arts standards call for argumentative writing at all levels, with high school students asked to engage in rhetorical analysis and to "use specific rhetorical devices to support assertions," including "logic through reasoning" and "emotion or ethical belief."[125]

122 Andrea A. Lunsford and Karen J. Lunsford, "'Mistakes Are a Fact of Life': A National Comparative Study," *CCC* 59.4 (2008): 781–806; Yancey et al. cited in Kathleen Blake Yancey, with Brian M. Morrison, "Coming to Terms: Vocabulary as a Means of Defining First-Year Composition," in *What Is "College-Level" Writing?*, ed. Patrick Sullivan and Howard Tinberg (Urbana, IL: NCTE, 2006), 268; Fulkerson, "Composition at the Turn."

123 Nancy Sommers and Laura Saltz, "The Novice as Expert: Writing the Freshman Year," *CCC* 56.1 (2004): 131.

124 CCCC Committee on the Major, "Writing Majors at a Glance" (2009), http://www.ncte.org/library/NCTEFiles/Groups/CCCC/Committees/Writing_Majors_Final.pdf (accessed November 15, 2011); Consortium of Doctoral Programs, "Current Members," http://www.cws.illinois.edu/rc_consortium/members.html (accessed November 17, 2011).

125 California State Board of Education, *Common Core Content Standards for English Language Arts* (2010), 36, http://www.scoe.net/castandards/agenda/2010/ela_ccs_recommendations.pdf (accessed November 15, 2011).

Unfortunately, some conditions have not improved. On the first page of the inaugural issue of the *English Journal* in 1912, Edwin M. Hopkins famously asked, "Can good composition teaching be done under present conditions?" His terse answer, "No," still resonates.[126] In colleges, most writing instruction at the freshman level is delivered by the least experienced and the least protected classes of instructors, graduate teaching assistants and contingent faculty. Writing instructors still frequently face high teaching loads and large class sizes, conditions that make it challenging to enact the pedagogies that most improve writing, particularly the opportunity to receive and respond to feedback on multiple drafts. Attempts have been made to address this issue; some colleges are creating independent and semi-independent writing programs with either tenure-line faculty or full-time lecturer positions, and pedagogical training for graduate students is increasingly more robust as the field expands.

It remains to be seen how these efforts will intersect with the larger socio-economic pressures that threaten writing at all levels, such as increasing dependence of universities on contingent faculty, decreasing public financing for public education, widespread demonization of teachers, and the increasing reliance on high-stakes testing, value-added assessment, and market-based reforms at the primary and secondary levels. In the schools in particular, pressures from testing and overcrowded classrooms often mean little time for writing instruction or the implementation of research-based practices, or, perversely, an emphasis on narrow modes or genres of writing.[127]

Also, despite remarkable advances *within* the field of writing studies, especially over the last thirty years, public perceptions about writing have remained largely static; for many citizens, the teaching of writing still largely means instruction in prescriptive grammar, and literacy remains a one-dimensional skill. Though the NCTE, CCCC, and Council of Writing Program Administrators (CPWA) have increased their literacy advocacy through the distribution of policy statements, action alerts, and instructional resources,[128] more coordinated and concerted efforts by greater numbers of writing scholars and teachers will be needed to address the full range of challenges that the twenty-first century will bring.

Further Reading

As our epigraph suggests, no overview of a period can be complete, and each will reflect, to some degree, the interests and idiosyncrasies of their authors. For readers interested in further perspectives on the development of writing instruction in the twentieth and twenty-first centuries, we suggest:

126 Edwin M. Hopkins, "Can Good Composition Teaching Be Done under Present Conditions?" *English Journal* 1.1 (1912): 1–8.
127 See, for example, Lisa Scherff and Carolyn Piazza, "The More Things Change, the More They Stay the Same: A Survey of High School Students' Writing Experiences," *Research in the Teaching of English* 39.3 (2005): 271–304.
128 See the NCTE's Take Action resources, http://www.ncte.org/action; CCCC's Position Statements, http://www.ncte.org/cccc/resources/positions; and the CWPA's Framework for Success in Postsecondary Writing, http://wpacouncil.org/framework, and Network for Media Action, http://wpacouncil.org/nma (all accessed November 15, 2011).

Gere, Anne Ruggles. "The Teaching of Writing, 1912–2000." In *Reading the Past, Writing the Future: A Century of American Literacy Education and the National Council of Teachers of English,* edited by Erika Lindemann, 93–121. Urbana, IL: NCTE, 2010.

Giberson, Greg A., and Thomas A. Moriarty, eds. *What We Are Becoming: Developments in Undergraduate Writing Majors.* Logan: Utah State University Press, 2010.

Lauer, Janice. "Rhetoric and Composition." In *English Studies: An Introduction to the Discipline(s),* edited by Bruce McComiskey, 106–52. Urbana, IL: NCTE, 2006.

Lunsford, Andrea, Kurt Wilson, and Rosa A. Eberly, eds. *The SAGE Handbook of Rhetorical Studies.* Los Angeles: SAGE, 2009.

MacArthur, Charles A., Steve Graham, and Jill Fitzgerald, eds. *Handbook of Writing Research.* New York: Guilford, 2006.

Miller, Thomas P. *The Evolution of College English: Literacy Studies from the Puritans to the Postmoderns.* Pittsburgh: University of Pittsburgh Press, 2010.

Smagorinsky, Peter, ed. *Research on Composition: Multiple Perspectives on Two Decades of Change.* New York: Teachers College Press, 2006.

Yancey, Kathleen Blake, ed. *Delivering College Composition: The Fifth Canon.* Portsmouth, NH: Boynton/Cook, 2006.

Not a Conclusion, But an Epilogue

James J. Murphy

Albertine Gaur remarks in her book *A History of Writing* that "The story of writing is a tale of adventure which spans some twenty thousand years and touches all aspects of human life."[1] It is with some temerity, then, that we have attempted to sketch the history of a small segment of this vast enterprise.

But we are inevitably interested in our own history more than we are in the histories of others, and our concentration on Western writing instruction is important to us because it tells us how we got to our present state of pedagogical affairs, and, hopefully, how we can improve our future performance.

Given the widely varying American approaches described in Chapter 8, however, it seems clear that no single Malthusian projection can provide us with an accurate forecast of the future of writing instruction in America.

A century of diverse views on the goals and methods of writing instruction has left us without a national consensus. On one hand, this is reasonable enough, since democracy not only permits but encourages diversity, and different segments of the population may have different needs and capacities. On the other hand, to the extent that human beings all have some elements in common, it may well be possible to identify more commonalities than appear at present.

The complete history of writing instruction in the twenty-first century, though, must necessarily be written by some scholars not yet born. It would be fruitless at this point for us to speculate about that history. Instead, it may be more useful to look at practical steps we can take to understand better the history which this book only begins to outline. One reviewer of the first edition of this book, John Flood of the University of London, wrote that "it is not short and it is not a history." In a sense he was right. No complete history of so complex a subject can be developed fully even in a volume of this length. We will be grateful if the book provides a general framework, a historical overview, which permits deeper investigation of a subject so important that people in our culture have devoted thousands of years to it.

Here, then, in no particular order of priority, are some possible realms of investigation that might further enhance our understanding.

1 Albertine Gaur, *A History of Writing* (rev. ed.,) (New York: Cross River Press, 1992) 7.

Comparative Studies

We seem to know little about how other societies have handled writing instruction in the past, or how they have developed their modern forms. An educated citizen of The Netherlands, for example, can speak and write fluently in English, German, and French as well as Dutch. It should be of interest to know how this is accomplished. Is Urdu writing instruction in India the same as the process inherited from the English? Do Japanese students learn writing the same way Europeans do? Where can we look to find useful lessons in other societies and cultures?

Research Tools

Writers about writing instruction have of course produced thousands of articles and book chapters on the subject, but the field still lacks some of the basic research tools common in almost every other area of study. An encyclopedia of teaching methods would be a useful tool, especially if it included historical as well as contemporary items. An anthology of statements about writing instruction could be compiled fairly easily. Pedagogical biographies of leading theorists and teachers could provide more personal insights into particular times and places. Above all, though, the field needs systematic bibliographic access in electronic form; printed bibliographies, while useful, are necessarily selective and slow to produce. A good model would be the *ITER* project operated jointly by the University of Toronto and Arizona State University for medieval and Renaissance studies with the assistance of the National Endowment for the Humanities and other foundations; it includes not only articles but book reviews, is continually updated, and provides a wide range of search modes. Can NCTE or MLA provide an analogous function?

A Book-Length History of Twentieth-Century Writing Instruction

As the preceding chapter demonstrates, this is an extremely complex period. Yet regular reading of contemporary journals and books would seem to indicate that some people in the field are unaware of many developments which affect the subjects they are writing about. A coherent account would enable instructors to place themselves in relation to what has gone before. The late James A. Berlin, the original author of Chapter 8, was well on his way to producing such a study. Now other scholars should consider this challenge as well.

The Role of Women

Much as already been done in this area, especially by recent writers like Andrea Lunsford, Cheryl Glenn, Molly Wertheimer, and Christine Sutherland and Rebecca Sutcliffe. Yet much remains to be done. Historians of rhetoric and of writing instruction are often accused of overlooking the contributions of women in the periods they cover; their response often is that historians must recount what actually occurred in male-dominated societies like the Roman or the medieval. But Carol Dana Lanham points out an analogous problem in

Chapter 3 in relation to records of schools in late antiquity—is it a fact that schools disappeared under the barbarian invasions, or is it fact instead that the written records of existing schools were lost? In other words, we may have to look beyond the obvious to find new categories of evidence. For another example the bibliographer Robin Alston of the British Library in London once said that he had identified 2,500 women writers of fiction of nineteenth-century England (though many used men's names to get their works published). His evidence was both direct and indirect, including title pages, diaries, correspondence, book-sellers' sales records, publishing contracts, book reviews, and references in literary journals of the time. In other words the investigator of the role of women in writing instruction, regardless of the period studied, may need to be just as inventive in searching for sources both direct and indirect.

The Role of Textbooks

Until the advent of printing there was very little likelihood that any teacher could offer a book to every student in the classroom. The "textbook" as we know it is a product of early modern times, the first one printed in England dating from 1480 when William Caxton published a Latin rhetorical text to be used by students in a class at Cambridge University. As we saw in the first four chapters in this book, ancient and medieval teachers relied heavily on oral reading, memorization, and repetition to bring written materials to the attention of their students. It might be profitable to examine more closely the question of whether the advent of textbooks changed teaching objectives and methods. And in modern America there is a particular question about textbooks which is seldom asked. Like the proverbial elephant in the living room that no one mentions, there is one subject too big to be noticed—the role of writing text-books in respect to curricula and method. Some aspects of this subject are obvious: the regulatory influence of the committee which chooses a single text-book for twenty sections of college composition, or the committee which chooses a secondary textbook for an entire state. But it may be useful to probe a whole range of other factors. One is the urge for novelty which seeks obsoles-cence of the familiar for the sake of sales; perhaps the fact that a textbook is in its sixth edition is proof enough that the book was not very good to begin with? If you have ever heard a publisher say, "The used-book market is killing us," you have heard a common expression of the "need" for a "new" edition. Another factor is the desire of writers to push variations on the same theme by using new titles rather than new ideas. Of course textbook publication also allows teachers to promote their instructional ideas beyond their own classrooms. This too is a complex subject, but it would be illuminating to unravel its inner workings.

The Influence of Quintilian

While there is an immense range of Quintilian studies in print, including a recent three-volume collection published in Spain to commemorate the 1,900th anniversary of his *Institutio oratoria* (95 CE), there is no definitive account of his influence over time. He is of course a major Renaissance force, but he is also cited by later figures such as Alexander Pope in the eighteenth century and John

Stuart Mill in the nineteenth. This historical account would indeed be a daunting task, but is hard to think of a single writer with a more long-lasting effect on the teaching of speaking and writing in Western culture. (Apart from this historical account, it might also be interesting for a skilled educational psychologist, perhaps teaming with a classical rhetorician, to re-examine the pedagogical principles of the Roman school system as described by Quintilian.)

Non-Departmental Writing Instruction

While this is partly a question of administrative history, the increase in the numbers of writing centers, projects, and institutes outside of English departments also has some philosophical/pedagogical implications. Coupled with calls for increased professionalism in the field and for an identity of writing-as-discipline, these distancing movements could possibly be shaping a new set of objectives for writing instruction. Recent events are always hard to study historically, since much of the needed data is not yet available, but it may well be that enough has been written already by and about these units that some analysis is now possible. Christina Murphy and Joe Law have begun this inquiry.

The History of English Departments

It is difficult for some American students to understand that English departments in their present form are barely more than a century old. Even the brief account of the events of the 1880s and 1890s provided here in Chapter 7 indicates the importance of far-reaching decisions made then at a small number of institutions to alter the national direction of instruction.

There is such a dearth of informed research on this subject that virtually every recent study still cites an article published nearly 45 years ago: William Riley Parker, "Where Do English Departments Come From?"[2] And Albert R. Kitzhaber's 1953 dissertation "Rhetoric in American Colleges: 1850–1900," now almost half a century old, has been printed as a book—presumably in the absence of a better account of the period. Yet this is such a critical period in this country's stance in respect to writing instruction that we ignore its details at our peril. One of the issues debated then was the question of who should teach writing—certainly a question of particular interest to today's part-time and adjunct faculty as well as tenured professors. Some of the other issues noted in Chapter 7 are still current today, which is yet another reason for learning more about how those issues were resolved in that period.

Reading and Writing after the Advent of Printing

It is generally understood that the more rapid reading which followed the increase in the number of texts available had some visible effects on the page— punctuation and paragraphing are two examples. Walter Ong and others have studied the impact of the visual on the oral, but were there concomitant changes in the ways in which students were prepared to write for print? On the face of it,

2 *College English* 28 (1967): 339–51.

it would seem not, since fifteenth- and sixteenth-century schools seemed to follow conservative methods; but then the question has not yet been explored directly. Printing was not universally welcomed in its early years; Paris book-sellers refused to buy any of the Gutenberg Bibles, for example, and the late fifteenth-century writer Trithemius, in a Latin work titled *In Defence of Scribes*, warned that printing would destroy careful writing, and ultimately grammar. Did writing instructors like or dislike the new medium, and what were their thoughts on the matter? Will modern texting destroy grammar? Are there analogues here to current thinking about other electronic aids?

Vernacular versus Latin

Chapters 5, 6, and 7 include reports on this issue. Their accounts are embedded in discussions of the schools and universities of their periods, but it might be useful to take the matter as a subject of its own. There are already a number of preliminary studies available, so that the project is not beyond possibility with what we already know. A related question for English-language users, too, is the history of the imposition of a traditional Latin grammar on a hybrid language with a Germanic base. This began to happen as early as the fifteenth century with English translations of the ancient Latin grammars of Donatus and Priscian. The historical basis of this development surely needs to be understood by anyone struggling with students who do not see any logic in the grammar we teach. This is an issue analogous to modern concerns about what levels of writing to teach to ESL students.

Old and New Technologies

This is a significant area to which little attention has been paid. The physical difficulty of writing was a factor in classroom teaching for most of the period covered in this book. Exploration of the means used over the centuries for coping with this problem may well provide us with clues to modern problems, especially at the lowest levels of instruction. We do not seem to know whether the fairly recent liberation from the inkpot, for example, or the ease of correction with a word processor have been matched by changes in pedagogy. We already see concerns about the putative erosion of grammatical standards in e-mail. The advent of voice-recognition technology may make computer writing once again the transcription of oral performance—an ironic return, perhaps, to the conditions in ancient Greece described in Chapter 1. If so, this would make it even more important that we understand the relationship of "dictation" to "text" in earlier periods, and to re-examine the age-old controversy over "oral" versus "written" styles. It is admittedly difficult to make historical assessments of current affairs, but a sure knowledge of the history of writing instruction can only enhance our ability to comprehend what is happening now.

The Death of Handwriting?

A British educator has proposed that government funding should no longer be used for the teaching of handwriting, since it is an obsolescing skill no longer worthy of such support. His argument is that keyboards and touch screens and other technologies not yet imagined have made it unnecessary for children to learn handwriting. If this argument were to prevail, what would be the implications for basic writing instruction?

These few suggestions, from among many possible ideas, may serve as illustrations of the many other things we do not yet know completely about the history of writing instruction. This is not simply a matter of filling in gaps in a chronological coverage. Rather, it is that chronological survey which makes it possible now to identify the key issues which have recurred over time. No doubt further research will continue to uncover more historical details of schools, their teachers, and their teaching methods, but it is also important to look at larger concerns.

Some of the approaches suggested above may require special skills, like a knowledge of computer programming or a grasp of nineteenth-century educational history, but exploring these issues (and many others) can only enhance our understanding both of history and of our own teaching situations.

Glossary of Key Terms in the History of Writing Instruction

Abbreviation. Compression of a given long text into a few lines of verse or prose. The reverse of **Amplification**.

Abecedaria. Letters of the alphabet that are written as an educational exercise for practice and memorization.

Adventure School. A private school which often specialized in teaching a particular skill, like dance. These schools were common in America from the seventeenth to the early nineteenth centuries.

After-lecture Summary. Proposal of George Jardine at Glasgow that students not take notes in class but instead write an abstract of the lecture's main points afterward.

Amplification. The dilation or verbal expansion of an idea or text. As an exercise in the "development" of concepts through additional detail, the main purpose is to give the student practice in handling multiple aspects of a given subject. See also *copia*, **progymnasmata**, and **Topic**.

Amplification of Outlines. Assignment of speech outlines prepared by the teacher for students to develop into complete orations for oral delivery in the classroom.

Analysis of a Text (*praelectio*). Detailed oral dissection of a text to evaluate the author's style and structure. The second stage in **Imitation**. This microanalysis as used in English schools led to the term "parsing" (from the Latin question *pars orationis?* (i.e., 'what part of speech is this word?').

Analysis of Authorial Choices. Detailed discussion of an author's rhetorical choices in a given text, with reasons proposed for authorial decisions at each point. A part of the **Imitation** process.

Analysis of Structure. Discussion of a work as a whole, with particular attention to Arrangement (e.g., arrangement of parts, methods of beginning and ending, or proportion of the work devoted to a particular theme).

Anthologies of Standard Texts. Conscious retention of certain texts as best for exemplifying both stylistic form and moral content. The *Liber Catonianus*, Virgil's *Aeneid*, and Lincoln's *Gettysburg Address* provide three examples.

Aoidoi. Oral composers who appear in Homer's *Iliad* and *Odyssey* and are the forerunners to the rhapsodes.

Apprenticeship. The practice of sending a student to live with and emulate a practicing professional. The method was used into the nineteenth century, especially in law, and continues in a modified form in modern medical internships.

Artificial Order. Artistic alteration of normal chronological order in a narrative, to achieve a rhetorical effect. Medieval commentators, for example, saw a double order in Virgil's *Aeneid*—artificial because it begins *in media res*, natural because the first six books illustrate the six stages of a man's life.

Assessment. Formal evaluation of student writing or writing programs. Holistic assessment of student papers often won out over strictly applied rubrics and more formal standards, outside of standardized testing situations where rater agreement must be produced and statistically demonstrated. Includes portfolio assessment.

Belletristic Writing. Writing with "taste" and aesthetic principles as the main features; greatly influenced by British and Scottish textbooks like Hugh Blair's *Lectures on Rhetoric and Belles Lettres* (1783).

Carlisle Indian School. Opened in 1879 by Colonel Richard Henry Pratt as the first off-reservation school designed to remove Indian children from their reservations to eradicate their tribal identities and assimilate them into white culture.

Catechetical System. Lecture followed by a period in which the lecturer questions the students over the material covered in the lecture.

Chreia. Amplification of what a person said or did. One of the **progymnasmata**.

Cognitive Model of Writing. Writing instruction based on cognitive psychology, which analyzes learning as a process susceptible to empirical investigation.

Commonplace. Casting a favorable or unfavorable light (i.e., "coloring") on something admitted. One of the **progymnasmata**. Also, a language device to aid recall.

Commonplace Book. See **Copy Book**.

Communications Course. A course combining writing, speaking, reading, and listening activities. Popular during the 1940s and 1950s.

Comparison. Treating two subjects in one composition, praising or dispraising both or praising one and dispraising the other ("contrast"). One of the **progymnasmata**.

Composition Based on Classical Rhetoric. Composition in this sequence occurs in four chronological interior steps—Invention (discovery) of ideas, their Arrangement, their wording (Style), and their retention in Memory—followed by one exterior step: for oral language the step of Delivery (through Voice, facial Expression, and Gesture), and for written language through the step of physical inscription (Orthography) of words on some receptor like papyrus, wax tablet, or paper.

Conference on College Composition and Communication (CCCC). Association of writing teachers formed in 1949.

Continuity of Method. Re-use of proven teaching methods from one period to the next, even as conditions change.

Copia. Term used by Desiderius Erasmus to denote the ability to express oneself in different ways; analogous to **Amplification**. The term includes variation, abundance, and eloquence. The term is not original to Erasmus, being a major feature of Roman educational practice.

Copy Book. Book of blank pages in which English grammar school students were expected to write commonplaces gleaned from the texts they read. Also called "**Commonplace Book**."

Correct Language as Social Status. The favorable effect, from Roman antiquity to present-day America, of the capacity to compose oral and written language according to accepted usage; the corollary has often been a heightened emphasis on grammatical "rules" and determined efforts to eliminate "dialects."

Correction. Public oral evaluation of student performance by the master and at times by the other students as well. The seventh stage in **Imitation**.

Courses in Composition. Separate courses in composition appear only in late nineteenth- and twentieth-century America, though (as the authors point out in Chapter 8) they are now the one element common to every level of education in America.

Craft Literacy. A system of writing that requires extensive time and energy for technical mastery, such as the training of an Egyptian scribe in hicroglyphics.

Cultural Studies. Language-centered pedagogy that begins by name in the 1990s, especially with postmodern and postcolonial theory, and focuses on the cultural level of composition studies, including classroom analyses of popular and high-culture artifacts, semiotic analyses, critical discourse studies, everyday life, and media studies.

Current-Rational Rhetoric. Writing as an extension of scientific method, with emphasis on inductive method. Prominent at Harvard in the late nineteenth century.

Current-Traditional Rhetoric. Formalist rhetoric dominating writing instruction in North America for much of the twentieth century. Inspired by Alexander Bain's texts, it features topic sentences, modes of discourse, and an emphasis on correctness.

Curriculum. A systematic educational program designed to achieve a particular objective. (The word literally means "little course," from the Latin *curru* "race-course" to which the diminutive *-ulum* has been added.) As Professor Enos points out in Chapter 1, the itinerant Sophists of ancient Greece could have little opportunity for systematic development of their ideas before they moved on; Isocrates, on the other hand, developed a purposeful curriculum over many years in one place, greatly influencing the Romans in their systematizing of education.

Dame School. A private school owned and operated by a woman. These schools were common in America from the seventeenth to the early nineteenth centuries.

Declamation. Classroom speeches on assigned issues, either political (*suasoriae*) or judicial (*controversiae*). Generally regarded as the most difficult of all the Roman exercises, since it included all the others. During the Roman Empire, Declamation also became a popular form of public entertainment, with adult speakers performing.

Description. Dilation of detail in vivid description, "bringing before the eyes what is to be shown." One of the **progymnasmata**.

Dictation. Oral reading of a text for the purpose of student transcription. It was used in the Roman system for early training in sentence structure, but in early modern Scottish universities, in the absence of textbooks, some "lectures" were delivered slowly enough to allow verbatim copying.

Dissenting Academy. A high-level secondary school, equivalent to today's colleges, run by English Nonconformists, or "dissenting" Protestants, unhappy with the Anglican control of education in England from the late seventeenth through nineteenth centuries.

Dominance of Latin. The assumption, from Roman times into the late eighteenth century, that Latin was the language of literacy.

Dominance of the Oration. The assumption, common into the nineteenth century, that oral discourse—and, therefore, the rhetoric that underlay it—was the highest form of language use and should therefore serve as a model for all types of discourse.

Eight Parts of Speech. A taxonomy of Latin words popularized by Aelius Donatus (fl. *ca.* 350 CE) in his Ars *Minor* and applied thereafter to large numbers of vernaculars as well.

Elliptical Exercise. Sentences with omitted words for students to supply.

Encomium. The praise of virtue or dispraise of vice in a person or a thing. One of the **progymnasmata**.

Epigraphy. The study of writing that appears on durable material such as marble, wood, or metal. Recent studies concentrating on marble inscriptions from Greece and Rome have yielded new primary evidence about writing practices.

Epistemic Rhetoric. (Sometimes called social-epistemic rhetoric.) Concept that language and writing help produce truth and knowledge through a process of interaction between the writer, the interlocutors, and the surrounding socio-cultural, political, and other external factors.

Examinators. Selected students in George Jardine's classes at Glasgow who would read and correct other students' written work.

Exemplification of Figures. Two forms: (1) short composition giving an example of one figure; (2) composition consisting entirely of examples of a standard set of figures of thought and figures of speech, in the order given by a standard source. A famous one is in Geoffrey of Vinsauf's *New Poetics* (*Poetria nova*), using the 64 figures from the *Rhetorica ad Herennium*.

Exercise Book. Book of blank pages for student compositions; a draft is written on the left-hand pages, then a final copy is written on the right-hand pages after the instructor has commented on the draft. (In sixteenth-century England the sales of blank sheets of paper ranked close to paper used for book printing.)

Expressionist Rhetoric. Writing as art, which can be learned by the student but cannot be taught directly. Thus the work of the teacher is to provide an environment in which students can learn what cannot be directly imparted in instruction. "Creative" and "expressive" writing are forms of this method.

Fable. Retelling of a fable from Aesop, either shorter or longer than the original. One of the **progymnasmata**.

Facility (*facilitas*). The term used by Quintilian to describe the ultimate objective of the Roman educational system, that is, the ability to improvise appropriate and effective language in any situation. See **Habit**.

Faults in Language Use. Deliberate study of imperfect texts to illustrate defects to be avoided.

Female Seminaries. Institutions created to provide women with an education similar to that found in men's colleges. Some notable early seminaries include Emma Willard's Troy Female Seminary, established in 1814; Catharine Beecher's Hartford Seminary, opened in 1823; and Mary Lyon's Mount Holyoke Female Seminary, founded in 1837.

Forms. Student groupings or classes in English grammar schools, with specific curricula and timetables laid out for each form.

Grammar. In antiquity, "the art of speaking correctly and the interpretation of the poets" (i.e., literature). In modern times, standards of correctness based on well-known textbooks. In Renaissance English grammar schools, however, the term denotes an integrated curriculum of oral and written composition combined with literary criticism.

Habit. The deep-rooted capacity (*facilitas*) to produce appropriate language under any circumstances. In Roman theory habit is the result of long practice in a carefully planned set of incremental exercises such as **Imitation** and the **progymnasmata**.

Hupogrammateus. A secretary used in ancient Athens for the purpose of recording the oral transactions of civil deliberations.

Imitation. A sequence of interpretive and reconstitutive activities using pre-existing texts to teach students how to create their own texts. One of the most pervasive and long-lasting methods of teaching writing and speaking, it appears in Greece in the fifth century before Christ; was systematized by the Romans; had continuing influence through the Middle Ages, the Renaissance, and early America; and continues in an altered form in many current textbooks. The complete Roman system has seven steps: reading aloud, analysis of text, memorization of model, paraphrase of model, transliteration of model, recitation of paraphrase or transliteration, and correction of the recited text.

Impersonation. Composition of an imaginary monologue that would fit the personality of an assigned person in certain circumstances. One of the **progymnasmata**.

Interactive Classroom. A Roman learning situation in which both students and teacher evaluated not only the model texts chosen for study but also each other's performance in recitation, in analysis, and in **Declamation**.

Language Acquisition. The natural process by which a child learns oral language on his own by listening to and imitating his elders; by contrast, writing requires external instruction and cannot be learned on one's own.

Laws. Composition of arguments either for or against a proposed law. The final and most difficult of the **progymnasmata**.

Lecture. The direct, uninterrupted, oral transmission of information by a teacher to a group of students. This method became popular only in early modern times, and was greatly spurred by the democratization of education that enlarged class sizes. See also **Dictation**.

Letteraturizzazione. Term used by George A. Kennedy to denote a movement from oral rhetoric ("primary rhetoric") toward written forms of discourse ("secondary rhetoric").

Letter Writing. A basic mode of writing practice from the early Middle Ages into the nineteenth century.

Liberal Culture. Writing based on literary works, with emphasis on appreciation of literature as "the best thoughts of the best minds." Prominent at Yale in the latter part of the nineteenth century.

Life Adjustment. A movement begun in the 1940s to use writing as a means to prepare students for specific real-life experiences they would encounter outside of school.

Literacy. A term once defined by the ability to sign one's own name but now serving as an umbrella for knowledge of various (rationally written) genres, forums, and discourses. For example digital literacy refers to the ability to read and write effectively in computer tasks, while health or media literacy refers to capabilities in those fields.

Lyceum. A nineteenth-century American institution found in cities across the country. Many had public buildings housing a lecture hall and library, with the aim of educating the public through access to libraries and lectures.

Melete **(see Declamation).** The Greek counterpart to the Roman *Declamatio*. Greek declamation stressed exercises in oral and written composition, as well as the study of **stasis**.

Memorization. Verbatim memorization of a text for either (1) oral recitation in the classroom or (2) analysis of the text as a part of **Imitation**.

Metics. Free, non-citizens who resided in Athens. Sophists who came to Athens were frequently given this status.

Modes of Discourse. Four types of composition stressed by Alexander Bain at Aberdeen: narration, description, exposition, argument, and poetry. Bain also urged frequent and sequenced writing assignments. Some others attribute the "modes" to the influence of faculty psychology, through the Scottish rhetorician George Campbell.

Multi-Purpose Exercises. *A* basic tenet of the Roman program, in which writing, speaking, listening, and reading are purposely combined wherever possible. Memorization for recitation was a common way to accomplish several ends in one exercise.

Narration as the Primary Step. Story-telling, and story retelling (as in **Imitation**), as prior to any instruction in persuasion; exercises in Vivid Description (*ecphrasis*) accentuate the details of a narration.

National Council of Teachers of English (NCTE). Association of teachers founded in 1911 in protest over uniform reading lists. The NCTE argued that teachers, rather than the colleges, should set reading and writing requirements for their students.

National Writing Project. A teacher-organized program of teacher training centers in virtually every state, organized initially as the Bay Area Writing Project in 1974.

Normal Schools. Early teacher-training institutions that began in the nineteenth century for the secondary education of young women thanks to the efforts of educators like Horace Mann. Some early normal schools developed into teachers' colleges and then into multi-purpose universities.

"Old Education." The family–tutorship–apprenticeship mode of education common in ancient Greece and Republican Rome up to the time of Cicero before the prevalence of rhetorical schools.

Oratory. The art of public speaking, also called by various other names, including expression and elocution, particularly in regard to late nineteenth- and twentieth-century women's speech education.

Orthography. The physical act of writing words on a page. By late antiquity, Orthography was a standard part of treatises on Grammar. Quintilian and other authors as late as the nineteenth century comment on the effects that writing instruments and writing surfaces could have on the thinking aspects of writing. Until very recently, the sheer labor of transcription with stylus or quill pens encouraged writers to think their texts through very carefully before starting the difficult physical process of transcription.

Oxbridge. Term coined for Oxford and Cambridge universities, reflecting their similar conservative curricula.

Paideia. The virtue of intellectual excellence in Greece. Also, the educational program to achieve it.

Paraphrase of Models. Re-telling of something in the student's own words. The fourth stage in **Imitation**.

Philology. The historical and comparative study of texts for their linguistic features and meanings. Philologists often studied texts as the key to cultural history.

Precept. The author of the *Rhetorica ad Herennium* (86 BCE) defines Precept as "a set of rules that provide a definite method and system of speaking." In Roman education, Precept included both rhetoric and grammar, and was linked in the pedagogical triad with **Imitation** and Practice.

Progymnasmata. A set of graded incremental composition exercises; each exercise builds on the ones before it but adds a new element to create a higher level of difficulty for the student. The twelve common in antiquity are described by Hermogenes, whose revival in Renaissance Europe transmitted them to America as well. They are: **Fable, Tales, chreia, Proverb, Refutation and Confirmation, Commonplace, Encomium, Comparison, Impersonation, Description, Thesis**, and **Laws**. See also **Modes of Discourse**.

Proverb. Amplification of an aphorism *(sententia)*. One of the **progymnasmata**.

Reading Aloud (*lectio*). Oral reading of a model as the first step in **Imitation**. Also used with a student's own composition as prelude for evaluation by the master and his fellow students.

Recitation of Paraphrase or Transliteration. Oral presentation by student of his version of the text; sometimes recited from memory, sometimes read aloud from a written text. The sixth stage in **Imitation**.

Redbricks. British universities founded in the nineteenth and twentieth centuries, so named because they were built of common red brick in contrast to the medieval stone structures of Oxford and Cambridge.

Refutation and Confirmation. Disproving or proving a narrative. One of the **progymnasmata**.

Regent System. System in eighteenth-century Scottish universities in which one professor taught all the subjects and stayed with one group of students during their entire education. Writing instruction was connected with every course.

Rhapsodes. Greek minstrels who preserved, transmitted, and composed oral epic tales such as those associated with Homer. Rhapsodes traveled throughout Greece, and some formed guilds. Some are known to have used writing and are credited with helping to preserve the text of the *Iliad* and the *Odyssey*.

Rhetoric. Originally its precepts concerned the "art of speaking," though many of its doctrines have been and continue to be applied to writing as well. The subject was central in Western education from the first century BCE until the late nineteenth century in America. Its traditional parts are Invention, Arrangement, Memory, Style, and Delivery. It is a term whose definitions have ranged broadly across the centuries, making it necessary to attach particular definitions to specific theorists and periods.

School. A system of group education under a dominant teaching master, who follows a plan of learning experiences designed to produce certain results in the knowledge-level and behavior of his students. The school in this sense is a Greek invention, though the Romans developed it further by establishing multiple sites with a common curriculum. Isocrates is the most influential Greek schoolmaster, being a major influence on Roman practice. His contemporaries Plato and Aristotle, on the other hand, operated "schools" devoted more to philosophical inquiry than to student development; they might rather be described in modern terms as "research institutes."

Self-Correction. Quintilian urges that adults continue throughout their whole lives to use the methods learned in school to evaluate their own writing, to determine what to add, take away, or alter.

Sentence Diagramming. A process of visualizing syntactic relationships, begun by Alonzo Reed and Brainerd Kellogg in the 1870s.

Sequencing. The systematic ordering of classroom exercises to accomplish two goals: Movement from simple to complex, and Reinforcement by reiterating each element of preceding exercises as each new one appears.

Short Compositions. Student writings, as short as one sentence, or a pair of opposing sentences, to provide practice in the use of particular techniques (e.g. a rhetorical figure, a contrast, or a description).

Shorthand. A method of rapid writing using simple strokes or other extremely abbreviated symbols instead of letters or words. Used in transcribing oral language, such as in courtrooms or legislatures.

Silent Reading. The dominant form of reading after the spread of printing, so that eventually writing became the medium for silent reading rather than the script for oral performance.

Social Efficiency. Writing instruction aimed at preparing students to be competent members of society.

Social-Epistemic Rhetoric. See **Epistemic Rhetoric**.

Sophists. Literally, "wise" individuals who taught at the most advanced level of ancient education. Sophists emerged in fifth-century Greece and continued well into the Roman Empire.

Speech Communication Association (SCA). Organization formed in 1915 when teachers of public speaking broke away from the **NCTE** to promote speech teaching separate from writing and literature classes. Now National Communication Association (NCA).

Stasis. A Greek inventional system which provided heuristics to help in identifying the point at issue in a controversy. *Stasis* is a central concept in Greek rhetorical education. Over the centuries, theoreticians constructed elaborate systems of *stasis*, but the most commonly named levels or focal points for argument are: fact, definition, quality, and appropriateness. The equivalent term in Roman rhetoric is *constitutio* or *status*.

Stichometry. The study of the patterns, habits, and tendencies of writing systems. In its most traditional form it is the study of the number of lines associated with different genres of written composition.

Structural Linguistics. Analysis of language structure, such as sentence combination, as an aid to learning how to write.

Student Literary and Debate Societies. Self-organized student groups begun in eighteenth-century America and Great Britain; members sponsored oral and written forums and competitions and evaluated each others' work.

Students' Right to Their Own Language (SRTOL). Conference on College Composition and Communication (CCCC) position statement (1974) promoting language diversity and linguistically informed pedagogical practices.

Sumposium (or *symposium*). A Greek term most commonly understood as a small gathering where (primarily) male aristocrats gathered to eat, drink, and discuss. The roots of the term, however, center on the practice of intimate family-oriented education where adult members of the household taught the youth. (See **"Old Education."**)

Syllabary. A writing system where characters represent clusters of vowels and consonants. The phonetic grouping of sounds is intended to approximate the vocalization of the referent. Often considered to be the forerunner to the alphabet. Linear B is an early Greek example of a syllabary.

Tales. Recounting of something that happened or may have happened. One of the **progymnasmata**.

Techne. A Greek term meaning "art" or "craft." Normally associated with a systematic method for facilitating oral or written expression. The Latin counterpart is the term *ratio*.

Theme. A prose composition as distinguished from a composition in verse.

Thesis. Composition of an answer to a General Question, that is, a question not involving individuals. One of the **progymnasmata**.

Thetes. The labor class of ancient Athenian Society. Thetes were often artisan writers whose craft skills included writing for public display on public buildings, or for inscriptions on objects such as vases intended as gifts.

Topic. A method of discovering ideas (**Invention**) through designated "places" or "regions of argument" (to use Cicero's term). Aristotle names twenty-eight in his *Rhetoric* II.23, though he discusses more than two hundred in his book *Topics*. Cicero's *Topica* treats fourteen, divided into those inherent in the subject at hand and those extrinsic to it. Each Topic is a mental process which directs the mind toward a certain activity that will recall pre-existent knowledge so that it may be used in composition. Common examples still used in modern textbooks (usually without acknowledgment) are definition, comparison and contrast, cause and effect, division, circumstances, and testimony.

Translation. The exercise of reproducing a text in another language. It was prominent in Roman times with Greek and, beginning with the late Middle Ages, with vernaculars. It is a form of **Transliteration** in the process of **Imitation**.

Transliteration of Models. Student re-casting of a text in a different form: prose to verse, or verse to prose, or from one language to another. The fifth stage in **Imitation**.

Tutorial System. One-on-one teaching program in which the tutor assigns theme topics, then evaluates the written text orally with the student individually; prevalent at Oxford and Cambridge universities since the seventeenth century.

Universal Grammar. Assumption that there is a grammar common to all languages, enabling Latin grammar to be applied to the English language.

WAC/WID. Writing program efforts that extend beyond traditional concerns with first-year composition. Writing Across the Curriculum and Writing in the Disciplines programs were found in most institutions by the new millennium. The second term is a later development that relies on particular analyses of a discipline's writing and publishing, purposes, and discourse communities, while the first was a more general descriptive term.

Web 2.0. Loose term that describes changes in patterns of internet use, primarily a shift from centralized, single- or institutional-authored websites delivering content, toward interactive and collaborative spaces such as community blogs, web forums, wikis, and social networking and file-sharing sites.

Whole Language Learning. Modern learning environment which stresses the integrated nature of reading, writing, speaking, and listening.

Word-Play as First Exercise. Medieval practice of introducing students to tropes and figures, complemented by memorization and recitation, before taking up Arrangement and finally Invention.

Writing as Academic Sorting. An effect of middle-class expansion in nineteenth-century America, as increasing class sizes made oral recitation and oral disputation unworkable, making writing a useful means of assessing student ability.

The Next Step in Your Research: A Bibliography for Further Study

If there is anything in the preceding pages that might spark some interest in learning more than these pages provide, we are happy to provide some ways to look further. This is not just a "list" but an additional quarry of information you can explore for yourself.

———. "The Renaissance." In *The Present State of Scholarship in the History of Rhetoric: A Twenty-First Century Guide*. Ed. Lynée Gaillet with Winifred Bryan Horner. Columbia: University of Missouri Press, 2010, 82–113.

Abbott, Don Paul. "Renaissance Rhetoric." In *Encyclopedia of Rhetoric*. Ed. Theresa Enos. New York: Garland, 1996, 594–600.

Adams, John Quincy. *Lectures on Rhetoric and Oratory*. 1810. New York: Russell, 1962.

Applebee, Arthur N. *Tradition and Reform in the Teaching of English: A History*. Urbana: NCTE, 1974.

Archer, R. L. *Secondary Education in the Nineteenth Century*. Cambridge: Cambridge University Press, 1921.

Ascham, Roger. *The Scholemaster*. 1863. Ed. John E. B. Mayor. New York: AMS, 1967.

Bain, Alexander. *English Composition and Rhetoric: A Manual*. London: Longmans, 1866.

Baldwin, T. W. *William Shakespere's Small Latine and Less Greek*. Urbana: University of Illinois Press, 1944.

Barnard, H. C. *A History of English Education From 1760*. 2nd Ed. London: London University Press, 1961.

Bazerman, Charles, Ed. *Handbook of Research on Writing: History, Society, School, Individual, Text*. New York: Lawrence Erlbaum Associates, 2009.

Beale, Dorothea. *History of the Ladies Colleges, 1853–1904*. London: n.p., 1905.

Beck, Frederick, A. B. *Album of Greek Education: The Greeks at School and Play*. Sydney: Cheiron, 1975.

———. *Greek Education, 450–350 B.C.* New York: Barnes, 1964.

Berlin, James A. *Rhetoric and Reality: Writing Instruction in American Colleges, 1900–1985*. Carbondale: Southern Illinois University Press, 1987.

———. *Rhetoric, Poetics, and Cultures: Refiguring College English Studies*. Urbana: NCTE, 1996.

Blair, Hugh. *Lectures on Rhetoric and Belles Lettres*. London: Strahan, 1783. Philadelphia: Aitken, 1784.

Bledstein, Burton J. *The Culture of Professionalism: the Middle Class and the Development of Higher Education in America*. New York: Norton, 1976.

Bonner, S. F. *Education in Ancient Rome from the Elder Cato to the Younger Pliny*. Berkeley: University of California Press, 1977.

Brinsley, John. *A Consolation for Our Grammar Schools*. 1622. New York: Scholar's Facsimiles, 1943.

———. *Ludus literarius*. English Linguistics 1500–1800 62. Menston, UK: Scolar Press, 1968.

Clark, Donald Lernen. *John Milton at St. Paul's School: A Study of Ancient Rhetoric in English Renaissance Education.* New York: Columbia University Press, 1948.

———. *Rhetoric in Greco-Roman Education.* New York: Columbia University Press, 1957.

Connors, Robert J. *Composition Rhetoric: Backgrounds, Theory, and Pedagogy.* Pittsburgh: University of Pittsburgh Press, 1997.

Crowley, Sharon. *Composition in the University: Historical and Polemical Essays.* Pittsburgh: University of Pittsburgh Press, 1998.

———. *Methodical Memory: Invention in Current-Traditional Rhetoric.* Carbondale: Southern Illinois University Press, 1990.

Curtis, S. J. *History of Education in Great Britain.* 4th Ed. London: University Tutorial Press, 1957.

Davie, George Elder. *The Democratic Intellect: Scotland and Her Universities in the Nineteenth Century.* Edinburgh: Edinburgh University Press, 1961.

Day, Angel. *English Secretorie.* English Linguistics 1500–1800 29. Menston, UK: Scolar Press, 1967.

Dionissotti, A. C. "From Ausonius' Schooldays? A Schoolbook and Its Relatives." *Journal of Roman Studies* 72 (1982): 83–125.

Diringer, David. *Writing.* London: Thames. 1962.

Enos, Richard Leo. *The Literate Mode of Cicero's Legal Rhetoric.* Carbondale: Southern Illinois University Press, 1988.

———. *Roman Rhetoric: Revolution and the Greek Influence.* Prospect Heights: Waveland, 1993.

Erasmus. *Adages.* Trans. Margaret Mann Phillips. Vol. 31 of *Collected Works of Erasmus.* Ed. Craig R. Thompson. Toronto: University of Toronto Press, 1978.

———. *The Ciceronian: A Dialogue on the Ideal Latin Style.* Trans. Betty I. Knott. Vol. 28 of *Collected Works of Erasmus.* Ed. Craig R. Thompson. Toronto: University of Toronto Press, 1978.

———. *Literary and Educational Writings: De copia/De ratione studii.* Trans. Betty I. Knott. Vol. 24 of *Collected Works of Erasmus.* Ed. Craig R. Thompson. Toronto: University of Toronto Press, 1978.

Freeman, Kenneth J. *Schools of Hellas.* New York: Teachers College Press, 1969.

Frykman, Erik. *W. E. Aytoun, Pioneer Professor of English at Edinburgh.* Ed. Frank Behre. Gothenburg Studies in English 17. Gothenburg: Elanders Boktryckeri Aktiebolag, 1963.

Gaff, Gerard. *Professing Literature: An Institutional History.* Chicago: University of Chicago Press, 1987.

Gaillet, Lynée Lewis, Ed. *Scottish Rhetoric and Its Influences.* Mahwah: Erlbaum, 1998.

———. (Ed., with Winifred Bryan Horner). *The Present State of Scholarship in the History of Rhetoric: A Twenty-first Century Guide.* Columbia: University of Missouri Press, 2010.

Gaur, Christine. *A History of Writing.* Revised Edition. London: British Library, 1992.

Gelb, I. J. *A Study of Writing.* Chicago: University of Chicago Press, 1963.

Geoffrey of Vinsauf. *The "Poetria nova" of Geoffrey of Vinsauf.* Trans. Margaret F. Nims. Pontifical Institute of Medieval Studies, Medieval Sources in Translation 49. Revised Edition. Introduction to Revised Edition by Martin Camargo. Toronto: PIMS, 2010.

Gere, Anne Ruggles. *Writing Groups: History; Theory and Implications.* Carbondale: Southern Illinois University Press, 1987.

Glenn, Cheryl. *Rhetoric Retold: Regendering the Tradition from Antiquity through the Renaissance.* Carbondale: Southern Illinois University Press, 1998.

Golden, James L., and Edward P. J. Corbett. *The Rhetoric of Blair, Campbell and Whately.* New York: Holt, 1968.

Goldhill, Simon. *The Invention of Prose.* Greece and Rome, New Surveys in the Classics, No. 32. Published for the Classical Association. Oxford: Oxford University Press, 2002.

Grafton, Anthony, and Lisa Jardine. *From Humanism to the Humanities.* Cambridge, MA: Harvard University Press, 1986.

Green, Lawrence and James J. Murphy, Eds. *Renaissance Rhetoric Short Title Catalogue 1460–1700*. Aldershot, UK: Ashgate, 2006.

Gwynn, Aubrey. *Roman Education from Cicero to Quintilian*. Oxford: Clarendon Press, 1926.

Hagaman, John. "Modern Use of the Progymnasmata in Teaching Rhetorical Invention." *Rhetoric Review* 5 (1986): 22–29.

Hans, Nicholas. *New Trends in Education in the Eighteenth Century*. London: Routledge & Kegan Paul, 1955.

Harris, Roy. *The Origin of Writing*. London: Duckworth, 1986.

Harris, William. *Ancient Literacy*. Cambridge, MA: Harvard University Press, 1989.

Hartley, James, Ed. *Technology and Writing: Readings in the Psychology of Written Communication*. Second Edition. London: Jessica Kingsley Publishers Ltd., 1992.

Harvey, David. "Greeks and Romans Learn to Write." In *Communication Arts in the Ancient World*. Eds. Eric A. Havelock and Jackson P. Hershbell. New York: Hastings, 1978. 63–80.

Havelock, Eric A. *The Literate Revolution in Greece and Its Cultural Consequences*. Princeton: Princeton University Press, 1982.

Hobbs, Catherine L., Ed. *Nineteenth-Century Women Learn to Write*. Charlottesville: University Press of Virginia, 1995.

Hoole, Charles. *A New Discovery of an Old Art of Teaching Schoole*. English Linguistics 1500–1800 133. Ed. R. C. Alston. Menston, UK: Scolar Press, 1969.

Horner, Winifred Bryan. *Nineteenth-Century Scottish Rhetoric: The American Connection*. Carbondale: Southern Illinois University Press, 1993.

Houlette, Forest. *Nineteenth Century Rhetoric: An Enumerative Bibliography*. New York: Garland, 1989.

Howell, Wilbur Samuel. *Eighteenth-Century British Logic and Rhetoric*. Princeton: Princeton University Press, 1971.

——. *Logic and Rhetoric in England, 1500–1700*. Princeton: Princeton University Press, 1956.

Humes, Walter M., and Hamish M. Paterson, eds. *Scottish Culture and Scottish Education: 1800–1980*. Edinburgh: Donald, 1983.

Isocrates. *Isocrates*. 3 vols. Trans. George Norlin. Loeb Classical Library. Cambridge, MA: Harvard University Press, 1954–56.

Jaeger, Werner. "The Rhetoric of Isocrates and Its Cultural Ideal." In *Landmark Essays on Classical Greek Rhetoric*. Ed. Edward Schiappa. Davis: Hermagoras, 1994: 119–41.

Jamieson, Alexander. *A Grammar of Rhetoric and Polite Literature*. New York: Armstrong, 1818.

Jardine, George. *Outlines of Philosophical Education Illustrated By the Method of Teaching Logic, or First Class of Philosophy in the University of Glasgow*. Glasgow: Duncan, 1818.

John of Salisbury. *The Metalogicon of John of Salisbury: A Twelfth-Century Defense of the Verbal and Logical Arts of the Trivium*. Trans. Daniel D. McGarry. 1955. Gloucester, MA: Smith, 1971.

Johnson, Nan. *Nineteenth-Century Rhetoric in North America*. Carbondale: Southern Illinois University Press, 1991.

Johnson, R. "Isocrates' Method of Teaching." *American Journal of Philology* 80 (1959): 25–36.

Kaster, Robert A. *Guardians of Language: The Grammarian and Society in Late Antiquity*. Berkeley: University of California Press, 1988.

Kellogg, Brainerd. *A Text-Book on Rhetoric*. New York: Maynard, 1896.

Kelly, Douglas. *The Arts of Poetry and Prose*. Typologie des sources du moyen âge occidental, Fasc. 59. Tournhout: Brepols, 1991.

Kelly, Louis G. *25 Centuries of Language Teaching: An Inquiry into the Science, Art, and Development of Language Teaching Methodology. 500 B.C.–1969*. Rowley: Newbury, 1969.

Kennedy, George A. *Classical Rhetoric and Its Christian and Secular Tradition from Ancient to Modern Times*. Chapel Hill: University of North Carolina Press, 1980.

——. *A New History of Classical Rhetoric: An Extensive Revision and Abridgment of The Art of Persuasion in Greece, The Art of Rhetoric in the Roman World, and Greek Rhetoric Under Christian*

Emperors, with Additional Discussion of Late Latin Rhetorics. Princeton: Princeton University Press, 1994.

Kimball, Bruce A. *Orators and Philosophers: A History of the Idea of Liberal Education.* New York: Teachers College Press, 1986.

Lanham, Carol Dana. "Freshman Composition in the Early Middle Ages: Epistolography and Rhetoric before the *ars dictaminis.*" *Viator* 23 (1992): 115–34.

——. *"Salutatio" Formulas in Latin Letters to 1200: Syntax, Style, and Theory.* Münchener Beiträge zur Mediävistik und Renaissance-Forschung 22. Munich: Arbeo-Gesselschaft, 1975.

Lentz, Tony M. *Orality and Literacy in Hellenic Greece.* Carbondale: Southern Illinois University Press, 1989.

Leonard, Sterling Andrus. *The Doctrine of Correctness in English Usage, 1700–1800.* 1929. New York: Russell, 1962.

Little, Charles E. *Quintilian the Schoolmaster.* 2 vols. Nashville: George Peabody College for Teachers, 1951.

Lunsford, Andrea A., Ed. *Reclaiming Rhetorica: Women in the Rhetorical Tradition.* Pittsburgh: University of Pittsburgh Press, 1995.

——. *Elizabethan Rhetoric: Theory and Practice.* Cambridge: Cambridge University Press, 2002.

Mack, Peter. "Humanistic Rhetoric and Dialectic." In *The Cambridge Companion to Renaissance Humanism.* Ed. Jill Kraye. Cambridge: Cambridge University Press, 1996, 82–99.

Marrou, H. I. *A History of Education in Antiquity;* Trans. George Lamb. Madison: University of Wisconsin Press, 1982.

Martin, Henri-Jean. *The History and Power of Writing.* Trans. Lydia G. Cochran. Chicago: Chicago University Press, 1994.

McLachlan, Herbert. *English Education under the Test Acts: Being the History of Non-Conformist Academies 1662–1820.* Manchester, UK: Manchester University Press, 1931.

McMurty, Jo. *English Language, English Literature: The Creation of an Academic Discipline.* Hamden: Archon, 1985.

Mailloux, Steven. "Disciplinary Identities: On the Rhetorical Paths between English and Communication Studies." *Rhetoric Society Quarterly* 30 (2000): 5–30.

Matthew of Vendôme. *The Art of Versification.* Trans. Aubrey E. Galyon. Ames: Iowa State University Press, 1980.

Michael, Ian. *The Teaching of English from the Sixteenth Century to 1870.* London: Cambridge University Press, 1987.

Miller, Thomas P. *The Formation of College English: Rhetoric and Belles Lettres in the American College, 1875–1925: A Documentary History.* Pittsburgh: University of Pittsburgh Press, 1995.

Morgan, Alexander. *Scottish University Studies.* London: Oxford University Press, 1933.

Morrison, Samuel Eliot. *Three Centuries of Harvard, 1636–1936.* Cambridge, MA: Harvard University Press, 1936.

Moss, Ann. *Printed Commonplace Books and the Structuring of Renaissance Thought.* Oxford: Clarendon Press, 1996.

Mulcaster, Richard. *Mulcaster's Elementarie.* Ed. E. T. Campagnac. Oxford: Clarendon Press, 1925.

Murphy, James J. "The Modern Value of Roman Methods of Teaching Writing, with Answers to Twelve Current Fallacies." *Writing on the Edge* 1 (1989): 28–37.

——, Ed. *Quintilian on the Teaching of Speaking and Writing: Translations from Books One, Two and Ten of the Institutio oratoria.* Carbondale: Southern Illinois University Press, 1987.

——. *Rhetoric in the Middle Ages: A History of Rhetorical Theory from St. Augustine to the Renaissance.* Berkeley: University of California Press, 1974.

——, Ed. *The Rhetorical Tradition and Modern Writing.* New York: MLA, 1982.

——. "The Teaching of Latin as a Foreign Language in the Twelfth Century." *Historiographia Linguistica* 7 (1980): 159–75.

Murphy, James J., and Richard A. Katula, Eds. *A Synoptic History of Classical Rhetoric*. 3rd Edition. Mahwah NJ: Hermagoras/Lawrence Erlbaum Associates, 2003.

Newman, Samuel B. *A Practical System of Rhetoric*. 10th Edition. New York: Dayton, 1842.

Ong, Walter J. *Orality and Literacy: The Technologizing of the Word*. London: Methuen, 1982.

——. *Ramus, Method, and the Decay of Dialogue*. Cambridge, MA: Harvard University Press, 1958.

Palmer, D. J. *The Rise of English Studies: An Account of the Study of English Language and Literature from its Origins to the Making of the Oxford English School*. London: Oxford University Press, 1965.

Parker, William Riley. "Where Do English Departments Come From?" *College English* 28 (1967): 339–51.

Parkes, Malcolm B. *Pause and Effect: An Introduction to the History of Punctuation in the West*. Berkeley: University of California Press, 1993.

Parks, E. Patrick. *The Roman Rhetorical Schools as a Preparation for the Courts Under the Early Empire*. Baltimore: The Johns Hopkins Press, 1945.

Pattison, Robert. *On Literacy: The Politics of the Word from Homer to the Age of Rock*. Oxford: Oxford University Press, 1982.

Plato. *Plato on Rhetoric and Language: Four Key Dialogues*. Ed. Jean Nienkamp. Mahwah: Erlbaum, 1999.

Quintilian. *The Institutio oratoria*. Ed. and Trans. by Donald A. Russell as *Quintilian: The Orator's Education*. 5 vols. Loeb Classical Library. Cambridge, MA: Harvard University Press, 2001.

——. *Institutio oratoria*. Book 2. Ed. Tobias Reinhardt and Michael Winterbottom. Oxford: Oxford University Press, 2006.

Rainolde, Richard. *The Foundation of Rhetoric*. English Linguistics 1500–1800 347. Menston, UK: Scolar Press, 1972.

Ramus, Peter. *Arguments in Rhetoric Against Quintilian: Translation and Text of Peter Ramus's Rhetoricae Distinctiones in Quintilianum. 1549*. Ed. James J. Murphy. Trans. Carole Newlands. Carbondale: Southern Illinois University Press, 2010.

Reed, Alonzo, and Brainerd Kellogg. *Higher Lessons in English*. New York: Clark, 1878.

Reynolds, Suzanne. *Medieval Reading: Grammar, Rhetoric, and the Classical Text*. Cambridge: Cambridge University Press, 1996.

Riché, Pierre. *Education and Culture in the Barbarian West, Sixth Through Eighth Centuries*. Trans. John J. Contreni. Columbia: University of South Carolina Press, 1976.

Robb, Kevin. *Literacy and Paideia in Ancient Greece*. London: Cambridge University Press, 1983.

Robinson, P. R., Ed. *Teaching Writing, Learning to Write: Proceedings of the XVIth Colloquium of the Comite International de Paleographie Latine*. London: Kings College London Centre for Late Antique and Medieval Studies, 2010.

Rudolph, Frederick. *The American College and University: A History*. New York: Vintage, 1962.

Schiappa, Edward. *The Beginnings of Rhetorical Theory in Classical Greece*. New Haven: Yale University Press, 1999.

Scholes, Robert. *Textual Power: Literary Theory and the Teaching of English*. New Haven: Yale University Press, 1985.

Scott, Izora. *Controversies Over the Imitation of Cicero as a Model for Style and Some Phases of Their Influence on the Schools of the Renaissance. 1910*. Davis, CA: Hermagoras, 1991.

Smith, Adam. *Lectures on Rhetoric and Belles Lettres*. Ed. J. C. Bryce. Indianapolis: Liberty Classics, 1985.

Spring, Joel. *The American School 1642–1985*. New York: Longman, 1986.

Stowe, A. Monroe. *English Grammar Schools in the Reign of Elizabeth*. New York: Teachers College Press, 1908.

Stromberg, Ernest. *American Indian Rhetoric of Survivance: Word Medicine, Word Magic.* Pittsburgh: Pittsburgh University Press, 2006.

——. (Ed.) *Education in Greek and Roman Antiquity*. Leiden: Brill, 2001.

——. *The Pedagogical Contract: the Economies of Teaching and Learning in the Ancient World*. Ann Arbor: Michigan University Press, 2000.

Too, Yun Lee. *Pedagogy and Power: Rhetorics of Classical Learning*. Leiden: Brill, 1995.

Vickers, Brian, Ed. *English Literary Criticism in the Renaissance*. Oxford: Oxford University Press, 1999.

Vives, Juan Luis. *On Education [De tradendis disciplinis]*. Ed. and Trans. Foster Watson. 1913. Totowa, NJ: Rowman & Littlefield, 1971.

Wagner, David L. *The Seven Liberal Arts in the Middle Ages*. Bloomington: Indiana University Press, 1983.

Ward, John. *A System of Oratory*. 1759. Hildesheim: Georg Olms Verlag, 1969.

Watson, Foster. *The English Grammar Schools to 1660*. [1908]. London: Cass, 1968.

Welch, Kathleen E. *The Contemporary Reception of Classical Rhetoric: Appropriations of Ancient Discourse*. Hillsdale: Erlbaum, 1990.

Wertheimer, Molly Meijer, Ed. *Listening to their Voices: The Rhetorical Activities of Historical Women*. Columbia: University of South Carolina Press, 1997.

Witherspoon, John. *Lectures on Eloquence and Moral Philosophy*. Philadelphia: Woodward, 1810.

——. *Classroom Commentaries: Teaching the "Poetria nova" across Medieval and Renaissance Europe*. Columbus: Ohio State University Press, 2010.

Woods, Marjorie Curry, Ed. *An Early Commentary on the "Poetria nova" of Geoffrey of Vinsauf*. Garland Medieval Texts 12. New York: Garland, 1985.

Wozniak, John Michael. *English Composition in Eastern Colleges, 1850–1940*. Washington: University Press of America, 1978.

Contributors

Don Paul Abbott is Professor in the Department of English at the University of California, Davis, CA 95616. E-mail: *dpabbott@ucdavis.edu*

James A. Berlin (1942–1994) was Professor in the Department of English at Purdue University, West Lafayette IN 47907.

Suzanne Bordelon is Associate Professor in the Department of Rhetoric and Writing Studies at San Diego State University, 5500 Campanile Drive, San Diego CA 92182–4452. E-mail: *bordelon@mail.sdsu.edu*

Martin Camargo is Professor of English, Classics, and Medieval Studies at the University of Illinois, Urbana IL 61801. E-mail: *mcamargo@illinois.edu*

Richard Leo Enos is Professor and Holder of the Lillian Radford Chair of Rhetoric and Composition in the Department of English, TCU Box 297270 at Texas Christian University, Fort Worth TX 76129. E-mail: *r.enos@tcu.edu*

Linda Ferreira-Buckley is Associate Professor of English and Rhetoric in the Department of English at the University of Texas at Austin, Austin TX 78712. E-mail: *linda-fb@uts.cc.utexas.edu*

David Gold is Associate Professor of English, University of Michigan. E-mail: *dpg@umich.edu*

S. Michael Halloran is Professor Emeritus in the Department of Language, Literature, and Composition at Rensselaer Polytechnic Institute, Troy NY 12180. E-mail: *shallora@nycap.rr.com*

Catherine L. Hobbs is Professor in the Department of English at the University of Oklahoma, Norman OK 73019. E-mail: *chobbs@ou.edu*

Carol Dana Lanham was Research Associate at the UCLA Center for Medieval and Renaissance Studies at Los Angeles CA.

James J. Murphy is Professor Emeritus in the Department of English and the Department of Communication at the University of California, Davis CA 95616. E-mail: *jermurphy@ucdavis.edu*

Marjorie Curry Woods is Professor of English and Comparative Literature at University of Texas at Austin, Austin TX, 78712–1164. E-mail: *marjorie.woods@austin.utexas.edu*

Elizabethada A. Wright is Professor in the Department of English at Rivier College, 420 Main Street, Nashua NH 03060. E-mail: *ewright@rivier.edu*

Index